Cisco NAC Appliance: Enforcing Host Security with Clean Access

Jamey Heary, CCIE No. 7680

Contributing Authors:
Jerry Lin, CCIE No. 6469
Chad Sullivan, CCIE No. 6493
Alok Agrawal

Cisco Press

Cisco Press
800 East 96th Street
Indianapolis, Indiana 46240 USA

Cisco NAC Appliance:
Enforcing Host Security with Clean Access

Jamey Heary, CCIE No. 7680

Contributing Authors:
Jerry Lin, CCIE No. 6469
Chad Sullivan, CCIE No. 6493
Alok Agrawal

Copyright © 2008 Cisco Systems, Inc.

Published by:
Cisco Press
800 East 96th Street
Indianapolis, IN 46240 USA

Library of Congress Cataloging-in-Publication Data

Heary, Jamey.

  Cisco NAC appliance : enforcing host security with clean access / Jamey Heary ; contributing authors, Jerry Lin ... [et al.].

     p. cm.

  ISBN 978-1-58705-306-1 (pbk.)

  1. Computer networks--Security measures. 2. Computers--Access control. I. Title.

  TK5105.59.H42 2007

  005.8--dc22

                         2007026204

Printed in the United States of America

First Printing August 2007

ISBN-13: 978-1-58705-306-1

ISBN-10: 1-58705-306-3

Warning and Disclaimer

This book is designed to provide information about Cisco NAC Appliance. Every effort has been made to make this book as complete and as accurate as possible, but no warranty or fitness is implied.

The information is provided on an "as is" basis. The authors, Cisco Press, and Cisco Systems, Inc. shall have neither liability nor responsibility to any person or entity with respect to any loss or damages arising from the information contained in this book or from the use of the discs or programs that may accompany it.

The opinions expressed in this book belong to the author and are not necessarily those of Cisco Systems, Inc.

Trademark Acknowledgments

All terms mentioned in this book that are known to be trademarks or service marks have been appropriately capitalized. Cisco Press or Cisco Systems, Inc., cannot attest to the accuracy of this information. Use of a term in this book should not be regarded as affecting the validity of any trademark or service mark.

Feedback Information

At Cisco Press, our goal is to create in-depth technical books of the highest quality and value. Each book is crafted with care and precision, undergoing rigorous development that involves the unique expertise of members from the professional technical community.

Readers' feedback is a natural continuation of this process. If you have any comments regarding how we could improve the quality of this book or otherwise alter it to better suit your needs, you can contact us through e-mail at feedback@ciscopress.com. Please make sure to include the book title and ISBN in your message.

We greatly appreciate your assistance.

Corporate and Government Sales

The publisher offers excellent discounts on this book when ordered in quantity for bulk purchases or special sales, which may include electronic versions and/or custom covers and content particular to your business, training goals, marketing focus, and branding interests. For more information, please contact:

U.S. Corporate and Government Sales
1-800-382-3419
corpsales@pearsontechgroup.com

For sales outside the United States, please contact:
International Sales international@pearsoned.com

Publisher	Paul Boger
Associate Publisher	Dave Dusthimer
Cisco Representative	Anthony Wolfenden
Cisco Press Program Manager	Jeff Brady
Executive Editor	Brett Bartow
Managing Editor	Patrick Kanouse
Development Editor	Andrew Cupp
Project Editor	Seth Kerney
Copy Editor	Mike Henry
Technical Editors	Prem Ananthakrishnan, Niall El-Assaad, Sheldon Muir
Editorial Assistant	Vanessa Evans
Book Designer	Louisa Adair
Composition	ICC Macmillan, Inc.
Indexer	Tim Wright
Proofreader	Karen A. Gill

Americas Headquarters	Asia Pacific Headquarters	Europe Headquarters
Cisco Systems, Inc.	Cisco Systems, Inc.	Cisco Systems International BV
170 West Tasman Drive	168 Robinson Road	Haarlerbergpark
San Jose, CA 95134-1706	#28-01 Capital Tower	Haarlerbergweg 13-19
USA	Singapore 068912	1101 CH Amsterdam
www.cisco.com	www.cisco.com	The Netherlands
Tel: 408 526-4000	Tel: +65 6317 7777	www.europe.cisco.com
800 553-NETS (6387)	Fax: +65 6317 7799	Tel: +31 0 800 020 0791
Fax: 408 527-0883		Fax: +31 0 20 357 1100

Cisco has more than 200 offices worldwide. Addresses, phone numbers, and fax numbers are listed on the Cisco Website at **www.cisco.com/go/offices.**

About the Author

Jamey Heary, CCIE No. 7680, is currently a security consulting systems engineer at Cisco Systems, Inc., and works with its largest customers in the Northwest United States. Jamey joined Cisco in 2000. He currently leads its Western Security Asset team and is a field advisor for the U.S. security virtual team. Prior to working at Cisco, he worked for the Immigration and Naturalization Service as a network consultant and project leader. Before that he was the lead network and security engineer for a financial firm whose network carries approximately 12 percent of the global equities trading volume worldwide. His areas of expertise include network and host security design and implementation, security regulatory compliance, and routing and switching. His other certifications include CISSP, CCSP, and Microsoft MCSE. He is also a Certified HIPAA Security Professional. He has been working in the IT field for 13 years and in IT security for 9 years. He has a BS from St. Lawrence University.

About the Contributing Authors

Jerry Lin, CCIE No. 6469, is a consulting systems engineer for Cisco and is based in southern California. He specializes in security best practices. Jerry has worked with a variety of Cisco enterprise customers in areas such as software development, local government agencies, K–12 and universities, high-tech manufacturing, retail, and health care, as well as managed web-hosting service provider customers. He holds his CCIE in routing and switching as well as in CCDP and CISSP. Jerry has been working in the IT industry for the past 12 years. During the late 1990s, he worked as a technical instructor. Jerry earned both a bachelor's degree and a master's degree in mechanical engineering from the University of California, Irvine.

Chad Sullivan, CCIE No. 6493 (Security, Routing and Switching, SNA/IP), CISSP, CHSP, is a senior security engineer and owner of Priveon, Inc., which provides leading security solutions to customers globally. Prior to starting Priveon, Chad worked as a security consulting systems engineer at Cisco. Chad is recognized within the industry as one of the leading implementers of the Cisco Security Agent product and is the author of both Cisco Press books dedicated to the Cisco Security Agent.

Alok Agrawal is the technical marketing manager for the Cisco NAC Appliance (Clean Access) product. He leads the technical marketing team developing technical concepts and solutions and driving future product architecture and features. He works with the Cisco sales and partner community to scale the adoption of the NAC Appliance product line globally. Prior to joining the Cisco Security Technology Group, he worked in the switching team of the Cisco Technical Assistance Center. He has a strong background in routing and switching and host security design and implementation. Alok holds a master's degree in electrical engineering from the University of Southern California and a bachelor's degree in electronics engineering from the University of Mumbai.

About the Technical Reviewers

Prem Ananthakrishnan is currently a technical marketing engineer for the Cisco NAC Appliance (Clean Access) product. He is responsible for global scalability of the product, documentation, partner/system engineer training, and critical escalations to ensure successful deployments. Prem has more than five years of hands-on experience as a systems/network engineer and in implementing managed services for data center operations. Prior to his current role, he worked at Cisco Technical Assistance Center (TAC) handling various security products. Prem holds an MS degree in telecommunications from the University of Colorado-Boulder and a BSEE from the University of Bombay.

Niall El-Assaad, CCIE No. 7493, is the Cisco NAC Appliance product manager for Europe, the Middle East, and Africa. Niall joined Cisco in 2000 and supported financial services customers with Cisco security solutions prior to his current role. Previously, he worked for a Cisco partner as head of the communications team and for a financial services organization. With more than 14 years of experience in the communications and security fields, Niall's areas of expertise include network and host security design and implementation and routing and switching. His other certifications include CCNP and CCDP.

Sheldon Muir is a consulting systems engineer within Cisco for the Cisco NAC Appliance product. Sheldon came over to Cisco with the acquisition of Perfigo in November 2004 where, with Perfigo, he was solely responsible for all technical channel development for North America. Sheldon holds a degree from UNLV and has been involved in the IT industry for 20 years, holding certifications with manufacturers such as Cisco, 3Com, and Juniper/Netscreen, with a supplemental CISSP to his credit. Prior to working for Cisco and Perfigo, he worked as an area escalation engineer and pre-sales engineer for 3Com, specializing in VoIP during the industry's early adoption.

Dedications

This book is dedicated to my wife Becca and two sons, Liam and Conor, without whose love and support little else would matter. A special thanks to my wife who continually motivated, encouraged, and supported me throughout this process. —Jamey

I would like to dedicate this book to my wife Christine, for supporting me through the last few weeks of completing this book. She gave me the boost of confidence to write about a special technology that I was passionate about. I truly enjoyed every minute I spent on this book. To all my customers who listened to me about NAC and have deployed NAC to secure their networks, thank you for believing in me. Together, we have and will continue to see the positive impact NAC is making. —Jerry

I would like to dedicate this book to my loving wife Jennifer and my energetic children Avery, Brielle, Celine, Danae, and Elliot. —Chad

I would like to dedicate this book to my loving parents and inspiring brother Aditya. —Alok

Acknowledgments

From **Jamey:**

A great big thanks to my wife Becca, for keeping me focused, giving me ideas, and proofreading my work during the whole process. Thank you, Becca, for all the sacrifices you made so that I could complete this book. Thank you to my parents for their never-ending support, prayers, and encouragement with everything I do. Thank you to my sisters for your advice and support over the years. A big thank you to my best man, Mike Ditta, for convincing the prison to let us use his self-portrait for the cover of this book. Thank you to Jerry Lin and Chad Sullivan; your drive, focus, and attention to detail throughout this process were awesome. Thank you to Alok Agrawal; your in-depth product knowledge was instrumental in the makeup of this book. Without all of your contributions, this book might never have made it to print. Thank you to the technical editors, Niall, Prem, and Sheldon; your observations and comments were instrumental in improving the readability and technical accuracy of this book. Thank you to Scott Henning for your backing and encouragement throughout this process. It played a critical role in my ability to start and finish this book. Thank you to the talented team in the Cisco NAC Appliance business unit for entrusting me with the writing of this book. Your help, advice, and support have been invaluable. Keep up the great work you are all doing with this product line—it rocks! Huge thank you to Cisco and Cisco Press, especially Brett Bartow and Drew Cupp, for this opportunity and your countless hours of hard work to make this book polished.

From **Jerry:**

I want to thank Jamey Heary for leading the effort on completing this NAC Appliance book. When I first heard about the writing of this book, I made up my mind to be one of the first customers to buy it. Never did I imagine that I would be given an opportunity to contribute to this project. Thank you, Jamey, for involving me in this book. This whole experience was all fun and play!

I also wanted to thank my manager, Nitesh Bondale, for words of support when I took on this project. Giving me a flexible work schedule definitely helped to complete this book on time.

To the NAC Appliance business unit team, Irene, Prem, Alok, Niall, and Sheldon, thanks for all of your invaluable inputs. You guys are a great team!

From **Chad:**

Thank you to my wife and children for your encouragement throughout my career. Thank you to my parents for providing me with the skills I needed to succeed. Thank you to my sister, Ashley, who continues to drive me to succeed. Thank you to my mother and father in-law for helping our family in what seems a continuous and endless cycle. Thank you to Jamey Heary for involving me in this project. Thank you to Cisco and Cisco Press for providing the guidance and information needed to best convey the material in this book to the reader. Thank you to all my coworkers and close friends who have assisted me over the years; your thoughts and prayers are not unnoticed. I would also like to thank God for continuing to provide these amazing opportunities to me and also for allowing to recognize and execute them. And, as always, thank you TiVo for allowing me to keep my schedule mine.

From **Alok:**

I would like to thank my colleagues on the dream product team Arvin, Rohit, Rajesh, Atif, Nick, Irene, Prem, Syed, Brendan, Niall, Mahesh, and the extremely talented NAC Appliance Development team for their passion in making the NAC Appliance a market leader, allowing us the opportunity to write this book. Thanks to Zeeshan Siddiqui, Shridhar Dhodapkar, Marty Ma, and Salman Zahid for being my mentors and for providing a strong platform to learn networking. Thanks to my brother, Aditya, and friend, Yash, who have always inspired me to do better. Lastly, but most importantly, I'd like to thank my parents for their constant encouragement, support, and confidence.

This Book Is Safari Enabled

The Safari® Enabled icon on the cover of your favorite technology book means the book is available through Safari Bookshelf. When you buy this book, you get free access to the online edition for 45 days.

Safari Bookshelf is an electronic reference library that lets you easily search thousands of technical books, find code samples, download chapters, and access technical information whenever and wherever you need it.

To gain 45-day Safari Enabled access to this book, do the following:

- Go to http://www.ciscopress.com/safarienabled
- Complete the brief registration form
- Enter the coupon code TKM4-Q2VM-9N13-P8M4-ALF9

If you have difficulty registering on Safari Bookshelf or accessing the online edition, please e-mail customer-service@safaribooksonline.com.

Contents at a Glance

Table of Contents

Command Syntax Conventions

The conventions used to present command syntax in this book are the same conventions used in the *IOS Command Reference*. The *Command Reference* describes these conventions as follows:

- **Boldface** indicates commands and keywords that are entered literally as shown. In actual configuration examples and output (not general command syntax), boldface indicates commands that are manually input by the user (such as a **show** command).

- *Italics* indicate arguments for which you supply actual values.

- Vertical bars (|) separate alternative, mutually exclusive elements.

- Square brackets [ ] indicate optional elements.

- Braces { } indicate a required choice.

- Braces within brackets [{ }] indicate a required choice within an optional element.

Introduction

Almost every contemporary corporation and organization has acquired and deployed security solutions or mechanisms to keep its networks and data secure. Hardware and software tools such as firewalls, network-based intrusion prevention systems, antivirus and antispam packages, host-based intrusion prevention solutions, and vulnerability scanners have proven effective to a certain degree, but only if they are kept up to date. For example, classic virus attacks sent via e-mail attachments, such as netsky and MyDoom, can easily be detected and prevented by any up-to-date antivirus and antispam software package. The key to stopping host attacks is being able to proactively enforce security policies that ensure all hosts must be fully patched and have up-to-date security software running before allowing them full network access. Existing security solutions do not proactively stop a PC from entering the network if its security software and operating system software are not current. Frequently, users will manually disable their host security software because it either reduces the overall performance of their PC or prevents an application from installing. When antivirus and antispam packages are out of date or not running, the likelihood of PC virus infections increases. This in turn increases the overall security risk to the organization.

The same principle applies to OS hotfixes. Take Microsoft Windows as an example. If you fail to implement new Windows security hotfixes in a timely manner to address newly discovered vulnerabilities, the probability of those unpatched hosts being compromised, or "owned," greatly increases. This can result in a loss of productivity due to system downtime, theft of company and personal confidential information, or unauthorized access to sensitive information. Unfortunately, loss of a client's confidential information usually leads to financial losses for affected individuals and the organization.

Data security laws and regulations such as the Health Insurance Portability and Accountability Act, the Sarbanes-Oxley Act, and the Peripheral Component Interconnect (PCI) standard are forcing organizations to implement and enforce tougher data security protection measures. Compliance regulations such as PCI speak directly to the antivirus and OS hotfix issues discussed previously. They make it mandatory that relevant hosts are kept up to date and run antivirus software, among other things. Increasingly, organizations are being forced by various data security laws and regulations to decrease their data security risk. Gone are the days when organizations had the flexibility to decide what their own data security risk tolerance and policy was. Given that many organizations used to choose to save money and time at the expense of data security, mandated security compliance is a welcome change for all.

The motivation for writing this book is to introduce the latest Cisco security technology, called Network Admission Control (NAC) Appliance. This security solution has proven to help minimize the chronic hard and soft dollar losses that corporations are experiencing due to security-related incidents. Additionally, it helps organizations enforce the use of already existing security investments such as antivirus software and patch management solutions. NAC brings to the table an innovative and proactive technique for improving the overall security posture of an organization's hosts and networks.

NAC allows organizations to enforce, for the first time, their previously unenforceable corporate host security policy. It works by authenticating users and posture assessing hosts before allowing them full network access. Hosts that fail the security posture checks (for example, if their OS or antivirus package is not up to date) are network quarantined and given remediation options. After the host is certified, it is allowed on the network. A user, based on a successful authentication, is granted the level of network access privileges appropriate for that user's role.

The objectives of this book are to provide IT and security teams all the information needed to understand, design, configure, deploy, and troubleshoot the Cisco NAC Appliance solution.

Who Should Read This Book?

This book will be of interest to the following professionals:

- IT directors and managers
- Network administrators
- Network and security engineers
- Security analysts and consultants
- Operating systems administrators
- Application developers

How This Book Is Organized

This book is divided into six parts with 15 chapters and an appendix.

Part I, "The Host Security Landscape," discusses the security landscape and challenges faced by corporations and organizations today. It discusses how Cisco Network Admission Control solutions can help and includes the following chapters:

- **Chapter 1, "The Weakest Link: Internal Network Security,"** provides an explanation of why network attacks and intellectual property losses are originating from the internal network.
- **Chapter 2, "Introducing Cisco Network Admission Control Appliance,"** provides an overview of Cisco NAC offerings and how NAC can help to minimize network outages. NAC's return on investment is covered.

Part II, "The Blueprint: Designing a Cisco NAC Appliance Solution," covers the building blocks and components that make up NAC and how each component works to build a NAC design. Part II includes the following chapters:

- **Chapter 3, "The Building Blocks in a Cisco NAC Appliance Design,"** explains the requirements to deploy NAC and the components involved.
- **Chapter 4, "Making Sense of All the Cisco NAC Appliance Design Options,"** explains the various NAC designs, such as out-of-band versus in-band, and discusses the advantages and disadvantages of each one.
- **Chapter 5, "Advanced Cisco NAC Appliance Design Topics,"** discusses the user authentication methods including MAC address authentication, active directory single sign-on (AD SSO), virtual private network SSO, and wireless SSO. Best practices for VoIP integration and redundancy considerations are covered.

Part III, "The Foundation: Building a Host Security Policy," covers a very important fundamental step of developing a robust security policy. It explains the foundation of building a host security policy and how to assign the appropriate network access privileges for various user roles. Part III includes the following chapter:

- **Chapter 6, "Building a Cisco NAC Appliance Host Security Policy,"** explains what makes up a NAC host security policy; the types of antivirus, antispam, and OS checks required to perform a posture assessment; and the user roles assigned to users. User roles define which access privileges are given to each user.

Part IV, "Cisco NAC Appliance Configuration," provides details of how to set up and configure the NAC appliance solution. Part IV includes the following chapters:

- **Chapter 7, "The Basics: Principal Configuration Tasks for the NAM and NAS,"** provides detailed instructions on how to set up and configure NAC Appliance Manager and NAC Appliance Server for a new deployment.

- **Chapter 8, "The Building Blocks: Roles, Authentication, Traffic Policies, and User Pages,"** explains what and why roles are created and how to manage each role effectively.

- **Chapter 9, "Host Posture Validation and Remediation: Cisco Clean Access Agent and Network Scanner,"** explains the checks and rules that the NAC agent uses for posture validation and remediation. For non-agent devices, Nessus scanning is used to assess the vulnerability of each machine. In addition, reports can be produced.

- **Chapter 10, "Configuring Out-of-Band,"** explains how to configure out-of-band deployment for Layer 2 and Layer 3 networks.

- **Chapter 11, "Configuring Single Sign-On,"** provides step-by-step instructions on how to configure AD SSO, VPN SSO, and wireless SSO.

- **Chapter 12, "Configuring High Availability,"** explains how high availability works and how to deploy it.

Part V, "Cisco NAC Appliance Deployment Best Practices," focuses on the roll-out phases of the NAC appliance solution. Part V includes the following chapter:

- **Chapter 13, "Deploying Cisco NAC Appliance,"** discusses the testing, pilot, and deployment phases of NAC.

Part VI, "Cisco NAC Appliance Monitoring and Troubleshooting," focuses on common monitoring, maintenance, and troubleshooting tasks and procedures. Part VI includes the following chapters:

- **Chapter 14, "Understanding Cisco NAC Appliance Monitoring,"** explains how to read the summary, online users, event logs, SNMP, and other user event pages. Detailed information on NAM and NAS monitoring is also provided.

- **Chapter 15, "Troubleshooting Cisco NAC Appliance,"** provides information on how to troubleshoot common issues related to licensing, agents not connecting, DNS, policy, design (in-band and out-of-band), certificates, high availability, and so on. This is especially useful for support during the first 30 days of NAC appliance deployment.

The **Appendix, "Sample User Community Deployment Messaging Material,"** provides sample NAC appliance deployment templates (e-mails, posters, bulletin board signs, and letters) for customers preparing to deploy NAC. The sample messages are tailored for education institutions but can be modified for any other business.

The Host Security Landscape

This chapter covers the following topics:

- Security Is a Weakest-Link Problem
- Hard Outer Shell with a Chewy Inside: Dealing with Internal Security Risks
- The Software Update Race: Staying Ahead of Viruses, Worms, and Spyware

CHAPTER 1

The Weakest Link: Internal Network Security

The rapid spread of e-commerce, e-learning, and e-business coupled with the growing reliance on information technology (IT) as a business enabler brings new information security challenges to organizations, including the following:

- Increased vulnerability-based attacks, which can cause large-scale business disruptions and directly result in productivity loss.

- Diminished security boundaries resulting in an increase in unauthorized access and internal attacks. The lack of an established security boundary increases an organization's risk of suffering the loss of intellectual property and disclosure of confidential information.

- Regulatory and compliance laws requiring specific security policies and procedures.

- Security policy enforcement challenges for clients connecting to the internal networks.

- Limited IT security budget and resources to counter the growing and complex security threats.

With today's security challenges and threats growing more sophisticated, perimeter defense alone is no longer sufficient. Organizations need to have internal security systems that are more comprehensive, pervasive, and tightly integrated than in the past. The purpose of this chapter is to make clear the internal security risks and challenges that drive the need for a solution such as Cisco Network Admission Control (NAC) Appliance.

Cisco NAC Appliance, formerly known as Cisco Clean Access, provides a powerful host security policy inspection and enforcement mechanism designed to meet these new challenges. Cisco NAC Appliance allows organizations to enforce their host security policies on all hosts (managed and unmanaged) as they enter the interior of the network, regardless of their access method, ownership, device type, application set, or operating system. Cisco NAC Appliance provides proactive protection at the network entry point. It allows for pervasive and in-depth security defenses throughout an organization's internal infrastructure with multiple points of protection. Cisco NAC Appliance integrates with current and advanced security products and technologies and serves as a critical component in an organization's overall security strategy.

Security Is a Weakest-Link Problem

Information security is commonly characterized as a weakest-link problem. The information you are trying to protect is only as secure as the weakest entry point to that information. Today's networks provide multiple access points to users in the form of virtual private network (VPN), wireless, dial-in, business-to-business (B2B) connections, web portals, and traditional onsite access to name but a few. Hardly any organizations today are closed entities with well-defined security perimeters. This leads to the concepts of ubiquitous access and perimeterless networks. Gone are the days when we had a nicely defined network security perimeter made up of a firewall that guarded against unauthorized access from the Internet. The rapid spread and adoption of e-commerce, B2B commerce, outsourcing, wireless, and VPN remote access have all helped to bring about the transformation of how we look at defending our networks and the information they contain. The demand to make network resources and information easily accessible will result in exposure to higher security risks. Security architecture is changing from a point defense perimeter approach to a defense-in-depth self-defending network design. Although this architecture change is happening, most networks are currently in the transition or adoption stage.

Today, networks are most secure at their traditional network perimeter: the Internet-facing access points. However, the security of the internal networks behind those impressive perimeter fortress walls is sorely lacking. By and large, after users gain access to the internal networks, they have free and unrestricted network access. In addition, a robust trust model usually exists between internal resources such as servers, applications, and databases. The model typically exists to make it easier to share information between systems and users.

The problem is that the trust model does not take into account who or what actually needs to be trusted; it defaults to trusting everything. Yes, these resources are located internally, but the same internal network that has very limited security in place has seen a dramatic increase in the number of entry points into it, and it gives everyone who connects free and unrestricted access. This is certainly a cause for concern. Internal network security is the weakest link in most organizations' network security architecture. IBM recently reported in a survey of 600 IT managers that 75 percent of respondents believed that threats to corporate security now come from within their own organizations.

NOTE   You can find information on the IBM survey at http://www.networkworld.com/news/2006/ 031406-ibm-survey-cybercrime.html.

The results from the 2006 CSI/FBI Computer Crime and Security Survey show the risks and damages that result from a breach of internal network security. The survey shows that 68 percent of respondents reported losses caused by insider threats. It also shows that insider abuse of the network takes third place in the most reported attack type. Unauthorized access to information takes fourth place in the survey. Viruses and theft of laptops took the first and second spots, respectively. The results of this survey draw attention to the pervasive lack of internal network security controls in today's organizations. This chapter provides an overview of the security threats and enforcement challenges common in the internal networks of today's organizations.

NOTE   You can find the 2006 CSI/FBI Computer Crime and Security Survey at http://
i.cmpnet.com/gocsi/db_area/pdfs/fbi/FBI2006.pdf.

Hard Outer Shell with a Chewy Inside: Dealing with Internal Security Risks

Ninety-nine percent of all networks today have a firewall in place to filter traffic coming from the Internet. In fact, most organizations have a robust set of outer defenses. These typically include one or more demilitarized zones, intrusion detection system or intrusion prevention system, spam filters, VPN concentrators, and antivirus scanners. These outer defenses are in place to protect the organization from very high-risk environments such as the Internet. The problem is that these defenses are virtually no help if an attacker, virus, or worm gains access to the internal networks behind the outer defenses.

Most organizations have extremely limited security on their internal networks. The same robust outer defenses just do not exist internally. The reasons for this deficiency vary, but typically include the following:

- It is seemingly too expensive, lacks scalability, and is overly complex.
- The perceived threat risk to the internal network is low.
- Too much internal security could impede business continuity requirements.

What organizations are starting to discover, however, is that the risk associated with having little or no security controls on their internal networks is becoming unacceptable. The previous reasons given to justify the lack of internal security are not holding up anymore. Because organizations have invested so heavily over the past several years in beefing up the security of their outer perimeters, the number of viruses and worms getting through from the Internet has greatly decreased. Given that security is a weakest-link problem, it comes as no surprise that organizations are increasingly finding that most of their virus or worm outbreaks originate from an internal or remote access source. Due to the proliferation of mobile, contract, and guest users needing access to the internal networks of organizations, it is very common for an outbreak to spread from a nonemployee or noncorporate PC. Additionally, most corporations are moving from desktop PCs to laptop PCs for their employees. This increase in mobile devices elevates the risk that hosts will become infected while offsite and introduce that virus back into the corporate network.

The vast majority of internal networks have no mechanisms in place that would allow an organization to control who can gain access to the internal network, what the security posture of the host they are using is, and based on these results determine what network rights the user will be granted. These three security controls are essential for properly locking down a network. They have existed for years on the network perimeter, but they are just now starting to make their way into the internal networks. It is startling that you can walk into almost any organization, sit down in an empty cube or office, plug into an Ethernet jack with your PC, and gain complete unrestricted access to the network. In too many cases this is true for wireless access as well, either because of lack of awareness or because an employee set up a rogue access point.

To proactively defend the internal networks from malicious users and virus and worm outbreaks, any security controls implemented must be able to do the following:

- **Control who is allowed access**   This is typically done by forcing the user to log in or authenticate before network access is granted. This authentication could be in the form of a username and password or a unique MAC address.

- **Determine whether the connecting client meets your host security requirements**   The goal is to reduce your exposure to viruses and worms by checking the host's security posture. This typically involves making sure that the host has up-to-date operating system patches, antivirus software, antispyware software, and that a virus or worm is not actively infecting it.

- **Quarantine any host that does not meet the host security requirements**   While in network quarantine, the host is given only the minimum network access required to patch and come up to compliance.

- **Control the amount of network access given to a connecting client**   The goal is to restrict network access, as much as is practical, to only those resources that the user truly needs. The amount of network access is typically determined based on the user's identity and the security posture of the user's host.

You must implement these network admission controls pervasively throughout your internal network for them to be effective. All clients trying to gain access to the internal network resources, by whatever means, must first be authenticated, authorized, and have their posture assessed as described earlier. Hardening your internal network in this way gives you ultimate control over who, how, when, where, and what connects to your internal resources. It also allows for the enforcement and verification of any endpoint security compliance regulations your organization must adhere to. These may include government regulations such as the Health Insurance Portability and Accountability Act and the Sarbanes-Oxley Act, or industry compliance regulations such as the Peripheral Component Interconnect (PCI) standard.

The Software Update Race: Staying Ahead of Viruses, Worms, and Spyware

How much more secure would your network be if every PC on it had the latest operating system patches, ran an up-to-date antivirus and antispyware client, and scanned for the top 20 known worms and viruses every time it reconnected? The answer is obvious, of course: It would be much more secure. But to find out just how much more secure, you would have to know how many security incidents would be mitigated by having the protections in place. If everything is up to date, the remaining risks are day zero attacks and misconfigured hosts. Day zero attacks are those released into the wild before a patch or signature is available to catch them. Most security studies indicate that day zero attacks, which actively propagate in the wild, make up only 1–2 percent of active attacks. So, just by patching, you are stopping 98 percent of what's out there.

Fortunately, the good guys discover most software vulnerabilities. This means that the vulnerability information is not disclosed publicly, which gives the affected company time to create a fix. After the company announces the fix or patch, the black hats get to work trying to create an exploit for the fixed vulnerability. At this point the exploit can infect only the weakest links: those systems that have not applied the patch. Unfortunately, many users do not keep their systems up to date and become easy prey for these attacks. In addition, the time between the public release of a software vulnerability notice and the release of the exploit that takes advantage of the vulnerability is rapidly shrinking. This is driving the need for organizations to make sure that only up-to-date systems are allowed full internal network access.

After the compromise or infection of a system, it needs cleaning or rebuilding. The cost incurred by an organization that needs to rebuild thousands of PCs can be staggering. Even though case study after case study proves that keeping PCs up to date results in decreased productivity loss and decreased IT expenditures, most organizations do not do a good job of it. In addition, it is not much use deploying a robust patch management system, such as Microsoft's Windows Server Update Services, if you cannot guarantee that it is enabled while users are connected to your network. This brings us back to the weakest-link problem: Your data is only as secure as the weakest access point to it. Any clients that disable their patch management software become glaring targets themselves and greatly increase the security risk to data in the organization as a whole. Add to this the enormous diversity present in today's networks, and the challenge gets even greater. Almost all organizations today have no way to dynamically and pervasively enforce a comprehensive host security policy on all hosts that connect to their network. The following are some of the challenges an organization faces when trying to keep all systems compliant with a host security policy and official regulations, and up to date:

- Supporting the myriad of operating system types and host security software available. For example, there are more than 20 antivirus software vendors.

- Detecting that an out-of-date system is on or attempting to gain access to the network. After detection, there must be a way to network quarantine that system until it is current.

- Dealing with mobile PCs. You must check to make sure that a system occasionally connecting via VPN is up to date before allowing it access to your network.

- Dealing with guest users. Guest users pose a unique problem. In general, the only thing guest users should be allowed to do while on the internal network is go to the Internet. They should be restricted from accessing all internal machines. If this enforcement is possible, there is no need to check and maintain the patch levels of a guest system.

- Dealing with PCs that are not owned or maintained by your organization but need access to your internal network resources. The machines of contract and temporary workers typically fall under this category.

- Enforcing—preferably at the network layer—that all systems have to be up to date before allowing them access.

- Enforcing—preferably at the network layer—that no host runs any applications that violate the corporate host security policy guidelines.

- Ensuring that all PCs are running the required security, backup, and encryption software necessary to satisfy compliance with official regulations (such as PCI) and your corporate host security policy guidelines.

- Distributing updates and patches to systems in a timely and scalable manner. Most organizations have patch management systems in place for their systems but provide no update services for the student, guest, and nonmanaged PCs that connect to their internal networks.

Summary

This chapter examined why, with today's security challenges and threats growing more sophisticated, perimeter defense alone is no longer sufficient. It discussed why organizations need to have internal security systems that are more comprehensive, pervasive, and tightly integrated than in the past. Cisco NAC Appliance is such a security system. It allows for pervasive and in-depth host security defenses throughout an organization's internal infrastructure with multiple points of protection. The chapter covered network security as a weakest-link problem and offered that the internal networks constitute the weakest link today. The internal networks are typically lacking the proper amount of security measures. This results in an increased likelihood of compromise to internal hosts and data by another internal host, not by an external source.

Also examined were the myriad of issues and challenges regarding the patch management update race of hosts. The chapter discussed that the time between the public release of a software vulnerability notice and the release of the exploit that takes advantage of the vulnerability is rapidly shrinking. This is driving the need for organizations to enforce that they allow full internal network access only to up-to-date systems.

This chapter covers the following topics:

- Cisco NAC Approaches
- Cisco NAC Appliance Overview
- Cisco NAC Return on Investment

CHAPTER 2

Introducing Cisco Network Admission Control Appliance

The primary goal of Cisco Network Admission Control (NAC) Appliance is to proactively enforce corporate host security policies on users and hosts accessing the network. A primary advantage of this solution is enabling ubiquitous user authentication at the network layer, and then using that information to grant network access based on the user's identity and characteristics of the device. For example, all guest users receive only limited Internet access and no internal access. Cisco NAC can leverage existing security technologies, such as antivirus, antispam, and operating system updaters to ensure that user machines are current with the latest patches. Cisco NAC can also collaborate with the network infrastructure to identify, assess, and authorize users according to the compliance status of the user's PC.

Cisco NAC Approaches

Cisco offers NAC as an appliance or as an embedded solution for an 802.1x-enabled infrastructure. This book focuses strictly on the appliance-based approach, but it may be helpful for the reader to understand the high-level differences between the two approaches.

NAC as an Appliance

Cisco NAC Appliance (formerly known as Cisco Clean Access) comes from the Cisco 2004 acquisition of Perfigo. NAC Appliance was designed as a self-contained NAC solution, able to authenticate, posture assess, quarantine, and remediate without the need to tie in multiple products from various certified vendors. Due to its rapid and flexible deployment capabilities, NAC Appliance has attained a 45 percent market share, according to a November 2006 Frost & Sullivan report. See Figure 2-1 for the components and architecture of NAC Appliance.

Figure 2-1   *NAC Appliance Components*

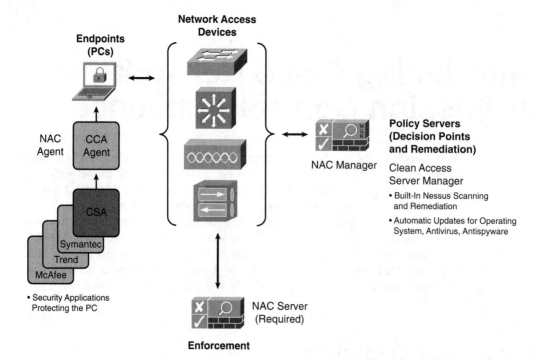

A NAC Appliance solution consists of NAC Appliance Manager (NAM), NAC Appliance Server (NAS), and NAC Agent (also known as Cisco Clean Access [CCA] Agent). This book provides more detail on each of these components throughout later chapters. For now, simply keep in mind that NAC Manager is the back-end central policy server hosting the user credentials and NAC policies. NAC Server is the workhorse of the NAC Appliance solution because it performs all authentication activities and enforces the user policies. You can think of NAC Server as a policy firewall. The free NAC Agent gathers username and password, antivirus, antispyware, and operating systems hotfix information from the user's machine and delivers it to NAC Server and NAC Manager.

User authentication occurs in two ways: agent and agentless (via web browser). The agent is the ideal and most effective use of NAC Appliance because the installed agent can easily read the details of the antivirus, antispyware, and operating system information via the registry. The agentless or web browser redirect authentication process can authenticate a user and scan the user's machine via the built-in Nessus scanner in NAC Server. Assuming that agentless machines do not have personal firewalls enabled, the Nessus scanner is effective in checking for current vulnerabilities.

Many customers see the primary strength of NAC Appliance as its off-the-shelf packaging with little customization required for deployment. NAC Appliance's proven flexibility in a myriad of network environments has led a majority of Cisco customers to quickly and successfully deploy a Cisco NAC Appliance solution.

NAC as an Embedded Solution

The initial Cisco vision of NAC, first introduced in 2003, leverages the Cisco IOS in Cisco routers and switches to deliver the NAC functionality. Also referred to as NAC Framework, it comprises Cisco Access Control Server (ACS), Cisco routers and switches, and an end point software agent called Cisco Trust Agent (CTA). To assist with posture assessment, device auditing, and software remediation, the embedded NAC solution relies on third-party software via application program interfaces (API). Third-party security software, such as antivirus and antispam programs from Symantec, McAfee, TrendMicro, and so on, is installed to protect the end points. These security applications use APIs to report their software version and status to Cisco Trust Agent. Cisco Trust Agent, acting as an application broker, collects the required software information regarding the machine and reports to Cisco ACS, which is the back-end authentication and policy server. See Figure 2-2 for components of the embedded NAC approach.

Figure 2-2   *Embedded NAC Components*

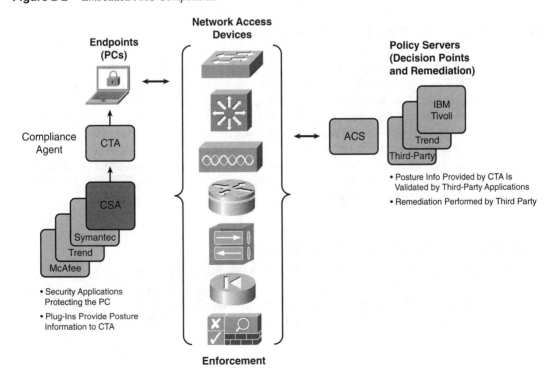

Based on the posture information provided by CTA, ACS compares the received information against its configured policies and informs the appropriate network device, such as a router or switch, to quarantine, permit, or deny network access. This process works well for PCs capable of running CTA. For devices incapable of running CTA (considered non-NAC–responsive devices), such as IP phones or network printers, NAC Framework allows for third-party auditing servers (that is, Qualys or Foundstone, now McAfee) to perform an audit of non-NAC responsive devices to determine the device type and its appropriate network access privileges. After the third-party auditing servers determine which devices on the network are printers, they can inform the routers or switches through ACS to assign those printers into the appropriate printer access role. For further details about the Cisco embedded approach to NAC, refer to http://www.cisco.com/go/nac/framework or *Cisco Network Admission Control Volume 1: NAC Framework Architecture and Design* from Cisco Press.

The embedded NAC approach is an elegant and deeply customizable technology, but the appliance-based approach is faster to deploy. Cisco recently introduced an integrated implementation strategy that combines the benefits of both approaches.

NOTE   This book does not cover the embedded (framework) NAC solution.

Cisco NAC Integrated Implementation

Cisco recently finalized a roadmap for an integrated implementation that enables both the NAC Appliance and embedded NAC approaches to interoperate within the same network. An existing example of this model is the Cisco firewall offering in both Cisco IOS routers and switches and dedicated appliances. Some customers deploy both IOS firewalls and dedicated firewall appliances as part of their defense-in-depth strategy. The integrated NAC implementation allows existing NAC appliance or embedded NAC customers to preserve their existing investments without having to worry about the long-term longevity of either NAC approach. The goal of Cisco is to provide interoperability and coexistence of either NAC approach where required. This integrated implementation is slated for availability in 2008. Contact your local Cisco account team for the latest developments.

Cisco NAC Appliance Overview

The leading Cisco NAC offering is Cisco NAC Appliance (formerly known as Cisco Clean Access). Cisco NAC Appliance is the focus of this book. Cisco NAC Appliance is an easily deployable NAC solution that leverages the existing Cisco network infrastructure to enforce network security policies and software compliance. NAC Appliance can authenticate a user or device and perform posture assessment before granting access to the network. Devices such as PCs found to be missing the latest required OS patch or antivirus and antispyware definition can be quarantined and remediated through the self-remediation process before assigning them an appropriate user access role. A key strength of NAC Appliance is its ability to dynamically assign user roles based on the posture of the PC or device. If an employee PC complies with corporate software policies, that PC can be placed in an employee role with full network access. If a guest user joins the network, that guest user is placed in the guest role with only limited guest access privileges such as web access only. Devices such as printers or IP phones typically do not respond to NAC and thus can bypass NAC and be placed in their appropriate network roles.

NAC can be applied to the following networks:

- High-speed LANs (optimized with out-of-band deployment)
- Hub-spoke networks across the WAN
- Remote-access IPsec and Secure Socket Layer Virtual Private Networks (SSL VPNs)
- Intranets and extranets
- Wireless networks

Cisco NAC provides the following benefits:

- **Minimize unauthorized access and potential breach of sensitive data**   By identifying users and PCs as they access the network and assigning access roles, users can access only data allowed in their access role.
- **Minimize network outages**   By ensuring that all end hosts have the latest antivirus and antispyware definitions and OS patches, the total number of virus and worm outbreaks is reduced.
- **Reduce the overall endpoint support cost**   Through the self-healing and remediation process, antivirus, antispyware, and OS updates are performed automatically or with little to no help from the IT help desk.

Cisco NAC Return on Investment

Many Cisco customers who have deployed the NAC appliance solution have quickly realized the immediate return on investment (ROI) of the NAC appliance. There are many references listed on the Cisco website at http://www.cisco.com/go/nac/appliance under Case Studies. The following four case studies give you an example of how a higher-education institute, healthcare medical center, clinical research lab, and local city agency are using the Cisco NAC solution to improve their overall endpoint security:

- **Arizona State University (ASU)**   With more than 58,000 users on campus, ASU is faced with unregulated laptops entering the residence halls and public access areas daily and potentially spreading viruses and worms. With Cisco NAC Appliance, the number of security incidents during the first six weeks of the fall semester of 2005 dramatically reduced from 1800 infected machines (2004) to 400 infected machines trying to access the network.

- **UK National Health Service**   NAC Appliance has been implemented at a new children's medical center based in southeast London. This new center hosts approximately 3500 employees and deployed a multilayer security model that included biometric fingerprint readers and Cisco NAC Appliance. The center uses Cisco NAC Appliance to authenticate users to the network based on fingerprint, and then checks the status of PCs and laptops for the latest antivirus and security software before granting them access to the network.

- **Charles River Labs (CRL)**   CRL is based in Wilmington, Massachusetts, and provides research models, preclinical services, and clinical services to the pharmaceutical and biotech markets. Its key IT driver was the construction of new research buildings known as Centers of Excellence. CRL relies on Cisco security products, including Cisco NAC Appliance, to make sure that it could meet and exceed the strict information security requirements mandated by the Food and Drug Administration, and to ensure that customers could trust CRL with their critical clinical data.

- **The City of Dublin, Ohio**   This city is home to more than 3000 businesses and continually strives to create an attractive economic environment by investing in information technology. The city implemented a Cisco secure wireless solution that uses Cisco NAC Appliance to enforce security policy compliance on every device accessing the wireless network. Doing so improves overall network health and maintains network availability for the public and private services that depend on it.

Summary

The main purpose of Network Admission Control is to enforce endhost policies. Example endhost policies are antivirus and antispam updates and operating system patches that must be current to mitigate potential virus and worm outbreaks and PC exploits. PCs that comply with corporate software policies are assigned a role and given appropriate network access. Devices that don't comply are quarantined and placed through the self-guided remediation process. Non-NAC–responsive devices, such as IP phones, printers, fax servers, and so on, can be configured to bypass NAC through exceptions. In general, NAC ensures that all PCs joining the network are compliant with corporate software policies, and it improves the overall network quality and availability.

The primary Cisco NAC offering is the NAC Appliance solution. NAC Appliance is prepackaged with minimal software customization and can be quickly deployed by any customer. NAC can apply to every component of the network such as high-speed Layer 2 and 3 LANs, across the WAN, remote-access IPsec and Secure Socket Layer virtual private networks, and wireless networks. Benefits of the Cisco NAC Appliance solution are minimized network outages due to virus and worm outbreaks, minimized unauthorized data access and sensitive data breach, and reduced overall endpoint support cost through its self-guided remediation process.

PART II

The Blueprint: Designing a Cisco NAC Appliance Solution

This chapter covers the following topics:

- Cisco NAC Appliance Solution Components
- Cisco NAC Appliance Minimum Requirements
- Scalability and Performance of Cisco NAC Appliance

CHAPTER 3

The Building Blocks in a Cisco NAC Appliance Design

Knowledge of how to properly design security solutions is what separates the professional from the amateur. Without a proper design, the eventual implementation will most likely be a disaster. One of the keys to success when designing a security solution is to first understand all the pieces you have to work with. I like to call these building blocks. After you achieve understanding, you then need to become skilled at manipulating the pieces in ways that best fit your environment. This chapter focuses on the building blocks available with the Cisco NAC Appliance solution. The purpose and function of each piece is covered. The requirements, scalability, and performance of these building blocks are also discussed. The next chapter discusses your options for manipulating these building blocks.

Cisco NAC Appliance Solution Components

A NAC Appliance solution is made up of the following components:

- Mandatory components:
  - Cisco NAC Appliance Manager (Clean Access Manager)
  - Cisco NAC Appliance Server (Clean Access Server)
- Optional components:
  - Cisco Clean Access Agent
  - Cisco NAC Appliance Network Scanner

Each piece has a distinct role to play in the solution. In this section, you examine the roles of each in more detail.

NOTE   Cisco NAC Appliance was formerly known as Cisco Clean Access. The legacy name Clean Access is still widely used in the industry, but this book will use the new name: Cisco NAC Appliance.

Cisco NAC Appliance Manager

The roles of NAC Appliance Manager are as follows:

- Central administration and monitoring
- Management of up to 40 NAC Appliance Server pairs
- Central configuration of security policy and requirements
- Performing automatic download of the latest Clean Access policies and updates
- Centrally controlling network devices
- Central user authentication to back-end authentication sources such as Lightweight Directory Access Protocol (LDAP), RADIUS, and Kerberos

NAC Appliance Manager is the administration server. It allows you to centrally manage and monitor your deployment of NAC Appliance Servers and Agents. It is here that you configure your security policies that define the checks your hosts will have to pass to be considered clean or up to date. The NAC Appliance allows you to build your own customized checks, but it also comes with many preconfigured checks. It is a big job to manually maintain and track all the new updates that come out for antivirus, antispyware, Microsoft Windows, and so on. That is why the NAC Appliance Manager is also responsible for receiving regular version and policy updates from Cisco. These policy updates contain information on the latest operating system patches, antivirus versions, and antispyware versions. The prepackaged software checks and security policies are automatically updated with this new version information. Using the policy update feature makes it easier to ensure your hosts are always checked for the latest versions before they are allowed network access.

NAC Appliance Manager is configured using a web console after a minimal bootstrapping process. NAC Appliance Manager is capable of scaling to administer up to 40 NAC Appliance Server pairs. NAC Appliance Manager's web console allows you to configure both global security policies and per-server local policies. Global security policies save time and are much easier to manage. For example, you could create a global policy that says all hosts connecting to the network through any NAC Appliance Server must have an up-to-date antivirus program installed. NAC Appliance Manager then pushes this policy out to all the NAC Appliance Servers for local checking and enforcement. If you have some specific local security policies that pertain to only a single NAC Appliance Server, you can use NAC Appliance Manager's web console to configure those as well. Figure 3-1 shows NAC Appliance Manager's web console.

NAC Appliance Manager is responsible for authenticating all users in the NAC Appliance deployment with the exception of single sign-on (SSO) users. SSO users are authenticated by the local NAC Appliance Server. NAC Appliance Manager can use either its local user database or an external user database such as LDAP or RADIUS as an authentication source.

Figure 3-1   *NAC Appliance Manager Web Console*

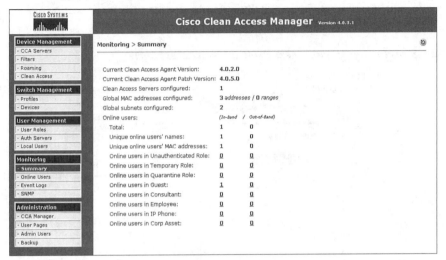

Cisco NAC Appliance Server

The roles of the NAC Appliance Server are as follows:

- Security policy assessment
- Security policy enforcement

NAC Appliance Server is the policy enforcer, or the policy firewall, between the untrusted networks and the trusted networks. NAC Appliance Server's job is to enforce the security policies created in NAC Appliance Manager. NAC Appliance Server, in conjunction with NAC Appliance Manager, actively checks the identity of users and the security posture of their host when they try to obtain access to the network. Based on the results of the check, NAC Appliance Server enforces the proper network access policy. It is important to note that NAC Appliance Server and NAC Appliance Manager act as a team in this process. NAC Appliance Server is mostly responsible for asking for authentication and posture information from the clients. This information is then forwarded to NAC Appliance Manager for checking. Based on the results, NAC Appliance Manager instructs the server to start enforcing a particular policy for that client.

For NAC Appliance Server to work, it must be physically or logically inline between the clients and their destinations during the initial posture assessment and remediation. After the clients pass the posture assessment, NAC Appliance Server can be removed from the dataflow (out of band) or remain in the dataflow (in band). The next chapter will discuss these different options in detail.

Clients can use either the Clean Access Agent or web login to trigger NAC Appliance posture assessment. Figure 3-2 illustrates the steps that trigger inspection of a client with a Clean Access Agent preinstalled.

Figure 3-2 *Steps to Trigger Assessment Using a Clean Access Agent*

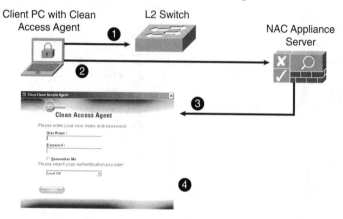

The following is an explanation of the numbered process in Figure 3-2.

Step 1 The host plugs into a switch port and requests a DHCP address. Acting as the DHCP server, NAC Appliance Server replies to the host's DHCP request. Clean Access Agent detects the new network connection.

Step 2 To find NAC Appliance Server, Clean Access Agent sends out discovery packets to all the default gateways present in the host's routing table. In Figure 3-2, NAC Appliance Server is the host's default gateway and receives the discovery packets.

Step 3 The discovery packets trigger NAC Appliance Server to perform assessment of the new host. First it checks to see whether the host MAC address is already permitted. If so, the host is allowed to pass through NAC Appliance Server. If not, NAC Appliance Server sends back a login request to Clean Access Agent.

Step 4 Clean Access Agent pops up the agent log in a dialog box and waits for the user to enter a username and password.

NOTE Clean Access Agent uses a proprietary discovery protocol called SWISS. SWISS runs on UDP port 8905 for Layer 2 users and 8906 for Layer 3 users. Clean Access Agent performs discovery every 5 seconds. The NAC Appliance Server listens on UDP 8905/8906 for the SWISS packets being sent from the agents.

Figure 3-3 illustrates the steps that trigger inspection of a client using the web login.

Figure 3-3 *Steps to Trigger Assessment Using Web Login*

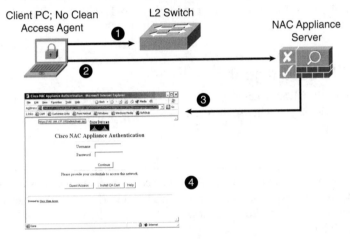

The following is an explanation of the numbered process in Figure 3-3.

Step 1   The host plugs into a switch port and requests a DHCP address. Acting as the DHCP server, NAC Appliance Server replies to the host's DHCP request.

Step 2   The user launches a web browser and requests a website. NAC Appliance Server sees this request. It checks the MAC address or IP address of the host to see whether it is already permitted. If so, the host is allowed on the network. If not, NAC Appliance Server intercepts the web request.

Step 3   The web page request triggers NAC Appliance Server to perform assessment of the host. The intercepted web page request is stopped, and a redirect to NAC Appliance Server's web login page is sent back to the user's web browser.

Step 4   The user is redirected and presented with the web login page. NAC Appliance Server waits for the client to log in or click on guest access.

CAUTION   Before a successful login, all clients are in the Unauthenticated role. Client traffic in this role will by default be dropped by NAC Appliance Server. The exceptions are DHCP and DNS queries, which are allowed through. Therefore, if other traffic types and services are required, you will have to customize the traffic filters. A common example of this is allowing clients to log in to the Windows Active Directory (AD) domain when they first boot up.

NAC Appliance Manager's web console is used to centrally manage NAC Appliance Servers. However, each server does have a local web console and supports Secure Shell (SSH). These can be useful for troubleshooting purposes but are not generally used for local configuration after NAC Appliance Server's initial setup script is run.

Cisco Clean Access Agent

Technically, Clean Access Agent and Network Scanner are optional components. However, in most cases, you will use the Clean Access Agent and Network Scanner in your deployment.

CAUTION   If you choose not to use either the Clean Access Agent or the Network Scanner, then you cannot perform any host security assessment checks (for example, checking for up-to-date antivirus definitions). You will, however, be able to perform user authentication checking via web login.

Clean Access Agent is a free software program that resides on client PCs. It is a read-only agent whose job is to gather information about the user and the host it is installed on. It then matches that against the requirements received for that user, role, or OS from NAC Appliance Server and sends back a report to NAC Appliance Manager via NAC Appliance Server. If the requirements are met, the host is allowed on the network. If the host fails, Clean Access Agent presents the user, via a dialog box, with the remediation instructions received from NAC Appliance Manager. The information it checks for is configured by you at the NAC Appliance Manager level and then pushed out to each NAC Appliance Server. The information that can be checked by Clean Access Agent includes applications, files, registry keys, and services. For example, Clean Access Agent could check for the presence of a Windows hotfix or check to see whether an antivirus program is current.

Hosts that fail a system check are then put into a Clean Access Agent Temporary role. This role is configured to restrict network access to only those resources they will need to remediate their host. This may include access to websites, such as update.microsoft.com, or access to antivirus vendor update servers (local or on the Internet). These restrictions are enforced at the closest NAC Appliance Server in the traffic path of Clean Access Agent. No enforcement is done locally at the Clean Access Agent level. Clean Access Agent will then help the user fix up, or remediate, the host. It uses pop-up dialog boxes to notify the user of security policy violations that have occurred. It also provides a remediation button to fix the violation. See Figure 3-4 for an example.

Figure 3-4   *Clean Access Agent Remediation Example*

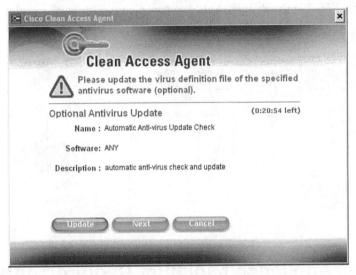

Cisco NAC Appliance Network Scanner

Network Scanner allows you to scan hosts to check for known vulnerabilities. Network Scanner is integrated into the NAC Appliance Manager and NAC Appliance Server software and is not a standalone piece. Network Scanner uses Nessus to scan hosts. You add in the Nessus plug-ins of your choice. For example, you can add the plug-ins that check to see whether music file-sharing applications are running on the host. If such programs are running, you could notify the end users that they must disable or uninstall the offending software before they are allowed on the network. Network Scanner can also be used to posture assess hosts that run operating systems not supported by Clean Access Agent, such as Linux.

TIP   For more information about the Nessus tool and its plug-ins, visit http://www.nessus.org or http://www.nessus.org/plugins.

The following simple example illustrates where the pieces of a Cisco NAC Appliance design are placed in a network. Figure 3-5 shows a NAC Appliance deployment using

Layer 2 in-band. Layer 2 means that NAC Appliance Server is Layer 2 adjacent to the clients it will control. In-band means that data traffic always flows through NAC Appliance Server.

Figure 3-5 *Cisco NAC Appliance Deployment Example (Layer 2 In-Band)*

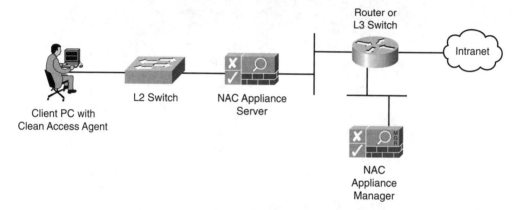

Cisco NAC Appliance Minimum Requirements

Cisco NAC Appliance Manager and NAC Appliance Server can be purchased two ways. You can buy only the software from Cisco and buy the hardware somewhere else, or you can buy the hardware and the software together in one of several appliance models available from Cisco. Typically, the term *appliance* means that the hardware and software come as a unit and you don't have the flexibility to buy your own hardware.

That is not the case with NAC Appliance. The NAC Appliance software-only option is packaged on a bootable CD or DVD in such a way that it completely self-installs everything you need on the hardware of your choice. There are no install scripts to run or questions to answer; just pop in the CD or DVD, boot up the system, wait a few minutes, and then you have NAC Appliance Manager or NAC Appliance Server ready to be configured.

However, the recommended path is to purchase the hardware and software NAC Appliance from Cisco. This is a true appliance and comes preinstalled and ready to go. It makes for a cleaner solution. There are three NAC Appliance hardware and software models. Table 3-1 shows the mapping of licenses to appliance models. A 3310 or 3350 appliance can be purchased as either NAC Appliance Manager or NAC Appliance Server—the hardware supports both. A 3390 supports only NAC Appliance Manager.

Table 3-1   *Cisco NAC Appliance 3300 Series*

	Cisco NAC Appliance 3310	Cisco NAC Appliance 3350	Cisco NAC Appliance 3390
Cisco NAC Appliance Server	Supported User Licenses: 100, 250, 500	Supported User Licenses: 1500, 2500, 3500	
Cisco NAC Appliance Manager	NAC Appliance Manager Lite—supports up to three NAC Appliance Server pairs	NAC Appliance Manager—supports up to 20 NAC Appliance Server pairs	NAC Appliance Super Manager—supports up to 40 NAC Appliance Server pairs

The 3350 and 3390 appliances both include an SSL accelerator card and a hard disk array. The sections that follow describe the requirements for each component of the solution.

Cisco NAC Appliance Manager and Server Requirements

Cisco NAC Appliance is sold as software only or as an appliance with hardware and software preinstalled. If you go the software-only route, you have to provide your own hardware. This hardware must be on the current supported server configurations list. Hardware not on the list will not be supported by Cisco Technical Assistance Center. To obtain the current supported server list, go to http://www.cisco.com and search for "supported server configurations nac." After you select a supported server vendor and model, make sure that it meets the NAC Appliance minimum requirements listed in Table 3-2. Of course, if you go with the Appliance-packaged version of NAC Appliance, you do not need to worry about any of this; it is already optimized.

Table 3-2   *NAC Appliance Manager and Server Minimum Requirements*

Component	Minimum Requirement
CPU	Single 2.4 GHz or greater.
RAM memory	1 GB or greater (see "Reasons to Exceed the Recommended minimum Requirements").
Hard disk space	10 GB or greater.
NICs[1]	Dual Fast or Gigabit Ethernet ports (see "Reasons to Exceed the Recommended minimum Requirements"). Intel or Broadcom recommended.
Web browser for web admin console	Internet Explorer 6.0 or above is required.

1.   network interface cards

CAUTION   Always check the latest NAC Appliance Release Notes at Cisco.com for the most up-to-date details about hardware and software requirements.

Reasons to Exceed the Recommended Minimum Requirements

It is generally a good idea to exceed the minimum requirement's but here are some specific reasons.

RAM Memory:

- Consider 2 GB of memory or greater if you plan to deploy NAC Appliance Manager with a large number of device filters, traffic policies, local users, or multiple NAC Appliance Servers fully loaded with more than 1000 users

- Consider 2 GB of memory or greater if you are deploying NAC Appliance Server as a DHCP server, configuring /30 subnets, or supporting close to 1500 users.

Network Interface Cards:

- If running NAC Appliance Servers in High Availability mode, it is recommended to configure a third NIC card. That NIC will be dedicated for high availability purposes.

- You should have 2 GB of memory if you have more than 500 users.

Cisco Clean Access Agent Requirements

The Cisco Clean Access Agent currently runs on Windows and Macintosh operating systems. Table 3-3 provides details as to the host requirements needed to run the Agent. Be sure to check Cisco.com to see whether additional operating systems or requirements have been added.

Table 3-3   *Clean Access Agent Requirements*

Host	Requirement
Supported operating systems	Microsoft Vista (all versions, including Japanese), Windows XP Professional, Windows XP Home, Windows XP MCE, Windows XP Tablet PC, Windows 2000, Windows 98, Windows SE, Windows Me, Japanese and simplified Chinese Windows XP SP2 Mac OS X[1]
Hard drive space	Minimum of 10 MB free
Hardware	No minimum requirements

1.   Mac OS X agent currently supports only user authentication. No host posture assessment checks are supported. This is a roadmapped feature; check with Cisco for availability.

Scalability and Performance of Cisco NAC Appliance

To ensure a good design, understanding the scalability and performance limits of NAC Appliance is important. Table 3-4 depicts the scalability and performance numbers that are relevant to properly designing a NAC Appliance solution.

Table 3-4 *Scalability and Performance of NAC Appliance*

NAC Appliance Manager	Maximum Managed Server Pairs/Manager	20
NAC Appliance Super Manager	Maximum Managed Server Pairs/Manager	40
NAC Appliance Server	Data Throughput/Server	~950 Mbps
	Maximum Users/Server	3500
	Maximum MAC Addresses/Server	8000

Summary

This chapter examined the various building blocks that make up the Cisco NAC Appliance solution. Those building blocks are as follows:

- Cisco NAC Appliance Manager
- Cisco NAC Appliance Server
- Cisco Clean Access Agent
- Cisco NAC Appliance Network Scanner

The purpose and function of each piece was covered and can be summarized as follows:

- NAC Appliance Manager is the administration server. It allows you to centrally manage and monitor your deployment of NAC Appliance Servers and Clean Access Agents.

- NAC Appliance Server is the policy enforcer, or the policy firewall, between the untrusted networks and the trusted networks. NAC Appliance Server's job is to enforce the security policies created in NAC Appliance Manager.

- Clean Access Agent is a free software program that resides on client PCs. It is a read-only agent whose job is to gather information about the user and host it is installed on.

- NAC Appliance Network Scanner allows you to scan hosts to check for known vulnerabilities. It uses the embedded Nessus vulnerability scanning software for this function.

The chapter finished with an overview of the minimum hardware and software requirements and performance metrics of the different building blocks. It was recommended that the newer appliance form factors be used for the NAC Appliance Manager and NAC Appliance Server pieces.

This chapter covers the following topics:

- NAC Design Considerations
- Deployment Options
- In-Band Mode
- Out-of-Band Mode
- Clean Access Agent and Web Login with Network Scanner

CHAPTER 4

Making Sense of All the Cisco NAC Appliance Design Options

In the previous chapter, you explored all the pieces, or building blocks, that can make up a Cisco NAC Appliance deployment. Now you will learn the multiple ways you can manipulate these building blocks so that they best fit into your environment. Given the complexity of today's networks, you need a Network Admission Control (NAC) solution that has options. Cisco NAC Appliance definitely has options. It has so many, in fact, that sometimes it can get confusing as to what to use where and why. The purpose of this chapter is to guide you through the different modes of operation and deployment that are available to you. Along the way, you receive explanations of the criteria you can use to make a use-case decision for various features.

This chapter starts with a brief explanation of the different Cisco NAC Appliance design decisions you will have to make. Then it moves into explaining, in detail, what each design element has to offer (depending on where you use it). Finally, it covers several traffic and work flow examples of common NAC Appliance deployment types.

NAC Design Considerations

When working through the design process for Cisco NAC Appliance, you will come up against multiple choices. Understanding what choices are available and how they work is incredibly important. Your environment will most likely use a few different deployment options, not a single one throughout. For example, you might choose to use Single-Sign-On (SSO) for your virtual private network (VPN) users but not for your wireless guest user and public space areas. Knowing how to best match the flexibility of NAC Appliance to your environment will make the deployment and adoption go smoothly.

These are some of the design decisions you will have to make in your environment:

- User Single-Sign-On versus dedicated NAC Appliance login
- In-Band versus Out-of-Band modes
- Layer 2 versus Layer 3 client adjacency
- Virtual Gateway versus Real IP Gateway modes
- Clean Access Agent versus Web Login with Network Scanner

Before explaining the specifics of each of the preceding features, it is useful to first describe the purpose of each new term or technology that will be relevant to subsequent discussions.

Single-Sign-On Capabilities

Single-Sign-On, or SSO, gives users the convenience of only having to log in to the network once. The way this works in a Cisco NAC Appliance solution is based on a trust model. For example, if a VPN concentrator has validated your login credentials successfully, NAC Appliance will trust these same credentials for its own user validation. This prevents the user from having to log in once to the VPN concentrator and a second time to NAC Appliance. Whenever possible, you should use SSO. Using SSO will greatly increase the satisfaction of the users' experience with NAC Appliance.

NAC Appliance has SSO integration support with the following platforms:

- Microsoft Active Directory (AD).
- Cisco VPN.
- Any VPN solution that can send a RADIUS accounting packet in an RFC-compliant format. (Microsoft's Internet Authentication Service is an example of this.)
- Cisco Wireless using lightweight access point technology.

In-Band Versus Out-of-Band Overview

In-Band (IB) and Out-of-Band (OOB) are modes of operation you choose for your NAC Appliance Servers. NAC Appliance Server can run in only one mode, not both simultaneously. However, a single NAC Appliance Manager can control servers of both mode types. NAC Appliance Server is similar in function, placement, and operation to a traditional stateless packet-filtering firewall. Like a firewall, NAC Appliance Server must be logically or physically in the traffic flow to work. Resembling a firewall, NAC Appliance Server's job is to regulate who and what can pass from the untrusted networks to the trusted networks. But unlike a firewall, you can choose to remove NAC Appliance Server from the traffic flow after its work—that is, posture assessment—is complete. This means NAC Appliance Server is now out-of-band. If you choose not to remove NAC Appliance Server after the host is certified, it is said to be in-band.

Configuring NAC Appliance Server for In-Band mode means that it is always in the flow of traffic between the untrusted networks and the trusted networks. This is regardless of whether or not the host on the untrusted side has passed assessment.

Configuring NAC Appliance Server for Out-of-Band mode means that it is not always in the flow of traffic. NAC Appliance Server remains in the flow of traffic between the untrusted networks and trusted networks until the host passes authentication and assessment. After a host is considered "clean," or certified, NAC Appliance reconfigures the host's switch port to be on a new VLAN. The new VLAN no longer has NAC Appliance Server in its path. Given that NAC Appliance Server is no longer in the path, network traffic to and from the certified host is routed and switched normally.

The choice of which mode to use, In-Band or Out-of-Band, will vary based on your environment and network. Like most of the choices you will make, this one is both function and location dependent. It is possible, even likely, that you will end up with both In-Band and Out-of-Band mode NAC Appliance Servers running in your deployment.

Layer 2 Versus Layer 3 Client Adjacency Overview

Layer 2 Adjacency means that NAC Appliance Server is a Layer 2 hop from hosts on its untrusted networks side. This allows NAC Appliance Server to see the real MAC address of every client it is controlling. In Layer 2 mode, a host's unique identity is defined using its MAC address only.

Layer 3 Adjacency means NAC Appliance Server is one or more Layer 3 network hops from the hosts on its untrusted networks side. In this mode, NAC Appliance Server cannot see the real MAC address of the host. In Layer 3 mode, a host's unique identity is defined using its IP address only. When using OOB mode, the client's MAC address is forwarded to NAC Appliance Server using either Clean Access Agent or the ActiveX or Java web login applet. However, this MAC address is not used by NAC Appliance to determine a host s identity; it is used only to determine the switch port a client resides on. Layer 3 OOB mode will be discussed in more detail later.

Using Layer 3 mode allows you more flexibility in your placement of NAC Appliance Servers. The drawback is it can be more complex to deploy. Deploying in Layer 3 mode behind a VPN device or wireless controller is simple and straightforward. However, deploying in a nontunneled environment, such as T1 attached branch offices, can add complexity. For some network areas, having a NAC Appliance Server be Layer 2 adjacent to the hosts it is controlling would not be possible. Some examples include VPN tunnel clients and clients coming from networks you don't control, such as business partner extranet clients. In some cases, it is not cost effective to deploy NAC Appliance Server in Layer 2 mode. In Layer 2 mode, if you have 80 small branch offices with only ten people each, you would have 80 NAC Appliance Servers—one NAC Appliance Server located at each site. In Layer 3 mode, you could have one NAC Appliance Server at the central site that posture assesses all hosts at the 80 branch offices.

Virtual Gateway Versus Real IP Gateway Overview

NAC Appliance Server can act as a network bridge or a router between its untrusted and trusted networks. When acting as a bridge between untrusted and trusted networks, it is in Virtual Gateway mode. When NAC Appliance Server is routing between untrusted and trusted networks, it is in Real IP Gateway mode. Virtual Gateway mode acts like a bump in the wire. NAC Appliance Server's presence is transparent to hosts.

In Real IP Gateway mode, NAC Appliance Server looks to hosts just like any other router would. In Layer 2 adjacent Real IP Gateway mode, NAC Appliance Server is the default router for the hosts on its untrusted side.

Deployment Options

Always keep in mind that every NAC Appliance Server must have three distinct deployment modes defined before it will operate. Together, these three modes define how NAC Appliance Server interacts with hosts and the rest of the network. The first mode is Client/Server Adjacency. This mode defines whether NAC Appliance Server and the clients on the untrusted interface are on the same network or multiple Layer 3 hops from each other.

The second mode is Post–Client Certification mode. This mode defines whether client traffic continues to flow through NAC Appliance even after a client is certified. There are never any network changes with In-Band mode, so client traffic always flows through NAC Appliance. With Out-of-Band mode, a certified client is moved to a new VLAN that removes NAC Appliance from the traffic path. Network mode, the last of the three modes, determines whether NAC Appliance Server acts as a bridge (Virtual Gateway) or a router (Real IP Gateway) between its untrusted and trusted interfaces. Table 4-1 presents the distinct modes and their options. Every NAC Appliance Server must have one option from each mode type defined.

Table 4-1 *Deployment Modes Required on NAC Appliance Servers*

Client/Server Adjacency Modes			Post–Client Certification Modes		Network Modes	
Layer 2	Layer 3	Layer 2 and 3	In-Band	Out-of-Band	Virtual Gateway	Real IP Gateway

NOTE It is possible to combine a mode option with any option from the other mode types. There are no restrictions on the combinations you can have across mode types. However, you can choose only one option within each mode type.

NOTE In NAC Appliance, you will see a third network mode option called Real IP NAT Gateway. Due mostly to performance reasons, this mode is not supported for production use. Therefore, this book does not discuss Real IP NAT Gateway mode.

The flowchart in Figure 4-1 is designed to help you select the appropriate features for your environment. This chart gives you a general idea of the dependencies each mode of operation has and the order you should make your choices in. The detailed information needed to make informed choices as you navigate this flowchart will be covered in this section.

Figure 4-1   *Design Selection Flowchart*

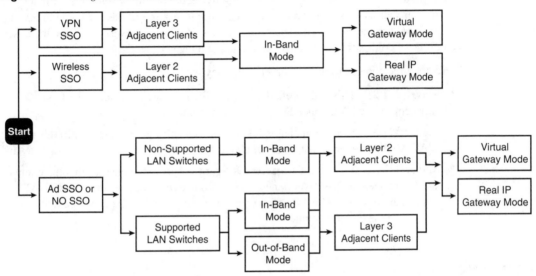

How to Choose a Client/Server Adjacency Mode

A NAC Appliance solution can be deployed in two ways: central and edge. It is possible, even likely, that most environments will end up with a design that uses both types. Central deployment means that you will position your NAC Appliance Servers in the core or hub sites of your networks. For example, if you have several remote sites coming into a hub site, you would position NAC Appliance Server at the hub site and not at each remote site. Usually this means that NAC Appliance Server is Layer 3 adjacent to the clients it is controlling. Edge deployment is the opposite of central deployment; so, using edge, you position your NAC Appliance Server as close as possible to the clients it is controlling. For example, if you have several remote sites coming into a hub site, you would position NAC Appliance Server at every remote site. Usually this means that NAC Appliance Server is Layer 2 adjacent to the clients.

NOTE	The preceding terms *central* and *edge* are used to describe the logical placement of the NAC Appliance Servers. To avoid confusion, you should be aware that the terms central and edge can also be used to describe the physical deployment method of NAC Appliance Servers. That is not how the terms are used here.

As discussed, the chosen deployment type influences the adjacency mode used in the design. Keep in mind that like most other security technologies, the closer you can get to the clients you want to control, the more secure your design will be. However, the tradeoff for pushing security to the client edge is usually higher costs and scalability issues. If an environment has a pure client edge deployment, NAC Appliance Servers are always Layer 2 adjacent to all clients everywhere. This is highly secure and allows you the ultimate control over your clients. However, to accomplish this task might mean deploying 30, 50, or more NAC Appliance Servers. This many servers drives up the overall cost and increases the burden of configuration, management, and maintenance.

There are three choices for client/server adjacency:

- **Layer 2 (L2)**   This is the default setting. All clients are expected to be Layer 2 adjacent to NAC Appliance Server's untrusted interface.

- **Layer 3 (L3)**   When you enable L3 support, you also get L2 support. In this mode, NAC Appliance Server listens to all clients from any number of network hops away.

- **Layer 2 Strict mode for Clean Access Agent**   This mode ensures that the clients are L2 adjacent to NAC Appliance Server. No network address translation (NAT) routers are allowed. This L2 enforcement requires the Clean Access Agent to be loaded on the client machine.

Layer 2 Mode

This mode is the default network setting for NAC Appliance Server. As such, it is the most commonly deployed as well. Layer 2 mode means that the clients are Layer 2 adjacent to the untrusted interface on NAC Appliance Server. In most LAN environments, L2 works just fine. If you have Layer 2 trunks between your access and distribution layer switches and your access switches do not use L3, you can usually use Layer 2 mode.

The most common reason to use Layer 2 mode in your environment is because of its ease of use. This is the most common and best understood deployment mode. It is the easiest to configure and troubleshoot. L2 mode adds the least amount of complexity to your network environment.

Layer 3 Mode

As mentioned, by enabling Layer 3 mode, you also get to use Layer 2 mode. Clean Access Agent always tries Layer 2 mode first and then tries Layer 3 mode. When NAC Appliance Server is in In-Band L3 mode, the client's MAC address is not needed because only the client's IP address is used to determine a host's identity. When NAC Appliance Server is in Out-of-Band L3 mode, the client's MAC address and IP address are used to determine a host's identity. For detailed information on Layer 3 mode's operations when used with Out-of-Band mode, see the section "Out-of-Band Mode."

Layer 3 In-Band mode is required if you use NAC Appliance to control clients coming in through a Cisco VPN on the concentrator, Adaptive Service Appliance, or Private Internet Exchange.

Here are some common reasons to use Layer 3 mode in your environment:

- Clients are coming in through a Cisco VPN.

- Access layer switches use L3 trunks to distribution switches.

- Cost of NAC Appliance Server at every remote office is prohibitive; instead, use a central NAC Appliance Server at headquarters.

- Protect sensitive network areas that are accessible only via a VPN, such as management and process control networks, by forcing clients to authenticate and certify before gaining entry.

- Need to authenticate and posture assess all clients accessing your network through third-party WAN connections. Common examples include business partners, vendors, and consultants that have direct routed connections into your network.

Layer 2 Strict Mode for Clean Access Agent

This mode was originally created for the universities that use NAC Appliance, but it is now being adopted by businesses as well. Many students were using wireless or wired NAT gateways in their dorm rooms. A NAT gateway causes NAC Appliance to authenticate and inspect only the first client and no subsequent clients. This is because the NAT device hides everyone behind a single IP and MAC address. This is also known as port address translation (PAT) or NAT overload. Therefore, regardless of how many clients are really behind the NAT gateway, NAC Appliance sees only a single MAC and IP pair. After this pair is certified, the gates are open to allowing subsequent—and potentially infected—hosts onto the network with no checking. Layer 2 Strict mode thwarts this problem by checking whether the client is behind a NAT or PAT device and denying the client access if it finds one.

NOTE	Layer 3 and Layer 2 Strict mode are mutually exclusive and cannot be used together.

L2 Strict mode can be used to combat the problem of users connecting rogue wireless access points or routers to the network. It is designed to sniff out the use of NAT gateways. Here is how it works:

1. Client's Clean Access Agent sends a login request to NAC Appliance Server. This request also sends the MAC addresses of all interfaces on the host.

2. NAC Appliance Server compares the MAC address in the packet header of the login request against the MAC addresses found inside the packet payload of the login request.

3 If there is no NAT gateway between the client and server, there will be a match of the MAC address in the header with one of those in the payload.

4 If there is a NAT gateway between the client and server, the match will fail and NAC Appliance will reject the login request. The reason the match fails is because the NAT gateway replaced the MAC in the packet header with a MAC of its own before sending it on to NAC Appliance. The user is forced to remove the NAT gateway to gain access to the network.

Here are some common reasons to use L2 Strict Mode for Clean Access Agent:

- Prevent the infection or compromise of your network through the use of multiuser NAT gateways.

- Prevent the spread and use of wireless NAT gateways. This is one way of stopping users from setting up their own wireless networks.

- If you charge for network access by the user, you can ensure that nobody sets up a wireless NAT gateway for freeloaders.

- Prevent NAT gateways from impeding the effectiveness of the network scanner.

NOTE   Layer 2 Strict mode requires the use of the Clean Access Agent. It does not currently support web login.

How to Choose a Network Mode

Cisco NAC Appliance supports two network modes: Virtual Gateway and Real IP Gateway. Network mode determines whether NAC Appliance Server bridges or routes traffic from its untrusted to trusted interfaces. Virtual Gateway is bridging, whereas Real IP Gateway is routing.

Virtual Gateway Mode

In Virtual Gateway mode, NAC Appliance acts like a Layer 2 transparent bridge or bump in the wire. This means it has no IP addresses on its interfaces and is essentially transparent to clients. It does, however, have one IP address for the management of NAC Appliance Server itself. In this mode, it acts much like a traditional Ethernet bridge does. Traffic is bridged as it flows from the untrusted to trusted side and vice versa. All the NAC Appliance security features will work in this mode. Virtual Gateway mode is the preferred method of deployment in most environments. This is because it does not require a re-architecture of the network and IP addressing.

For example, you have a Layer 2 802.1Q trunk between your access switch and your distribution switch. Your L3 distribution switch is configured to be the default router for clients on the access switch. You would like to have NAC Appliance posture assess the clients on the access switch. If you break the 802.1Q trunk by placing NAC Appliance Server between the two switches and use Virtual Gateway mode, you will not have to change anything on your clients' or network topology. The clients continue to use the same default gateway, and NAC Appliance is transparent to clients. If you use the same example but instead use Real IP Gateway mode on NAC Appliance Server, you will have to make changes. The default gateway of clients has to be changed to be NAC Appliance Server, not the distribution switch as before. In addition, a new subnet is needed for the trusted side of the NAC Appliance Server.

Here are some common reasons to use Virtual Gateway mode in your environment:

- Ease of use. It does not require a redesign of the network topology.

- No changes to subnets or client IP addresses are required.

- Routing protocols such as Enhanced Interior Gateway Routing Protocol (EIGRP) and Open Shortest Path First (OSPF) can flow through NAC Appliance uninhibited.

- Static routes are not required.

Real IP Gateway Mode

In Real IP Gateway mode, NAC Appliance Server acts just like a router. Traffic flowing from the untrusted side is routed to the trusted side. In this mode, NAC Appliance Server acts as the default gateway and, typically, as the DHCP server for clients on the untrusted networks.

Here are some common reasons to use Real IP Gateway mode in your environment:

- Guest or new network segments where you do not have a router already.

- You want NAC Appliance to be the DHCP server for your untrusted networks. The DHCP server embedded in NAC Appliance Server works only in Real IP Gateway mode. Given a Class C IP subnet, this feature can auto-generate /30 micro-subnets within that class C address space, allowing you to further segment your client traffic.

- You want NAC Appliance to be the default gateway for clients on the untrusted side.

In-Band Mode

In-Band has strengths and weaknesses. The purpose of this section is to bring those to light.

In-Band and Out-of-Band refer to the post client certification mode NAC Appliance Server is in. NAC Appliance Manager is used to centrally configure this mode on the servers. The first method to configure NAC Appliance is In-Band. In-Band means that NAC Appliance Server is *always* in the flow of traffic between the untrusted networks and trusted networks. This is regardless of whether or not the host on the untrusted side has passed assessment.

Figure 4-2 depicts an In-Band NAC Appliance Server design. As you can see, all traffic from the client machine must flow through NAC Appliance Server before it can leave the subnet.

Figure 4-2 *In-Band Server Design*

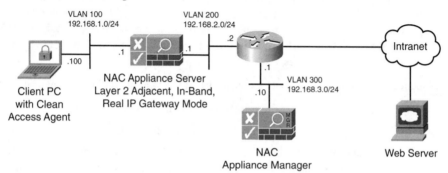

The Certification Process in In-Band Mode

This section will give an example of the Clean Access Agent certification process and the web login certification process. Certification, in the NAC Appliance world, is the process of user authentication and host security checks that a client must go through before it is allowed on the network. For a client to become certified, it must have properly authenticated with username and password and passed all the host security policies defined by the user's role. A host security policy is made up of all the checks and vulnerability scans configured for a given user role. A user's role is typically determined by some Active Directory or RADIUS attribute, such as group membership. Host security policies could include checking to make sure that antivirus definitions and Windows XP are up-to-date and using Network Scanner to check whether the machine is infected with a worm.

Certification Steps for Host with Clean Access Agent

These certification steps are based on the perspective of the host in Figure 4-2. The host has the Clean Access Agent installed.

Steps for Client to Acquire an IP Address

The steps for the client to acquire an IP address are as follows:

1 The host plugs into an Ethernet switch port. The switch port is a member of VLAN 100.

2 The host sends out a DHCP request to obtain an IP address.

3 NAC Appliance Server, also on VLAN 100, sees the DHCP request come into its untrusted network interface.

4 NAC Appliance Server, configured to be a DHCP server, replies to the host with a free IP address of 192.168.1.100/24 and a default gateway address of 192.168.1.1.

Clean Access Agent Authentication Steps

The Clean Access Agent authentication steps are as follows:

1 The host is now a member of the NAC Appliance Unauthenticated role. By default, hosts in this role will not be allowed to send any traffic, except DHCP and Domain Name System (DNS) queries, through their local NAC Appliance Server. You can modify the allowed traffic list as necessary for your environment.

2 Clean Access Agent, noticing the network connectivity, begins to send SWISS discovery packets to its default gateway. The SWISS discovery packets are sent first on UDP port 8905 (L2). If that fails, Clean Access Agent tries UDP 8906 (L3). Clean Access Agent is trying to locate a NAC Appliance Server in the network.

3 NAC Appliance Server, listening on the SWISS ports, hears the request and checks to see whether the host is already authenticated. Because it is not, NAC Appliance Server responds with the equivalent of an "I'm here; you need to log in" message.

4 NAC Appliance Server's reply message prompts the host's Clean Access Agent to pop up its login dialog box on the user's screen (see Chapter 3's Figure 3-2).

5 The user enters a username (Liam), password, and optionally an authentication provider, and then clicks **Log In**. An authentication provider defines the user database NAC Appliance will use to verify authentication. In this example, the local user database will be used.

6 Liam's login credentials are forwarded by NAC Appliance Server to NAC Appliance Manager for verification.

Clean Access Agent Host Security Posture Assessment Steps

The Clean Access Agent host security posture assessment steps are as follows:

1 After user authentication succeeds, NAC Appliance Manager moves to stage two: host security posture assessment. The user group that Liam is a member of determines his login role. The user's login role establishes what host security checks will be performed.

2 NAC Appliance Manager tells Clean Access Agent what security checks to perform on the host.

3 Clean Access Agent performs these checks and sends the results back to NAC Appliance Server, which forwards them to NAC Appliance Manager for certification.

4 If the host passes all Clean Access Agent security checks, skip Steps 5–7 and go to the "Clean Access Agent Network Scanner Steps" section.

5   For any failed checks, NAC Appliance Manager instructs NAC Appliance Server to tell Clean Access Agent to pop up a remediation dialog box on the user's screen. This dialog explains the issue found and gives details on how to repair it. See Figure 3-4 for a sample remediation dialog box.

6   NAC Appliance Manager then moves the user's role from Unauthenticated to Clean Access Temporary. This Temporary role is typically configured to allow the host access to only those networks or services from which it might need to obtain remediation patches or fixes.

7   The user then takes any necessary actions to fix the issues found. Failed checks are presented for remediation one at a time. If multiple failed checks occur, they must be repaired in the order presented. Skipping remediation of a failed check is an option only if the requirement was configured as optional.

Clean Access Agent Network Scanner Steps

The Clean Access Agent network scanner steps are as follows:

1   If no network scans are configured for the user's role, skip this section and go to the "Agent Post-Certification Steps" section.

2   If network scans (Nessus scans) are configured for the user's role, they are now performed. The host's local NAC Appliance Server is responsible for performing the network Nessus scans.

3   If any vulnerabilities are found on the host, Clean Access Agent displays them. This informs the user of the vulnerabilities found and alerts that user that he is in Quarantine mode. Figure 4-3 shows Clean Access Agent's vulnerability dialog box.

Figure 4-3   *Clean Access Agent Scanning Vulnerability Dialog Box*

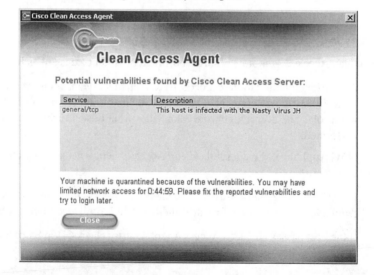

4   NAC Appliance Manager moves the user from the current role to the temporary role.
    The temporary role restricts the host's capability to talk freely on the network.
    Figure 4-4 shows Clean Access Agent's temporary access user notification dialog box.

5   After all the vulnerabilities are patched, the user has to log out and log back in again
    to be rescanned.

6   The network vulnerability scan is performed again, but this time the client passes.

Figure 4-4   *Clean Access Agent Temporary Access User Notification Example*

Agent Post-Certification Steps

The Clean Access Agent post-certification steps are as follows:

1   The host is now considered certified or "clean" and is put into its proper normal login
    role.

2   Optionally, the user is shown the acceptable use policy for the normal login role.

3   After the policy is accepted, NAC Appliance Manager adds the user and host to the
    certified devices list.

4   Any network bandwidth limits or network access lists configured for this normal login
    role take effect on the host traffic as it flows through NAC Appliance Server.

Login Steps for Host Using Web Login (No Clean Access Agent)

These login steps are based on the perspective of the host in Figure 4-2. The web login steps
will be shown. This host does *not* have the Clean Access Agent installed.

Web Login Authentication Steps

The web login authentication steps are as follows:

1 The host plugs into an Ethernet switch port. The switch port is a member of VLAN 100.

2 The host sends out a DHCP request to obtain an IP address.

3 NAC Appliance Server, also on VLAN 100, sees the DHCP request come into its untrusted network interface.

4 NAC Appliance Server is configured to be a DHCP server, so it replies to the host with a free IP address of 192.168.1.100/24 and a default gateway address of 192.168.1.1.

5 At this point, NAC Appliance Manager checks to see whether the host is already authenticated. If not, the host is put into the Unauthenticated user role. Hosts in this role are not allowed to send any traffic, except DHCP and DNS queries, through their local NAC Appliance Server.

6 If the host is already authenticated, it is put back into its final normal user login role (for example, Employees).

7 NAC Appliance Server now waits for the user to open a web browser. It will drop any through traffic, except DHCP and DNS queries, sent from the unauthenticated host.

8 The user launches a web browser and requests a website. NAC Appliance Server intercepts the web page request.

9 The web page request triggers NAC Appliance Server to perform certification of the host. The original web page request is replaced with a redirect to NAC Appliance Server's web login page. This starts the authentication process, the first step toward becoming certified.

10 The user's web browser is redirected to the NAC Appliance web login page. The user must enter a username and password. NAC Appliance Server forwards the user's login credentials to NAC Appliance Manager for verification. See Figure 3-3 for a sample web login page.

Web Login Network Scanning Steps

The web login network scanning steps are as follows:

1 After user authentication succeeds, NAC Appliance Manager moves to stage two: network scanning. The user group that the user is a member of determines the login role he is in.

2 The web login process also sends the host's operating system type to NAC Appliance. The host's operating system type and user role are used to decide which Nessus plug-ins will be used for the network scan.

3 NAC Appliance Manager instructs NAC Appliance Server which Nessus plug-ins to use for the network scan.

4 After performing the network scan, NAC Appliance Server sends the results to NAC Appliance Manager. Each plug-in will return no value if nothing was found, or will result in a security hole, warning, or info alert.

5 NAC Appliance Manager then matches the plug-in alert results (hole, warning, or info) against the alert results considered necessary for the specific plug-in to be considered a vulnerability. For example, plug-in XYZ is a vulnerability if the alert result is a security hole. This criterion is specific to the host's role and operating system.

6 Any matches result in the host being put into a quarantine role or blocked from the network completely.

7 If set to block network access, the user is shown the blocked access web page. No further steps are performed. This is a rather harsh way to treat users and is not frequently used.

8 If set to quarantine, the user is shown a user agreement page that must be acknowledged in order to complete the login.

9 Typically, the network vulnerability scan report web page is opened for the user. This report contains a description of the vulnerabilities found, and instructions and URL links to facilitate patching them. See Figure 4-5 for a scan report example.

Figure 4-5   *Sample Vulnerability Scan Report*

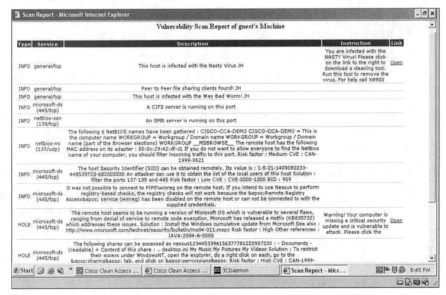

10 Hosts in the quarantine role have a configurable amount of time to patch or fix themselves. After the session timer runs out, the host is automatically logged out.

11 After the user patches all the vulnerabilities, that user has to be rescanned. The expiration of a relogin or session timer triggers a new network scan.

12 The network vulnerability scan is performed again, but this time the host passes.

Post–Web Login Steps

The post–web login steps are as follows:

1 The host is now considered clean and is put into its proper normal login role.

2 Optionally, the user is shown the user agreement page for the normal login role.

3 After the agreement page is accepted, NAC Appliance Manager adds the user and host to the online user list.

4 Any bandwidth limits or network access lists configured for the normal login role take effect on traffic as it flows through NAC Appliance Server.

Advantages of Using In-Band Mode

When designing any security solution, it is important to understand the advantages and disadvantages of the various product features and modes of operation. There are several compelling reasons to use In-Band instead of Out-of-Band mode. The following is a list of the major advantages In-Band has to offer:

- It is the easiest mode to design, configure, deploy, and troubleshoot.

- It is less intrusive in environments with IP phones.

- It is the only mode that allows you to use bandwidth rate-limiting and traffic control (access lists) on certified clients.

- It allows for the use of the heartbeat timer to automatically log off users who have been inactive for a set time.

- It is required for VPN and wireless clients.

- In-Band mode works regardless of the type of Ethernet switches in your network.

- In-Band mode works even if your hosts are connected to Ethernet switches that you do not control, such as switches controlled by another department or another company.

Disadvantages of Using In-Band Mode

In-Band mode has a few disadvantages when compared to Out-of-Band mode. You should check these disadvantages against your security policy and network environment requirements for relevancy. The following is a list of the major disadvantages of using In-Band mode:

- In-Band does not provide true switch port–level host control. In certain situations, it is possible for an unauthenticated host to talk to other hosts in the same Layer 2 domain (VLAN) without first passing NAC Appliance assessment.

- Because the traffic from hosts always flows through NAC Appliance in this mode, the server is another possible point of failure in the network. If the server dies in In-Band mode, all host traffic stops flowing. Using NAC Appliance Server high availability and failover decreases the risk of that occurring.

- A NAC Appliance Server in In-Band mode that loses communication with its NAC Appliance Manager could affect traffic. If set to fail closed, existing certified hosts will not be affected but any new hosts will be denied access. If set to Fallback mode, NAC Appliance Server will fail open, allowing all traffic to flow through unchecked.

- In-Band mode could adversely affect the performance of your network. Each server has a maximum throughput of approximately 950 Mbps. If your network infrastructure (uplinks) is faster than 950 Mbps, NAC Appliance could theoretically be a bottleneck.

- In-Band mode, unlike Out-of-Band mode, does not give you the ability to set which switch ports you want to be posture assessed and which you do not. It can only posture assesses whole subnets or VLANs. MAC address exceptions must be made for those hosts in a VLAN that you do not want to posture assess.

- If you use In-Band in Real IP Gateway Layer 3 adjacency mode, NAC Appliance will not support any routing protocols and relies solely on static routing. If you put NAC Appliance in the middle of a routed topology, it will break any routing protocols trying to flow through NAC Appliance Server. When designing for this mode, think of NAC Appliance Server as a router that supports only static routing.

Where You Can Use In-Band Mode

In-Band mode is by far the most flexible deployment mode available. It can be used almost anywhere. It is the only mode that can be used behind VPN and wireless networks. And, of course, it can be used in a LAN. It is great for protecting guest networks and conference rooms. These areas can really take advantage of In-Band mode's always-available bandwidth rate limiting, session timeout, and traffic control (access control list or ACL) features. There are currently no known areas of a network where In-Band mode does not work.

Out-of-Band Mode

Out-of-Band mode was created to fill some of the perceived gaps of In-Band mode operating in a LAN environment. OOB is designed for one purpose: to control hosts that connect directly to Cisco LAN switches. It is not capable of operating in wireless or VPN environments or those with non-Cisco switches. Businesses wanted true switch port–level network admission control, and they did not want the appliance to be a bottleneck on their high speed LANs.

To accomplish this, OOB uses switch port–level VLANs—two VLAN types, in fact. The first type is the authentication VLAN, and the second type is the access VLAN. While clients are in the authentication VLAN, all their traffic passes through NAC Appliance just as in In-Band mode. However, after the client is authenticated and certified, it is moved into the access VLAN where all the client traffic bypasses NAC Appliance completely. The effect of this behavior is that NAC Appliance is In-Band with the client traffic *only* during the process of authentication, certification, and remediation. After that process completes, client traffic no longer flows through NAC Appliance.

OOB works by changing the VLAN of the host's switch port. OOB mode provides the ability to communicate with and reconfigure Cisco Catalyst switches real-time via Simple Network Management Protocol (SNMP). It is the job of NAC Appliance Manager to reconfigure switch ports using SNMP write commands. For this to work, NAC Appliance must be told when and where new hosts connect to the network. This is accomplished by configuring the LAN switches to send SNMP traps when new hosts connect to the network.

TIP   SNMP is critical to the operation of Out-of-Band mode. When using Layer 3 Out-of-Band to control clients across WAN links (for example, remote site clients controlled by a central NAC Appliance Server), it is highly recommended that priority quality of service (QoS) for SNMP traffic be configured on the relevant WAN routers.

When a new host connects to a switch port, NAC Appliance is notified using one of the following trap types:

- **MAC-Notification Trap**   This type of SNMP trap is triggered and sent anytime a new MAC address is detected on a switch port. It includes the MAC address and port number of the new host. This trap triggers even if there are multiple clients or a hub on a single switch port. This is the preferred notification method, but it is not supported by all Cisco switches. See the "Switches Supported by NAC Appliance Out-of-Band" section in this chapter for details. Example 4-1 shows a MAC-notification trap message.

Example 4-1 *MAC Notification Message*

```
Internet Protocol, Src: 192.168.1.250 (192.168.1.250), Dst: 192.168.3.20
(192.168.3.20)
User Datagram Protocol, Src Port: 51493 (51493), Dst Port: snmptrap (162)
Simple Network Management Protocol
    Version: 1 (0)
    Community: public
    PDU type: TRAP-V1 (4)
    Enterprise: 1.3.6.1.4.1.9.9.215.2 (SNMPv2-SMI::enterprises.9.9.215.2)
    Agent address: 192.168.1.250 (192.168.1.250)
    Trap type: ENTERPRISE SPECIFIC (6)
    Object identifier 1: 1.3.6.1.4.1.9.9.215.1.1.8.1.2.0 (SNMPv2-
SMI::enterprises.9.9.215.1.1.8.1.2.0)
    Value: Hex-STRING: 01 00 C8 00 0C 29 42 DF C1 00 08 00
```

This captured SNMP MAC-Notification trap message shows the client's
MAC address as 000C-2942-DFC1.

- **SNMP Linkup Trap**   This trap is triggered and sent anytime a switch port changes
  its state to operational. This occurs only when a port goes from not being used
  (disconnected) to being used (connected). Because of this, only the first client on a
  port is ever detected. This trap includes the port number but does *not* include the MAC
  address of the client. To obtain the vital client MAC address, NAC Appliance Manager
  issues an SNMP query or get request to the switch. The query looks up the MAC
  address for the port sent by the linkup trap. It is because of the extra query that linkup
  traps are not the preferred method. Example 4-2 shows a linkup trap.

Example 4-2 *Linkup Trap*

```
Internet Protocol, Src: 192.168.1.250 (192.168.1.250), Dst: 192.168.3.10
(192.168.3.10)
User Datagram Protocol, Src Port: 52464 (52464), Dst Port: snmptrap (162)
Simple Network Management Protocol
    Version: 3 (3)
    PDU type: TRAP-V2 (7)
    Object identifier 2: 1.3.6.1.6.3.1.1.4.1.0 (SNMPv2-MIB::snmpTrapOID.0)
    Value: OID: IF-MIB::linkUp
    Object identifier 3: 1.3.6.1.2.1.2.2.1.1.10006 (IF-MIB::ifIndex.10006)
    Value: INTEGER: 10006
    Object identifier 4: 1.3.6.1.2.1.2.2.1.2.10006 (IF-MIB::ifDescr.10006)
    Value: STRING: FastEthernet1/0/6
    Object identifier 6: 1.3.6.1.4.1.9.2.2.1.1.20.10006 (SNMPv2-
SMI::enterprises.9.2.2.1.1.20.10006)
    Value: STRING: "up"
```

When a host disconnects, the switch sends a linkdown SNMP trap message to NAC
Appliance. The linkdown trap message includes the switch port number that disconnected.
Example 4-3 shows a captured linkdown SNMP trap message.

Example 4-3 *Linkdown SNMP Trap Message*

```
Internet Protocol, Src: 192.168.1.250 (192.168.1.250), Dst: 192.168.3.20
(192.168.3.20)
User Datagram Protocol, Src Port: 51493 (51493), Dst Port: snmptrap (162)
Simple Network Management Protocol
    Version: 1 (0)
    Community: public
    PDU type: TRAP-V1 (4)
    Agent address: 192.168.1.250 (192.168.1.250)
    Trap type: LINK DOWN (2)
    Object identifier 1: 1.3.6.1.2.1.2.2.1.1.10006 (IF-MIB::ifIndex.10006)
    Value: INTEGER: 10006
    Object identifier 2: 1.3.6.1.2.1.2.2.1.2.10006 (IF-MIB::ifDescr.10006)
    Value: STRING: FastEthernet1/0/6
    Object identifier 4: 1.3.6.1.4.1.9.2.2.1.1.20.10006 (SNMPv2-
SMI::enterprises.9.2.2.1.1.20.10006)
    Value: STRING: "down"
```

Notice that the trap message has the interface number as well as the **"down"** message. This is all the information NAC Appliance needs to reset the switch port's security policy.

The big advantage of OOB is that hosts are within the control of NAC Appliance only during authentication, assessment, and remediation. After the host is authenticated and certified, its switch port moves to the access VLAN, which is external to NAC Appliance. At this point, the host never interacts with NAC Appliance again until it logs out or disconnects from the network.

All OOB designs have the following two VLAN types:

- **Authentication (Auth) VLAN**   When a host first connects to the switch, this is the VLAN type it is placed into. While in an authentication VLAN, the host is always In-Band with NAC Appliance Server. All client traffic is forced to pass through NAC Appliance Server. Client authentication, posture assessment, and remediation are performed in this VLAN.

- **Access VLAN**   After a host completes authentication and certification, it moves into the access VLAN type. A client in this VLAN never interacts with NAC Appliance and is considered Out-of-Band. While on the access VLAN, no client traffic flows through NAC Appliance Server.

NAC Appliance uses port profiles to define the VLAN name or number these VLAN types are set to. The host's switch port location is used to determine which port profile to use. For example, a port profile for switch IDF2 port 3/1 assigns VLAN 30 for authentication and VLAN 100 for access. A port profile is used to determine whether a particular switch port is controlled or uncontrolled by NAC Appliance. If a port is controlled, the port profile will define what authentication and access VLANs should be used, as well as other port behavior. The following are the four types of port profiles for switch ports:

- **Unmanaged/Uncontrolled**   Ports of this type will not be controlled by NAC Appliance. Common uses of this type include any nonclient switch ports, such as printers, servers, and other network devices.

- **Managed/Controlled Port with Auth VLAN and Default Access VLAN**   This managed port profile type defines the auth VLAN and the access VLAN explicitly and statically. If a port is a member of a profile of this type, both the auth and access VLANs will be the same for all other ports in this profile. This is regardless of their user role, location, or any other criteria.

- **Managed/Controlled Port with Auth VLAN and Switch Initial VLAN**   This type statically defines the auth VLAN but not the access VLAN. The access VLAN value is always set to whatever the switch port VLAN was before the user moved to the auth VLAN. The initial VLAN value is learned and stored by NAC Appliance Manager during the initial discovery of the LAN switch. If necessary, the original initial VLAN can be changed or updated later in NAC Appliance Manager.

- **Managed/Controlled Port with Auth VLAN and User Role VLAN**   The auth VLAN is statically configured for this type, but the access VLAN changes depending on the user's ultimate role. The access VLAN is defined in the user's role. The access VLAN will, therefore, change depending on who authenticates and what user role they are put into. Each user role has a field that defines that role's access VLAN name or number.

Figure 4-6 shows the port profile configuration screen.

Figure 4-6   *Port Profile Configuration Screen*

Determines Uncontrolled or Controlled

Auth & Access VLAN Values

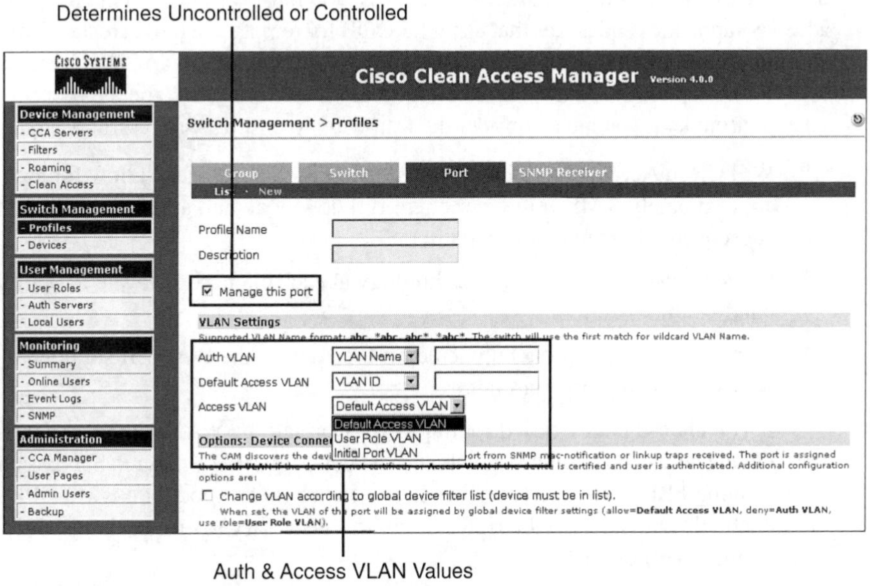

How the Adjacency Mode Affects Out-of-Band Operation

Out-of-Band mode supports both Layer 2 and Layer 3 Adjacency modes on the NAC Appliance Server. The adjacency mode you choose will change the flow of operations for OOB.

In Layer 2 OOB mode, all clients in the authentication VLAN are Layer 2 adjacent to NAC Appliance Server. This means that NAC Appliance Server is in the same IP subnet as the clients and is able to see the real MAC address of all its clients. As described earlier, after certification finishes and the client moves to its access VLAN, NAC Appliance Server is no longer in-band. If possible, using Layer 2 OOB instead of L3 OOB is recommended. Layer 2 OOB mode is much easier to design, configure, deploy, and support.

In Layer 3 OOB mode, all clients are one or more routed L3 hops away from the NAC Appliance Server. This means that for the client to reach the NAC Appliance Server, it must pass through one or more routers. Layer 3 mode also supports Layer 2 adjacent clients, so when you turn on Layer 3 mode, you also get Layer 2 mode as well. L3 OOB was designed for customers with routed links to their campus access layer switches.

Traditionally, the link between access and distribution switches was an 802.1q or Inter-Switch Link Layer 2 trunk. It is becoming increasing popular to enable L3 routing on uplink trunks between the access and distribution layer switches. This means that there is an L3 hop between clients and NAC Appliance Server. The most common use case for L3 OOB is campus networks with routed uplinks to the access layer. You can also use L3 OOB to centralize the NAC Appliance Servers at your network core or hub site, and use those NAC Appliance Servers to control hosts at WAN remote sites.

The biggest benefit of using L3 OOB for remote site NAC is that it allows you to centralize your NAC Appliance Servers at the core and saves you the expense of having NAC Appliance Server at every WAN remote site. Nevertheless, you must weight this benefit against the added complexities and issues that using L3 OOB for remote site NAC creates. Typically, you will find that positioning either an L2 In-Band or L2 OOB mode NAC Appliance Server at every WAN remote site is the best solution. If L3 OOB turns out to be the best solution for your environment, you must consider the following to ensure a successful design:

- Will Clean Access Agent be deployed using the WAN? If so, allow for an approximately 8 MB initial per client full download and approximately 4 MB for subsequent client updates thereafter.

- Consider using a file-caching technology at each client remote site to optimize WAN bandwidth utilization.

- Is the Network Scanning engine being used across the WAN? If so, how much bandwidth will it use per client?

- If you choose policy-based routing (PBR), are all the WAN routers and every L3 device between the client switch and the central NAC Appliance Server capable of running PBR? What performance hit will your router model take when PBR is enabled? Do you have the rights or control necessary to ensure that PBR is enabled on these L3 devices?

- How much additional traffic will be created over the WAN for remediation downloads, authentication, SNMP traffic, and other auth VLAN–type activities?
- QoS should be configured on all WAN routers to prioritize SNMP traffic from NAC switches. SNMP traffic is critical to the operation of NAC Appliance and must be given priority over the WAN.
- Consider using QoS in WAN routers to prefer access VLAN traffic over authentication VLAN traffic. This will ensure that business-critical traffic is not affected by spikes in client-remediation traffic.
- The first few weeks of NAC Appliance deployment will create a large spike in WAN traffic as clients download required patches and updates. Make sure that your WAN can accommodate the traffic loads during this initial deployment stage. Consider using the bandwidth control feature of NAC Appliance to help with this.
- Each time a new security check or requirement is enforced, you will see a temporary spike in WAN traffic as clients download the files necessary to pass the new check. Consider how often you anticipate these updates to occur and the WAN bandwidth necessary during these times.

The following are some common reasons to use Layer 3 Out-of-Band mode:

- L3 OOB is for wired LAN deployments only. Wireless and VPN deployments are not currently supported.
- L3 OOB is best used in routed access or campus deployments where port-level NAC is desired.
- L3 OOB can also be used for remote WAN sites, but other deployment types should be considered as well.
- L3 OOB should be used in environments that use Layer 3 switch trunks instead of L2 trunks.
- In most cases, using Layer 3 Out-of-Band mode results in having to deploy fewer NAC Appliance Servers throughout your network.

Because the client is not Layer 2 adjacent, NAC Appliance Server cannot view the real MAC address of its clients. Due to normal network behavior, each router along the path replaces the MAC address of the client's packets with its own MAC Address before forwarding them. This causes a problem for NAC Appliance. NAC Appliance needs the MAC address of the client in order to match it with a switch's MAC notification message. This matching process is how the NAC Appliance determines which switch port a particular client is connected to. The following are two ways for NAC Appliance to learn the client's real MAC address:

- Using the Clean Access Agent v4.0 or greater.
  - Clean Access Agent sends the client's MAC address to NAC Appliance.
  - Clean Access Agent is the preferred method for detecting the client MAC address when using L3 OOB mode.

- Using the ActiveX or Java applet with web login.
  - The web login page downloads the ActiveX control or Java applet. The control or applet then discovers and sends the MAC address of the client to the NAC Appliance.
  - The control or applet is downloaded only to detect the client MAC address when Clean Access Agent cannot detect the MAC address.
  - For Internet Explorer browsers, the ActiveX control is preferred and faster than the Java applet.

The following is an example of the MAC address discovery process in L3 OOB mode:

1 Host A connects to switch A.

2 Switch A sends MAC-notification and linkup SNMP traps to NAC Appliance. The MAC-notification trap includes the MAC address of the host and the switch port it is located on.

3 NAC Appliance Manager records and stores these traps.

4 Clean Access Agent sends the client's MAC address, along with a login request, to NAC Appliance.

5 NAC Appliance Manager then performs a lookup to match the MAC address from Clean Access Agent with a MAC address it received via a switch MAC-notification trap. When it finds a match, it knows exactly what switch and port the Clean Access Agent login request is originating from.

6 NAC Appliance Manager now has a complete IP-MAC-port mapping.

After the location is known, NAC Appliance Manager then looks up the port profile for the switch port and goes from there.

Layer 3 Out-of-Band Traffic Control Methods

Another important design requirement of using Layer 3 Out-of-Band is traffic control. While in the authentication VLAN, no client traffic should be allowed to roam freely throughout the network: It must be controlled. Because NAC Appliance Server is not Layer 2 adjacent to the client, the client's traffic is not forced through NAC Appliance Server. If you do not implement controls on the authentication VLAN traffic, it can route to anywhere the local default router allows it to go. Of course, this defeats the purpose of NAC, which is controlling clients until they are authenticated and certified. The following are the methods you can use to control the traffic of clients in the authentication VLAN:

- Policy-based routing
- Access control lists

- VPN routing and forwarding (VRF)
- Virtual private networks

The recommended methods are PBR and ACLs. PBR and ACL methods will be discussed in detail, but first a brief overview of the VRF and VPN methods is necessary. VRF and VPN are tunneling technologies that you can use to tunnel the client auth VLAN traffic back to a central NAC Appliance Server. VRF and VPN are typically used for WAN remote sites configured for L3 OOB. To properly capture the client traffic, you would configure a tunnel with one endpoint being the remote site's auth VLAN router and the other endpoint being the central NAC Appliance Server's untrusted network router. This tunnel ensures that all auth VLAN client traffic is forced to flow through the central NAC Appliance for authentication, certification, and remediation. You might consider these technologies for your design if you are already using them on your WAN and you own or manage the tunnel endpoint routers. VPN and VRF design is out of the scope of this book.

When deciding which traffic control method to use, PBR and ACLs should be at the top of your list. It is also likely that you will end up using both in some environments. Policy-based routing works by forcing defined traffic to follow a set path through the network. In this case, you would define the auth VLAN traffic and force it to always go through a central NAC Appliance Server. PBR overrides the normal routing path traffic would normally take with its own predetermined path that leads to NAC Appliance Server. This requires that a PBR policy be configured in every L3 device along the set path.

ACLs work by filtering traffic based on a set of rules, just like a firewall. In this case, you would configure inbound ACLs on each remote site router. You want to use the router or L3 switch interface that is closest to the clients you are going to filter. The closest L3 device to auth VLAN clients would be the default router for the auth VLAN. Given that each remote site will typically have only one authentication VLAN, the ACL method can scale fairly well in a large remote site topology. It works out to a 1:1 ratio; you have to configure one router ACL for each remote site being protected with NAC. For large networks, the ACL method will be easier to deploy than the PBR method. This is mainly because with the PBR method, you still have the 1:1 ratio of one PBR policy on every remote site router. In addition, you will have to add or modify the PBR policy of each router in the path from the remote client to the central NAC Appliance Server.

The ACLs you configure on the remote site routers allow only the traffic types that you determine clients need while they are in the authentication VLAN. Remember the auth VLAN is used for authentication, certification, and remediation. So, your allowed traffic would typically include access to NAC Appliance Server, remediation servers, DNS, limited ping, and AD demilitarized zone servers if AD SSO is being used.

When using the ACL method, client traffic is not forced to go through NAC Appliance Server at any time. This is why web login does not automatically redirect users with only the ACL method. A workaround for guest users is to print out for them the URL address for web login. They can then put that in their browser to gain access to web login. Clean Access

Agent works just fine because it is preconfigured with the IP address of NAC Appliance Server or a device behind NAC Appliance Server. This allows Clean Access Agent to discover, communicate with, and receive instructions from NAC Appliance Server. Table 4-2 shows the strengths of PBR and ACL traffic control methods.

Table 4-2 *PBR and ACL Traffic Control*

Traffic Control Method	Clean Access Agent Support	Client Web Login Support	Client Is Two or Fewer L3 Hops from NAC Server	Client Is More Than Two L3 Hops from NAC Server	All L3 Devices Between Client and NAC Server Are *Not* Manageable by You
Policy-Based Routing	Strong	Strong	Strong	Weak	Not Supported
Access Control Lists	Strong	Limited support; requires URL or limited PBR implementation	Average	Strong	Strong

Policy-based routing makes an excellent control method for routed campus networks and WAN remote sites with only one or two hops between the clients and the NAC Appliance Server. Remember that the more L3 hops there are between clients and the NAC Appliance Server, the greater the number of devices you have to configure for PBR. This is why PBR becomes a less and less attractive option as the hop number increases. Another strong benefit PBR has is its support for both Clean Access Agents and web login, or Clean Access Agent–less, clients. Web login requires that auth VLAN web traffic must flow through NAC Appliance Server. Because PBR does exactly that, it can support web login.

A routed campus network typically has tens or hundreds of L2 access switches collapsing via L3 uplinks to the distribution layer. In that campus topology, you would position NAC Appliance Server in the distribution layer. The topology gives you a natural PBR traffic choke point: the distribution routers or L3 switches. All auth VLAN traffic coming from the access switches passes through the distribution switches. By configuring policy route statements at the distribution layer, you can force any traffic coming from the access switches' auth VLAN to go to NAC Appliance Server's untrusted IP address or interface number. Using PBR in this way allows you to control the auth VLAN client traffic with minimal effort and complexity. PBR typically doesn't work well for WAN remote sites.

The ACL method works well for remote sites. This is especially true when the remote clients are several L3 hops away from the central NAC Appliance Server. The ACL method is the preferred method if the L3 devices in your network don't support PBR or all are not managed by you. This method is popular in environments where the ISP owns the routers at each remote site or where the remote site device is a firewall not capable of running PBR.

The biggest disadvantage of using ACLs is that doing so requires the use of Clean Access Agent and provides limited support for web login. As stated previously, this is because in order for web login to work, client web traffic must be forced to flow through the central NAC Appliance Server. The ACL method, by itself, has no way of forcing traffic to follow a set path through to NAC Appliance Server. Not being able to support the web login service is a big problem. The web login service will be needed in most environments because rarely will Clean Access Agent be supported by and deployed to everyone's PC at all times. In addition, it is a common practice to use the web login service to distribute clean access agents to new users. The following are some of your options for using the ACL method but still supporting web login:

- Distribute an authentication URL to Clean Access Agent–less users that points to or goes through NAC Appliance Server. This causes the redirect to happen and the login page to display.
- Implement a limited deployment of PBR.

The first option is straightforward. When new users arrive at your site, they are given a username and password in addition to the URL they must go to for authentication. If NAC Appliance Server were running in Real IP Gateway mode, the URL could point to either NAC Appliance Server's trusted interface or a web server reachable only by going through NAC Appliance. It might look something like this: http://guest.companyxyz.com. Your DNS would resolve this to the IP address of the trusted interface of the NAC Appliance Server or the web server.

TIP   If you use the trusted interface of your NAC Appliance Server as the destination for your authentication URL, be sure to send users to a prespecified web page after they successfully log in. By default, NAC Appliance sends the user to the previously or originally requested URL. If left unchanged, that URL will point to the trusted interface of NAC Appliance and will result in the user receiving a 404 page not found error in the web browser. This would not be pleasant for the user. To change the URL, edit the user role page. Specify a specific URL, such as a company welcome page, in the appropriate field next to the option **After Successful Login Redirect To**.

A user going to that page is redirected to the web login page. Normal web login procedures would then be followed. If NAC Appliance Server were in Virtual Gateway mode, you would hand out a URL of a web server that was on the trusted side of NAC Appliance Server. This web server must be reachable only by going through NAC Appliance Server. When the user attempts to go to this web server, NAC Appliance Server redirects him to the web login page. Handing out URLs is not the most efficient method and could result in additional help desk calls from those users who were not given a URL to use. However, it is the simplest and easiest method by far and should work efficiently in environments that require guests to sign in at a front desk. The front desk personnel could be assigned the task of handing out the necessary information. Figure 4-7 shows a workflow example of how this could work.

Figure 4-7   *ACL Traffic Control Method Using Authentication URL*

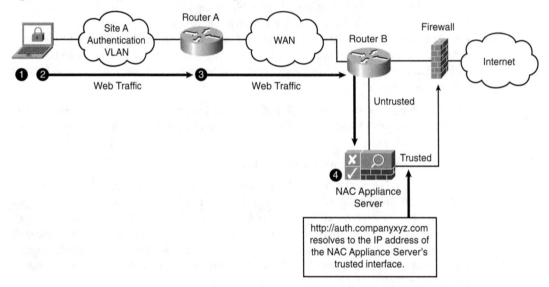

The following is an explanation of the steps presented in Figure 4-7:

1 On arriving, a user receives a username and password. He is told that to gain access to the network, he has to go to a website and enter his credentials. This website would be your authentication URL.

2 The user opens a web browser and enters the authentication URL, such as http:// auth.companyxyz.com. The HTTP connection heads toward the web server.

3 Web traffic to the auth URL is permitted by router A's ACL. For example:

Permit any traffic to remediation resources

Permit any web traffic to auth URL site (that is, NAC Server)

4 NAC Appliance Server redirects the user to the web login page.

The second option is implementing a limited deployment of policy-based routing. This option does not rely on the user having prior knowledge of how to access the system—it works automatically. This implementation of PBR is limited to forcing web traffic through to only the central NAC Appliance Server. This is accomplished by implementing

PBR on only the routers that sit in front of your company's Internet connection. The untrusted interface of NAC Appliance Server should be Layer 2 adjacent to an interface on an Internet-facing router. The PBR policy forces TCP port 80 and 443 traffic coming from any remote site auth VLAN to go through the NAC Appliance Server. Any auth VLAN user who opens a web browser and attempts to contact an Internet website is forced by the PBR policy to go through the NAC Appliance Server. NAC Appliance Server then issues a redirect to the web login page. Normal web login operation takes over from there. For this to work and be secure, you must do the following:

- Add ACL statements to every remote site auth VLAN router that denies traffic from the auth VLAN to any internal host and permits any other TCP port 80 and port 443 traffic. This permitted traffic is Internet bound and is caught by the PBR policy. These ACL additions are typically added at the bottom of the existing ACL. This allows the permits for remediation servers, AD, and so on to continue to function.

- The PBR policy must include the IP subnets for all remote site auth VLANs. If a remote site auth VLAN is missed, those clients will have full unrestricted Internet access.

TIP   A best practice is to use IP address ranges for all remote site auth VLANs that could be easily super-netted in the PBR policy. For example, always use the 10.10.X.0/24 address space when carving out subnets for remote site auth VLANs. This allows you to super-net them to 10.10.0.0/16 in a PBR policy.

Figure 4-8 gives a flow example when using ACLs for L3 OOB traffic control.

Figure 4-8   *L3 OOB Traffic Control Using ACLs and Web Login*

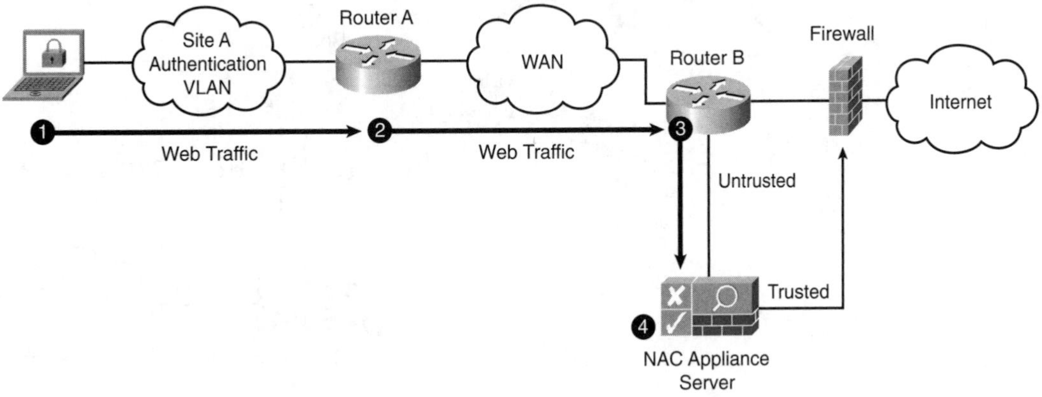

The following is an explanation of the steps presented in Figure 4-8:

1 The user opens a web browser and enters an external URL, such as http://
www.google.com. The HTTP connection heads toward the Internet.

2 Web traffic to the Internet is permitted by router A's ACL. For example:

Permit any traffic to remediation resources

Deny any traffic to internal hosts

Permit any web traffic to anywhere (for example, the Internet)

3 The PBR on router B (Internet router) forwards web traffic sourced from site A auth
VLAN to NAC Appliance Server.

4 NAC Appliance Server redirects the user to the web login page.

Policy-based routing is a Cisco IOS router feature. PBR can be used to force all
authentication VLAN traffic to follow a predetermined path through the network. PBR
allows you to route traffic based on its source IP address, or other criteria, rather than just
its destination IP address as is typical of routing. This path will of course take the traffic to
NAC Appliance Server. It is not possible for traffic to deviate from this predetermined path.
For simplicity's sake, you can think of PBR as a tunnel through the network that traffic from
the authentication VLAN is forced to go through. At the end of the tunnel is the untrusted
interface of NAC Appliance Server. This accomplishes the goal of making sure that all
traffic of hosts still on the authentication VLAN is forced to pass through NAC Appliance
Server. See Figure 4-9 for a look at policy-based routing.

Figure 4-9   *Policy-Based Routing Overview*

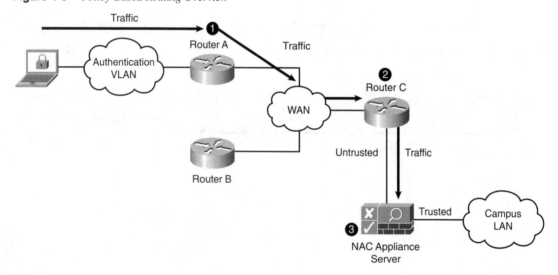

The following is a breakdown of the numbered process shown in Figure 4-9:

1   PBR policy on router A: All traffic coming from the authentication VLAN is forwarded to router C.

2   PBR policy on router C: All traffic coming from the authentication VLAN is forwarded to NAC Appliance Server.

3   NAC Appliance Server performs authentication, certification, and remediation. It also controls what traffic can flow through to the trusted side.

NOTE   After a client moves to its access VLAN, PBR, ACL, VPN, and VRF policies no longer affect its network traffic.

How the Network Mode Affects Out-of-Band Operation

Out-of-Band mode supports both Virtual Gateway and Real IP Gateway network modes on NAC Appliance Server. Given that OOB mode relies on VLANs for segmentation of clients, you need to be aware of the process NAC Appliance goes through to change a client's IP address as it transitions from the authentication VLAN to the access VLAN. If you choose to use Real IP Gateway mode, you are required to have different IP subnets for the authentication VLAN and the access VLAN. This is because NAC Appliance is routing between the VLANs, and routers can't route traffic between two identical IP subnets. If you choose Virtual Gateway mode, you have the flexibility of having the auth VLAN and access VLAN be the same or different IP subnets. This is because NAC Appliance is bridging and uses VLAN remapping.

If you choose to have separate subnets for the auth and access VLANs, you need to consider how you can force the client to change its IP address at the appropriate times. The issue revolves around the difficulty in forcing a client to change its IP address. After a client receives an IP address from a DHCP server, it doesn't like to relinquish that IP address for a new one. In fact, a number of operating systems—some Linux variants, for example—require you to reboot if you change IP addresses. To deal with the IP address change problem, NAC Appliance uses switch port bouncing and DHCP Release/Renew. Bouncing a port simply means disconnecting and reconnecting it. This port reset action forces the client's operating system to clear its existing IP address and request a new one. The problem is that this method does not work with all operating systems, Linux being one example.

The second way NAC Appliance can force a client to change its IP address is using DHCP release/renew functionality. The way this works is that Clean Access Agent or the web login applet sends a DHCP release/renew instruction to the host's operating system. This is the equivalent of typing **ipconfig /release** followed by **ipconfig /renew** in a Windows command prompt. The problem with this method is that only Windows operating systems are unconditionally supported as of this writing. Macintosh systems support release/renew only when using the web login applet; the Clean Access Agent release/renew is not supported as of this writing.

CAUTION In IP telephony environments, port bouncing must be avoided and is not an acceptable method. You must either preserve the client's IP address as it moves from the authentication VLAN to the access VLAN or use the DHCP release/renew method. Because of the port bounce, IP phones on those client ports will also be reset. This is because the client is plugged into the IP phone and the phone is then plugged into the switch. See Figure 4-10 for an example of this arrangement.

Figure 4-10 *Client with an IP Phone*

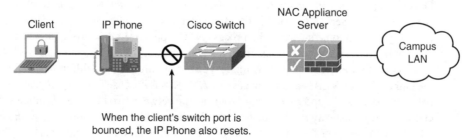

When the client's switch port is
bounced, the IP Phone also resets.

If the host's IP address needs to be changed, the DHCP release/renew method is recommended. However, if port bouncing is enabled, its physical Ethernet switch port is bounced by NAC Appliance. Port bouncing is an option because it forces the operating system of the host to release the old IP address and request a new one. One of the undesirable effects of port bouncing is that if the host is connected to an IP phone, the IP phone is also bounced.

It is recommended that Virtual Gateway mode be used in any IP telephony environment in which hosts are plugged into IP phones. Only Virtual Gateway mode can be configured to never change the IP address of the host and therefore mitigates the need for port bouncing or DHCP release/renew. This in turn reduces the complexity of the design. Virtual Gateway (transparent bridging) mode can be configured so that the IP address the client receives in the authentication VLAN is also valid in the access VLAN. NAC Appliance will not bounce the switch port because the IP address never changes. Because the switch port never bounces, the IP phone is not affected in any way. The downside to using this method is that you cannot use role-based VLAN assignment. Everyone must be assigned to the same access VLAN. See Figure 4-11 for a look at how IP addressing is typically handled with OOB in Virtual Gateway mode.

Figure 4-11 *IP Addressing with OOB in Virtual Gateway Mode*

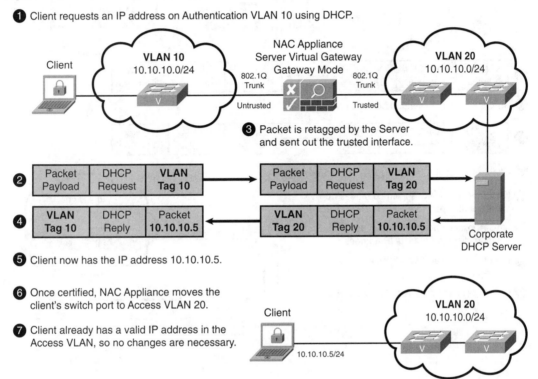

In Real IP Gateway (Routing) mode, the client's IP address is always changed when it transitions between the authentication and access VLANs. To force this change on the client, the switch port must be bounced or DHCP release/renew must happen. Typically, NAC Appliance Server acts as the DHCP server for the authentication VLAN, but not in the access VLAN. See Figure 4-12 for a look at how IP addressing is typically handled with OOB in Real IP Gateway mode.

Figure 4-12 *IP Addressing with OOB in Real IP Gateway Mode*

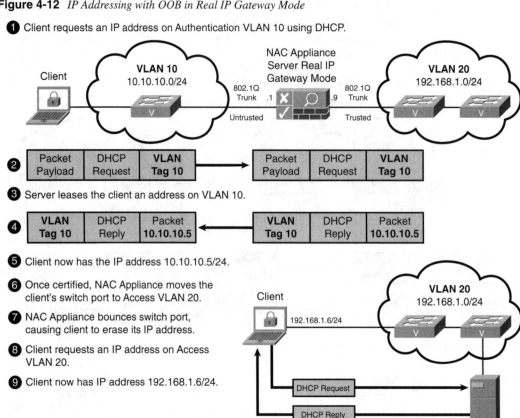

① Client requests an IP address on Authentication VLAN 10 using DHCP.

② (figure: Packet Payload | DHCP Request | VLAN Tag 10 → Packet Payload | DHCP Request | VLAN Tag 10)

③ Server leases the client an address on VLAN 10.

④ (figure: VLAN Tag 10 | DHCP Reply | Packet 10.10.10.5 ← VLAN Tag 10 | DHCP Reply | Packet 10.10.10.5)

⑤ Client now has the IP address 10.10.10.5/24.

⑥ Once certified, NAC Appliance moves the client's switch port to Access VLAN 20.

⑦ NAC Appliance bounces switch port, causing client to erase its IP address.

⑧ Client requests an IP address on Access VLAN 20.

⑨ Client now has IP address 192.168.1.6/24.

Login Steps with OOB in L2 Adjacency, Virtual Gateway Mode

These certification steps are based on the perspective of the host and user in Figure 4-13. The host has Clean Access Agent installed and is Layer 2 adjacent to NAC Appliance Server. NAC Appliance Server is in Virtual Gateway mode and bridging between the untrusted and trusted networks. NAC Appliance is not configured for network scanning, only Clean Access Agent posture assessment. The Cisco LAN switch is configured to send both linkup or linkdown and MAC-notification SNMP traps to NAC Appliance Manager. NAC Appliance Manager is set up for OOB control of the Cisco switch. This example shows NAC Appliance failing open.

Figure 4-13 *OOB in L2 Virtual Gateway Mode*

Pre-Certification Topology

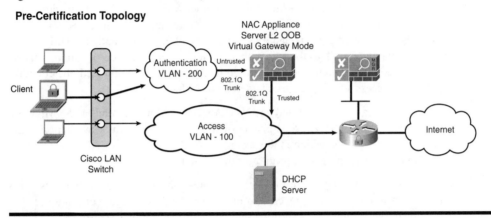

Post-Certification Topology

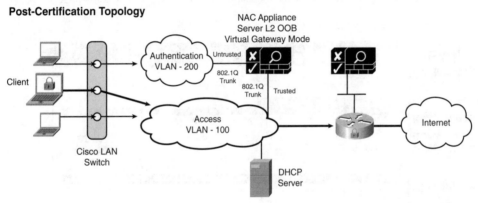

NOTE   NAC Appliance recognizes both VLAN IDs and names as valid VLAN values. This allows you the flexibility of using either the ID (for example, 100) or the name (for example, Authentication-VLAN) when defining your VLAN values.

Initial Steps for OOB Clients

The initial steps for OOB clients are as follows:

1   The host plugs into an Ethernet switch port.

2   The switch immediately sends linkup and MAC-notification SNMP traps to NAC Appliance Manager. These traps include the MAC address of the client and the port number it is plugged into.

3   NAC Appliance Manager checks to see whether the MAC address is already certified (that is, whether it is on the certified list). In other words, is the client certified but logged off the network? If true, you can either put the client on the access VLAN or force the user to authenticate again by putting the client on the authentication VLAN. The client will go through authentication again but not certification. This is because the client remains on the certified list. After it is authenticated, the client is put on the access VLAN and is considered out-of-band.

4   If the client is not on the certified list, NAC Appliance Manager sends an SNMP write to the switch. This SNMP write tells the switch to move the client's switch port to the authentication VLAN, which in this example is 200. The exact VLAN number is determined based on the port profile for that switch port.

5   NAC Appliance Manager adds the client to its out-of-band discovered clients list. This list shows all the clients discovered from SNMP MAC-notification or linkup or linkdown traps. Figure 4-14 shows a sample OOB discovered clients page.

Figure 4-14 *Out-of-Band Discovered Clients Page*

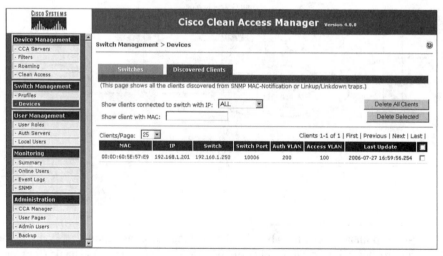

6   At this point, the client is on VLAN 200, which is the untrusted side of NAC Appliance Server. All traffic from the client is now forced to pass through NAC Appliance Server by the network. NAC Appliance Server is configured to allow only certain traffic types through to its trusted side. Common examples are DHCP requests and DNS queries.

7   The client requests a DHCP address.

8   The request is seen by NAC Appliance Server on its untrusted interface (VLAN 200.) Because it is not a denied traffic type, it is retagged for VLAN 100 and forwarded out its trusted interface. The DHCP request continues on to a DHCP server. This VLAN retagging happens based on the preconfigured rules in NAC Appliance Manager's

VLAN mapping tables. In this example, there is a rule to retag traffic from VLAN 200 to VLAN 100 and another rule to retag return traffic from VLAN 100 to VLAN 200.

9 The DHCP request is received by the DHCP server in access VLAN 100. From the DHCP server's viewpoint, this request has come from a client on VLAN 100. As such, it replies to the client with an IP address in VLAN 100.

10 NAC Appliance Server receives the DHCP reply on its trusted interface. It then retags the reply from VLAN 100 to VLAN 200 and forwards the DHCP reply to the originating client.

11 The client now has an IP address in the authentication VLAN that is part of the same subnet as the access VLAN. This is allowed because NAC Appliance is bridging, not routing, between the two VLANs.

Clean Access Agent Authentication Steps in OOB

The Clean Access Agent authentication steps in OOB are as follows:

1 The client is now a member of the NAC Appliance Unauthenticated role. By default, hosts in this role are not allowed to send any traffic, except DHCP and DNS queries, through their local NAC Appliance Server. You can modify the allowed traffic list as necessary for your environment.

2 Clean Access Agent, noticing the network connectivity, begins to send SWISS discovery packets to its default gateway. The agent is trying to locate a NAC Appliance Server.

3 NAC Appliance Server, listening on the SWISS ports, intercepts the request and checks to see whether the host is already authenticated. Because it is not, NAC Appliance Server responds with the equivalent of an, "I'm here; you need to log in" message.

4 NAC Appliance Server's reply message prompts the host's Clean Access Agent to pop up its login dialog box on the user's screen.

5 The user enters a username (Liam), password, and optionally an authentication provider, and then clicks **Log In**. An authentication provider defines the user database that NAC Appliance will use to verify authentication. In this example, the local user database will be used.

6 Liam's login credentials are forwarded by NAC Appliance Server to NAC Appliance Manager for verification.

Agent Host Security Posture Assessment Steps for OOB

The agent host security posture assessment steps for OOB are as follows:

1 After user authentication succeeds, NAC Appliance Manager moves to stage two: host security posture assessment. The user group that Liam is a member of determines the login role he is in. The user's login role determines what host security checks will be performed.

2 NAC Appliance Manager tells NAC Appliance Server to tell Clean Access Agent what security checks to perform on the host.

3 Optionally, the user is shown the acceptable use policy for the normal login role.

4 Clean Access Agent performs these checks and sends the results back to NAC Appliance Server, which forwards them to NAC Appliance Manager for certification.

5 If the host passes all Clean Access Agent security checks, skip to the "Agent Post-Certification Steps for OOB" section.

6 For any failed checks, NAC Appliance Manager instructs NAC Appliance Server to tell Clean Access Agent to pop up a remediation dialog box on the user's screen. This dialog informs the user of the issue found and how to fix it.

7 NAC Appliance Manager moves the user's role from Unauthenticated to Clean Access Temporary.

8 All traffic permitted for remediation is allowed through NAC Appliance Server. NAC Appliance Server retags the remediation traffic from the authentication VLAN to the trusted side, which is the access VLAN. VLAN retagging happens here just as in the initial steps covered earlier.

9 The user then takes the necessary actions to fix the issues found. Failed checks are presented for remediation one at a time. The user cannot continue to any subsequent failed checks until the current one is solved (unless it is an optional requirement).

Agent Post-Certification Steps for OOB

The agent post-certification steps for OOB are as follows:

1 The host is now considered certified or clean and is put into its proper normal login role.

2 At this point, NAC Appliance Manager instructs the switch to move the client's switch port from the authentication VLAN 200 to the access VLAN 100. The access VLAN value is specified in the port profile.

3 The client is now considered out-of-band. This is because the client's traffic no longer flows through NAC Appliance. It is routed and switched normally by the network.

4 Because the original IP address given to the client came from and is valid on the access VLAN, the client does not need to change it now.

5 NAC Appliance Manager adds the client to the out-of-band online user list and the user and host to the certified devices list.

Login Steps for OOB in L3 Adjacency, Real IP Mode

These certification steps are based on the perspective of the host and user in Figure 4-15. The traffic control method used is policy-based routing. The host has Clean Access Agent installed and is multiple Layer 3 hops from NAC Appliance Server. NAC Appliance Server is in Real IP Gateway mode and routing between the untrusted and trusted networks. NAC Appliance is not configured for network scanning, only Clean Access Agent posture assessment. The Cisco LAN switch is configured to send both linkup and linkdown and MAC-notification SNMP traps to NAC Appliance Manager. NAC Appliance Manager is set up for OOB control of the Cisco switch. The routers in the network are configured to policy route all traffic in the authentication VLAN to the untrusted interface of NAC Appliance Server.

Figure 4-15 *Out-of-Band in Layer 3 Real IP Gateway Mode*

Pre-Certification Topology

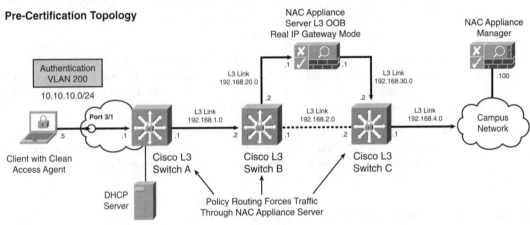

Post-Certification Topology

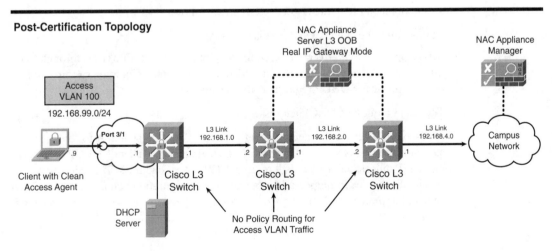

Initial Client Steps for L3 OOB

The initial client steps for L3 OOB are as follows:

1 The host plugs into switch A port 3/1.

2 The switch immediately sends linkup and MAC-notification SNMP traps to NAC Appliance Manager. These traps include the MAC address of the client and the port number it is plugged into.

3 NAC Appliance Manager checks to see whether the MAC address is already certified (that is, already on the certified list). In other words, is the client certified but logged off the network? If true, you can either put the client on the access VLAN 100 or you can force the user to authenticate again by putting the client on the authentication VLAN 200. If put back on the access VLAN, the client bypasses the NAC process. If put on the authentication VLAN, the client is authenticated again but does not go through the certification process. After it is authenticated, the client is put on the access VLAN and is considered out-of-band.

4 If the client is not on the certified list, NAC Appliance Manager sends an SNMP write to the switch. This SNMP write tells the switch to move the client's switch port 3/1 to the authentication VLAN, which in this example is 200. The exact VLAN number is determined based on the port profile for that switch port.

5 NAC Appliance Manager adds the client to its out-of-band discovered clients list. This list shows all the clients discovered from SNMP MAC-notification or linkup or linkdown traps. Figure 4-12 shows a sample OOB discovered clients page.

Steps to Obtain an IP Address in L3 OOB

The steps to obtain an IP address in L3 OOB are as follows:

1 At this point, the client switch port is on VLAN 200.

2 NAC Appliance Server is configured to allow only certain traffic types through to its trusted side. These firewall rules are called network filters. Common examples of allowed traffic are DHCP requests and DNS queries.

3 The client requests a DHCP address.

4 A Cisco IOS DHCP relay agent is configured on Cisco L3 switch A for the authentication VLAN. The DHCP relay agent changes the client's DHCP broadcast into an IP unicast and forwards it to the DHCP server's address. This address is specified using the **ip helper-address** interface configuration command on the Cisco switch. For more information, go to http://www.cisco.com and search for *IOS DHCP Relay Agent*.

TIP	A design best practice is to use the existing DHCP server in the network. A new DHCP scope should be created for the authentication VLAN. If a DHCP server is not available, NAC Appliance Server can be used.

5 The relayed DHCP request is received by the corporate DHCP server. From the DHCP server's viewpoint, this request has come from a client on the authentication VLAN 200. As such, it replies to the client with an IP address in VLAN 200.

6 The client now has an IP address in the authentication VLAN of 10.10.10.5/24. The client's default gateway is set to 10.10.10.1.

Client Authentication and PBR Steps in L3 OOB

The client authentication and PBR steps in L3 OOB are as follows:

1 The client's Clean Access Agent, noticing the network connectivity, begins to send Layer 2 UDP port 8905 SWISS discovery packets to its default gateway. The agent is trying to locate a NAC Appliance Server.

2 Because there is no NAC Appliance Server between the Clean Access Agent and its default gateway, it does not get a response.

3 Clean Access Agent then tries Layer 3 SWISS discovery. Clean Access Agent sends UDP port 8906 unicast packets to its configured discovery host. The discovery host is NAC Appliance Manager in this example, but it can be set to any host on the trusted side of NAC Appliance Server.

4 The Clean Access Agent includes the host's MAC address in the discovery messages.

5 Because the client is not L2 adjacent to NAC Appliance Server, Cisco IOS PBR or VRF features must be used. PBR and VRF ensure that all authentication VLAN traffic is forced to follow a predetermined network path that goes through NAC Appliance Server. This example will use policy-based routing.

6 The configuration for policy-based routing on Cisco L3 switch A would look something like Example 4-4.

Example 4-4 *PBR Sample Configuration*

```
access-list 1 permit ip any
!
interface vlan 200
 ip policy route-map auth-vlan
!
route-map auth-vlan permit 10
 match ip address 1
set ip next-hop 192.168.1.2
```

This configuration instructs switch A to send all IP traffic coming in on interface VLAN 200 to switch B's 192.168.1.2 interface. This PBR policy effectively prevents any host on the authentication VLAN from going anywhere except to switch B.

TIP   Each L3 device between the authentication VLAN and NAC Appliance Server must have PBR configured appropriately. Do not forget to make sure that the client's return traffic is also forced to go through NAC Appliance Server. This can be done using routing tables, PBR, or VRF.

---

7   Clean Access Agent's Layer 3 SWISS discovery packets are routed to NAC Appliance Server (10.10.20.1) via policy-based routing.

8   NAC Appliance Server, listening on the SWISS ports, hears the request and checks to see whether the host is already authenticated. Because it is not, NAC Appliance Server responds with the equivalent of an "I'm here; you need to log in" message.

9   NAC Appliance Server's reply message prompts the host's Clean Access Agent to pop up its login dialog box on the user's screen.

10   The user enters a username, password, and optionally an authentication provider, and then clicks **Log In**. An authentication provider defines the user database NAC Appliance will use to verify authentication. In this example, the local user database will be used.

11   The user's login credentials are forwarded by NAC Appliance Server to NAC Appliance Manager for verification.

Client Certification and Post-Certification Steps in L3 OOB

The client certification and post-certification steps in L3 OOB are as follows:

1   After the user passes authentication, client certification is performed. This process is almost identical to the in-band certification process found in the "Agent Host Security Posture Assessment Steps for OOB" section. The one difference is that in L3 OOB mode, policy-based routing is used to ensure that NAC Appliance Server is in-band for all client traffic in and out of the authentication VLAN. This is regardless of the user's role (that is, quarantine, temporary, and so on).

2   After the client passes certification, NAC Appliance Manager matches the MAC address received from Clean Access Agent with a MAC address sent via a MAC-notification SNMP trap. When a match is made, NAC Appliance Manager looks into the MAC-notification trap to find the switch port information.

3 Now that NAC Appliance Manager has a complete MAC/IP/port mapping, it instructs switch A to change port 3/1 to access VLAN 100.

4 NAC Appliance Manager instructs the client to perform DHCP release/renew operations. Optionally, NAC Appliance Manager instructs the switch to bounce port 3/1. Either of these methods forces the client to erase its current IP address and request another one. DHCP release/renew is the preferred method.

5 The client sends out a DHCP request on access VLAN 100. It receives a new IP address of 192.168.99.9/24 with a default gateway of 192.168.99.1.

6 The client is now considered out-of-band. Traffic flows through the network unrestricted because no PBR policies are configured for access VLAN traffic. NAC Appliance is now totally out of the picture.

Advantages of Using Out-of-Band Mode

When designing any security solution, it is important to understand the advantages and disadvantages of the various product features and modes of operation. There are several compelling reasons to use Out-of-Band mode instead of In-Band mode. The following is a list of Out-of-Band mode's major advantages:

- Typically the biggest advantage OOB has over IB is that client traffic no longer flows through NAC Appliance after authentication and certification are complete.

- OOB provides true switch port–level Network Admission Control. Given that OOB uses VLANs to dynamically control client traffic at the switch port–level, it could be considered more secure than IB. With In-Band mode, there is only a single policy enforcement point: NAC Appliance Server. With Out-of-Band mode, there are two policy enforcement points: the switch port VLAN and the NAC Appliance Server.

- NAC Appliance OOB poses no throughput limitations on traffic while the client is on the access VLAN.

- NAC Appliance is removed from being a single point of failure in the traffic path while the client is on the access VLAN.

- OOB mode allows administrators to configure NAC Appliance to fail-open (sort of). If the server fails in In-Band mode, all traffic from the untrusted side stops flowing regardless of the client's certification status. If the server fails in Out-of-Band mode, all hosts remain in the VLAN configured on their switch port. This means anyone already on an access VLAN sees no impact. But anyone on the authentication VLAN is blocked from network access.

Disadvantage of Using Out-of-Band Mode

Out-of-Band mode has a few disadvantages when compared to In-Band mode. These disadvantages should be checked against your security policy and network environment requirements for relevancy. The following is a list of the major disadvantages:

- Out-of-Band requires specific Cisco switches and software versions be used. See the "Switches Supported by NAC Appliance Out-of-Band" section in this chapter for details.

- OOB works *only* in wired LAN environments where VLANs can be used. Wireless and VPN clients are not currently supported in Out-of-Band mode.

- The ability to control traffic by using bandwidth limiting and traffic filtering after the client is certified is not available in OOB mode. This is because traffic does not flow through NAC Appliance after clients are in the access VLAN. External controls such as Cisco IOS QoS and ACLs may be used instead.

- OOB requires privileges to manage and change the configuration on the Cisco switches that NAC Appliance will control. This is done through the use of SNMP.

- Due to conflicts, Out-of-Band mode and 802.1X cannot coexist on the same switch ports.

- Switch clusters are not supported in OOB mode. However, OOB mode does support Cisco's StackWise technology. The workaround is to assign a unique IP address to each switch in the stack.

Where You Can Use Out-of-Band Mode and Where You Cannot

NAC Appliance Out-of-Band excels when deployed in campus LAN environments with lots of access-layer switch ports. OOB mode can be used *only* in wired switched LAN environments that can support VLANs. Additionally, you must use a supported Cisco switch and software version. NAC Appliance Out-of-Band mode cannot be used in wireless, VPN, 802.1X, or any non-Cisco switched environments. Note that 802.1x will be supported in a future release.

Switches Supported by NAC Appliance Out-of-Band

This section details the Cisco switch models and the required minimum software version you must have in your environment if you plan to use NAC Appliance in Out-of-Band mode. This information is constantly being updated, so be sure to check the latest NAC Appliance Release Notes on http://www.cisco.com. Table 4-3 lists the supported switches as of this writing.

Table 4-3   *Supported Switches for Cisco NAC Appliance Out-of-Band*

Minimum Cisco NAC Appliance Version[1]			Switch Model	Minimum Supported OS Version[2,3]
4.0(0)+	3.6(1)+	—	Cisco Catalyst Express 500 Series (CE500)[4]	Cisco IOS Release 12.2(25)SEG
	3.6(0)+	3.5(4)+	Cisco Catalyst 2900 XL[5,6]	Cisco IOS Software Release 12.0(5)WC7
			Cisco Catalyst 2940	Cisco IOS Software Release 12.1(6)EA2
		3.5(0)+	Cisco Catalyst 2950[7]	Cisco IOS Software Release 12.1(14)EA1
			Cisco Catalyst 2950 LRE[7]	Cisco IOS Software Release 12.1(14)EA1
	3.6(1)+	—	Cisco Catalyst 2955	Cisco IOS Software Release 12.1(14)EA1
	3.6(0)+	3.5(7)+	Cisco Catalyst 2960	Cisco IOS Software Release 12.2(25)
		3.5(4)+	Cisco Catalyst 3500 XL[5,6]	Cisco IOS Software Release 12.0(5)WC7
		3.5(0)+	Cisco Catalyst 3550	Cisco IOS Software Release 12.1(8)EA1b
		3.5(1)+	Cisco Catalyst 3560	Cisco IOS Software Release 12.2(25)SEE
		3.5(0)+	Cisco Catalyst 3750[8,9]	Cisco IOS Software Release 12.2(25)SEE
		3.5(8)+	Cisco Catalyst 4000	Cisco Catalyst OS Release 7.1
				Cisco IOS Software Release 12.2(31)SG
		3.5(0)+	Cisco Catalyst 4500	Cisco Catalyst OS Release 7.1
				Cisco IOS Software Release 12.2(31)SG
		3.5(8)+	Cisco Catalyst 6000[10]	Cisco Catalyst OS Release 7.5
				Cisco IOS Software Release 12.1(8a)EX
		3.5(0)+	Cisco Catalyst 6500[10]	Cisco Catalyst OS Release 7.5
				Cisco IOS Software Release 12.1(8a)EX

continues

Table 4-3 *Supported Switches for Cisco NAC Appliance Out-of-Band (Continued)*

Min. Cisco NAC Appliance Version[11]	3750 Service Modules Supported for Cisco 2800/3800 Integrated Services Routers[12,13]	Minimum Switch Cisco IOS Version	Minimum Router Cisco IOS Version
4.0(1)+ 3.6(4)+	NME-16ES-1G	12.2(25)SEC	12.3(14)T3
	NME-16ES-1G-P	12.2(25)EZ	12.3(14)T
	NME-X-23ES-1G	12.2(25)SEC	12.3(14)T3
	NME-X-23ES-1G-P	12.2(25)EZ	12.3(14)T
	NME-XD-24ES-1S-P	12.2(25)EZ	12.3(14)T
	NME-XD-48ES-2S-P	12.2(25)EZ	12.3(14)T

1. The "+" designation in the **Minimum Cisco NAC Appliance Version** column indicates the switch model or OS that is supported starting from the CCA version listed and for subsequent versions.

2. If running a deferred Cisco IOS, make sure to run a nondeferred version that is higher than the minimum supported OS version.

3. OS versions support SNMP V3 except where noted.

4. With Cisco IOS release 12.2.25(SEG) for CE500, MAC-notification SNMP traps are supported on all Smartport roles (including DESKTOP and IPPHONE roles). After upgrading to 12.2.25(SEG), customers can configure MAC-notification for CE500 under **Switch Management > Devices > List > Config [Switch IP] > Config > Advanced** on the Content-Addressable Memory (CAM). For CCA 3.6.2, 3.6.3, 4.0.0, 4.0.1, 4.0.2, CE500 supports linkup and linkdown SNMP notifications by default and the "OTHER role" warning message can be ignored when changing to MAC-notification traps. Note that in future CCA releases, this warning message will removed and the default control method for CE500 will be MAC-notification traps. Note: If running a Cisco IOS version *lower* than 12.2(25) SEG, the CE500 switch ports must be assigned to the OTHER role (not Desktop or IP phone) on the switch's Smartports configuration, otherwise, MAC-notification will not be sent out.

5. CCA OOB supports Cisco Catalyst 2900 XL, 3500 XL, and 5500 only until the product (switch) end of support. For details, see http://www.cisco.com/en/US/partner/products/hw/switches/prod_category_end_of_life.html.

6. 3500 XL and 2900 XL do not support SNMP V3.

7. Cisco IOS 12.1(14)EA1 or above is required for 2950/2950 LRE switches. 2950s running 12.1(11)–12.1(13) might experience caveat CSCea56777, which prevents the VLAN from being changed on the switch itself. For additional details, see http://www.cisco.com/pcgi-bin/Support/Bugtool/onebug.pl?bugid=CSCea56777.

8. Cisco IOS 12.2(25)SEE or above is required for 3750 L3 switches. For details, see *Stacked Cisco Catalyst 3750 Switches and NAC Appliance Out-of-Band Deployment*.

9. CCA OOB supports 3750 StackWise technology. Clusters are not supported. With stacks, when MAC-notification is used and there are more than 252 ports on the stack, MAC-notification cannot be set or unset for the 252nd port using the CAM. There are two workarounds: Use linkup/linkdown SNMP notifications only or if using MAC-notification, do not use the 252nd port and ignore the error; the other ports will work fine.

10. Catalyst 6000/6500 on Cisco IOS do not support MAC-notification.

11. The "+" designation in the Minimum Cisco NAC Appliance Version column indicates the switch model or OS supported starting from the CCA version listed and for subsequent versions.

12. For further details on which ISRs support the preceding service modules, refer to the following table: http://www.cisco.com/en/US/partner/products/hw/modules/ps2797/products_module_installation_guide_chapter09186a008069418f.html#wp1124185.

13. Adding 3750 NME modules to the CAM for OOB switch management requires the same steps as if adding a 3750 switch. When configuring the switch profile for these 3750 NMEs, choose **Cisco Catalyst 3750 Series** under **Switch Management > Profiles > Switch > New | Switch Model**.

Clean Access Agent and Web Login with Network Scanner

This section will deal with how to best use the web login with Network Scanner and Clean Access Agent in your Cisco NAC Appliance design. Understanding where and when to use Clean Access Agent or web login is critical to producing a successful design. For this discussion, it should always be assumed that web login will include the Network Scanner function. The Network Admission Control Appliance solution has three main functions: authentication, posture assessment, and remediation. Each of these functions requires the NAC Appliance solution to interact with the clients it is attempting to control. Each of the main functions requires client information and interaction that is unique to their purpose. The agent and web login differ in their capabilities to gather information and interact with a client. An examination of these differences will help in the decision-making process of which approach to use for a given situation.

The first function's purpose, authentication, identifies who is connecting to the network. Authentication requires the gathering and validating of a user's credentials, typically username and password. Authentication can also include performing the SSO process. Both Clean Access Agent and web login can perform basic authentication. However, only the Clean Access Agent can perform the duties of SSO. As a result, if you choose to use any of the SSO methods, VPN, Wireless, or AD, you must use Clean Access Agent for authentication. A nice feature of Clean Access Agent is that it self-discovers when the user needs to authenticate to NAC Appliance and pops up a Windows dialog box to do so. Web login has no equivalent discovery function. It requires the user to know when to open a web browser to log in. Figure 4-16 shows the Clean Access Agent Login dialog box.

Figure 4-16 *Clean Access Agent Login*

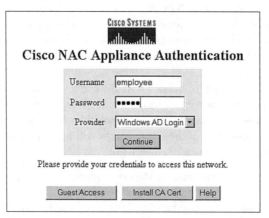

Web login is shown in Figure 4-17.

Figure 4-17 *Web Login Authentication*

The second main function is posture assessment of the user's host PC. Posture assessment involves validating that a given host complies with the requirements set forth in your host security policy. To accomplish this task, NAC Appliance gathers relevant information about the host and compares it against the requirements set forth in the host security policy. Both Clean Access Agent and the Network Scanner part of web login are capable of performing a host posture assessment. However, Clean Access Agent is by far the more widely deployed of the two. During the creation of your host security policy, you will determine what host posture assessment checks you want to perform. Based on those checks, ask yourself these questions:

- What information do I need to gather to perform the checks?

- Where is this information stored? Can it be accessed using a network scan, or must it be gathered by a local agent? If both, which is easiest?

- Will hosts have personal firewalls enabled that will thwart the NAC Appliance network scanner?

- If the information is only available locally, the agent must be used. Are all the clients running operating systems that the Clean Access Agent supports?

- The installation of Clean Access Agent requires the user to have admin rights. Will users have the admin rights necessary to install Clean Access Agent on their PC? If not, a software distribution method, such as Short Message Service, should be used.

- One way to get around the previous requirement is to distribute an agent stub first. A stub provides a convenient way to allow users to install Clean Access Agent without admin rights. But the stub program itself requires the network administrators to have admin rights on the PC it will be installed on. Do you control or have admin rights on all the PCs you want to control?

- How will the posture assessment checks change based on user role and host location? For example, in the public areas you might want to scan only for infected hosts and not use an agent.

Clean Access Agent is built to do local checks of a host's file system, registry, running services, and applications. Clean Access Agent provides an effective mechanism to allow NAC Appliance to check for things such as the running state of antivirus clients, virus definition file versions, Windows hotfixes and service packs, and so on. Figure 4-18 shows Clean Access Agent kicking off its posture assessment process.

Figure 4-18 *Clean Access Agent Posture Assessment*

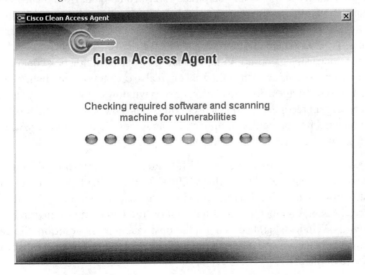

The Network Scanner function is built to scan a host to detect known security vulnerabilities and active worm infections. Nessus is the scanning engine used by Network Scanner. Network Scanner has hundreds of vulnerability plug-ins for you to choose from. For example, you can run plug-ins that scan to see whether a host is infected with the Zotob worm or is vulnerable to a dcom buffer overflow attack. The big downside of Network Scanner is that it performs the scans from the NAC Appliance Server across the network to the host. This means that simple things like a host personal firewall or Intrusion Prevention System will block Network Scanner from gathering any information. Figure 4-19 shows the vulnerability report screen that web login displays.

Figure 4-19 *Web Login Vulnerability Report*

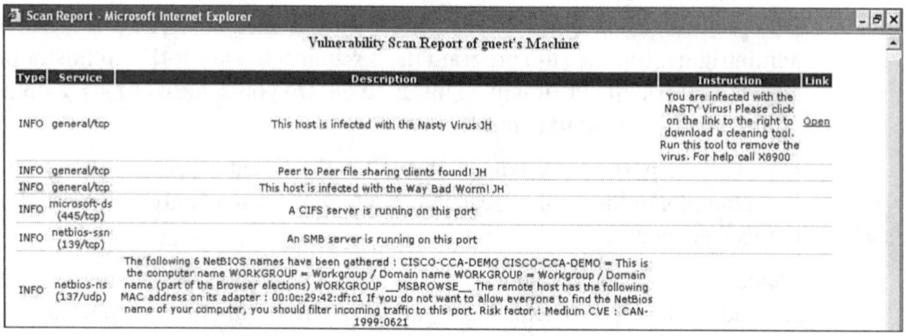

The purpose of the third function, remediation, is to provide noncompliant users with the necessary tools and information they need to become compliant. This requires that NAC Appliance be able to deliver the tools and information to the user and be able to validate that the changes required for compliancy were completed. Both the agent and the network scanner function of web login are capable of performing the remediation function. However, the capabilities of Clean Access Agent are far superior to Network Scanner. Clean Access Agent's remediation process walks the user through each individual failed check. This is done using a pop-up Windows dialog box. This dialog box contains information and instructions pertaining to the failed check. It also contains a remediation button. This button can link to web pages, download files, or start windows or antivirus update programs. Clean Access Agent recognizes when a user completes a fix and when the host becomes compliant. After the user is compliant, Clean Access Agent notifies NAC Appliance, which then grants the client access to the network.

Network Scanner works a little bit differently. After performing its vulnerability scan, a web page containing all the vulnerabilities found is displayed on the client's PC. Instructions and a URL link are provided for each vulnerability listed. Unlike Clean Access Agent, this method does not support the launching of any update programs— antivirus, Windows, and so on—on the host machine. In addition, the capability to recognize when a user completes a fix is not automatic. The user must log out and log in to be rescanned.

As discussed, NAC Appliance interacts with and gathers information from clients in three ways: through Clean Access Agent, Web Login, or both. Either method can be used to accomplish the three main functions—authentication, posture assessment, and remediation—as set forth in the preceding discussion. By and large, the Clean Access Agent method is the recommended design choice. However, both Clean Access Agent and web login have advantages and disadvantages. A good rule of thumb is to use Clean Access Agent on hosts that you or the users have admin rights on. Using web login is a popular choice for guest users that will be given extremely limited access to your internal resources, such as Internet only. And, of course, web login is used for hosts that you cannot install Clean Access Agent on.

The type of interaction method chosen is role dependent. For a given role, both Clean Access Agent and web login can be made available or Clean Access Agent can be made mandatory. For example, the Guest role users might have both methods available, but the Employee role users must use the Clean Access Agent.

Summary

This chapter examined the various design options available in a Cisco NAC Appliance deployment. The function and pros and cons of each option were studied in detail. The following design options were covered:

- Single-Sign-On
- In-band
- Out-of-band
- Layer 2 adjacency
- Layer 3 adjacency
- Virtual gateway mode
- Real IP gateway mode
- Clean Access Agent
- Web login and Network Scanner

This chapter covers the following topics:

- External Authentication Servers
- Single Sign-On
- NAC Appliance and IP Telephony Integration
- High Availability and Load Balancing

CHAPTER 5

Advanced Cisco NAC Appliance Design Topics

This chapter will build on the basic NAC Appliance design concepts covered in the preceding chapter. It focuses on those advanced features essential to designing the most secure, user-friendly, scalable, and fault-tolerant NAC Appliance environment possible. This chapter by no means covers all the advanced features available, but instead focuses on the most widely deployed, or popular, advanced options. You will undoubtedly use most of these options in your design. The use of external authentication servers and high availability as design options is highly recommended. Be sure to read through those sections to get a good idea of the choices available to you.

External Authentication Servers

A key component of the NAC process is user authentication. In fact, identifying, or authenticating, who is connecting to the network is the first step in the NAC Appliance process. A user's identity determines which user role that user will be a member of. The user role in turn determines or influences almost every other NAC process. For example, if you are user John Doe, you are a member of the Employee user role. Everyone in the Employee user role is scanned for the latest hotfixes and, if clean, is granted unlimited network access.

In most environments, building a local user database in NAC Appliance is not practical given the sheer amount of users. Except for perhaps in test and guest environments, an external authentication server should be used to authenticate users. The process that NAC Appliance goes through when authenticating is pretty straightforward. It starts with the user typing in credentials to log in to NAC Appliance. These credentials, a username and a password, are sent from NAC Appliance Manager to the external authentication server. The external authentication server then validates the user credentials against its user database and return a pass or fail result to NAC Appliance Manager.

NAC Appliance can optionally be configured to request a specific attribute's value from the authentication server. The attribute's returned value can then be used to determine what user role a particular client should be made a member of. For example, for any particular user, NAC Appliance can query the external authentication server for the value of the attribute *group membership.* If the authentication server returns a value of *domain users,* this user is put into the Employee user role of the NAC Appliance solution. Here is the complete process of authentication when an external authentication server is used:

Step 1 The user connects to the network.

Step 2 The user supplies credentials, username, and password, using either web login or Clean Access Agent.

Step 3 These credentials are sent to NAC Appliance Server, which forwards them on to NAC Appliance Manager.

Step 4 NAC Appliance Manager sends the user's credentials to the external authentication server.

Step 5 The external authentication server validates the credentials and sends a pass or fail result to NAC Appliance Manager.

Step 6 If the credentials pass, NAC Appliance Manager can optionally request the value(s) of some attribute(s) from the external authentication server.

Step 7 NAC Appliance will then use the received attribute values to map the user into a user role. An example of the attribute-to-role mapping configuration screen is shown in Figure 5-1.

Figure 5-1 *Role Mapping Configuration Screen*

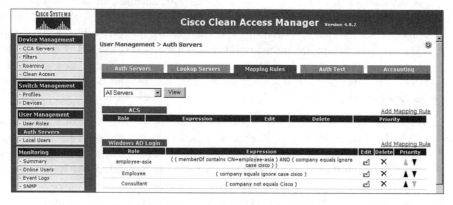

Several of the most popular authentication server types are supported by NAC Appliance. Here are the supported external authentication server types:

- Remote Authentication Dial-In User Service (RADIUS)
- Lightweight Directory Access Protocol (LDAP)
- Kerberos/Active Directory

NOTE	Windows NT LAN manager (NTLM) is still supported, but because Windows NT is end-of-life, this type will not be covered.

One or more authentication server types can be used simultaneously within a NAC Appliance solution. If you configure two or more authentication servers, NAC Appliance uses the provider field to determine which authentication server a particular user wants to use. A provider is a configured authentication server. You configure web login and Clean Access Agent to display a list of available providers to the user. Be sure to use provider names that your user community will understand. The user then must choose a server from a drop-down list, called the provider list. Figure 5-2 shows an example of a web login drop-down provider list.

Figure 5-2 *Web Login Provider List*

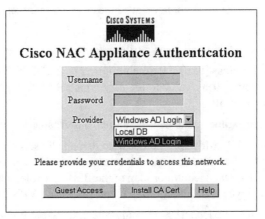

Mapping Users to Roles Using Attributes or VLAN IDs

Probably the most complex external authentication server design option you will deal with is mapping users to a user role. During the design phase, you will want to determine how many user roles you will need and how you will map users into these roles. For example, if you want faculty and students to be granted different network access privileges, you will need two roles: faculty and students. Then you could use the returned value of an LDAP group membership query to assign the users to their proper role. If the LDAP query returns a value of *faculty,* the Faculty role is used. Traffic policies are then used to determine how much network access a particular role is allowed. Three parameters can be used to assign a user to a role:

- **VLAN ID**   NAC Appliance uses the virtual LAN (VLAN) ID of the user traffic on the untrusted side of NAC Appliance Server.

- **Authentication attributes** NAC Appliance uses the values of various attributes passed from LDAP, Cisco VPN, and wireless devices, or RADIUS servers.

- **Default role** If the previous two parameters are not configured or receive no match, the user is put into the default role configured for that external authentication server.

NAC Appliance uses a set of mapping rules to determine which user maps to which role. Cisco NAC Appliance allows the administrator to specify complex Boolean expressions when defining mapping rules. Mapping rules are broken down into conditions. You can combine these conditions using Boolean operators to create a string of criteria. For example, a user is a member of the Employee role if his VLAN ID is *100* and the LDAP query returned a group membership of either *employee-USA* or *employee-Asia* and a company value of *acme corp*. As you can see, a mapping rule can be as simple or as complex as you need it to be for your environment. During the design phase of NAC Appliance, you will want to determine what your mapping rules will look like.

Here are some of the most common attributes used in mapping rules for RADIUS and LDAP:

- **RADIUS** Commonly used attributes are as follows:
    - **IETF class [025]** If so configured in RADIUS, you can use the *class* attribute string value to identify which RADIUS group a user is a member of.
    - **User_Name** Can be used to map a username to a user role.
    - **NAS_IP_Address** Can be used to map all users on a given virtual private network (VPN) concentrator to a user role. For example, all users on the B2B VPN concentrator map to the B2B user role, whereas all users on the employee concentrator map to the Employee-VPN user role.

An example of a RADIUS mapping rule is shown in Figure 5-3. Unlike LDAP, a RADIUS rule provides you with a list of attributes to pick from.

- **AD LDAP** Commonly used attributes and value examples are as follows:
    - **memberOf** Sample values are *CN=employee-asia, CN=Users, DC=jheary, DC=com*.
    - **company** Sample value is *ACME Corp.*
    - **department** Sample value is *Engineering*.

Figure 5-4 shows an example of a compound mapping rule for an AD LDAP Server. Notice the rule logic says that both conditions #1 and #2 must be true for the rule to succeed. If it succeeds, the user is mapped into the employee-Asia user role.

Figure 5-3   *Mapping Rule Example for a RADIUS Server*

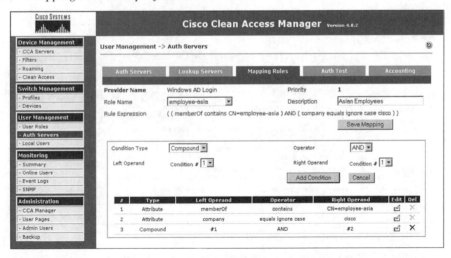

Figure 5-4   *Mapping Rule Example for an LDAP Server*

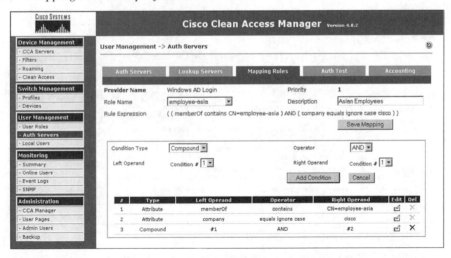

TIP   An LDAP browser program allows you to find, and verify the spelling of, all the available attributes in a given LDAP server. Many free LDAP browsers are available at sites like http://www.downloads.com.

MAC Address Authentication Filters

In some cases, you will want to bypass authentication, posture assessment, role assignment, or any combination thereof for certain network devices or users. NAC Appliance relies on matching the device's MAC address or MAC/IP address pair to determine whether bypass is enabled. Common examples of bypassed device types are printers, IP phones, servers, nonclient machines, and network devices. Another less common use of MAC Address filtering is for allowing corporate desktops to bypass authentication and perform only posture assessment and role assignment. By doing this, you can save the end user the time and hassle of performing authentication but maintain the security that posture assessment and user roles provide. The MAC filter example shown in Figure 5-5 allows corporate PCs to bypass authentication and move directly to posture assessment and role assignment. Given that client desktops typically use DHCP for their IP address, only the MAC address is used to identify hosts. If this were a statically addressed host, both the MAC/IP pair would be used.

Figure 5-5 *MAC Filter with Checking*

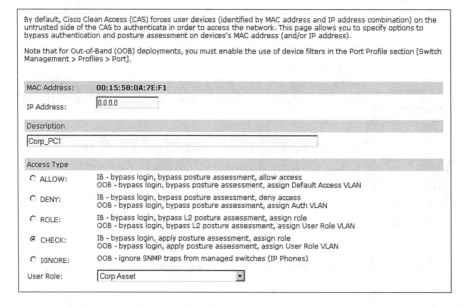

Figure 5-5 shows the client access type options. As you can see, you can use five different access types. Each access type gives a description of what actions it will take. These actions can differ between in-band (IB) and out-of-band (OOB), so the actions are separated out accordingly. Pay special attention to how the OOB VLAN is assigned because it differs for each access type.

When using Out-of-Band mode, it is very important to add all your IP phones to this MAC filter list and set them to *ignore*. For In-Band mode, it is recommended that you configure your network to have all voice traffic bypass the NAC Appliance solution altogether. However, if this is not possible, you must import the MAC addresses of all the IP phones and set them to *allow*.

Single Sign-On

This section covers the design best practices for the various NAC Appliance–supported Single Sign-On (SSO) methods. SSO gives users the convenience of having to log in to the network only once. For example, without SSO enabled, a VPN user would have to enter credentials into the VPN client, connect, and then enter credentials again to the Clean Access Agent pop-up dialog. With SSO enabled, the Clean Access Agent uses the credentials supplied to the VPN client, thus eliminating that step and creating a one-time login user experience. Cisco NAC Appliance currently supports three methods of Single Sign-On:

- Active Directory SSO
- VPN SSO
- Cisco Wireless SSO

Making the right SSO design decisions will help ensure a successful SSO deployment. The first decision is to pick which SSO method you would like to be able to use. This is not necessarily the method you will ultimately end up using, but the one whose use you would like to initially explore. This is arguably the easiest decision because it is mostly predetermined based on the access method of the client. If your clients are connecting through a NAC Appliance–supported VPN device, you would use VPN SSO there. If your clients are connecting through a supported Lightweight Access Point Protocol (LWAPP) wireless controller, you would use Wireless SSO. Finally, if your clients are logging in to a Windows Active Directory (AD) domain, you would use AD SSO. If your environment combines two of the supported access methods—wireless and AD login for instance—a good rule of thumb is to use the SSO method that would happen first. For example, clients in an environment that uses both wireless and AD Login access methods follow an order of operations. First the wireless connection is established, and then the AD login is performed. The best SSO method would be wireless SSO because the wireless connection happens first.

The selected SSO method must now be looked at in greater detail to make sure that it is the correct design choice for your environment.

Active Directory SSO

Cisco NAC Appliance 4.0 or greater supports Single Sign-On with Windows Active Directory. You can configure NAC Appliance to use a back-end Kerberos Domain Controller (Active Directory server) to automatically authenticate Clean Access Agent users. This feature permits users who are already authenticated to an Active Directory server to bypass the normal Clean Access Agent login and skip right to posture assessment and certification.

Active Directory SSO Prerequisites

The following are prerequisites for Active Directory SSO:

- NAC Appliance Clients must use the Clean Access Agent software.
- NAC Appliance 4.0 or greater software is required.
- Time must be synchronized between NAC Appliance and Active Directory servers.
- The supported AD servers are as follows:
  - Windows 2000 Server SP4
  - Windows 2003 Standard SP1
  - Windows 2003 Enterprise SP1
  - Windows 2003 Enterprise R2

How Active Directory SSO Works

The NAC Appliance Active Directory SSO process works by using the Kerberos ticket exchange process built into the Windows 2000 and 2003 server architecture. A NAC Appliance Server that will support AD SSO clients must have a username configured in Active Directory. You can share this username among multiple NAC Appliance Servers that will support SSO. This username must be set up to use DES encryption, not the default RC4. This is because the Linux OS on NAC Appliance Server does not support RC4 encryption.

To change the encryption for the NAC Appliance Server user, a program called ktpass.exe must be used. This program is a part of the Windows Support Tools and is available on the Windows Server CD or online at Microsoft.com. The NAC Appliance Server user and ktpass.exe program need to be set up only on the Domain Controller (DC) Server that the NAC Appliance Server will talk to. NAC Appliance Server will use this server for user authentication requests. So, if your AD domain has 10 DC servers, you have to run ktpass.exe only on the server that NAC Appliance Server is configured to use. In the design phase, you should pick which AD Domain Controller you will use for this purpose. Figure 5-6 shows the details of how AD SSO works with the Kerberos ticket exchange process.

After the Kerberos SSO process authenticates the user, NAC Appliance then performs user role mapping. NAC Appliance Manager sends an LDAP lookup request to the Active Directory Server. The results are run through the mapping rules, and the user is put into the correct NAC Appliance role. The NAC certification process now initiates. The host is checked to make sure that it meets the security requirements defined by the user's role.

Figure 5-6   *Active Directory Single Sign-On Kerberos Exchange*

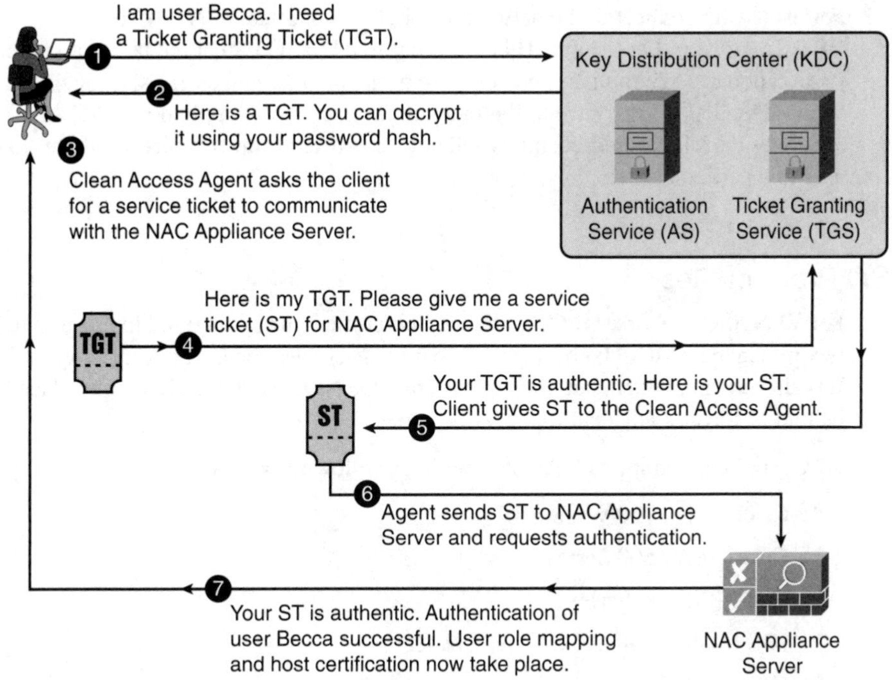

I am user Becca. I need
a Ticket Granting Ticket (TGT).

❶

Key Distribution Center (KDC)

❷

Here is a TGT. You can decrypt
it using your password hash.

Authentication   Ticket Granting
Service (AS)   Service (TGS)

❸

Clean Access Agent asks the client
for a service ticket to communicate
with the NAC Appliance Server.

Here is my TGT. Please give me a service
ticket (ST) for NAC Appliance Server.

TGT   ❹

Your TGT is authentic. Here is your ST.
Client gives ST to the Clean Access Agent.

ST   ❺

❻

Agent sends ST to NAC Appliance
Server and requests authentication.

❼

Your ST is authentic. Authentication of
user Becca successful. User role mapping
and host certification now take place.

NAC Appliance
Server

NOTE   For a detailed explanation of the Kerberos ticketing process, see Microsoft's Kerberos
website at http://www.microsoft.com/kerberos.

During the SSO authentication process, the end user sees the Clean Access Agent dialog
box shown in Figure 5-7. This dialog box disappears after the end user passes
authentication.

Figure 5-7   *Clean Access Agent AD SSO Authentication Dialog Box*

VPN SSO

For users who connect to the network through a supported VPN device, you can use the VPN Single Sign-On feature. This is similar to AD SSO in that the user authentication portion of the NAC Appliance process is transparent to the end user. Users logging in through their VPN client do not have to log in again to Cisco NAC Appliance. NAC Appliance leverages the VPN user credentials and any VPN user group and class attributes to map the user to a particular role.

VPN SSO Prerequisites

For VPN SSO to work, NAC Appliance Server must run in In-Band mode, and it is recommended, although not required, that the user have the Clean Access Agent installed. It is also recommended, but not required, that the NAC Appliance Server be placed directly behind or Layer 2 adjacent to the VPN device.

NAC Appliance supports VPN SSO with the following VPN devices:

- Cisco VPN 3000 Version 4.7
- Cisco ASA 5500 Series
- Cisco PIX 500 Series
- IOS Routers with security feature set
- Cisco VPN Client (IPsec)
- Cisco SSL VPN (full tunneling client)

NOTE   Cisco NAC Appliance supports *any* VPN device that uses and can send RFC-compliant RADIUS accounting messages to NAC Appliance. However, only the devices in the preceding list are officially supported by Cisco Technical Assistance Center. Be sure to check the NAC Appliance release notes at http://www.cisco.com for the latest details about the devices and codes supported with VPN SSO.

How VPN SSO Works

VPN SSO operates using a trust model. NAC Appliance trusts the VPN device to correctly perform user authentication for the client VPN tunnels. After this authentication is complete, the VPN device sends a RADIUS message to NAC Appliance with the necessary details of who just successfully authenticated. Given that NAC Appliance trusts the VPN device's messages, the VPN client is allowed to bypass NAC authentication and proceed directly to posture assessment or certification. Figure 5-8 shows how the VPN SSO process works.

Figure 5-8   *VPN SSO Process*

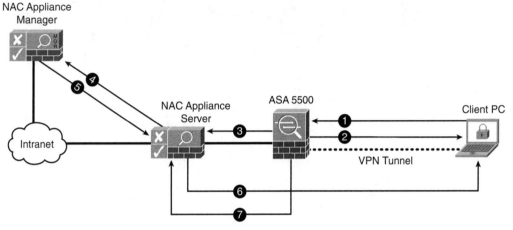

Here are the steps represented in Figure 5-8:

Step 1   The client PC sends a VPN tunnel request to the ASA VPN device. In this request is the username and password of the user.

Step 2   The ASA 5500 performs a verification of the user's credentials. If the user passes authentication, a VPN tunnel is established between the ASA and the client PC.

Step 3   The ASA sends a RADIUS accounting start message to NAC Appliance Server. A start message indicates that a new client has successfully passed authentication. This message also contains the client's IP address, username, and miscellaneous other RADIUS attribute values such as class [025]. During this process, the Clean Access Agent on the client machine pops up the dialog box shown in Figure 5-9.

Step 4   At this point, NAC Appliance considers the user successfully authenticated. If user role mapping is configured, the server forwards the RADIUS attributes received from the ASA to the manager. For example, *RADIUS attribute class = employee*. The manager holds the mapping rule table that matches VPN users with NAC Appliance user roles.

Step 5   NAC Appliance Manager performs a mapping rule table lookup using the RADIUS attributes it has received. After it finds a match, it maps that user into the matched user role. See Figure 5-10 for a sample mapping rule. This rule says that if the RADIUS attribute class [025] equals Admin, put this user in the user role Admin.

Figure 5-9   *VPN SSO Authentication Dialog Box*

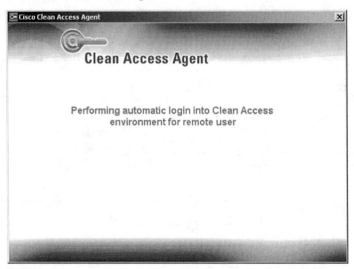

Figure 5-10   *RADIUS Mapping Rule Configuration Screen*

Step 6   NAC Appliance Server now performs the normal posture assessment or certification of the client. The security requirements for the client are dependent on the user's role. The posture assessment process is the same regardless of whether VPN SSO is used.

Step 7   The client is logged off NAC Appliance when a RADIUS stop record is received from the ASA.

Cisco Wireless SSO

In a supported wireless environment, it is recommended that the NAC Appliance perform SSO. This means that the end user will have to enter credentials into only the wireless client. These same credentials will then be used transparently to log on the user to NAC Appliance, thus bypassing the manual user authentication step. NAC Appliance performs wireless single sign-on in just about the same manner as it does VPN single sign-on. It uses a trust relationship between the Airespace wireless LAN controller (WLC) and NAC Appliance. NAC Appliance trusts the user authentication results reported by the WLC. NAC Appliance logs a user on when it receives a RADIUS start record. NAC Appliance logs a user off when it receives a RADIUS stop record.

Cisco Wireless SSO Prerequisites

For wireless SSO to work, NAC Appliance Server must be running in In-Band mode. It is recommended, although not required, that the NAC Appliance Server be placed Layer 2 adjacent to the WLC.

NAC Appliance supports wireless SSO with Cisco Airespace 4400 Series Wireless LAN Controllers.

NOTE   Be sure to check the NAC Appliance release notes at http://www.cisco.com for the latest details about the devices and codes supported with wireless SSO.

How Cisco Wireless SSO Works

Figure 5-11 shows the process by which NAC Appliance performs single sign-on in a WLC environment.

Figure 5-11 *Wireless SSO Process*

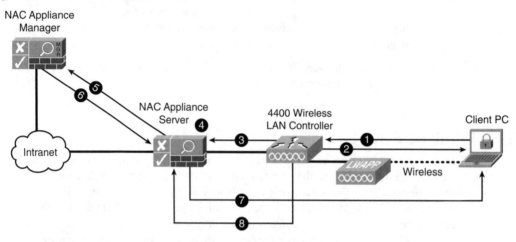

Here are the steps shown in Figure 5-11:

Step 1   The client PC sends a wireless association/connection request to the 4400 WLC. This request contains the user's username and password for authentication.

Step 2   The 4400 WLC performs a verification of the user's credentials. If the user passes authentication, the client is permitted to associate to the wireless access point.

Step 3   The WLC sends a RADIUS accounting start message to NAC Appliance Server. A start message indicates that a new client has successfully passed authentication. This message also contains the client's MAC Address, IP address, username, and miscellaneous other RADIUS attribute values such as class [025]. During this process, the Clean Access Agent on the client machine pops up the dialog box shown previously in Figure 5-9.

Step 4   At this point, NAC Appliance considers the user successfully authenticated. If the optional role-to-attribute mapping rules are configured, NAC Appliance Server forwards the RADIUS attributes received from the WLC to the NAC Appliance Manager.

Step 5   NAC Appliance Manager matches the RADIUS attributes with a user role. After a match is found, the client is put into that role.

Step 6   The NAC Appliance Server now performs the normal posture assessment or certification of the client. The security requirements for the client are dependent on the user's user role. The posture assessment process is the same regardless of whether wireless SSO is used.

Step 7   The wireless client is logged off NAC Appliance when a RADIUS stop accounting record is received from the WLC.

NAC Appliance and IP Telephony Integration

With careful design and planning, NAC Appliance and IP telephony can coexist harmoniously. This section is dedicated to the design best practices of integrating NAC Appliance into an IP telephony environment. When designing NAC Appliance to work in an IP telephony environment, the ultimate goal is to have clients inspected by NAC Appliance while all voice traffic bypasses NAC Appliance completely.

The best practices that help accomplish this goal are most relevant when client PCs plug directly into IP phones behind a NAC Appliance Server or are on a switch controlled by NAC Appliance. If your clients do not connect directly to IP phones, it is recommended that you design your network so that the voice traffic completely bypasses the NAC Appliance solution. Because IP phones are not capable of performing NAC, they should not have to go through the NAC solution. Removing IP telephony in this way greatly reduces the complexity of your design. Given that voice should be on its own VLAN, separate from the client VLANs, this should be a relatively straightforward solution. Just make sure that all voice VLANs never pass through NAC Appliance Server. If you are using OOB mode, you must also ensure that the switch ports with IP phones attached are set to *Uncontrolled* in NAC Appliance. This means that NAC Appliance completely ignores these ports, letting their behavior remain unchanged.

When your environment includes clients that plug directly into IP phones, you have to pay special attention to how you design your NAC Appliance solution. Here are some best practices that will make your integration go smoothly. They are broken up into two groups: in-band and out-of-band. The groups correspond to the mode your voice-facing NAC Appliance Server is using.

IP Telephony Best Practices for In-Band Mode

Here are the design recommendations you should consider when your voice-facing NAC Appliance Server is running in In-Band mode:

- It is highly recommended that the network be configured in such a way as to allow all voice traffic to bypass the NAC Appliance Servers. NAC Appliance does not support quality of service (QoS) and adds small amounts of latency and jitter to any voice streams that flow through it.

- If it is not possible to allow voice to bypass NAC Appliance, be sure to exempt all voice subnets from NAC inspection. This can be done using Allow filters on NAC Appliance Manager. Given that the Allow filter uses the bandwidth management settings of the unauthenticated role, be sure to set the unauthenticated role's bandwidth setting to *unlimited*.

IP Telephony Best Practices for Out-of-Band Mode

If your voice-facing NAC Appliance Server is running in OOB mode, your design becomes a little bit more complex. This makes sense given that with OOB mode you are controlling the actual switch port that the IP phone and its connected client are attached to. The basic rule of thumb is that if you will not have a client connecting to an IP phone, make sure that the phone's switch port is still set to be controlled in NAC Appliance Manager. Use MAC address filters to identify and permit your IP phones. This practice ensures that rogue users cannot gain access by disconnecting an IP phone and plugging in a laptop. If your clients do connect directly to the IP phones, you should consider the following design recommendations:

- Set your switch profiles to never bounce a switch port.

- The MAC addresses of all IP phones must be added and maintained in NAC Appliance Manager's Filter list.

- If you use NAC Appliance in Layer 3 adjacency Out-of-Band mode, you must rely on the DHCP release and renew functionality built into the Clean Access Agent and web login applet.

- If you configure NAC Appliance to change port VLANs dynamically, you must rely on the DHCP release and renew functionality built into the agent and applet to change the client's IP address.

- Use the certified timer in environments where the clients connect to the IP phone and not the switch port.

- You must configure NAC Appliance and your switches to use the MAC Notification SNMP trap and not the Linkup SNMP trap.

The following paragraphs explain these recommendations in more detail.

Be sure to set your port profiles to never bounce a switch port. Switch port bouncing is used to force the client to renew its IP address when it transitions from the authentication VLAN to the access VLAN. However, if you bounced the switch port, it would take down your IP phone as well as your client. Instead of port bouncing, use either virtual gateway mode with the authentication and access VLAN being the same subnet (also called virtual gateway same IP subnet design), or rely on the DHCP release and renew feature built into the Clean Access Agent and web login applet.

The virtual gateway same IP subnet solution is designed to eliminate the client IP address change when moving from the authentication VLAN to the access VLAN. It works by forwarding the client's initial DHCP request to the access VLAN. This means that the client is given a legal address that works for both the authentication VLAN and access VLAN. Therefore, the client never has to change its IP address when it transitions between the authentication and access VLANs. If you choose the DHCP release and renew feature, the agent or web login applet will issue a DHCP release request followed by a DHCP renew request to the host operating system. This works basically the same way as running the **ipconfig /renew** command on a Windows PC.

The MAC addresses of all IP phones must be added to the NAC Appliance Manager's filter list. Set these MAC exceptions to *Ignore*, meaning that when NAC Appliance receives a MAC notification trap for an IP phone, it should ignore it and take no action. You can quickly populate the IP phone MAC Exception list by using the bulk administration tool in CallManager and by using MAC address wildcards.

The reason IP phones must be added to the exception list is because when a switch port is controlled using OOB mode, it sends a MAC notification SNMP trap every time a new MAC address is detected. This action does not differentiate between the IP phone connecting and the client PC attached to the IP phone connecting. Therefore, if the IP phone's MAC address is not ignored in the Filter list, NAC Appliance considers it a new client and changes the port's VLANs to the authentication VLAN. It will then wait forever for an authentication request from the new MAC address (the IP phone), but one will never come. This whole time, the client PC connected to this port is stuck on the authentication VLAN as well. It is important to note that the voice VLAN, or aux VLAN, and by extension voice traffic, is not affected by this behavior. Only the data VLAN is manipulated by NAC Appliance.

If you use NAC Appliance in Layer 3 adjacency Out-of-Band mode, you must rely on the DHCP release and renew functionality built into Clean Access Agent and web login applet. Version 4.1 or greater of this feature updates the client's IP address as it transitions from the authentication VLAN to the access VLAN. You cannot use the virtual gateway same IP subnet design referred to previously because it requires NAC Appliance to be Layer 2 adjacent to the clients.

If you configure NAC Appliance to set the access VLAN to the user role VLAN, you must rely on the DHCP release and renew functionality built into Clean Access Agent and applet to change the client's IP address. You cannot use the virtual gateway same IP subnet design. This is because each user role VLAN must have a unique IP subnet of its own. It is not possible for the single shared authentication VLAN to have the same IP subnet as the multiple user role access VLANs. All clients are initially put into a single authentication VLAN, where they receive an IP address. After clients become certified, they are moved to the access VLAN ID configured for their particular user role. As a result, the client must be forced to change its IP address to match the user role access VLAN. Given that port bouncing cannot be used to force this change, the only alternative is to use the DHCP release and renew feature.

You should use the certified timer in environments where the clients connect to the IP phone and not the switch port. This helps with the problem of removing stale users from the certified device list. NAC Appliance normally relies on the switch to send a linkdown trap to the NAC Appliance Manager when a user disconnects from the network. The NAC Appliance Manager then logs out the user previously connected to that port. Relying on the linkdown trap to log off users in an IP telephony environment poses a problem in that an IP phone is always up. When a client disconnects from the IP phone port, the switch never sees it. It still sees linkup on the port because the IP phone is plugged into it. Therefore, the switch never sends a linkdown trap when the client disconnects from the network. The result of this is that the Certified Devices list never ages out and users are never logged off NAC Appliance.

To address this issue, using the certified device timer is recommended. This feature clears the certified devices list at regularly scheduled intervals. This clearing is intrusive, however, because it moves the client's switch port back to the authentication VLAN. It then forces the user to reauthenticate and run through the certification process. Because of this, it is recommended that the clearing be done during nonbusiness hours and about every seven days. Figure 5-12 shows the Certified Devices Timer configuration page.

Figure 5-12 *Certified Devices Timer Page*

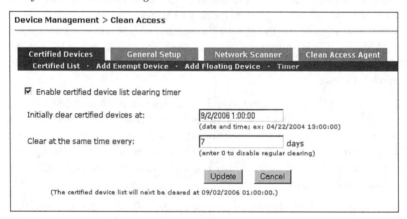

You must configure NAC Appliance and your switches to use the MAC Notification SNMP trap and not the Linkup SNMP trap. In an IP telephony environment where clients connect to IP phones, a linkup trap cannot be relied on as an indicator of when a new user connects to the network. This is because from the switch's point of view, it already has linked up with the IP phone and doesn't transition the link state for the user connecting through an IP phone. However, each time a new user connects to the phone port, the downstream switch port does learn the new user's MAC address and generates a MAC notification trap message.

High Availability and Load Balancing

Maintaining a highly available and fault-tolerant network is paramount in today's high-tech world. The services that today's networks are providing have become engrained into even our most rudimentary daily routines. When these services go down, the impact can be devastating. This is why, when designing your NAC Appliance solution, special attention must be paid to making it as reliable as possible. To create a scalable and reliable design, you must first be aware of the impact and risk to the clients and services when pieces of the solution fail. To this end, some of the impacts and risks that a failure can bring will be discussed. After the risks are laid out, the various design options you can use to mitigate those risks are discussed.

There are three main components to a NAC Appliance solution: NAC Appliance Manager, NAC Appliance Server, and Clean Access Agent. If OOB mode is used, Ethernet switches can be added to the list of main components. Outside of the main components are the supporting components. This includes mechanisms such as authentication servers, VPN devices, wireless LAN controllers, log servers, routers, and general network availability. All these pieces, some more than others, can affect the availability and fault tolerance of a NAC Appliance solution. Table 5-1 examines some failure scenarios and their impact if no high availability features are used.

Table 5-1   *NAC Appliance Failure and Risk Analysis*

Failure Scenario	Impact/Risk
NAC Appliance Manager fails or network communication between the NAC Appliance Manager and NAC Appliance Servers fails. NAC Appliance Server has the fallback feature enabled.	When NAC Appliance Server detects that NAC Appliance Manager is no longer responding, it can be configured to fail open, closed, or do nothing. If configured to fail open, all traffic is allowed to pass through NAC Appliance Server unchecked. If configured to fail closed, all traffic is blocked. And if configured to do nothing, the behavior would be the same as having fallback disabled (explained later in this table.)
NAC Appliance Manager fails or network communication between the NAC Appliance Manager and NAC Appliance Servers fails. NAC Appliance Server has the fallback feature disabled.	Clients that have passed authentication and certification before the failure continue to operate normally. Be aware that expiration of certain NAC Appliance timers can log clients out.
	New In-Band mode clients, clients in quarantine, and clients in any state other than authenticated and certified will not be able to log in to NAC Appliance. In most cases, this means they are denied network access.
	OOB mode clients in the access VLAN are not affected by the outage. Clients in the authentication VLAN are denied network access.
	For new clients, the behavior is not predictable. If the client plugs in to a port that has been previously set with the access VLAN, it is not affected. However, if the port is configured with the authentication or initial VLAN, the client will not be able to communicate on the network. The reason this behavior is unpredictable is that NAC Appliance OOB does not reset the switch port VLAN back to a default setting when a user disconnects or logs off the network. This results in switch ports that remain in the VLAN state they were last set to.

continues

Table 5-1 *NAC Appliance Failure and Risk Analysis (Continued)*

Failure Scenario	Impact/Risk
L2 In-Band NAC Appliance Server fails.	All traffic flow from clients on the untrusted side of NAC Appliance Server fails.
L3 In-Band NAC Appliance Server fails.	All traffic destined for networks on the trusted side of the NAC Appliance Server fails. Traffic flow on the untrusted networks is not affected. For example, if you put a NAC Appliance Server in front of your Internet connection and it fails, only Internet traffic is stopped. All internal, non-Internet-bound traffic continues unaffected.
L2 Out-of-Band NAC Appliance Server fails.	All clients on the access VLAN are unaffected. Clients on the authentication VLAN lose network connectivity. For new clients, NAC Appliance Manager still moves the switchport into the authentication VLAN. But because the failed NAC Appliance Server is in-band in the authentication VLAN, the traffic is dropped.
L3 Out-of-Band NAC Appliance Server fails.	All clients on the access VLAN are unaffected. Clients on the authentication VLAN lose the capability to access networks on the trusted side of NAC Appliance Server. Communication to networks on the untrusted side is unaffected. For new clients, the behavior is not predictable and acts just like the L2 OOB mode failure described previously.
Loss of the external user authentication server.	New clients will be unable to log in to NAC Appliance. Clients that have passed authentication and are certified are not affected.

High Availability

There are several approaches to ensuring high availability and mitigating the failure risks described previously. The most popular are as follows:

- Stateful failover of NAC Appliance Manager
- Stateful failover of NAC Appliance Server

- Fallback feature on NAC Appliance Server
- Spanning Tree N+1

The following sections discuss these approaches in detail.

Stateful Failover of NAC Appliance Manager

The following are the prerequisites for stateful failover of NAC Appliance Manager:

- Must have two NAC Appliance Managers—one primary and one secondary.
- The two NAC Appliance Managers must be Layer 2 adjacent.
- Works with all NAC Appliance design options.

NAC Appliance Manager is the highest-risk component in the solution. This is because if it fails, all servers—up to 40 of them—are affected. It is highly recommended that you deploy the failover NAC Appliance Manager bundle. This includes two servers; one serves as the primary, and the other serves as the secondary. Under normal conditions, the primary server takes the entire workload. The secondary machine maintains state with the primary and constantly polls to make sure that the primary is working properly.

Two methods are used for polling. The first is a User Datagram Protocol heartbeat signal; the second is a serial heartbeat signal. In the event the primary machine fails, the secondary takes over. Clients are unaffected by the failure because all state information is known by the new primary machine. The old secondary machine is now the new primary; it remains the primary until it fails. After the old primary comes back online, it assumes the role of secondary machine.

The failover solution requires that both the primary and secondary machines be on the same IP subnet and should not be geographically separated. This is because they advertise a common IP address called a service IP address and exchange high availability information, such as heartbeat messages and configuration information, across a separate Ethernet cross-over network. The service IP address is the virtual IP address that is advertised to NAC Appliance Servers and used for Secure Sockets Layer (SSL) certificate generation. The solution works very much like Hot Standby Router Protocol or Virtual Router Redundancy Protocol. The primary and secondary machines both have their own interface IP address but share a virtual service IP address.

To create the high-availability exchange network on which failover information passes, you put the second Ethernet port of both NAC Appliance Managers on an IP subnet that is not routed in your environment. This network can be built by using a simple Ethernet cross-over cable and connecting the two NAC Appliance Managers or by creating a nonrouted VLAN on a switch. For extra resilience, you can enable the serial heartbeat signal by connecting the second serial port of each NAC Appliance Manager using a null modem cable. Figure 5-13 illustrates a high-availability design example.

The high-availability feature of NAC Appliance Manager detects the following failures of the primary NAC Appliance Manager:

- Power failure or shutdown of the primary NAC Appliance Manager
- Loss of heartbeat messages over eth1 or serial port

Figure 5-13 *High-Availability Design Diagram*

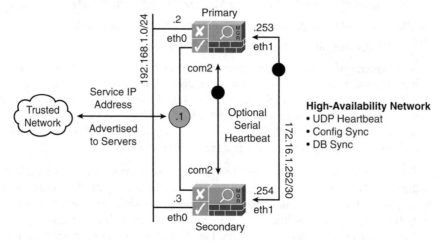

Stateful Failover of NAC Appliance Server

The following are the prerequisites for stateful failover of NAC Appliance Server:

- Must have two NAC Appliance Servers—one primary and one secondary.
- Two NAC Appliance Servers must be Layer 2 adjacent.
- Works with all NAC Appliance design options.

NAC Appliance Server supports stateful failover just like the NAC Appliance Manager does. It uses the same primary and secondary design in which the primary server takes the entire load and the secondary takes over if the primary fails. In addition to configuration and state sync, NAC Appliance Servers sync all DHCP information when they are configured as a DHCP server. Designing high availability into your NAC Appliance Servers is a best practice, especially in an in-band deployment where traffic always flows through it. Of course, the decision of whether to add high availability to a design requires a cost-to-risk analysis. This analysis should be done on a per-server basis given that each server will support different parts of the network, with some parts more critical than others. NAC Appliance Manager can control redundant servers and standalone servers simultaneously. This gives you the flexibility to use fault tolerance where it makes the most sense.

When configuring high-availability failover on a NAC Appliance Server pair, you can use the eth0 interface or a third Ethernet interface, eth2, if available. The heartbeat polling options, Ethernet and serial, work the same way as described previously for NAC Appliance Manager. Figure 5-14 shows a NAC Appliance Server high-availability design example.

Figure 5-14   *NAC Appliance Server High-Availability Design Example*

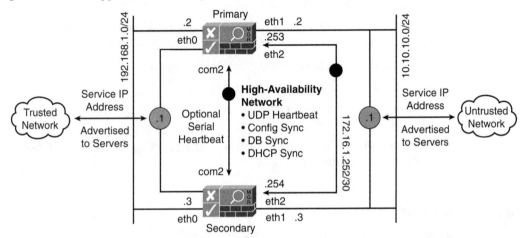

The high-availability feature of NAC Appliance Server detects the following failures of the primary NAC Appliance Server:

- Power failure or shutdown of the primary NAC Appliance Server.
- Loss of heartbeat messages over the eth1 or serial port.
- Loss of link on either eth0 or eth1.
- Link-based failover via icmp requests. If the Server cannot ping the configured host, failover occurs.

Fallback Feature on NAC Appliance Server

Starting in Version 4.1, NAC Appliance Server supports the fallback feature. This feature increases the fault tolerance of NAC Appliance during a communication failure between the NAC Appliance Server and NAC Appliance Manager. This communication failure could be the result of a failed manager, failed LAN or WAN segment, misconfigured access control list or firewall rule, or any number of things that could disrupt NAC Appliance Server to NAC Appliance Manager communications. The fallback server is configured per server, not globally. With the fallback feature enabled, NAC Appliance Server continuously monitors its connection with NAC Appliance Manager. When the connection fails, NAC Appliance Server can be configured to fall back to one of three states:

- **Fail-open**   This state turns off the NAC checks and controls and allows all clients to go through that NAC Appliance Server.

- **Fail-closed**   This state denies all clients access, regardless of their previous state from traversing the NAC Appliance Server.

- **Do nothing**   This state's behavior would be the same as not turning on the feature. Those clients on the Certified list continue unaffected. New clients or clients in the quarantine phase are denied access.

The fallback feature of NAC Appliance Server detects the following failures of communication between NAC Appliance Server and NAC Appliance Manager:

- Power failure or shutdown of NAC Appliance Manager

- Loss of link on eth0 of NAC Appliance Manager

- A WAN or LAN failure that disrupts communication between NAC Appliance Server and NAC Appliance Manager

- Any fault software fault on NAC Appliance Manager that prevents it from responding to the fallback heartbeat messages

Spanning Tree N+1

The following are the prerequisites for Spanning Tree N+1:

- NAC Appliance Server must be in In-Band Virtual Gateway mode.

- NAC Appliance Server must not be configured for 802.1q trunking with VLAN mapping or with VLAN interfaces.

- You must use either Per VLAN Spanning Tree Plus (PVST+) or Multiple Instance Spanning Tree Protocol (MISTP) as the Spanning Tree Protocol (STP) algorithm.

It is possible to use the network to bypass a failed NAC Appliance Server and provide per-network load distribution among several NAC Appliance Servers. The goal is to distribute the client load, on a per-VLAN basis, among several NAC Appliance Servers and support an N+1 redundancy model. This is done using spanning tree and 802.1q trunks. It is important to note that the redundancy this solution provides is not stateful. As a result, clients moved to the backup NAC Appliance Server must go through authentication and certification again. This high-availability method is most common in large campus or wireless networks that abide by the access, distribution, and core layered network architecture.

The NAC Appliance Servers would be placed between the distribution and core layers. Figure 5-15 depicts just such a design.

As shown in Figure 5-15, NAC Appliance Servers are sandwiched between the distribution switch and the core switch. Clients plug into the access layer switches, which have an 802.1q trunk to the distribution switch. The distribution switch has three 802.1q trunks to the core switch. All the NAC Appliance Servers are configured for In-Band Virtual Gateway mode. They do not have 802.1q or any VLAN interfaces configured. They are simply acting as Layer 2 bridges with one notable exception: They will pass, unmodified, any bridge protocol data units (BPDUs) they receive from attached switches. BPDUs carry the STP information that switches exchange to determine the best Layer 2 paths. Because the BPDUs pass through NAC Appliance Server unmodified, the distribution and core switches believe that they have point-to-point 802.1q trunks between each other. They are not aware that NAC Appliance Server is in the middle.

Figure 5-15 *NAC Appliance Load Balancing Using STP*

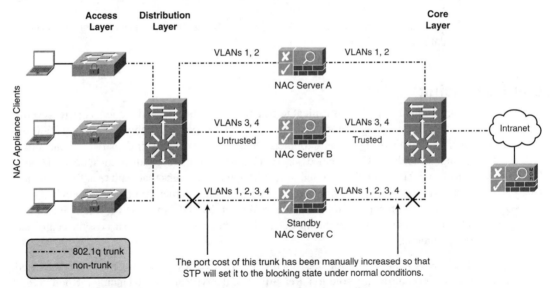

The Spanning Tree Protocol distributes the load across the individual trunk links and provides failover in the case of a primary trunk failure. To accomplish this, STP uses the concept of path cost to determine which trunks are forwarding (active) and which are blocking for a given VLAN. STP calculates the path cost using two values: media speed (bandwidth) of the links and port cost (a value assigned to individual switch ports). Spanning Tree selects the best path based on the lowest path cost. The trunk with the lowest path cost is put into the STP forwarding state and begins passing traffic. All other alternate paths are put into the STP blocking state and pass no traffic.

The trunk going through standby server C in Figure 5-15 has had its port cost on both sides increased to the point that its path cost is higher than the cost of the other trunks. This results in the trunk being put into the STP blocking state for VLANs 1-4. The other two trunks are put into the forwarding state for the VLANs they carry. As a result, server A will take the client load for VLANs 1 and 2. Server B will take the client load for VLANs 3 and 4. And server C will act as the standby or backup server for all the active servers. Under normal conditions, server C does not receive client traffic. When a failure occurs with either server A or B, STP recalculates the path cost for the VLANs on the lost trunk. The trunk through server C will now have the lowest path cost available. STP will move this trunk from the blocking state to the forwarding state. Now all the VLAN traffic that used to pass over the failed trunk will be redirected to this new trunk. The result is that the standby server C will take the client load for the failed NAC Appliance Server.

The Spanning Tree N+1 method detects the following types of NAC Appliance Server failures:

- Power failure or shutdown of NAC Appliance Server.
- Loss of link on either eth0 or eth1.
- Software failures that cause NAC Appliance Server to stop forwarding bridge protocol data units (BPDU).

Load Balancing

In larger environments, it is critical to be able to load-balance (LB) clients across several NAC Appliance Servers. A single NAC Appliance Server is capable of handling 2500 clients simultaneously. For environments that must have a greater density of clients flow through a single NAC Appliance Server, a load-balancing mechanism must be used. Large densities of clients could be found in NAC Appliance designs that want to authenticate and posture assess users only when they try to access the Internet. Another common high-density environment would be a centralized L3 in-band deployment for multiple remote sites, in which clients are authenticated and certified when they try to access the central site or the Internet.

The NAC Appliance solution does not provide a native load-balancing mechanism. Instead, it relies on a third-party solution. Regardless of the type of load-balancing method used, it must allow for the symmetric flow of traffic. This means that a client must be consistently balanced to the same NAC Appliance Server in both directions. The reason for this requirement is that no state information is being shared between the servers in the NAC Appliance Server farm. So, if a client was balanced to server A for one traffic flow and server B for its next flow, server B would not be aware that the client already passed authentication and certification on server A. Therefore, it would start the login process again. In addition, if a flow tries to return through a NAC Appliance Server different from the one it went out on, the flow will be denied. The recommended load-balancing techniques are as follows:

- Cisco Content Switching Module (CSM), Application Control Engine Module (ACE), or standalone Content Services Switch (CSS)
- Policy-based routing (PBR) load balancing

It is important to note that some load-balancing methods offer load balancing and fault tolerance, whereas others are strictly load-balancing solutions. Table 5-2 lists the redundancy capabilities of each LB solution.

Table 5-2 *Load-Balancing Methods and Their Capabilities*

Method	Can Provide Fault Tolerance?
CSM, CSS	Yes
Policy-based routing LB	Yes, with Object Tracking turned on

Cisco Content Switching Module or Standalone Content Services Switch

The following are the prerequisites for Cisco Content Switching Module or standalone Content Services Switch:

- Must have either two CSS or one CSM Appliance.
- NAC Appliance servers must be in Real-IP Gateway mode.

The CSM and CSS are advanced Layer 4–to–Layer 7 load-balancing appliances. Using CSM or CSS load balancing allows you to scale NAC Appliance protection by distributing traffic across multiple NAC Appliance Servers on a per-client basis. The CSS and CSM are capable of providing both persistent load balancing and failover to NAC Appliance Servers that are in In-Band Real-IP Gateway mode. Out-of-Band and Virtual Gateway modes are not supported because the CSM or CSS has to be configured for L3 LB.

The CSM or CSS provides the most robust method available for load balancing a NAC Appliance solution. The CSM is a module that fits in the Catalyst 6500 switch. The CSS is a standalone load-balancing appliance. These methods provide an N+1 failover model, where N equals the number of NAC Appliance Servers plus one more server that serves as the backup for the group. This means that the first server to fail will be backed up by the single secondary server. Any additional servers that fail will be taken out of the load-balancing server pool but will not be backed up. The danger here is that the remaining servers might not be able to manage the additional load. If necessary, it is possible to have multiple servers in the backup pool to make an N+2 or N+3 failover model. The CSS and CSM detect the following types of server failures:

- Power failure or shutdown of NAC Appliance Server.

- Loss of link on either eth0 or eth1.

- Software failures that cause the NAC Appliance Server to not respond to pings or login requests. This is done through the use of health-monitoring probes. Health probes can be configured to check the HTTP, Internet Control Message Protocol, or TCP services running on the NAC Appliance Servers.

When using the CSS appliances for load balancing NAC Appliance Servers, the design requires two sandwiched CSS appliances. See Figure 5-16 for a sample CSS design.

Figure 5-16 *NAC Appliance Load Balancing Using CSS Appliances*

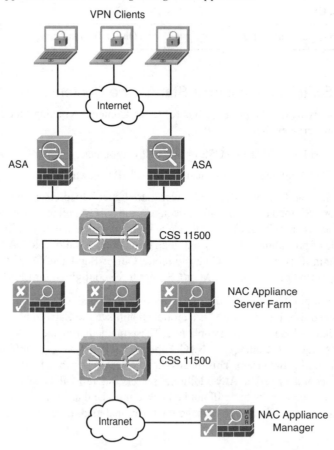

When using the CSM as your solution, only a single CSM is required. See Figure 5-17 for a sample CSM design. The figure shows a single physical CSM broken into two logical ones.

Figure 5-17 *NAC Appliance Load Balancing Using a CSM*

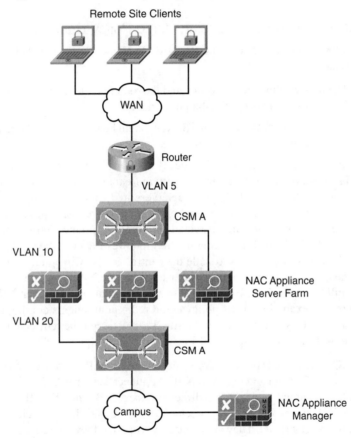

The CSS or CSM design and configuration necessary to achieve load balancing and failover with the NAC Appliance solution closely mirrors the design and configuration for CSS or CSM firewall load balancing. Details on the firewall load-balancing design can be found by searching for *CSM firewall load-balancing* at Cisco.com.

NAC Appliance Server Load Balancing Using Policy-Based Routing

The following are the prerequisites for NAC Appliance Server load balancing using policy-based routing:

- The router on the untrusted side and the router on the trusted side of NAC Appliance Server must support policy-based routing.

- Traffic flow to NAC Appliance Server should be symmetric in both directions. This is not a requirement but a best practice.

This load-balancing technique was developed specifically for a centralized NAC Appliance Server deployment model with more than 2500 clients. In a centralized NAC Appliance model, the NAC Appliance Servers are located at a central site that is multiple layer three hops away from the remote clients they are inspecting. For example, the clients at a remote office are inspected by a NAC Appliance Server that resides at the HQ site. The PBR load-balancing method requires Layer 3 client adjacency. The goal of the PBR LB technique is to scale the centralized NAC Appliance deployment model past the 2500 client limit imposed by using a single NAC Appliance Server. This is accomplished by using PBR policies to spread clients across several NAC Appliance Servers. For example, a PBR policy could redirect all clients coming from site A IP subnet to NAC Appliance server A. Site B clients could be redirected to server B. Figure 5-18 shows a sample PBR load-balancing design.

The HQ routers PBR policies are set up to redirect all client traffic coming from the 10.1.1.0/24 subnet at site A to NAC Appliance server A. All traffic coming from the 10.1.2.0/24 subnet at site B is redirected to server B, and all traffic coming from the 10.1.3.0/24 subnet at site C is redirected to server C. The PBR policies on 6500 A mirror those on the HQ router. They are identical except that they are redirecting based on traffic going to the sites, not traffic coming from them. This is necessary because of the requirement that client traffic must flow symmetrically. This means that a client must be consistently balanced to the same NAC Appliance Server in both directions. Here is the traffic flow for the clients in Figure 5-18.

Figure 5-18 *NAC Appliance Load Balancing Using PBR*

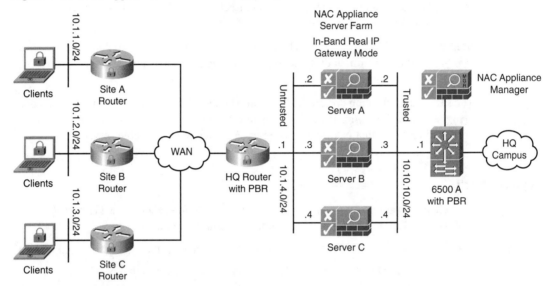

Step 1 The Clean Access Agent on a client at site A sends out discovery packets to the IP address of 6500 A, 10.10.10.1. The Clean Access Agent is searching for a NAC Appliance Server.

Step 2 The site A router forwards the packets to the HQ router.

Step 3 The HQ router does a lookup in its PBR policies looking for a source IP address match. It finds a match associated with the 10.1.1.0/24 subnet. The action for the match says to set the next hop router to NAC Appliance Server A, 10.1.1.2.

Step 4 The HQ router forwards the client's discovery packets to server A.

Step 5 Server A intercepts the Clean Access Agent discovery packets and notifies the client's Clean Access Agent that it should perform user authentication and certification.

Step 6 The user passes authentication and certification. From now on, all traffic from site A to a trusted side network, such as HQ campus, will be redirected by PBR on the HQ router and sent through NAC Appliance server A.

Step 7 Return traffic from a trusted side network, such as HQ campus, to the untrusted site A network will be redirected by PBR on 6500 A and sent through NAC Appliance server A.

Step 8 The PBR policies on the HQ router and 6500 A are configured to send traffic sent from or destined to site B through server B and site C through server C.

The PBR load-balancing design supports failover and fault tolerance. This is typically done using object tracking with PBR. In the event that a NAC Appliance Server fails, all clients being redirected to that NAC Appliance Server switch to an available server.

Summary

This chapter examined some of the advanced design topics related to a Cisco NAC Appliance solution. The following recommendations were made:

- Use an external user authentication database instead of the internal user database.

- Use Active Directory or RADIUS attributes to map users into a NAC Appliance user role.

- Whenever possible, configure the network to allow voice traffic to bypass the NAC Appliance solution.

- If it is not possible to allow voice to bypass an In-Band mode NAC Appliance, be sure to exempt all voice subnets from NAC inspection.

- In an OOB deployment, be sure to set your port profiles never to bounce a switch port that has an IP phone connected to it.

- You should use the certified timer in OOB environments where the clients connect to the IP phone and not the switch port.

- When you have NAC Appliance clients connecting through a supported VPN or wireless device, configuring single sign-on is recommended.

- When using VPN or wireless SSO, it is recommended that the NAC Appliance Server be placed Layer 2 adjacent to the VPN concentrator.

- It is highly recommended that you deploy the NAC Appliance Manager using the stateful failover bundle.

- The recommended load-balancing techniques are as follows:
  - The Cisco Content Switching Module (CSM) or standalone Content Services Switch (CSS)
  - Policy-Based Routing LB
- The Fallback feature of the NAC Appliance Server can mitigate the risks of losing communication between the NAC Appliance Server and NAC Appliance Manager.
- A Cisco NAC Appliance solution can be designed to support both load balancing and fault tolerance.

PART III

The Foundation: Building a Host Security Policy

This chapter covers the following topics:

- What Makes Up a Cisco NAC Appliance Host Security Policy?
- Determining the High-Level Goals for Host Security
- Defining the Security Domains
- Understanding and Defining NAC Appliance User Roles
- Establishing Acceptable Use Policies
- Checks, Rules, and Requirements to Consider
- Defining Network Access Privileges

CHAPTER 6

Building a Cisco NAC Appliance Host Security Policy

For any host-centric security solution to be successful, a solid host security policy (HSP) must first be in place. After a policy is in place, NAC Appliance enforces that policy networkwide. A host security policy defines, in as much detail as is practical, the protection strategy for the different clients within an organization. Given that host security threats are constantly changing, a host security policy must also be a living, changeable document. This book does not attempt to assemble an all-encompassing host security policy but instead focuses on the building of policies that are relevant to a NAC Appliance solution. This chapter will guide you through the process of creating a comprehensive host security policy that can be used in a NAC Appliance environment. Building a host security policy is not always straightforward and can be frustrating at times, but stick with it; your hard work will be rewarded in the end.

What Makes Up a Cisco NAC Appliance Host Security Policy?

One of the hardest things about writing a comprehensive host security policy is figuring out what should be included in the policy. This chapter will guide you through the parts and pieces that, at a minimum, should be included in any host security policy written for a NAC Appliance solution. For your NAC Appliance solution to be most effective, it is necessary to first determine exactly what an acceptable host security posture is under different circumstances. After this is done, you can then easily translate your host security policy into the proper checks and security requirements that NAC Appliance will use to posture assess hosts. For example, if the host is a corporate asset and connected to the wireless network, a strict host security policy should be enforced. However, if the same host moves to the wired network, a less strict security policy should be in place. It is also necessary to determine what the host security policy should be for different types of hosts, either based on their operating system or based on who the end user is. For example, if a contractor logs on to your network using a Windows XP laptop, the security policy would differ from the same user logging in with a Mac OS X system.

Host Security Policy Checklist

Here is a checklist of the most common steps considered necessary to create a NAC Appliance host security policy. Each checklist item will be explained in detail in the subsequent sections of this chapter. Use this checklist, along with the detailed explanations, to give you a head start in the creation of your own unique host security policy.

- ☐ Obtain senior management sponsors who will support you through the creation of the host security policy and the deployment of the NAC Appliance solution.

- ☐ Determine what people and departments need to be involved in the creation of the host security policy. Make sure that they are included up front, right from the start of the project.

- ☐ Determine what your high-level goals for host security are.

- ☐ Break up your organization into security domains. The requirements of the host security policy can then be customized for each security domain as necessary.

- ☐ Define user roles that are relevant for your organization.

- ☐ Establish an acceptable use policy (AUP) for your network.

- ☐ Define NAC Appliance's host security checks, rules, and requirements for each user role.

- ☐ Define the network access privileges that should be granted to each user role.

- ☐ Establish an HSP lifecycle process that allows for the regular updating and changing of the host security policy's checks, rules, and requirements.

Involving the Right People in the Creation of the Host Security Policy

At the very beginning of the planning for a NAC Appliance deployment or purchase, it is extremely important to obtain project sponsorship from senior-level management. Given that NAC Appliance will force a change on the user community's behavior and network access, this is a mandatory step. Without senior-level sponsorship, your NAC Appliance deployment could be derailed by a few users who are not happy with or willing to accept the new policy changes.

Having the endorsement of senior management grants you the power to push back on those users in a constructive way. Too often the security group spends the time to develop sound security policies and practices only to be told that they are too restrictive and need to be changed. This can be avoided by making sure that you keep your sponsors involved and up to date on the progress and content of your host security policy. It is also critical that you have your final version approved by your sponsorship committee prior to releasing it to the public. Try to anticipate the type of reaction, resistance, and questions the user community will have. Be ready with solid rebuttals, facts, and collateral to combat their arguments, answer their questions, and make them feel more comfortable that the new host security policy is the correct one.

One of the first steps in the creation of any HSP is the creation of the host security policy committee. This committee should be made up of the principal persons whose group or users will be most affected by or have some ownership in the new policy. It is a best practice to try and keep the committee small in the beginning phases of the policy creation. After this core team has an HSP with a clear direction, some substance, and some content, the HSP committee should be expanded to include more key persons. When the HSP reaches a completed draft format, the HSP committee should again be expanded. This time the expansion is to include those principal persons who do not have any direct ownership or responsibility for the creation of the HSP but do have a sizeable user community that will be directly affected by the policies' proposed changes.

This last group will serve to scrutinize the policies in your HSP draft to make sure that the policies do not inhibit business practices or workflow, are practical, and have achieved the proper balance of security risk versus network access for the organization. After a final HSP version has been created, the entire committee must agree to present a united front once the new policy begins to be enforced inside the organization. A nonunited, or splintered, HSP committee almost always results in the splintering or haphazard adoption of the host security policy within the organization.

Here is a list of the most common principal persons that should be a part of the creation of a host security policy. You should adapt this list for your environment.

- Sponsorship
  - CSO/CIO must be a sponsor or core committee member
  - At least one CxO level sponsor other than the CSO/CIO
  - At least one company board member sponsor
  - One sponsor or core committee member from the legal department
- Core HSP committee members should be made up of key persons from the following groups:
  - Ideally the CSO/CIO would be a core member
  - Security group
  - Networking group
  - Server group
  - Desktop support group
  - Operations group
  - Security incident response team
- Extended HSP committee members should be made up of key persons from the following groups:
  - Human Resources group
  - Legal group
  - Audit group

- Final HSP committee members should be made up of key persons from the following groups:

    — Managers of large end-user groups within the organization (such as division heads, department heads, and so on)

    — Key individuals from the end-user community for feedback

This list should be used as a guideline and is not meant to be all-inclusive. The goal of HSP committee member selection is to ensure that the committee has adequate representation from all key stakeholders, budget holders, management, legal council, and technical staff. Each group will have a slightly different role to fulfill on the committee.

Determining the High-Level Goals for Host Security

Determining what your high-level goals are for host security is a critical step toward the completion of a comprehensive host security policy. These high-level goals will serve as your benchmarks and guides throughout the HSP creation process. The final HSP document should represent a detailed plan that achieves these high-level goals. It is important to periodically refer to these high-level goals to ensure that your HSP remains focused and on target to meet your stated security goals.

The following comes from RFC 2196, "Site Security Handbook" (http://www.ietf.org/rfc/rfc2196.txt):

Your goals will be largely determined by the following key tradeoffs:

(1) services offered versus security provided -

Each service offered to users carries its own security risks. For some services the risk outweighs the benefit of the service and the administrator may choose to eliminate the service rather than try to secure it.

(2) ease of use versus security -

The easiest system to use would allow access to any user and require no passwords; that is, there would be no security. Requiring passwords makes the system a little less convenient, but more secure. Requiring device-generated one-time passwords makes the system even more difficult to use, but much more secure.

(3) cost of security versus risk of loss -

There are many different costs to security: monetary (i.e., the cost of purchasing security hardware and software like firewalls and one-time password generators), performance (i.e., encryption and decryption take time), and ease of use (as mentioned above). There are also many levels of risk: loss of privacy (i.e., the reading of information by unauthorized individuals), loss of data (i.e., the corruption or erasure of information), and the loss of service (e.g., the filling of data storage space, usage of computational resources, and denial of network access). Each type of cost must be weighed against each type of loss.

NOTE   For more detailed information about the creation of host security goals and security policies in general, see the IETF's RFC 2196 at http://www.ietf.org/rfc/rfc2196.txt.

Your final high-level host security goals will be the result of the fine balancing act of the above trade-offs. The result of each trade-off will be different for each organization or possibly division within an organization.

Common High-Level Host Security Goals

Here are some examples of host security goals that are frequently instituted in organizations that deploy a NAC Appliance solution. These examples are meant to be a sampling and not a comprehensive list.

- Protect the network from unauthorized access, both internally and externally originated.
- Authenticate all users attempting access to the network.
- Authorize all users attempting access to the network. Restrict access for nonemployees and guests.
- All users must acknowledge an acceptable use policy before being granted network access.
- All hosts must be running an approved antivirus program that is up to date.
- All hosts must be running an approved antispyware program that is up to date.
- All hosts must be running an approved operating system that is up to date.
- All hosts must pass a network scan for virus and worm activity before being granted network access.
- Any host found running banned software applications will be denied network access.
- All hosts must be running an approved personal firewall or Host Intrusion Prevention System before being granted network access.
- All guest hosts will be granted access only to the Internet and not internal resources.
- All guest hosts will be bandwidth limited to 256 kbps.

It is common for an organization to modify its host security goals based on a specific network location or access type. For example, an organization might have a policy that states all hosts connecting through wireless in the Denver data center must be running an approved antivirus program that is up to date in order to gain network access.

Many organizations choose to gradually enforce their host security policies and the deployment of a NAC Appliance solution. Initially, host security policy enforcement is instituted at the highest risk areas of the network. This would include virtual private network (VPN) or remote access, wireless, conference rooms, guest access, and common areas. Then, as the adoption of the NAC Appliance solution grows, the host security policy enforcement is spread ubiquitously throughout the organization.

Figure 6-1 summarizes the process for determining the exact host security policy that will be enforced for a given host or in a given network location.

Figure 6-1   *Host Security Policy Decision Matrix*

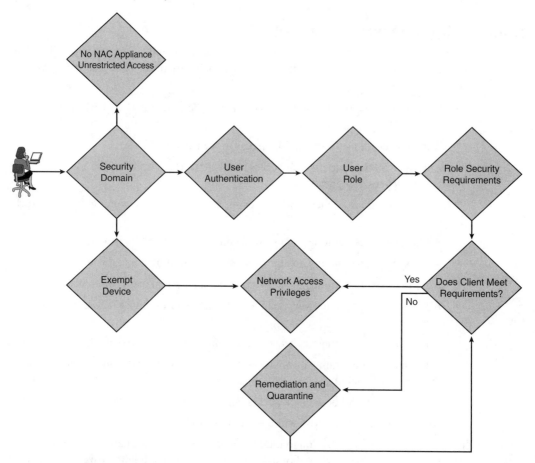

Here is the explanation of the host policy decision steps shown in Figure 6-1. Following this list are several sections that will describe these decision steps in greater detail.

1 The host connects to a location of the network.

2 The host is determined to be a member of a certain security domain. The HSP must define what the security domains are for the organization.

3 The HSP must define one of three choices for each unique security domain.

   a Which security domains will not have NAC Appliance deployed, thus allowing unrestricted network access. The host security policy for this security domain states that no host security policies are to be enforced in this domain.

b Which hosts or devices will be a member of the exemption list and thus will be able to bypass the NAC Appliance authentication and posture assessment phases.

c Which security domains will force hosts to comply fully with the NAC Appliance solution.

4 If the host is a member of the exemption list, it will flow directly to the network access privileges. The remaining steps in this list are bypassed. The HSP must define exactly what the network access privileges will be for each type of exempt host. It is possible to have different network access policies for different types of exempt devices. For example, you can have an exempt host security policy that allows IP phones to access the network unrestricted, but exempt printers are restricted to communicating using TCP port 9100 only.

5 If the host is part of a security domain that requires full compliance with the NAC Appliance solution, the client is forced to authenticate. The HSP should determine exactly how the user's credentials are authenticated and verified.

6 After successfully authenticating, the client is then moved to the user role it is a member of. The HSP should identify how user roles are defined and which users are members of which user roles.

7 The host is checked to make sure that it meets all the host security requirements defined for that user role. The HSP should define what the security requirements are for each user role.

8 If the host complies with all of its security requirements, it is moved to the network access privileges. The HSP should define the type of network access that should be granted to clients. This is typically defined per user role.

9 If the host fails to meet its security requirements, it is moved into network quarantine. Typically, self-remediation functions are also provided here. The HSP should clearly specify what network access privileges, remediation functions, and time limits should be imposed on quarantined hosts.

Defining the Security Domains

A security domain is used to group network areas, host types, and locations under a common host security policy. The goal of creating security domains for a NAC Appliance solution is to define which networks and locations will require hosts to use the NAC Appliance solution and which locations will not. It is also necessary to define the devices that will require exemption from the NAC Appliance solution within a given security domain. Figure 6-2 shows an example of security domains.

Figure 6-2 *Sample Security Domains*

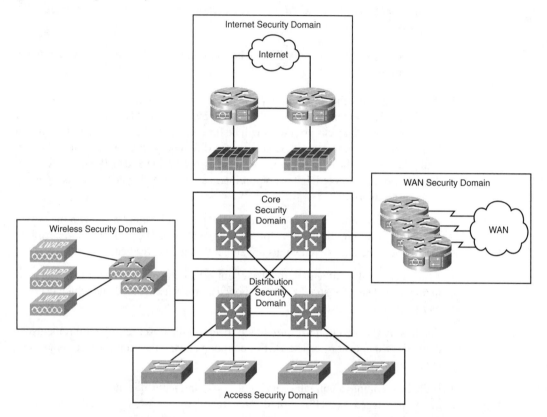

Most organizations will need to define the security domains that are depicted in Figure 6-2. Almost all organizations have an Internet connection, use VPN, have a WAN and campus LAN, and use wireless. Each one of these network access types or locations usually requires its own unique host security policy and thus should be its own security domain. The separating of these areas into unique security domains allows you to create unique host security polices for each. The more compartmentalized your HSP is, the more granular and targeted it can be. This results in a more locked-down host security policy for your organization. To make the point, if you had an HSP that did not use security domains and treated all hosts the same no matter what, you would be forced into using a global policy based on those hosts that required the weakest security policies. That said, however, sometimes it makes more sense to keep your security policy as simple and global as possible. This could be for political reasons or business reasons. As long as it meets your security objectives and is effective, go with it. Again, there is a trade-off: a comprehensive multidomain policy versus a simple global policy. A multidomain policy should be inherently more secure, but a simple global policy could be easier to manage and maintain.

Here are some commonly used security domains:

- **Remote Access**   This domain includes any host that is accessing the network remotely via VPN or dial-up modems.

- **OOB Management**   This domain includes any host that resides on the out-of-band network management network. This is typically a highly secured domain.

- **Internet**   This domain includes any host that accesses the Internet. A sample policy here could be the following: Before a host is allowed to access the Internet, its operating system and antivirus software must be up to date.

- **Guest**   This domain includes any host that is a guest on the network. Many times this domain is segmented into access types as well, such as guest wireless, guest VPN, and guest LAN domains. This allows for the creation of granular host security policies for guests.

- **Campus LAN**   This domain includes any host that connects to the network via a wired switch port. It is common to separate security domains by virtual LAN (VLAN) or location at the LAN level. This allows the HSP to have policies for specific VLAN and locations instead of one generic policy for all wired hosts.

- **Wireless**   This domain includes any host that uses wireless to access the network. It is common for the wireless domain to be separated by VLAN or location, such as a guest wireless security domain or a Denver campus wireless security domain.

This is by no means a comprehensive list, but it should serve to give you a good start in the creation of your own security domains.

Here is a list of devices that are commonly exempted from the NAC Appliance solution in all security domains. If a device resides on an untrusted domain and is not capable of authenticating itself and running through the remediation process, it must be exempted. A device exemption is made up of either a device's MAC address or its MAC and IP address pair. It is possible to use wildcards and ranges for MAC addresses. An exemption can also be defined using IP subnet and mask values.

- **IP phones**   Phones do not have the capability to participate in the NAC process today. A best practice is to segment voice onto its own VLAN and make sure that VLAN never passes through NAC Appliance. With Out-of-Band mode, make sure that the MAC addresses of all phones are put into the exemption list.

- **Printers**   Printers do not have the capability to participate in the NAC process today. However, they can still be subjected to the network access controls. This can be effective in limiting the ports and protocols that can reach your printers.

- **Network-attached fax machines**   Same as printers.

- **Servers**   Given that nobody sits at the console of servers, and servers are usually in a secure area, NAC Appliance should be bypassed for servers. However, network access controls can be used if necessary to control what traffic can flow to and from servers. Bandwidth rate-limiting can also be used if applicable.

- **Wireless access points** If wireless access points are permitted, they should bypass NAC Appliance. The clients that connect to them, however, will not be exempt.

- **Routers and routing protocols** When deploying NAC Appliance in Virtual Gateway L3 In-Band mode, it is possible to have routers present on the untrusted side. In this case, they should be exempt and their routing protocols should be allowed to pass.

- **Switches** Same as for routers.

- **Game consoles** Given that game consoles do not have the capability to participate in the NAC process today, they should be exempt. However, it is a best practice to deploy bandwidth rate-limiting and tight network access control rules on this device type.

This is by no means a comprehensive list, but it should serve to give you a good start in the creation of your own exempt device list. It should be noted that several non-Cisco products are available that can auto-discover exempt devices for NAC Appliance; Great Bay Software has such a product.

Understanding and Defining NAC Appliance User Roles

The effective use of user roles is a key component to any successful NAC Appliance deployment. NAC Appliance is role based; a user role defines the host security policies that will be required for its members. The concept of user roles is the backbone of NAC Appliance. User roles are analogous to groups in Active Directory (AD). Like groups, users are assigned membership to a specific user role. Unlike groups, however, users can be a member of only one user role at a time. NAC Appliance moves clients into a user role as soon as the client system is detected on the network. The moment an Ethernet frame is seen from a new client, it is moved into the Unauthenticated role by NAC Appliance. Given that a client or user can be a member of only one user role at a time, it is important to understand the role assignment priority. The order for role assignment is as follows:

1 **MAC address** The physical MAC address of the client is matched to assign it to a user role.

2 **Subnet/IP address** The IP address or IP subnet of the client is matched to assign it to a user role.

3 **Login information** The login credentials of the client are matched to assign it to a user role.

The login information could consist of the user's login credentials, the VLAN ID of the host, or attributes obtained from an external authentication server such as the Lightweight Directory Access Protocol (LDAP) or RADIUS.

TIP	It is a best practice to map attributes from an external authentication server (such as LDAP or RADIUS) to a user role in NAC Appliance. A common attribute matched on is MemberOf in Windows AD. This allows user roles to be based on existing AD groups within your organization. For example, an LDAP user Conor is a MemberOf AD group employee. A mapping can then be configured in NAC Appliance that reads **if MemberOf=employees then map the client to user role employee**.

The user role has policies that determine which NAC Appliance functions will be performed on client members. All clients that are members of the user role will be subjected to its security requirements. Some of the functions that can be controlled by user roles are as follows:

- Dynamic VLAN assignment
- Authentication method
- Bandwidth restrictions
- Traffic policies
- Session duration
- Clean Access Agent posture assessment
- Network Scanner
- Acceptable use policy
- Quarantine policy
- Clean Access Agent use
- Web login features
- External authentication server features

As you can see, user roles are integral to the functioning of NAC Appliance.

Built-In User Roles

NAC Appliance comes with three built-in, or default, user roles and one user role type. These roles are used for the basic policy functions of NAC Appliance. The traffic control and bandwidth control policies can and should be modified on all the built-in user roles. Let's examine each role in detail.

Unauthenticated Role

Clients are members of this role until they are successfully authenticated, scanned, and posture assessed. The one built-in role that must be used and cannot be deleted is the Unauthenticated role. The reason for this is NAC Appliance moves users into the Unauthenticated user role as soon as the client system is detected on the network. Specifically, the moment an Ethernet frame is seen from a new client, NAC Appliance implicitly moves that client into the Unauthenticated role.

Normal Login Role

The normal login role is not a role in and of itself but rather it represents a type of user role. The user role that a client is moved to when it has passed authentication, scanning, and posture assessment is always of type normal login role. The final or desired user role that a client will be in if it successfully authenticates and is found to be clean is always of type normal login role. Another way to define it is that any role that is not a Temporary, Quarantine, or Unauthenticated role will be of type normal login role. User roles of this type will make up the bulk of the roles you will define in your NAC Appliance solution.

Here is a sample scenario: User Liam passes authentication, scanning, and posture assessment. NAC Appliance then does an LDAP lookup to find the normal login role that Liam should be a member of. The LDAP server responds that Liam is a member of group student. Group student has been mapped to user role student. Liam is now moved to user role student, which is of type normal login role.

Clients can be assigned to a normal login role in the following ways:

- By MAC address, MAC/IP address pair, or IP subnet of the client.
- By mapping attributes from an external authentication server to a NAC Appliance user role. This is the most common method.
- By creating users in the local user database in NAC Appliance and assigning the users to a role. This is not common for production environments and should typically be used only for testing purposes.

Temporary Role

The Temporary role is reserved for only those clients that use the Clean Access Agent software to log in to NAC Appliance. If web login is used, the Temporary role does not apply. Clients must have passed authentication to be eligible for membership in the Temporary role. After successful authentication, clients are moved to the Temporary role only if they fail any of the Clean Access Agent security requirements or checks. The Temporary role has a session timer setting. When the timer reaches zero, the client is kicked out of the Temporary role and moved back to the Unauthenticated role. The user must then reauthenticate.

The purpose of the Temporary role is to quarantine the host on the network and provide access to remediation resources. For that reason, hosts in this role should be granted network access to the resources necessary for them to remediate and nothing more. In fact, while the user is clicking through the remediation screens shown by Clean Access Agent, the client is in the Temporary role. Therefore, it is critical that the proper network access be granted to clients in the Temporary role in order for the remediation methods to work. It is equally important that clients in the Temporary role be restricted from accessing network resources they do not absolutely require. This will serve to keep those noncompliant hosts from potentially doing harm to the rest of the network. For noncompliant hosts, the Temporary role serves as a policy stopgap between the Unauthenticated role and the normal login role.

If you enable Network Scanner for Clean Access Agent clients, it is important to note that a failed scan will result in the host being moved into the Quarantine role, not the Temporary role. Note that performing network scanning when using Clean Access Agent is possible, but it is not commonly done. The scan of the host happens after the Clean Access Agent security requirements and checks are performed. The following is a possible scenario:

1 The client connects to the network. NAC Appliance detects the new client and moves it into the Unauthenticated role.

2 The user successfully authenticates using the Clean Access Agent software. The client moves into the Temporary user role.

3 Clean Access Agent checks the host to see whether it meets the security requirements defined in the client's desired final normal login role.

4 The client fails a check and is presented with a remediation option to download a file. The client downloads and installs the file.

5 The client now passes the security checks. Network Scanner kicks off and scans the host for viruses and worms.

6 Network Scanner finds a worm on the host. NAC Appliance moves the host to the Quarantine user role. The user is presented with a web link to a tool to clean the worm.

7 The user uses the tool to clean the worm. The user is rescanned, and the scan now passes.

8 The user is moved to the normal login role of student.

Quarantine Role

The purpose and function of the Quarantine role is identical to that of the Temporary role. The difference is that this role is used by hosts that use web login, or clientless mode, and Network Scanner. As mentioned previously, it is also used by Clean Access Agent hosts that are found to have a vulnerability during the network scan. The purpose of the Quarantine role is to restrict the client's network access to only those resources it requires to fix the vulnerabilities found during the network scan. This role also has a session timer that, if allowed to expire, will kick the user out of the Quarantine role and move it back into the Unauthenticated role. The user will then have to reauthenticate to NAC Appliance.

It is possible to have more than one Quarantine role in NAC Appliance. Each Quarantine role is assigned to a normal login role and, optionally, to an operating system type. For example, clients in the Employee user role that are using Windows XP will be quarantined using the employee_winxp_quar role. Clients in the Guest role that are using Mac OS will be quarantined using the guest_mac_quar role. Consequently, it is possible to have the quarantine security policies change to match the needs of different user groups or roles and different operating systems. This allows for the creation of much more granular host security policies. For instance, it would be possible to have a Windows Quarantine role and a Mac OS Quarantine role for a particular normal login role. The Windows policy would allow access to http://www.windowsupdate.com. The Mac OS policy would not have that access but would instead have access to http://www.apple.com.

Commonly Used Roles and Their Purpose

This section will focus on the normal login roles commonly found in the host security policies of organizations that use the NAC Appliance solution. The goal is to present you with a solid starting point on which to base the user role needs of your organization's host security policy.

Start with the built-in user roles. As discussed previously, it is mandatory that you use the Unauthenticated user role. Therefore, make certain that your HSP has a section that addresses the Unauthenticated role. If you use Clean Access Agent for posture assessment, it is also mandatory for you to use the Temporary user role. Again, make sure that your HSP has a section for this. If you must use the Network Scanner function, it is mandatory for you to use a Quarantine user role and have a supporting HSP section.

However, given that NAC Appliance Manager can accommodate more than one role of type Quarantine, you do not necessarily have to use the Quarantine role provided by default. It is typical for a larger organization to create separate Quarantine roles. The purpose is to allow for the creation of separate quarantine HSP sections. These quarantine HSP sections are then assigned to hosts in quarantine either based on their operating system, their normal login role membership, or both. The following are some sample HSP sections for using multiple Quarantine roles:

- **Guest users Quarantine role**   While in quarantine, all guest users should have access to only Internet remediate resources and Domain Name System (DNS). No access to internal remediation servers or other network resources should be allowed. Commonly allowed Internet remediate resources could include, but are not limited to, http://update.microsoft.com, http://mcafee.com, http://nai.com, and http://trendmicro.com. It is recommended that the default remediation hosts listed under the Quarantine role in NAC Appliance be allowed.

- **Employee Quarantine role**   While in quarantine, all members of the employee role should have access to only internal remediation resources and DNS. No access to external remediation servers, Internet, or internal resources should be allowed. Commonly allowed internal remediation resources could include, but are not limited to, corporate Windows Server Update Services servers, antivirus servers, and antispyware servers.

Next you will explore some of the most commonly used normal login roles. Remember, a normal login role defines the rights and privileges that a client will have after it passes authentication and posture assessment. All organizations must have their own customized normal login roles. The number and purpose of these roles will vary according to your environment. Each of the roles you choose should have a separate policy definition section in your host security policy document. The following are some of the most commonly configured roles; all are of type normal login role:

- Guest/visitor role
- Employee role
- Corporate user role
- Contractor/temp role
- Student role
- Faculty role
- Roles based on network location, such as Denver user role
- Job-based roles, such as sales, engineering, and so on
- Admin role
- Staff role
- Wireless user role
- VPN user role
- Printers and other exempt devices role

The printers and other exempt devices role can be used to put noninteractive network devices, such as printers, faxes, IP phones, and so on, into a user role. This allows for the creation of strict network access policies for these devices. These policies should allow them to communicate only using protocols that match the services they provide.

TIP   Creating roles for exempt device types is optional and can be time-consuming. The other option is to allow exempt devices full network access. However, taking the time to lock down the network access polices for exempt devices can greatly increase the security of those devices and your network as a whole.

Establishing Acceptable Use Policies

A network acceptable use policy is a clear and concise document that defines what users can and cannot do on a network. However, the focus of the AUP is on communicating to users what they cannot do. It also lays out the penalties for noncompliance and gives contact information. Ideally, before users are granted network access, they must first accept the organization's AUP. The problem has always been enforcing this requirement. Without some kind of network admission control system, ubiquitous enforcement is not possible. The NAC Appliance solution supports the enforcement of acceptable use policies.

Before creating your acceptable use policy for NAC Appliance users, determine who needs to be involved and what the approval process for a final policy will look like. Create an AUP committee that includes, at a minimum, persons from the Legal and IT departments. Draft a flow chart of the expected approval process the AUP will have to go through. Next, decide what documents the committee will have to produce to successfully complete the AUP. For example, to have an AUP approved in the education space, it is customary to need the following documents:

- **Justification and purpose for creating an AUP**   This typically needs to be presented to the school board and must be approved in the beginning to allow for the creation of the AUP committee.

- **A high-level AUP specifically created for or by the school board to establish the framework from which the final detailed AUP will be crafted**   It establishes the major security goals and network use guidelines. This must be approved by the school board.

- **A parent letter and permission form informing them of the AUP and the use of NAC Appliance to enforce this AUP**   This must be approved by the school board.

- **The final acceptable use policy document**   Typically, this is created by the committed and presented to the school board for approval. This is the document that will be used by the NAC Appliance solution.

In general, an acceptable use policy will include these parts or sections:

- **AUP Overview or Purpose**   Serves as an introduction to the AUP.

- **AUP Scope or Coverage**   Defines who must comply with this acceptable use policy.

- **Acceptable Network Use Guidelines**   Conveys the appropriate use of the network.

- **Unacceptable or Prohibited Network Uses**   This section might have several subsections, such as a subsection each for e-mail, copyrighted material, virus and worms, unauthorized access, illegal activity, and so on.

- **Violation or Enforcement Policy**   Communicates the penalties and legal action that could be taken against AUP violators.

- **Privacy Disclaimer**   Indicates that the organization assumes no responsibility or liability for a user's privacy while using the network.

- **Definitions**   Fully defines all acronyms and terms used in the document.

- **Legal Disclaimer**   Releases the organization from any and all legal liabilities resulting from the AUP itself or network use. Let the lawyers define this one.

- **Right to Modification**   This disclaimer communicates your ability to modify this policy at any time without notice.

- **Contact Information**   Provides users with a contact for additional information, questions, and complaints.

Your AUP might include additional or fewer sections than those listed here. The sections in the previous list should give you a rough idea of what to include in your AUP.

TIP   To find additional information on AUPs, such as how-to guides and examples, search Google using the keywords *network acceptable use policy*. For AUP samples, check out the SANS policy site at http://www.sans.org/resources/policies/. For K-12 organizations, check out the state of Washington's AUP guides at http://www.k12.wa.us/K-20/AUP.aspx.

The NAC Appliance solution has two methods for enforcing an acceptable use agreement. One is called a user agreement page and is used only by users who log in via web login. The other is called a network usage policy and is used only by users who log in via Clean Access Agent. Both methods can, and typically do, use and enforce the same acceptable use policy. Both methods enforce the policy by denying users network access until they acknowledge or accept the network acceptable use policy. After they accept the policy, they are granted network access.

The enforcement of an acceptable use policy is an optional feature. Enforcement can be selectively enabled as well. Enforcement can be turned on and off based on the client's user role, operating system type, or a combination of both. Additionally, it can be enabled and disabled based on the use of web login or the Clean Access Agent. For example, you might want to enable AUP enforcement for clients in the user role of Guest using a Windows XP host and either Clean Access Agent or web login. Figure 6-3 illustrates such a configuration for web login clients on NAC Appliance Manager.

Figure 6-3 *NAC Appliance Manager Web Login AUP Configuration*

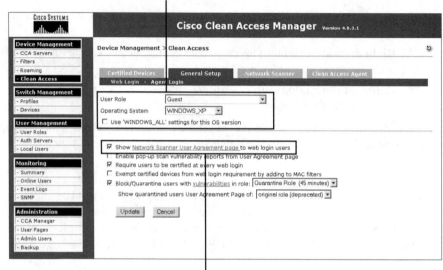

Here you determine the user role and OS
that will be affected by the below changes.

This enables the AUP.

Figure 6-4 illustrates the same configuration for Clean Access Agent clients.

Figure 6-4 *NAC Appliance Manager Clean Access Agent AUP Configuration*

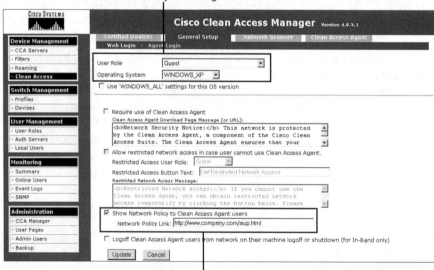

Here you determine the user role and OS
that will be affected by the changes below.

AUP is enabled here.

It is important to understand the different delivery mechanisms and user experiences provided by the two enforcement methods. The user agreement page method used only by web login users makes use of a web page AUP delivery mechanism. After users have passed authentication and network scanner checks, the user agreement page can be presented to the user for acceptance. Users will be granted network access only if they accept the user agreement presented. Figure 6-5 shows a screen shot of the web login user agreement page that is presented to end users.

Figure 6-5   *Web Login User Agreement Page*

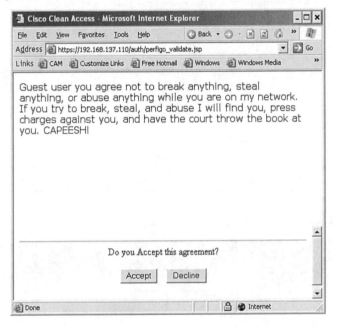

Figure 6-6 shows an example of the web page that displays if the user declines the user agreement. As you can see, network access is being blocked.

The network usage policy method used only by Clean Access Agent clients makes use of the Clean Access Agent dialog box to deliver the AUP for acceptance. After users have passed authentication and posture assessment, the user is presented with a link to the network usage policy and asked to accept it. If accepted, network access will be granted; if declined, network access will be denied. Figure 6-7 shows the Clean Access Agent–displayed network usage policy screen.

Figure 6-6 *Web Login—Declined User Agreement*

Figure 6-7 *Clean Access Agent Network Usage Policy Screen*

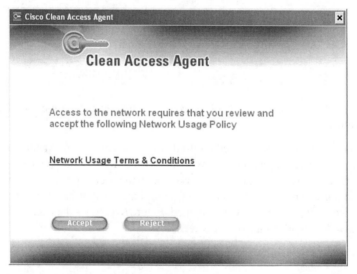

Figure 6-8 shows a screen shot of Clean Access Agent if the user declines the network usage policy. As you can see, network access is being blocked.

If users decline the AUP using either method (web login or Clean Access Agent), they will be moved back into the Unauthenticated role and forced to complete authentication again.

Figure 6-8   *Clean Access Agent—Declined Network Usage Policy*

Checks, Rules, and Requirements to Consider

This section covers how to include the host posture assessment and remediation checks, rules, and requirements into an organization's host security policy document. One of the major benefits to using Clean Access Agent is its capability to perform granular host posture assessments and remediation on Windows hosts. Therefore, your host security policy should contain the checks, rules, and requirements that NAC Appliance should look for, enforce, and remediate on Windows hosts. Because Clean Access Agent is loaded on the host, it has the capability to read into the host's registry, applications, services, and file system. Clean Access Agent also offers robust remediation capabilities for a host that fails a security requirement. The remediation capabilities include file distribution, link distribution, delivery of instructions, and auto update mechanisms for Windows, antivirus, and antispyware programs. The host security policy should include the details on how hosts will be remediated under different circumstances.

All posture assessment and remediation configuration is done at NAC Appliance Manager. It is here that you will configure the checks, rules, and requirements that will satisfy the policies contained in your corporate HSP document. Before creating your host security policy for NAC Appliance, it is important to understand the process that NAC Appliance goes through for posture assessment. This process uses a combination of checks, rules, and requirements that are applied to user roles and optionally operating system types. Checks like the one shown in Figure 6-9 are configured at NAC Appliance Manager.

NAC Appliance rules, like the one shown in Figure 6-10, can be made up of several checks combined using Boolean operators. They can also be operating system specific.

Figure 6-9 *Check Configuration Example*

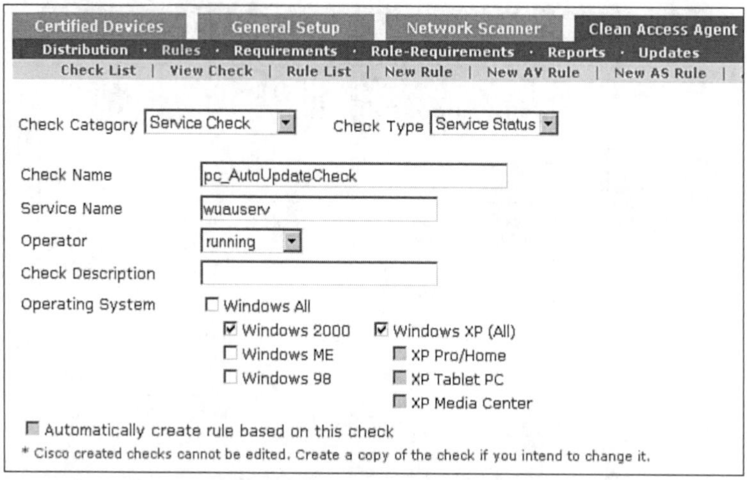

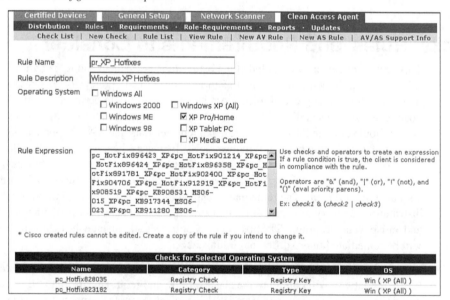

Figure 6-10 *Rule Configuration Example*

A NAC Appliance requirement, like the one shown in Figure 6-11, defines what remediation mechanism is offered to any noncompliant users. In this example, the Windows auto-update service is being turned on and configured to download and install the most current updates.

A requirement to rules mapping, like the one shown in Figure 6-12, is then performed.

This mapping specifies that all the rules must succeed in order for the requirement to be met. The two rules that must succeed are pr_AutoUpdateCheck_Rule and pr_XP_Hotfixes. It also specifies a specific operating system type: Windows XP Pro/Home.

Figure 6-11 *Requirement Configuration Example*

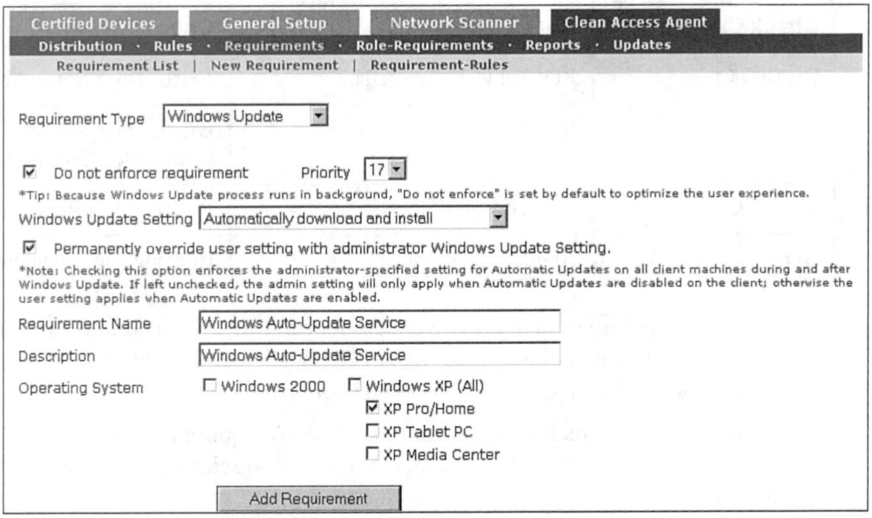

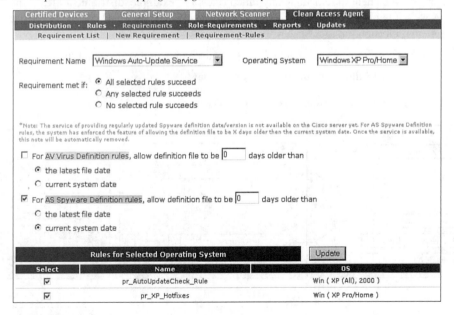

Figure 6-12 *Requirement-Rules Mapping Configuration Example*

Finally, the requirements are mapped to one or more user roles. In addition, it is possible to further classify the requirements by operating system type. The order of operations NAC Appliance uses is as follows:

- Checks are condition statements that examine the client to find the state or presence of a file, service, application, or registry key. Table 6-1 presents the different check categories and their associated check types and operators.

Table 6-1 *Checks*

Check Category	Check Types	Check Operators
Registry Check	Key, Value, Value (default)	Exists, Does Not Exist
File Check	File Existence, Date, Version	Exists, Does Not Exist, Earlier Than, Later Than, Same As
Service Check	Service Status	Running, Not Running
Application Check	Application Status	Running, Not Running

- Rules are made up of one or more checks that can be combined into an expression using the Boolean operators and "&", or "|", not "!", and evaluation priority parentheses "()". If the result is true, the client passes the rule.

- Requirements are made up of one or more rules. A requirement can specify that a host must pass any selected rule, all selected rules, or no selected rules in order for the host to pass the requirement.

- Requirements also define the mechanism to use and the instructions that will allow the client to remediate any failed rules. For example, distribute a file or link with the instructions "Click the link and download, install, and run the XYZVirus cleaning tool."

- Requirements are mapped to user roles and operating system types.

Figure 6-13 illustrates the order of operations.

Figure 6-13 *Clean Access Agent Posture Assessment Process*

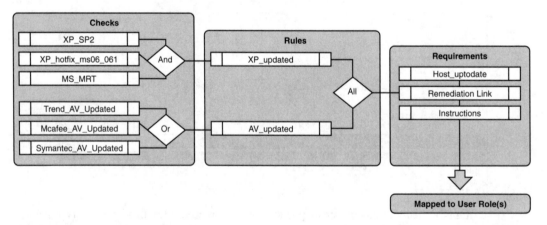

This posture assessment process can be thorough or simple. The flowchart in Figure 6-14 shows an example of the authentication and remediation process NAC Appliance could follow.

Figure 6-14 *Sample Authentication and Remediation Flowchart*

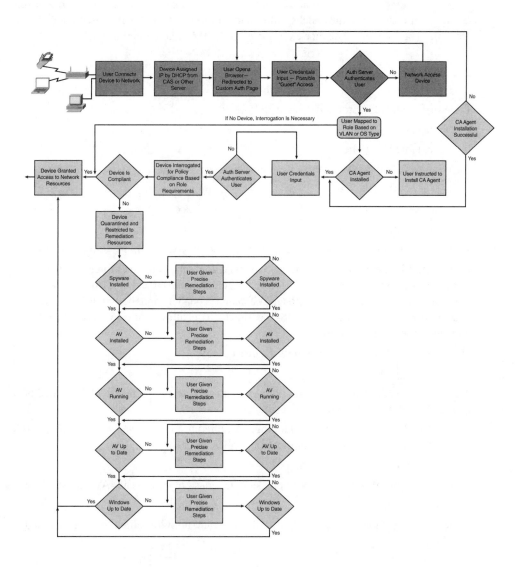

Sample HSP Format for Documenting NAC Appliance Requirements

As discussed, the NAC Appliance uses several mechanisms to define what it should look for, or posture assess, on a given host. It also has several mechanisms for the proper remediation of any failed security requirements. Ultimately, the host security requirements and remediation steps that are performed on a client are based on the user role of the client. With this in mind, your HSP should have sections for each user role. Under each user role section, you would have the checks, rules, and requirements that pertain to clients of that user role. The following is a nice example of an HSP formatted in this way:

Employee User Role

Table of Contents for Employee Security Policy:

I. Members – Any user who is a member of the Employees group in Active Directory.

II. Acceptable Use Policy – Reference which AUP, if any, is to be enforced by the employee user role. For example, you might reference an AUP called Trusted_User_AUP. It is common that only a reference to an AUP name is put here and the actual AUP document lives in its own section within the HSP document. This allows for easy reuse of AUP policies across multiple roles.

III. Windows 2000 and XP Security Requirements

1. Trend_AV_Installed

Trend_AV_Requirement – Link distribution that points to the Trend client download page on the Trend Micro corp. antivirus server.

Trend_AV_Requirement to Rule Mapping – Map requirement *Trend_AV_Installed* to rule *Trend_AV_Installed*. Requirement met if any rules succeed.

    a. Security Rules –

Trend_AV_Installed rule – Rule expression includes only the Trend_AV_Installed check.

    b. Security Checks –

Trend_AV_Installed check – Corporate Trend Micro antivirus client must be installed on all Windows hosts.

The NAC Appliance solution has lots of prebuilt checks and rules that you can use to build your requirements. All the built-in checks have a *pc* preceding their name, such as pc_AutoUpdateCheck. The built-in rules have either a *pr* preceding their name, such as pr_AutoUpdateCheck_Rule, or are special antivirus or antispyware rules. It is recommended that you use the newer special antivirus and antispyware rules rather than the pr rules where applicable. pr rules can only check whether an antivirus definition version is exactly equal, whereas an antivirus rule understands greater than as well. These checks and rules are constantly updated by Cisco and are automatically downloaded by your NAC Appliance Manager. Out of the box, NAC Appliance has auto-update support for Microsoft Windows, 24 antivirus vendors, and 17 antispyware vendors. This means that NAC Appliance automatically keeps up to date with the latest versions, .dat files, and hotfixes available for each of the supported vendors. Keep this in mind when creating your NAC Appliance host security policy. It is recommended that you use these built-in checks and rules wherever possible.

Common Checks, Rules, and Requirements

Here are some of the most common checks, rules, and requirements implemented by administrators of the NAC Appliance solution. All the examples given have corresponding built-in checks and rules written and are auto-updated by NAC Appliance.

- An antivirus program must be installed, running, and up to date. Most organizations specify specific antivirus programs for certain user roles. For example, employee user role clients must use the corporate Trend Micro antivirus client, whereas guest user role clients are allowed to use any of the 24 NAC Appliance–supported antivirus vendors.

- An antispyware program must be installed, running, and up to date. Most organizations specify specific antispyware programs for certain user roles. For example, employee user role clients must use the corporate Webroot antispyware client, whereas guest user role clients are allowed to use any of the 17 NAC Appliance–supported antispyware vendors.

- All Windows XP clients must be running Service Pack 2. The built-in check is called pc_Windows-XP-SP2.

- All Windows 2000 clients must be running Service Pack 4. The built-in check is called pc_Windows-2K-SP4.

- All Windows XP and 2000 clients must have the Windows auto-update service running. By default, NAC Appliance looks to make sure that the wuauserv service is running. The built-in check is called pc_AutoUpdateCheck. The built-in rule is called pr_AutoUpdateCheck_Rule.

- All Windows XP, 2000, NT, Me, and 98 clients must be running the latest Microsoft security hotfixes as defined by the NAC Appliance rules pr_XP_Hotfixes, pr_2K_Hotfixes, pr_NT_Hotfixes, pr_ME_Hotfixes, and pr_98_Hotfixes, respectively. These rules, and their corresponding checks, are continuously updated by Cisco. They include the most critical security hotfixes for XP, 2000, NT, Me, and 98. They do not, however, include every security update that Microsoft has ever released for each operating system. If you require additional hotfixes, you can edit the relevant pr_??_Hotfixes rule to include them.

- All Windows clients must have either Cisco Security Agent or Symantec Personal Firewall installed and running.

- All requirements dealing with the updating of antivirus and antispyware programs use the built-in AV Definition Update type. These rules are preconfigured to map to the matrix of 24 antivirus and 17 antispyware vendors and products supported by NAC Appliance. These rules do not require you to configure any checks and are continuously updated by Cisco. If the user fails these requirements, the user is presented with an Update button. When clicked, the Update button auto-launches the update program for the antivirus or antispyware program that failed to pass the policy.

Method for Adding Checks, Rules, and Requirements

Many organizations do not have a process in place that they can follow to determine if, when, and how a security update should be added to their host security policy document. Organizations that lack this type of process, or method, are in greater danger of making bad decisions about the security updates they choose to install. For this reason, it is important for organizations to establish and follow a formal method for adding checks, rules, and requirements. This subsection will deal with this topic as it pertains to the initial creation and subsequent revisions of the host security policy document. Knowing which security patches to enforce using NAC Appliance is a big job. The goal is to provide the information necessary for you to set up your own method, or process, for determining which checks, rules, and requirements you want to include in your initial host security policy for NAC Appliance. A secondary goal is to provide the information necessary for you to set up your own method, or process, for determining when to add, change, and delete new checks, rules, and requirements to your HSP.

Research and Information

The NAC Appliance solution comes with many preconfigured checks and rules, such as the ones described previously. Simply implementing these built-in policies goes a long way toward increasing the security posture of most organizations' hosts and networks. However, these are by no means the only security checks and rules available. In many cases, your organization might choose to implement checks, rules, and requirements beyond the scope of the built-in policies. When this occurs, it is vital that you are able to find the information and research needed to make the most informed decision possible. Regardless of whether the security fixes you put in place use the built-in policies, custom policies, or a combination of both, it is vital that you understand what the fixes are for, their impact, and their severity level. It is also necessary to remain informed about the emergence of new vulnerabilities, exploits, and viruses. Obtaining this information is not always trivial. Here are some of the commonly used security websites, blogs, and resources available online. Most are free, but some also offer a paid service.

- **SecurityFocus (http://www.securityfocus.com)**   This is one of the best websites for obtaining security information.
- **Full Disclosure Mailing Lists (http://seclists.org/#fulldisclosure)**   This site is made up of various security mailing lists, like the extremely popular bugtraq list and the sometimes controversial full disclosure list. New vulnerabilities and exploits are frequently announced on bugtraq before anywhere else in the world.
- **Microsoft TechNet Security Center (http://www.microsoft.com/technet/ security)**   This web portal serves as a good jumping-off point for investigating any Microsoft security vulnerabilities, updates, and exploits.
- **Microsoft Security Bulletin (http://www.microsoft.com/technet/security/ bulletin)**   This website has a nice search engine for Microsoft security bulletins. The site also has a link to sign up to receive security bulletins via e-mail, Really Simple Syndication, or instant message. The search engine allows you to search for vulnerabilities based on severity level and operating system type and version.
- **McAfee Threat Center (http://www.mcafee.com/us/threat_center/)**   McAfee has a well laid out and informative security information portal here.
- **Cyber Alert System (http://www.us-cert.gov/cas/)**   The national Cyber Alert System was created to ensure that you have access to timely information about security topics and threats. You can sign up to receive the alerts here.
- **Government sites like National Vulnerability Database (http://nvd.nist.gov) and U.S. Computer readiness team (http://www.us-cert.gov)**   These are filled with timely security alert information and are vendor agnostic.
- **metasploit (http://www.metasploit.com/)**   This site does not offer any security information but does provide an easy-to-use security tool to help you test the security of your hosts.
- **Cisco MySDN (http://www.mysdn.com)**   This website, hosted by Cisco Systems, serves as a security portal to find information regarding security bulletins from all the major application and operating system vendors. It also has a paid service called IntelliShield that provides customers with a customizable, web-based threat and vulnerability alert service.

These websites and others like them can be found throughout the Internet. They can be powerful tools for gathering the security information you need to make an informed decision on which security patches NAC Appliance should enforce.

Establishing Criteria to Determine the Validity of a Security Check, Rule, or Requirement in Your Organization

A host security policy should have a section that documents the criteria to be used to decide whether a proposed security check, rule, or requirement needs to be added to NAC Appliance. The establishment of set criteria will serve to improve the accuracy of the decision process. The criteria used should be tailored for your specific environment and should refrain from using generalities whenever possible. The more fine-grained the criteria used, the more informed the decision process will be.

For every security fix proposed for and existing in the HSP, and subsequently in NAC Appliance, you should be familiar with or know where to obtain the following information regarding a security vulnerability:

- What products, applications, and versions are affected?
- What is the vulnerability's severity level?
- What is the potential impact or risk to the organization if the vulnerability is exploited? This point should be explored in detail, noting a best and worst case scenario.
- Can the vulnerability be exploited remotely?
- Are the exploits publicly available?
- Is the use of the affected software widespread in your organization?
- Are the ports, protocols, and hosts in question already being blocked using a firewall, Intrusion Prevention System, Personal Firewall, or NAC Appliance? If so, to what extent does this mitigate the exploit risk?
- Is a patch available for the vulnerability?
- If yes, is it possible to test the patch to make sure that it works as advertised?
- If no testing can be done, is the risk of deploying a faulty patch less than the risk of the vulnerability?
- If no patch is available, is it possible to use any of the security features in NAC Appliance to help mitigate this feature? If no, is it possible to use any other security products to do so?

Before taking action, it is important to understand what the expected overhead on the IT staff might be if the new patch or fix is implemented. This should be explored in detail, noting the best case and worst case scenarios. The following are some of the topics for consideration:

- Will there be additional help desk load?
- Will there be additional IT staff load?
- What is required of the end-user community?

- Will there be additional network load created due to deployment of new patches? If deploying patches over the WAN, what is the potential impact?

- Who will perform any testing needed? What resources are required to perform the testing?

- What is needed to set up the deployment method for distributing the patch or update?

- What is the expected impact on and reactions from the user community if the fix for the vulnerability is rolled out?

Method for Determining Which User Roles a Particular Security Requirement Should Be Applied To

After it is decided that a security fix or patch should be deployed in your environment, the next step is to decide what user roles should receive the fix. Additionally, it is important to determine whether the fix should be mandatory or optional. This might vary based on user role; some roles will be deployed as optional, whereas other roles will be mandatory. It is a best practice to deploy new security requirements as optional first and then, after a set amount of time, make them mandatory. This results in the least impact possible on the user community. However, if a vulnerability poses significant risk to the organization, the new security requirement should be rolled out as mandatory. The following are some things to consider when deciding what roles should receive a new security requirement:

- Do all roles run the affected software?

- Do any of the roles pose a greater risk than others if the patch causes adverse affects on clients? In other words, do certain user roles contain clients that, if debilitated due to a bad patch, would significantly affect the organization? If so, would starting with less risky user roles first to further assess the robustness of the patch make sense?

- Do any user roles have an elevated exposure to the vulnerability in question? If so, does this elevated exposure warrant mandatory enforcement of the new security requirement?

- Does the security requirement apply to the guest user role?

Method for Deploying and Enforcing Security Requirements

After it has been decided that a security requirement should be added to the HSP and NAC Appliance, it is necessary to come up with a deployment strategy. The security requirement could be made up of one or more files, actions, or patches. Keep in mind that deployment of the security patches will happen while clients are in either a Quarantine role or Temporary role. If they are using Clean Access Agent, patch deployment will always happen while in the Temporary role.

The requirement type chosen might affect the decision process regarding deployment type. As previously discussed, a requirement type has the following options for remediation: File Distribution, Link Distribution, Message Only, AV Definition Update, AS Definition Update, Launch Program, and Windows Update. The easiest types to deploy are the update types. This is because they use the already built-in deployment and updating mechanisms configured on the local host. For example, the requirement type of Windows Update uses the Windows update service already present on and configured for the client that needs the updates. Regardless of the requirement type chosen, the following deployment questions should be considered:

- Should the deployment method be the same for all user roles?

- Which deployment method would be the most efficient in reaching the user roles in question?

- Should the enforcement of the new security requirement be optional or mandatory in the beginning? Does this vary by user role?

- If optional, should the requirement be made mandatory at some point in time? If so, define the period between optional and mandatory. Does this vary by user role?

- Do clients in the Quarantine and Temporary user roles have privileges to access the proposed deployment resources? For example, if you use a link to http://www.fixme.com as your deployment method, you need to ensure that access to this URL is not restricted. To be sure, it is always best to test it.

Defining Network Access Privileges

The NAC Appliance solution has several methods available to grant and restrict the network access privileges of clients. Most of these methods are defined per user role; however, it is possible to define some of them per MAC or IP address. A host security policy for NAC Appliance should include details on what network access privileges should be given to what user roles and devices. Device details are typically reserved for devices, such as printers, that are exempt from NAC Appliance authentication and posture assessment but are still subjected to network access restrictions.

Here is an example that uses traffic control rules in NAC Appliance. A client in the guest user role should be granted access only to the Internet on TCP ports 80 and 443; all other network access should be denied. The following common and easily understandable syntax can be used for documenting NAC Appliance traffic control policies in the HSP. Typically, these rules would be found under their corresponding user role section in the HSP.

<line #> Permit|Deny <protocol> from <host(s) | network(s)> to <host(s) | network(s)> equaling | not equaling port(s) <list of port numbers or names>

Description: <explanation of rule>

The previous example would be written in the HSP under the guest user role/traffic control subsection as follows:

10 Deny IP from any to any internal network.

Description: Block IP traffic from anyone to any internal subnet or host.

20 Permit TCP from guest user role to any equaling port 80 or 443.

Description: Allow web traffic from clients in the guest user role to the Internet.

30 Deny IP from guest user role to any.

Description: Block everything else.

Formatting the rules in this way not only makes them unambiguous but allows them to be easily translated into the traffic control rules configured in the NAC Appliance Manager.

Enforcement Methods Available with NAC Appliance

Not all enforcement methods supported by NAC Appliance are supported in all modes of operation. This issue applies mostly to the In-Band and Out-of-Band operating modes. Many of the features are not available for out-of-band clients that have passed authentication and posture assessment. This is because once clients are certified, they are moved to the appropriate access VLAN. This access VLAN completely bypasses the NAC Appliance solution, making the use of some enforcement methods unfeasible. Table 6-2 lists the different network access control methods available, gives a brief description for each, and shows whether they will work with Out-of-Band and In-Band modes.

Table 6-2   *NAC Appliance Network Access Control Methods*

Enforcement or Control Method	Description	Supported in OOB Mode?	Supported in In-Band Mode?
Traffic Control Rules	The equivalent of network access control lists. They permit and deny traffic like a firewall does.	Partial support. Supported only while client is in a Quarantine or Temporary user role and going through NAC Appliance Server.	Yes.
Allowed Hosts	A list of DNS-resolvable hostnames of permitted hosts. Useful for allowing access to websites that have multiple or changing IP addresses. For example, *.mcafee.com allows access to any host with a .mcafee.com suffix.	Partial Support. Supported only while client is in a Quarantine or Temporary user role and going through NAC Appliance Server.	Yes.

continues

Table 6-2   *NAC Appliance Network Access Control Methods (Continued)*

Enforcement or Control Method	Description	Supported in OOB Mode?	Supported in In-Band Mode?
VLAN Segmentation	Dynamically changes the access port's Layer 2 VLAN based on the user role of the connected client. The authentication VLAN type is used for new or noncompliant hosts. The access VLAN type is reserved for authenticated and compliant hosts. The authentication VLAN type is forced through NAC Appliance and all the accompanying enforcement, whereas the access VLAN type bypasses NAC Appliance.	Yes.	No.
Bandwidth Control	Provides the ability to rate-limit the amount of data a client or group of clients can send. The bandwidth rule includes the upstream Kb/S, downstream Kb/s, and burst rate fields. Bandwidth control is set per user role. The bandwidth limits are either shared by all clients in the user role or are granted to each client in the user role.	Partial support. Supported only while client is in a Quarantine or Temporary user role and going through NAC Appliance Server.	Yes.
Session Timer	The session timer serves as an absolute time limit for a client in a given user role. When the timer expires, the client is kicked off the network and must reauthenticate. The user will be dropped regardless of connection status or activity. This enforcement method is used to force clients to pass authentication and posture assessment again.	Yes.	Yes.

Commonly Used Network Access Policies

In short, a network access policy defines what a host can and cannot do on the network. The exact rules that make up any network access policy are customized for a particular environment but, nevertheless, there are some commonalities between organizations. This section will focus on those common elements. The network access policy defined in your

HSP will typically cover all the enforcement methods that NAC Appliance supports. To review, those enforcement methods are VLAN segmentation, traffic control (access control lists or ACLs), bandwidth control, and session duration limits.

VLAN segmentation applies only if you use Out-of-Band mode. Additionally, for OOB mode traffic control, bandwidth control and session duration limits apply only while the client is in the authentication VLAN. After the client moves to the access VLAN, these controls no longer apply. You can optionally and manually configure switch or router ACLs and QoS to control clients while they are on the access VLAN. Traffic control policies are always tied to a user role in NAC Appliance. Some user roles (such as guest) have restrictive network access policies, whereas others are wide open (such as employee). In addition, it is always a best practice to lock down the network access policy on any Unauthenticated, Temporary, or Quarantine user role.

Here are some popular or mandatory user roles shown with a common example of their associated network access policy. This is formatted for a NAC Appliance host security policy. You can choose to use this HSP format or develop your own. The important thing is that your network access policy is well documented. Note that these pick up where the earlier sample HSP left off, at section IV. (See the section "Sample HSP Format for Documenting NAC Appliance Requirements.")

Employee User Role

Table of Contents for Employee Security Policy:

...

IV. Network Access Policies

1. VLAN Segmentation – Yes, out-of-band will be used.

   a. Authentication VLAN Name/ID = auth-vlan/100

   b. Access VLAN Name/ID = employees/10

2. Traffic Control – N/A. Refer to traffic control policy for Temporary and Quarantine user roles. Due to OOB mode, traffic control applies to clients only while they are in Temporary or Quarantine user role.

3. Bandwidth Control – N/A. Refer to Bandwidth Control policy for Temporary and Quarantine user roles. Due to OOB mode, bandwidth control applies to clients only while they are in Temporary or Quarantine user role.

4. Session Duration – Unlimited.

The subsequent examples will not show the full host security policy format. Only the sections relevant to the network access policy will be shown.

Unauthenticated User Role

1. VLAN Segmentation – Yes, out-of-band will be used.

   a. Authentication VLAN Name/ID = auth-vlan/100

2. Traffic Control –

10 Permit UDP from any to "dmz DNS Server" equaling DNS.

Description: Allow DNS but only to the DMZ DNS server.

20 Deny IP from any to any.

Description: Block everything else.

3. Bandwidth Control –

Limits: 1 Mbps upstream, 1 Mbps downstream, 3X burst.

Shared mode: Each user owns the specified bandwidth.

Description: Bandwidth is restricted to provide denial of service protection for the DMZ DNS server.

4. Session Duration – Unlimited.

Quarantine User Role

1. VLAN Segmentation – Yes, out-of-band will be used.

   a. Authentication VLAN Name/ID = auth-vlan/100

2. Traffic Control –

10 Permit TCP from any to "Link-based remediation resources" equaling 80 or 443.

Description: Allow web traffic to the appropriate remediation resources.

20 Permit TCP from any to "CAM for file-based remediation" equaling 80 or 443.

Description: Allow web traffic to the CAM for remediation file distribution.

30 Permit UDP from any to "dmz DNS Server" equaling DNS.

Description: Allow DNS to only the DMZ DNS server.

40 Permit hosts ending with *.symantec.com, *.trendmicro.com, and *.microsoft.com.

Description: Allow remediation traffic to hosts at our antivirus, antispyware, and Microsoft.

50 Deny IP from any to any.

Description: Block everything else.

3. Bandwidth Control –

Limits: 512 kbps upstream, 1 Mbps downstream, 3X burst.

Shared mode: All users share the specified bandwidth.

Description: Bandwidth is restricted to provide denial of service protection for the network.

4. Session Duration – 30 minutes.

Temporary User Role

1. VLAN Segmentation – Yes, out-of-band will be used.

   a. Authentication VLAN Name/ID = auth-vlan/100

2. Traffic Control –

5 Permit TCP from any to "AUP web server" equaling 80.

Description: Allow anyone to access the acceptable use policy link.

10 Permit TCP from any to "Link-based remediation resources" equaling 80 or 443.

Description: Allow web traffic to the appropriate remediation resources.

20 Permit TCP from any to "CAM for file-based remediation" equaling 80 or 443.

Description: Allow web traffic to the CAM for remediation file distribution.

30 Permit UDP from any to "dmz DNS Server" equaling DNS.

Description: Allow DNS only to the DMZ DNS server.

40 Permit hosts ending with *.symantec.com, *.trendmicro.com, and *.microsoft.com.

Description: Allow remediation traffic to hosts at our antivirus, antispyware, and Microsoft.

50 Deny IP from any to any.

Description: Block everything else.

3. Bandwidth Control –

Limits: 512 kbps upstream, 1 Mbps downstream, 3X burst.

Shared mode: All users share the specified bandwidth.

Description: Bandwidth is restricted to provide denial of service protection for the network.

4. Session Duration – 30 minutes.

Guest User Role

1. VLAN Segmentation – Yes, out-of-band will be used.

   a. Authentication VLAN Name/ID = auth-vlan/100

   b. Access VLAN Name/ID = guests/20

2. Traffic Control –

10 Deny IP from any to any internal network.

Description: Block IP traffic from guests to any internal subnet or host.

20 Permit TCP from guest user role to any equaling port 80 or 443.

Description: Allow web traffic from clients in the guest user role to the Internet.

21 Permit TCP from any to any equaling 20 or 21.

Description: Allow guests to FTP files from the Internet.

25 Permit VPN from any to any.

Description: Allow guests to VPN to anywhere on the Internet.

30 Deny IP from guest user role to any.

Description: Block everything else.

Traffic control is applicable only while on the auth VLAN.

3. Bandwidth Control –

Limits: 512 kbps upstream, 1 Mbps downstream, 3X burst.

Shared mode: All users share the specified bandwidth.

Description: Bandwidth is restricted to provide denial of service protection for the network. Bandwidth control is applicable only while on the auth VLAN.

4. Session Duration – 30 minutes.

Summary

This chapter examined the intricacies of creating a host security policy for a Cisco NAC Appliance deployment. The following recommendations were made:

- Create and follow an HSP checklist.

- Make sure to get executive buy-in for the creation and subsequent enforcement of an HSP.

- Create an HSP committee. Be sure to involve the right people.

- Determine your organization's high-level host security goals. Use these as guides when creating the detailed host security policy.

- Break up your organization into security domains. Determine which security domains will use NAC Appliance and which will not. For those that will, you must determine what modes NAC Appliance should use in each domain (for example, In-Band, Out-of-Band, Real-IP-Gateway, and so on).

- Determine and create the user roles necessary for your organization.

- Create one or more acceptable use policies.

- Determine what checks, rules, and requirements will be enforced for each user role.

- Establish and follow a method for adds, moves, and changes to user role checks, rules, and requirements.

- Determine a method for deploying Clean Access Agent and remediation resources.

- Determine what network access policy should be assigned to each user role.

- Either use the host security policy formatting shown throughout this chapter or pick your own formatting. The important thing is to document your host security policy in a concise and easily understood manner.

PART IV

Cisco NAC Appliance Configuration

This chapter covers the following topics:

- Understanding the Basic Cisco NAC Appliance Concepts
- NAM Overview
- NAS Overview
- Configuring NAS Deployment Mode
- Understanding NAS Management Within the NAM GUI
- Adding Additional NAS Appliances

CHAPTER 7

The Basics: Principal Configuration Tasks for the NAM and NAS

This chapter explains the basic configuration tasks required to install and configure the NAC Appliance Manager (NAM) and NAC Appliance Server (NAS).

The NAM and NAS are software packages that are installed on top of their own dedicated server appliance. The software is built on a hardened Linux kernel and will turn each dedicated server into a Cisco appliance. This means you cannot install any other third-party software on top of the Linux kernel. Prior to 4.0.3, you could buy the software from Cisco and install them on top of Cisco-certified servers or buy both software and hardware from Cisco directly to avoid any unexpected hardware and software incompatibilities. From 4.0.3 on, all new NAC 33xx appliance series have come with software preinstalled from Cisco. This means that you only have to apply new updates and patches when you receive your 4.0.3 or higher appliances.

Understanding the Basic Cisco NAC Appliance Concepts

A Cisco NAC Appliance solution consists of NAM, NAS, and Cisco Clean Access (CCA) Agent. The majority of the configurations are performed in NAM because it oversees all deployed NAS appliances and agents. Installation and configuration of NAM and NAS are very straightforward. Here is a high-level summary of how to perform the initial installation and configuration:

Step 1 Connect a keyboard and monitor to NAM and NAS. The mouse is not required. There is no need to plug either appliance into the network yet. An alternative to the keyboard and monitor is using the serial console connection.

Step 2 Insert the NAC Appliance installation CD into the NAM or NAS appliance.

Step 3 Reboot.

Step 4 Follow the step-by-step command-line interface (CLI) setup script to configure NAM and NAS.

Step 5 Connect NAM and NAS to the network and verify connectivity.

NAM Overview

NAM is the central administration server for monitoring and configuring the deployment of NAC Appliance servers and agents. This section covers details on NAM installation, connection, and initial configuration. It also covers NAC Appliance licensing and the NAM GUI.

NAM Hardware Installation Requirements

For performance reasons, it is generally a good idea to acquire servers that exceed the minimum required hardware specifications in any enterprise deployments. For the NAM, two physical 10/100/1000 Ethernet interfaces are required for a high-availability (HA) deployment. For non-HA deployments, only one physical interface is needed. In either deployment scenario, Ethernet 0 is the primary network interface. For a NAM HA scenario, Ethernet 1 is the designated failover interface to the standby NAM for failover heartbeats and stateful connection information.

NAM Software Installation Requirements

The software installation requirements are as follows:

- Cisco NAC Appliance – Clean Access CD
- NAM or "CiscoCleanAccess" license key

How to Connect NAM

There are two methods available to connect the NAM initially. Both methods will access the CLI required to perform the initial configuration. Option 1 is the preferred method, but both are listed.

- Connect a keyboard and monitor to the back of the NAM appliance. A mouse is not required.
- Connect a serial cable from a laptop or desktop PC to the serial port (typically DB9 connector) on the NAM appliance. Open a terminal emulation program, such as HyperTerminal or SecureCRT, on the laptop or desktop PC to access the NAM CLI. The port settings for the terminal emulation programs are as follows:
  - Bits Per Second – 9600
  - Data Bits – 8
  - Parity – None
  - Stop Bits – 1
  - Flow Control – None
  - Terminal Emulation – VT100

After the initial configuration is complete and NAM is connected to the network, you can securely connect to NAM via common browsers such as Internet Explorer (IE) or FireFox using **https://***NAM_IP_address*. An example is https://192.168.137.4.

Performing Initial NAM Configurations

If your NAM is preinstalled with the NAM software from Cisco, you may skip the manual installation that follows and proceed from Example 7-3. From the CLI, simply type in **service perfigo config** to run the setup script.

If your NAM is not preinstalled with the NAM software from Cisco, you will need to manually install the NAM software via the Cisco NAC Appliance – Clean Access CD. Insert the NAC installation CD into the CD-ROM drive of the NAM appliance and reboot the appliance.

Your NAC appliance should boot from the CD-ROM and display the NAC installation display. Example 7-1 shows the NAC installation output.

Example 7-1   *Initial NAC Installation Output*

```
Cisco Clean Access 4.0-3 Installer (C) 2006 Cisco Systems, Inc.

                    Welcome to the Cisco Clean Access 4.0-3 Installer!
  -  To install a Cisco Clean Access device, press the <ENTER> key.

  -  To install a Cisco Clean Access device over a serial console,
     enter serial at the boot prompt and press the <ENTER> key.
boot:
Pressing <ENTER> key at the above boot prompt will continue the NAC installation via
keyboard, monitor, and mouse. Entering the word, serial, at the boot prompt will
continue via the serial cable.

There will be a large amount of installation data being displayed on screen. Since
this is an installation example, only the interactive portions of the installation
will be shown here.

The next interactive installation point is where you the administrator need to choose
the NAM or NAS. Choose CCA Manager and press OK. Pressing the Tab key on your keyboard
should allow you to jump to the OK button.

Welcome to Cisco Clean Access

                          ++ Package Group Selection ++
                          ¦                             ¦
                          ¦ Total install size: 678M    ¦
                          ¦                             ¦
                          ¦    [*] CCA Manager          ¦
                          ¦    [ ] CCA Server           ¦
                          ¦                             ¦
                          ¦                             ¦
                          ¦                             ¦
                          ¦                             ¦
                          ¦                             ¦
                          ¦                             ¦
                          ¦                             ¦
                                                              continues
```

Example 7-1 *Initial NAC Installation Output (Continued)*

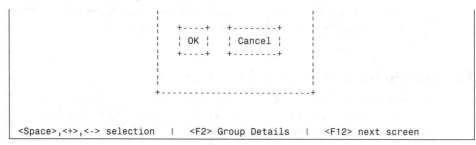

```
                        +----+    +--------+
                        | OK |    | Cancel |
                        +----+    +--------+


                    +----------------------------+

  <Space>,<+>,<-> selection   |   <F2> Group Details   |   <F12> next screen
```

Next, you will see the HDD formatting portion, as displayed in Example 7-2. Don't be alarmed if the formatting process stops at 11% for a while. The total amount of formatting time will depend on the HDD space of the appliance. Be patient. Give yourself about an hour or so to complete the entire installation process.

Example 7-2 *NAC Manager Installation Screen*

```
       +-------------------+ Formatting +--------------------+
       |                                                     |
       | Formatting / file system...                         |
       |                                                     |
       |                        11%                          |
       |                                                     |
       +-----------------------------------------------------+
```

Next, you will see many more Package Installation messages with filename info, size, time remaining, and so forth on your screen. Be patient, and it will eventually finish. When complete, you should see the setup script walking you through the configuration of the NAM. Example 7-3 shows the NAM setup/configuration script. Simply follow the script through.

NOTE   By default, the NAM Installation software assigns private IP addresses to all required IP address fields. Enter your own IP addresses for your network.

If you have completed the setup and configuration script and need and decide to reconfigure certain parameters, simply access the CLI via Secure Shell (SSH); keyboard, monitor, and mouse; or serial console, and type **service perfigo config** to rerun the script. Although not required, Cisco best practices recommend that the administrator reboot the NAM after making any changes in the setup script.

Example 7-3 *NAM Setup/Configuration Script*

```
Welcome to the Cisco Clean Access Manager quick configuration utility.

Note that you need to be root to execute this utility.

The utility will now ask you a series of configuration questions.
Please answer them carefully.

Cisco Clean Access Manager, (C) 2006 Cisco Systems, Inc.
Configuring the network interface:

Please enter the IP address for the interface eth0 [10.0.2.15]: 192.168.137.3
You entered 192.168.137.3 Is this correct? (y/n)? [y]

Please enter the netmask for the interface eth0 [255.255.255.0]:
You entered 255.255.255.0. Is this correct? (y/n)? [y]

Please enter the IP address for the default gateway [192.168.137.1]:
You entered 192.168.137.1. Is this correct? (y/n)? [y]

Please enter the hostname [localhost.localdomain]: nam1
You entered nam1. Is this correct? (y/n)? [y]

Please enter the IP address for the name server: [10.0.2.1]: 192.168.100.100
You entered 192.168.100.100. Is this correct? (y/n)? [y]

The shared secret used between Clean Access Manager and Clean Access Server is the
default string: cisco123

This is highly insecure. It is recommended that you choose a string that is unique
to your installation.

Please remember to configure the Clean Access Server with the same string. Please
enter the shared secret between Clean Access Serv3
You entered: cisco123
Is this correct? (y/n)? [y] y

>>> Configuring date and time:

The timezone is currently not set on this system.
Please identify a location so that time zone rules can be set correctly.
Please select a continent or ocean.
 1) Africa
 2) Americas
 3) Antarctica
 4) Arctic Ocean
 5) Asia
 6) Atlantic Ocean
 7) Australia
 8) Europe
 9) Indian Ocean
10) Pacific Ocean
11) none - I want to specify the time zone using the Posix TZ format.
```

continues

Example 7-3 *NAM Setup/Configuration Script (Continued)*

```
#? 2
Please select a country.
 1) Anguilla            18) Ecuador              35) Paraguay
 2) Antigua & Barbuda   19) El Salvador          36) Peru
 3) Argentina           20) French Guiana        37) Puerto Rico
 4) Aruba               21) Greenland            38) St Kitts & Nevis
 5) Bahamas             22) Grenada              39) St Lucia
 6) Barbados            23) Guadeloupe           40) St Pierre & Miquelon
 7) Belize              24) Guatemala            41) St Vincent
 8) Bolivia             25) Guyana               42) Suriname
 9) Brazil              26) Haiti                43) Trinidad & Tobago
10) Canada              27) Honduras             44) Turks & Caicos Is
11) Cayman Islands      28) Jamaica              45) United States
12) Chile               29) Martinique           46) Uruguay
13) Colombia            30) Mexico               47) Venezuela
14) Costa Rica          31) Montserrat           48) Virgin Islands (UK)
15) Cuba                32) Netherlands Antilles 49) Virgin Islands (US)
16) Dominica            33) Nicaragua
17) Dominican Republic  34) Panama
#? 45
Please select one of the following time zone regions.
 1) Eastern Time
 2) Eastern Time - Michigan - most locations
 3) Eastern Time - Kentucky - Louisville area
 4) Eastern Time - Kentucky - Wayne County
 5) Eastern Standard Time - Indiana - most locations
 6) Eastern Standard Time - Indiana - Crawford County
 7) Eastern Standard Time - Indiana - Starke County
 8) Eastern Standard Time - Indiana - Switzerland County
 9) Central Time
10) Central Time - Michigan - Wisconsin border
11) Central Time - North Dakota - Oliver County
12) Mountain Time
13) Mountain Time - south Idaho & east Oregon
14) Mountain Time - Navajo
15) Mountain Standard Time - Arizona
16) Pacific Time
17) Alaska Time
18) Alaska Time - Alaska panhandle
19) Alaska Time - Alaska panhandle neck
20) Alaska Time - west Alaska
21) Aleutian Islands
22) Hawaii
#? 16

The following information has been given:

        United States
        Pacific Time

Is the above information OK?
```

Example 7-3 *NAM Setup/Configuration Script (Continued)*

```
1) Yes
2) No
#? 1
Updating timezone information...

Current date and time hh:mm:ss mm/dd/yy [05:50:43 12/06/06]:
You entered 05:50:43 12/06/06 Is this correct? (y/n)? [y]
Wed Dec  6 05:50:43 PST 2006

You must generate a valid SSL certificate in order to use the Clean Access Manager's
secure web console.
Please answer the following questions correctly.
Information for a new SSL certificate:
Enter fully qualified domain name or IP: nam1.selab.net
Enter organization unit name: selab
Enter organization name: se_org
Enter city name: san jose
Enter state code: ca
Enter 2 letter country code: us

You entered the following:
Domain: cam1.selab.net
Organization unit: selab
Organization name: se_org
City name: san jose
State code: ca
Country code: us
Is this correct? (y/n)? [y]
Generating SSL Certificate...
CA signing: /root/.tomcat.csr -> /root/.tomcat.crt:
CA verifying: /root/.tomcat.crt <-> CA cert
/root/.tomcat.crt: OK
Done

For security reasons, it is highly recommended that you change the default passwords
for the root user.
User: root
Changing password for user root.
New UNIX password: ********

Retype new UNIX password: ********
passwd(pam_unix)[2087]: password changed for root
passwd: all authentication tokens updated successfully.

Changes require a RESTART of Clean Access Manager.

Configuration is complete.

Logrotate configuration
Initializing Clean Access Manager Database...
Done
Install has completed. Press <ENTER> to reboot.
```

NAC Licensing

After setting up NAM and accessing the GUI (**https://**NAM_IP) for the first time, you will be prompted to enter a valid product license. Without it, you cannot proceed with further NAC configurations. See Figure 7-1 for initial license installation.

Figure 7-1   *NAC Manager Licensing Page*

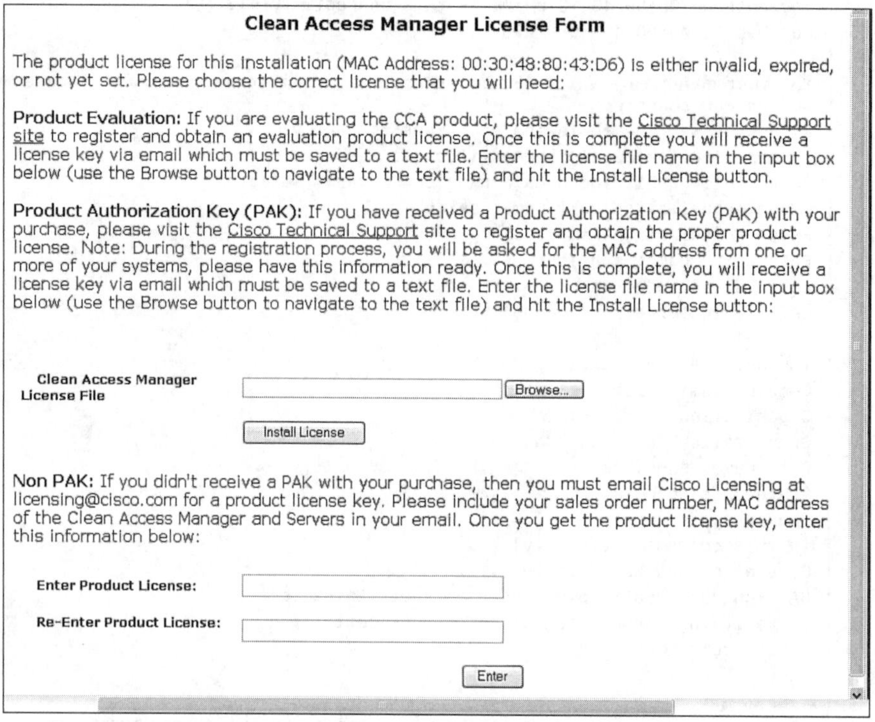

Clean Access Manager License Form

The product license for this installation (MAC Address: 00:30:48:80:43:D6) is either invalid, expired, or not yet set. Please choose the correct license that you will need:

Product Evaluation: If you are evaluating the CCA product, please visit the <u>Cisco Technical Support site</u> to register and obtain an evaluation product license. Once this is complete you will receive a license key via email which must be saved to a text file. Enter the license file name in the input box below (use the Browse button to navigate to the text file) and hit the Install License button.

Product Authorization Key (PAK): If you have received a Product Authorization Key (PAK) with your purchase, please visit the <u>Cisco Technical Support</u> site to register and obtain the proper product license. Note: During the registration process, you will be asked for the MAC address from one or more of your systems, please have this information ready. Once this is complete, you will receive a license key via email which must be saved to a text file. Enter the license file name in the input box below (use the Browse button to navigate to the text file) and hit the Install License button:

Clean Access Manager License File   [   ] [Browse...]

[Install License]

Non PAK: If you didn't receive a PAK with your purchase, then you must email Cisco Licensing at licensing@cisco.com for a product license key. Please include your sales order number, MAC address of the Clean Access Manager and Servers in your email. Once you get the product license key, enter this information below:

Enter Product License: [   ]

Re-Enter Product License: [   ]

[Enter]

There are two available licensing options.

- **Clean Access FlexLM License Files**   If you have a product activation key from your order, go to http://www.cisco.com/go/license with your Cisco.com ID and enter the PAK to receive a license file via e-mail. You will have to enter the MAC address of the primary NAM Ethernet0 interface. For failover, you will have to enter the Ethernet0 MAC address of the backup NAM as well. After you have the license file on your computer, click the **Browse** button to locate the license file on your computer and then **Install License**.

- **Perfigo Product License Key**   Legacy Pre-Cisco license key format. If you have a legacy key, you can enter it at the bottom where it states **Enter Product License**. Then click **Enter**.

After the license file or legacy product license is installed, you will be redirected to the admin login page of NAM. The default NAM login is **admin/cisco123**.

For future license additions and updates, simply go to **Administration > CCA Manager > Licensing** and upload additional licenses. See Figure 7-2 for updated licenses.

Figure 7-2   *NAM Licensing Page with Installed Server Count*

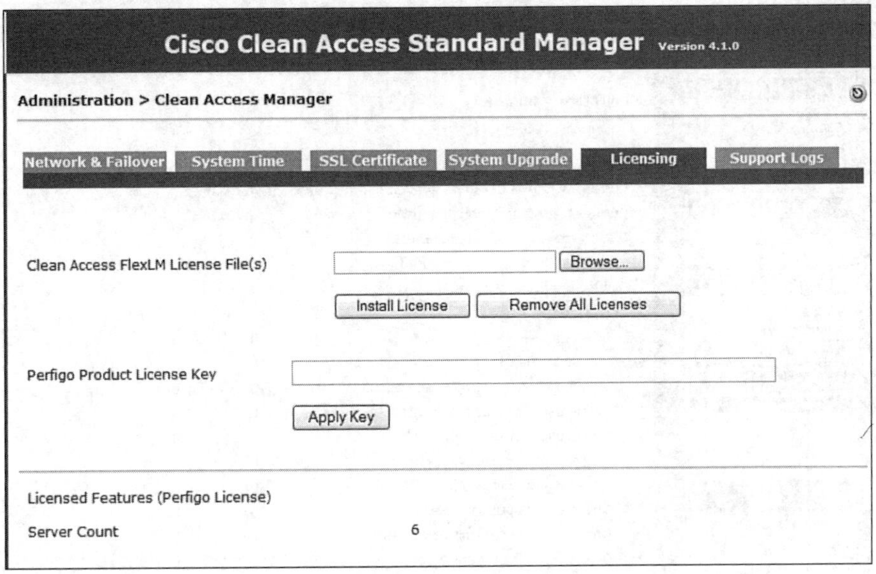

NAM GUI Description

After the initial licensing, all NAM configurations are performed via a secured web browser session at **https://***NAM_IP*. Figure 7-3 shows the initial NAM login screen.

Figure 7-3   *Initial NAM Login Screen*

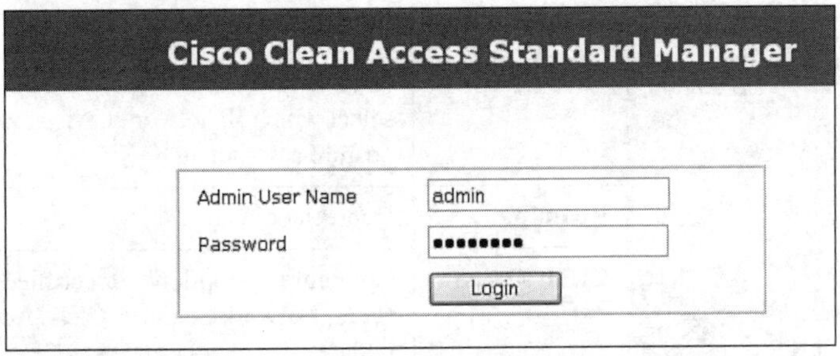

After you enter the NAM GUI, you can change the admin account and password under the **Administration > Admin Users** page. After logging in, the main NAM configuration screen is displayed, as shown in Figure 7-4.

Figure 7-4 *Main NAM Configuration Screen*

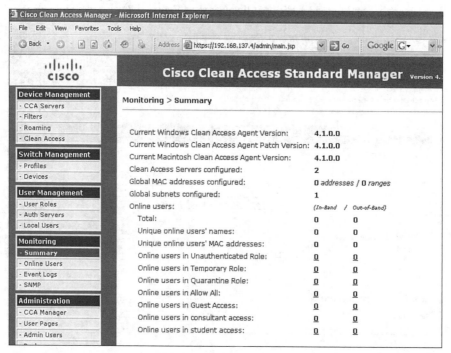

The main NAM configuration screen is divided into five sections on the left side of the screen, as described in Table 7-1.

Table 7-1 *NAM Configuration Screen*

Section	Feature	Description
Device Management	**CCA Servers**	NAS server configuration.
	Filters	Used to create MAC address authentication or to select which IP network devices will bypass login and posture assessment.
	Roaming	Deprecated feature.
	Clean Access	Configuration options for certified devices, general setup, Network Scanner, Clean Access Agent, and updates (for checks and rules).
Switch Management (Used for out-of-band deployments only)	**Profiles**	Creating out-of-band switch profiles.
	Devices	Adding and configuring out-of-band switches.

Table 7-1   *NAM Configuration Screen (Continued)*

User Management	User Roles	Creating user roles and access policies.
	Auth Servers	Configuring various back-end authentication servers such as Kerberos, RADIUS, Windows NT, LDAP[1], Active Directory SSO[2], Windows NetBIOS SSO, Cisco VPN[3] SSO, and Allow All. Also used for attribute mapping.
	Local Users	Local user database on NAM appliance.
Monitoring	Summary	Main NAM summary page.
	Online Users	Summary of online users.
	Event Logs	NAM/NAS event logs.
	SNMP	SNMP[4] configuration.
Administration	CCA Manager	NAM configuration.
	User Pages	Creation of clientless web access pages and Agent access for various device platforms, such as Windows, Mac OS, Linux, and so on. Must configure this step as part of initial configuration.
	Admin Users	Configuration of administrator users and group accounts.
	Backup	NAM configuration backup. This also backs up all NAS configurations.

1.   LDAP = Lightweight Directory Access Protocol

2.   SSO = Single Sign-On

3.   VPN = Virtual Private Network

4.   SNMP = Simple Network Management Protocol

NAS Overview

NAS is the policy enforcer between the trusted and untrusted networks. This section describes how to install and configure NAS (also known as the CCA server).

NAS Hardware Installation Requirements

Because NAS is the true workhorse of the NAC architecture, it requires high performance hardware. In the In-Band mode, all traffic will pass through NAS between its Untrusted and Trusted Ethernet interfaces. In Out-of-Band mode, only the authentication traffic passes through the NAS. Thus, OOB is typically used for higher-performance LAN deployments.

If HA is desired, three interfaces are required. Ethernet0 is the trusted inside interface. Ethernet1 is the untrusted client networks. The third Ethernet interface is used for failover purposes. An option for the failover interface can be the serial interface on the NAS appliance. However, the third Ethernet interface is recommended for higher-speed transfer of failover data.

NOTE For NAM and NAS HA, Cisco recommends enabling and connecting both the Ethernet and serial failover interfaces.

NAS Software Installation Requirements

The only software requirement is the Cisco NAC Appliance – Clean Access CD.

NAS Software License Requirement

There is no license key to enter into the NAS during installation. The NAM controls how many NAS devices can be deployed and managed. All licensing is handled through the NAM licensing GUI.

How to Connect NAS

NAS is configured using the same process as described for the NAM installation, with the following options available:

- Use a keyboard and monitor; no mouse required.
- Connect to NAS via a serial cable from a laptop or desktop PC running HyperTerminal or any other similar terminal emulation application.

After the installation of the NAS software, **https://*NAS_IP*/admin** is used to access the NAS directly. An example is https://192.168.137.10/admin.

Performing Initial NAS Configurations

If your NAS is preinstalled with the NAS software from Cisco, you may skip the following manual CD installation discussion and proceed directly to the setup script. To run the setup script from the CLI, simply type in **service perfigo config**.

If your NAS is not preinstalled with the NAS software from Cisco, you will have to manually install the NAS software via the Cisco NAC Appliance – Clean Access CD. Insert the NAC CD into the CD-ROM drive of the NAM appliance and reboot the appliance.

The NAC Appliance should boot from the CD-ROM and display the NAC installation status. The NAS installation process is very similar to the NAM installation process described earlier. For the sake of conserving space, the full installation process will not be shown here, although Example 7-4 provides a condensed version:

Step 1   Insert the Cisco NAC Appliance – Clean Access CD and reboot NAS Appliance.

Step 2   When prompted to select CCA Manager or CCA Server, choose **CCA Server**.

Step 3   Be patient. NAS installation can take up to 1 hour. When the setup and configuration script launches, enter all required IP information. The NAS setup script and configuration script is shown in Example 7-4.

NOTE   If you have completed the setup and configuration script and decide to reconfigure certain parameters, simply access the CLI via SSH, keyboard and monitor, or serial console and type **service perfigo config** to rerun the script. Cisco best practice recommends a reboot after running the setup script.

Example 7-4 *Sample NAS Setup Script*

```
Welcome to the Cisco Clean Access Server quick configuration utility.

Note that you need to be root to execute this utility.

The utility will now ask you a series of configuration questions.
Please answer them carefully.

Cisco Clean Access Server, (C) 2006 Cisco Systems, Inc.
Configuring the network interfaces:

Please enter the IP address for the interface eth0 [10.1.110.2]:
You entered 10.1.110.2. Is this correct? (y/n)? [y]

Please enter the netmask for the interface eth0 [255.255.255.0]:
You entered 255.255.255.0. Is this correct? (y/n)? [y]

Please enter the IP address for the default gateway [10.1.110.1]:
You entered 10.1.110.1. Is this correct? (y/n)? [y]

[Vlan Id Passthrough] for packets from eth0 to eth1 is disabled.
Would you like to enable it? (y/n)? [n]

[Management Vlan Tagging] for egress packets of eth0 is disabled.
Would you like to enable it? (y/n)? [n]
```

continues

Example 7-4 *Sample NAS Setup Script (Continued)*

```
Please enter the IP address for the untrusted interface eth1 [10.1.111.2]:
You entered 10.1.111.2. Is this correct? (y/n)? [y]

Please enter the netmask for the interface eth1 [255.255.255.0]:
You entered 255.255.255.0. Is this correct? (y/n)? [y]

Please enter the IP address for the default gateway [10.1.111.1]:
You entered 10.1.111.1. Is this correct? (y/n)? [y]

[Vlan Id Passthrough] for packets from eth1 to eth0 is disabled.
Would you like to enable it? (y/n)? [n]

[Management Vlan Tagging] for egress packets of eth1 is disabled.
Would you like to enable it? (y/n)? [n]

Please enter the hostname [cas1]:
You entered cas1. Is this correct? (y/n)? [y]

Please enter the IP address for the name server: [10.1.112.105]:
You entered 10.1.112.105. Is this correct? (y/n)? [y]

Would you like to change shared secret? (y/n)? [y]
Please enter the shared secret: cisco123
You entered: cisco123
Is this correct? (y/n)? [y]

>>> Configuring date and time:


The timezone is currently set to:America/Los_Angeles
Would you like to change this setting? (y/n)? [y] n

Current date and time hh:mm:ss mm/dd/yy [14:26:55 12/08/06]:
You entered 14:26:55 12/08/06. Is this correct? (y/n)? [y]
Fri Dec  8 14:26:55 PST 2006

You must generate a valid SSL certificate in order to use the Clean Access Server's
secure web console.
Please answer the following questions correctly.
Information for a new SSL certificate:
Enter fully qualified domain name or IP: cas1.SElab.net
Enter organization unit name: SElab
Enter organization name: SE
Enter city name: San Jose
Enter state code: ca
Enter 2 letter country code: us

You entered the following:
Domain: cas1.SElab.net
Organization unit: SElab
Organization name: SE
City name: San Jose
```

Example 7-4 *Sample NAS Setup Script (Continued)*

```
State code: ca
Country code: us
Is this correct? (y/n)? [y] y
Generating SSL Certificate...
CA signing: /root/.tomcat.csr -> /root/.tomcat.crt:
CA verifying: /root/.tomcat.crt <-> CA cert
/root/.tomcat.crt: OK
Done

For security reasons, it is highly recommended that you change the default password
for the root user.
User: root
Changing password for user root.
New UNIX password:
Retype new UNIX password:
passwd: all authentication tokens updated successfully.


Would you like to change the default password for the web console admin user
password? (y/n)? [y]
Please enter an appropriately secure password for the web console admin user.

New password for web console admin:
Confirm new password for web console admin:
Web console admin password changed successfully.
Configuration is complete.
[root@cas1 ~]#
```

NAS GUI Description

There are two ways to connect to NAS via the GUI: through the NAM GUI and by connecting directly to the NAS GUI.

To connect to the NAS through the NAM GUI, do the following:

Step 1 Within the NAM interface, select **Device Management > CCA Servers**.

Step 2 Click the **Connection** icon under the **Manage** column. See Figure 7-5.

To connect to the NAS GUI directly, do the following:

Step 1 Type **https://***NAS_IP***/admin**. For example, **https://192.168.137.3/ admin**.

Step 2 When prompted to log in, enter the web console login and password. The default should be **admin/cisco123**. After you log in, the NAS GUI screen is shown. Within this screen, you can make IP information changes and reboot if necessary. See Figure 7-6 for NAS IP configuration.

Figure 7-5 *Managing a NAS Within the NAM GUI*

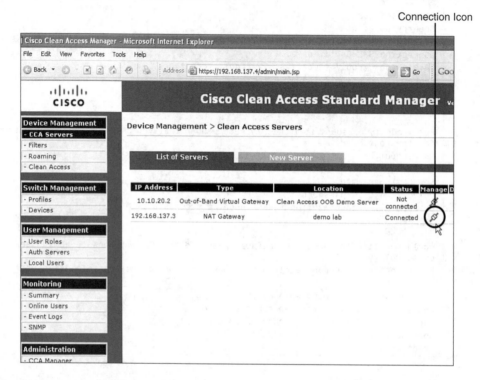

Figure 7-6 *NAS IP Address Configuration*

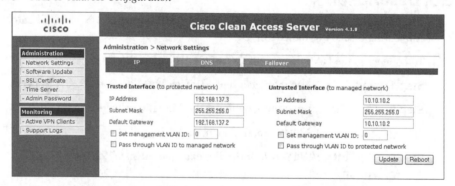

The Administration panel on the left side is fairly self-explanatory:

- **Network Settings**   Used for IP info, Domain Name System (DNS), and failover changes. For monitoring HA failover, the failover screen here is useful in showing the connection status of this NAS versus the standby NAS. Figure 7-7 shows the NAS Failover GUI status page.

Figure 7-7 *NAS Failover Configuration Page*

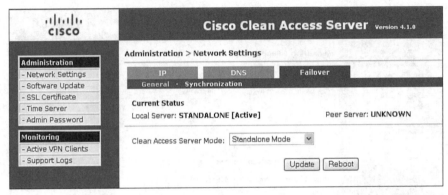

- **Software Update**   Used to update the NAS software. Can also be done from the NAM GUI.

- **SSL Certificate**   Used to generate, import, and export digital certificates. Secure Sockets Layer certificates should typically be generated from the NAM GUI.

- **Time Server**   Used to synchronize NAS with a dedicated NTP server. The NAS and NAM time difference must be less than 5 minutes for NAC to function properly. *This is very important.*

- **Admin Password**   Update admin password.

The Monitoring panel includes the following:

- **Active VPN Clients**   This feature is used for monitoring RADIUS accounting packets received from the wireless LAN Controller or VPN concentrator. During SSO, the **List All VPN Clients** button will show info relating to client IP, client name, and the VPN server IP based on the received RADIUS accounting packets.

- **Support Logs**   Very useful for troubleshooting and debugging communications from the clients to NAS and to NAM. Cisco best practices recommend enabling logging levels to **ALL** only during troubleshooting at the Cisco Technical Assistance Center's request. Set logging level to **Severe** during normal operations. The **Download** button allows admins to review local log files for troubleshooting. See Figure 7-8.

Figure 7-8 *Viewing and Setting NAS Support Logs*

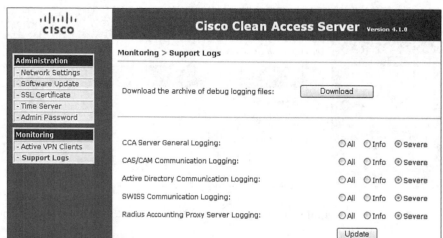

Configuring NAS Deployment Mode

NAS can be deployed in several modes.

In-Band Virtual Gateway (VGW), Real-IP Gateway, or NAT (Network Address Translation) Gateway

Out-of-Band Virtual Gateway, Real-IP Gateway, or NAT Gateway

In-Band Deployment Options

The in-band deployment options are as follows:

- **VGW** Virtual Gateway is probably the easiest and quickest way to deploy NAC. NAS simply acts as a bridge and policy enforcement gateway between the end clients and the upstream router. Figure 7-9 shows a sample in-band VGW deployment.

- **Real-IP** Real-IP gateway turns the NAS appliance into a routing gateway. Both Ethernet0 (trusted network) and Ethernet1 (Untrusted client network) are assigned unique IP addresses. Static routes are configured within NAS to maintain network connectivity. Figure 7-10 shows a sample in-band Real-IP deployment.

Figure 7-9   *In-Band VGW Deployment*

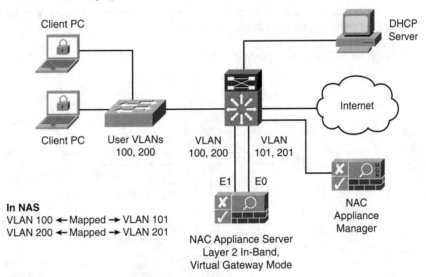

In NAS
VLAN 100 ← Mapped → VLAN 101
VLAN 200 ← Mapped → VLAN 201

Figure 7-10   *In-Band Real-IP Deployment*

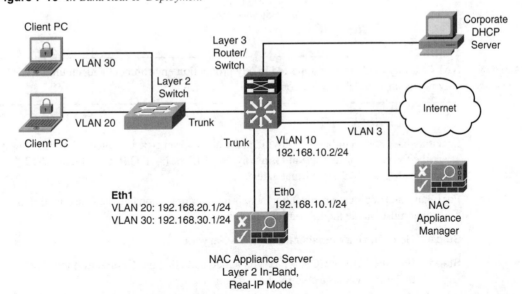

- **NAT Gateway**   NAT gateway mode is basically the same as the Real-IP mode. The only difference is that private NAT addresses are assigned to the Ethernet1 (untrusted client network) interface. NAS can perform dynamic NAT, one-to-one NAT, or Port Address Translation between the Ethernet0 and Ethernet1 interfaces. However,

NAT functionality consumes additional CPU resources and limits the total performance of the NAS Appliance. Figure 7-11 shows an example of an in-band NAT gateway lab-only deployment.

Figure 7-11   *In-Band NAT Gateway Lab-Only Deployment*

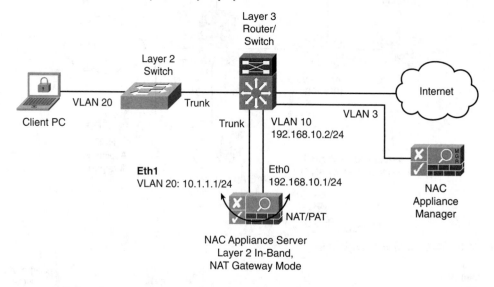

CAUTION   NAT Gateway mode is *not* supported in any production environment and should be used only in a controlled lab test network.

For either an L2 or L3 in-band deployment, the NAS server type is treated the same. Simply select the **Server Type** as **Virtual Gateway**, **Real-IP**, or **NAT Gateway**. Figure 7-12 shows how to add NAS as a virtual gateway.

For L3 in-band deployment, meaning there is a router or L3 hop between the clients and the NAS, you must enable the L3 routing check box:

Step 1   Go to **Device Management > CCA Servers**.

Step 2   Find the NAS or CCA server you added and click the **Connection** icon under the **Manage** column. See Figure 7-5.

Step 3   Select the **Network** tab and check **Enable L3 Support**. See Figure 7-13.

Figure 7-12 *Adding NAS as a Virtual Gateway*

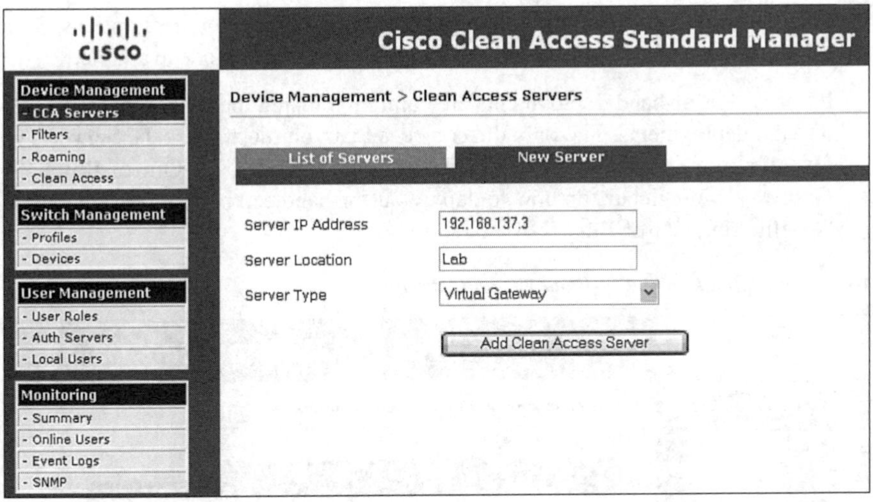

Figure 7-13 *Enabling L3 Support in NAS*

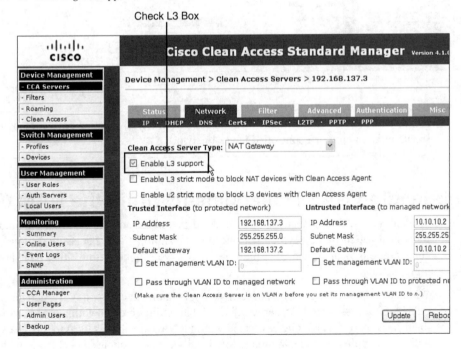

Out-of-Band Deployment Options

Out-of-band deployment options are similar to in-band deployment options. Simply select the mode best suited for your environment from the three mode available.

L2 or L3 out-of-band deployments are configured using the same process as L2 or L3 in-band deployments. The only difference is that you must select the **Server Type** as **Out-of-Band** <mode>. Figure 7-14 shows how to add NAS as **Out-of-Band Virtual Gateway**. More details on how to deploy out-of-band can be found in Chapter 10, "Configuring Out-of-Band."

Figure 7-14 *Adding NAS as an Out-of-Band Virtual Gateway*

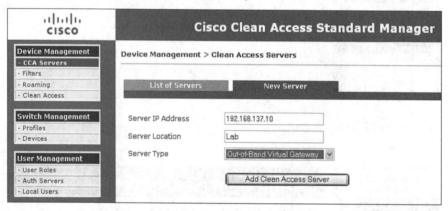

NOTE Out-of-Band NAT Gateway mode is *not* supported in any production environment and should be used only in a controlled lab test network.

Understanding NAS Management Within the NAM GUI

All deployed NAS appliances will fall under the administration of one NAM appliance for typical enterprise deployments. Therefore, the administrator can easily deploy configurations to an individual or multiple NAS servers quickly from either global or local policy settings.

Within the NAM configuration page, the administrator can create, modify, and delete policies for all managed NAS servers. Any global settings created within NAM are applied to all NAS servers. Any policies created within a NAS are always local to that NAS and will not be applied as a global policy. Any locally created policies and changes within a NAS override the global setting by the NAM.

Global Versus Local Settings

The concept of global versus local settings can help with quick and efficient NAC deployments. Most parameters are configured globally and automatically applied to all NAS servers.

Global Settings

Global settings include fields that apply to all added NAS servers. Figure 7-15 shows the global settings in the NAM GUI.

Figure 7-15 *Global Settings for All NAS Servers*

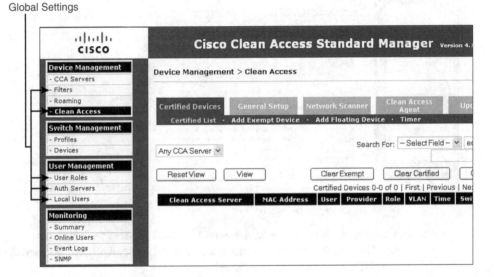

The global parameters are as follows:

- **Device Management > Filters**   This is where you set login and posture assessment exceptions for IP and MAC addresses and subnets. Typically, this is used when specific devices such as IP phones, printers, and other non-NAC responding devices should bypass login and posture assessment. For an IP phone, you can enter its MAC address, select **IGNORE** under **Access Type**, and it will bypass NAC. Figure 7-16 shows an IP phone added to the filter list with the IGNORE action assigned to that device.

Figure 7-16 *NAC Bypass or Filter Entry GUI*

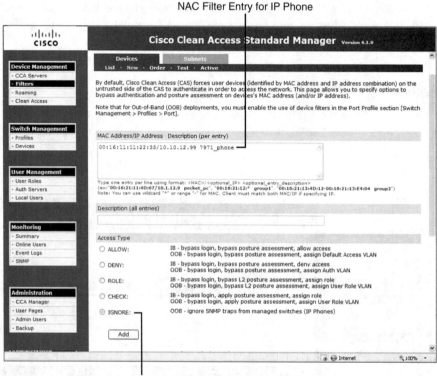

- **Device Management > Clean Access > Certified Devices > Certified List**   The certified devices list shows all authenticated and posture assessed devices. Figure 7-17 has a certified user "jdoe".

- **Device Management > Clean Access > General Setup**   This is where you set requirements for web login and Clean Access Agent login. Under Clean Access Agent login, if you require all employees with any Windows machine to install the NAC agent on their PC, simply select User Role: **Employee,** Operating System: **WINDOWS_ALL,** and check the **Require Use of Clean Access Agent** box. See Figure 7-18.

- **Device Management > Clean Access > Network Scanner**   This is where you set loading and configuration of the built-in Nessus scanner for web login posture assessments. Figure 7-19 shows the web login scanner configuration page.

Figure 7-17 *User "jdoe" Shown as a Certified Device on a Network*

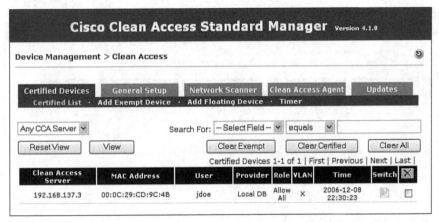

Figure 7-18 *Web and Agent Login Requirement GUI*

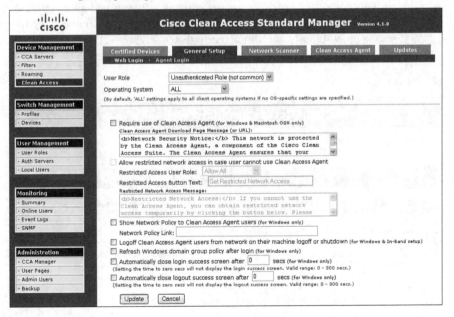

Figure 7-19 *Network Scanner Configuration GUI for Web Login Users*

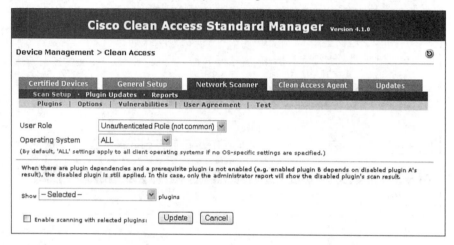

- **Device Management > Clean Access > Clean Access Agent** Here you configure all NAC compliance policies such as hotfixes, antivirus and antispyware definitions, and so on. This is a very useful page. You will spend some initial setup time here setting up NAC software compliance policies. Figure 7-20 shows a NAC software compliance configuration page.

Figure 7-20 *NAC Agent Policy GUI*

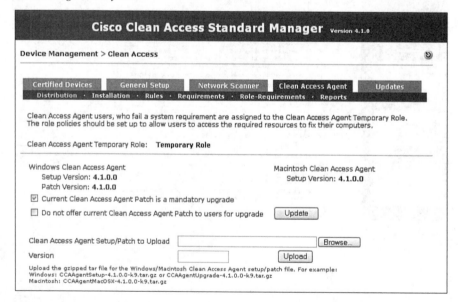

- **Device Management > Clean Access > Updates**   This shows the version summary of Cisco checks and rules, supported antivirus and antispyware product count, and agent upgrade version info. Figure 7-21 provides an overall summary. All the updates received here come directly from a Cisco server. This helps to keep NAM updated and saves the administrator time from manually going to all supported antivirus and antispyware vendors to download the latest definitions. The same applies to OS hotfixes as well.

Figure 7-21 *Summary of Updates for Checks and Rules, Antivirus and Antispyware List, and Clients*

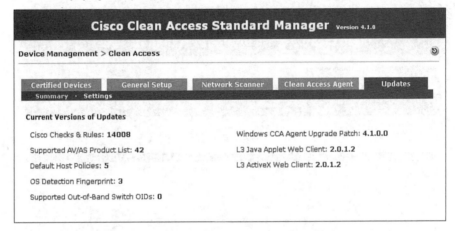

- **User Management > User Roles**   Use this section for creating user roles, such as Unauthenticated, Quarantine, Allow All, Guest, and so on, which authenticated users are assigned to. For In-Band mode, traffic control policies and bandwidth per role assignment are configured here. See Figure 7-22.

Figure 7-22 *User Roles and Policies Configuration GUI*

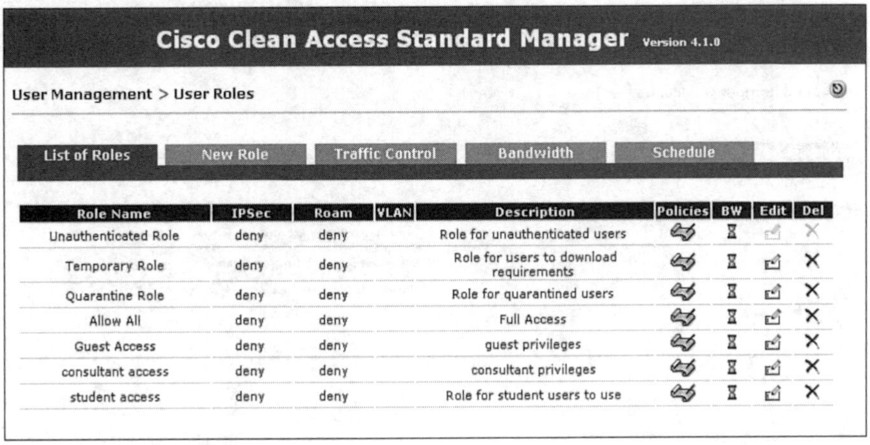

Cisco Clean Access Standard Manager Version 4.1.0

User Management > User Roles

| List of Roles | New Role | Traffic Control | Bandwidth | Schedule |

Role Name	IPSec	Roam	VLAN	Description	Policies	BW	Edit	Del
Unauthenticated Role	deny	deny		Role for unauthenticated users				✕
Temporary Role	deny	deny		Role for users to download requirements				✕
Quarantine Role	deny	deny		Role for quarantined users				✕
Allow All	deny	deny		Full Access				✕
Guest Access	deny	deny		guest privileges				✕
consultant access	deny	deny		consultant privileges				✕
student access	deny	deny		Role for student users to use				✕

- **User Management > Auth Servers**   Use this section to define which back-end authentication server will be used to authenticate users. Authentication server types include Kerberos, RADIUS, Window NT, LDAP, Active Directory Single-Sign-On, Windows NetBIOS SSO, Cisco VPN SSO, and Allow All. Figure 7-23 shows four authentication server types. A detailed example of how to configure Active Directory Single-Sign-On is shown in Chapter 11, "Configuring Single Sign-On." You can also test whether your authentication server is configured correctly via the **Auth Test** tab (not available for Active Directory SSO due to Kerberos implementation).

Figure 7-23 *Multiple Authentication Servers Configured*

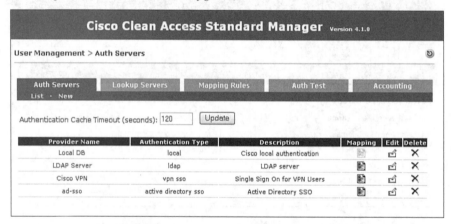

- **User Management > Local Users**   This is where you set the local user database internal to NAM. The guest user is typically created here. This local database is used when an external database is not available. See Figure 7-24 for an example of multiple users created within the local database.

Figure 7-24 *Sample User Created Within the NAM Local Database*

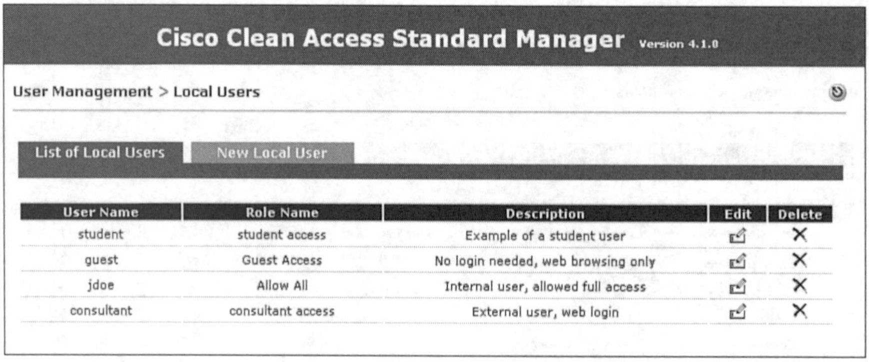

Cisco Clean Access Standard Manager   Version 4.1.0

User Management > Local Users

| List of Local Users | New Local User |

User Name	Role Name	Description	Edit	Delete
student	student access	Example of a student user	🖉	✕
guest	Guest Access	No login needed, web browsing only	🖉	✕
jdoe	Allow All	Internal user, allowed full access	🖉	✕
consultant	consultant access	External user, web login	🖉	✕

Local NAS Settings

Beyond the global settings you can apply in the NAM GUI, there are local settings you can apply to each NAS in the GUI for that NAS. The word *local* here refers to all settings that directly apply to the NAS being configured. There is no setting inheritance across multiple NAS appliances. To configure a specific NAS, you would access **Device Management > CCA Servers** and click the **Manage** icon for a specific NAS. Figure 7-25 shows the six tabs available for each NAS.

Figure 7-25 *NAS Status GUI*

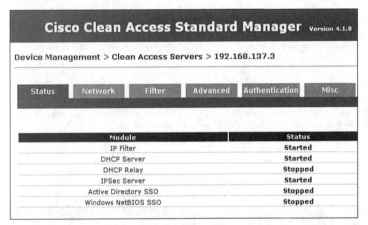

The list that follows explains each functional local NAS setting tab and subtab and its use:

- **Device Management > CCA Servers > Status**   As shown in Figure 7-25, the **Status** tab shows the status of the services running on the NAS.

- **Device Management > CCA Servers > Network > IP**   This is the IP configuration page for trusted and untrusted interfaces. For Layer 3 deployment (one or more router hops between the clients and NAS server), the **Enable L3 Support** box must be checked. Be sure to click **Update** after changing or updating settings. NAS will notify you if a reboot is required. See Figure 7-26.

- **Device Management > CCA Servers > Network > DHCP > DHCP Status**   This is where you set NAS DHCP services. If you are keeping your corporate DHCP server in use and not using the NAS DHCP services, make sure to select **None**. Figure 7-27 shows the NAS DHCP configuration page.

- **Device Management > CCA Servers > Network > DHCP > Subnet List**   This is the NAS DHCP manual IP subnet creation page.

- **Device Management > CCA Servers > Network > DHCP > Reserved IPs**   This shows a list of MAC addresses associated with reserved IP addresses.

- **Device Management > CCA Servers > Network > DHCP > Auto-Generate**   This allows automatic generation of IP subnets by NAS. The administrator defines the subnet sizes.

Figure 7-26 *NAS IP Configuration GUI*

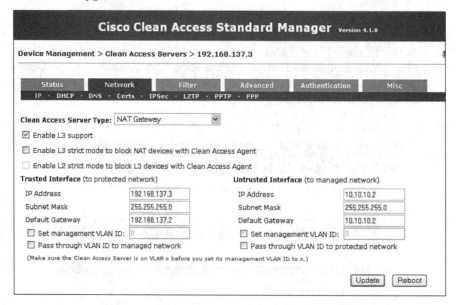

Figure 7-27 *NAS DHCP Services Configuration GUI*

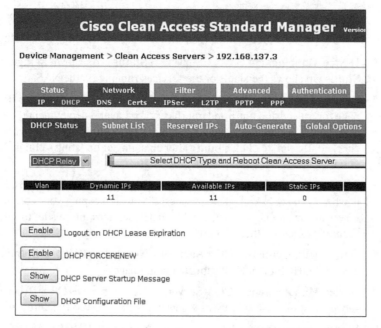

- **Device Management > CCA Servers > Network > DHCP > Global Options**   This is where you enable user-specific DHCP options.

- **Device Management > CCA Servers > Network > DHCP > Global Action**   This allows global changes to be made to all DHCP subnets defined on NAS without manually editing each DHCP subnet.

- **Device Management > CCA Servers > Network > DNS**   This is the NAS DNS configuration page. Figure 7-28 shows where you configure the hostname, domain name, and DNS server IP addresses. Make sure to click the **Update** button after entering DNS information.

Figure 7-28 *NAS DNS Configuration GUI*

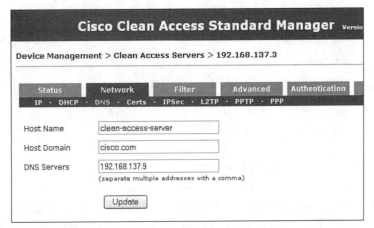

- **Device Management > CCA Servers > Network > Certs**   This is the NAS Certificate import, export, and generation page as shown in Figure 7-29.

- **Device Management > CCA Servers > Network > IPsec**   Deprecated feature in 4.x.

- **Device Management > CCA Servers > Network > L2TP**   Deprecated feature in 4.x.

- **Device Management > CCA Servers > Network > PPTP**   Deprecated feature in 4.x.

- **Device Management > CCA Servers > Network > PPP**   Deprecated feature in 4.x.

- **Device Management > CCA Servers > Filter > Devices**   This is where you set login and posture assessment exceptions for IP and MAC addresses and subnets. Typically, this is used when specific devices such as IP phones, printers, and other non-NAC responding devices should bypass login and posture assessment. For an IP phone, if you enter its MAC address and select **IGNORE** under **Access Type**, it will bypass NAC. See Figure 7-16 earlier where non-NAC responding devices can be added to bypass NAC.

- **Device Management > CCA Servers > Filter > Subnets**   Individual IP or IP subnets entered here can be **allow**, **deny**, or assigned to specific user roles. "**allow**" bypasses NAC. **deny** means no network access through NAS.

Figure 7-29 *NAS Certificate Management GUI*

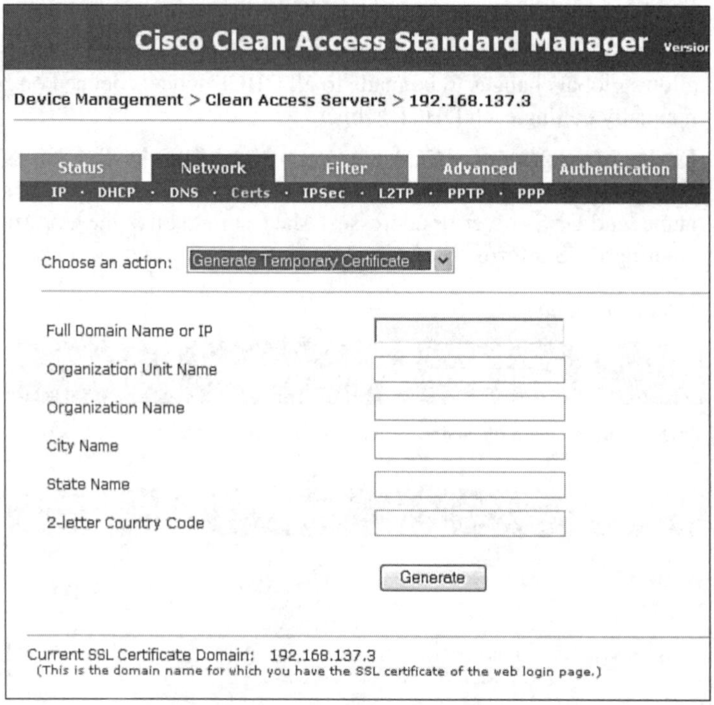

- **Device Management > CCA Servers > Filter > Roles > Traffic Control** This is where you set network access policies assigned to each access role within the selected NAS. Cisco best practices recommend that any policy modifications to any defined roles should be performed at the global level under **User Management > User Roles** to keep policy administration in one central location.

- **Device Management > CCA Servers > Filter > Roles > Allowed Hosts** This is where you set hosts allowed during remediation while in the Quarantine or Temporary role. Cisco best practices recommend that any policy modifications to any defined roles should be performed at the global level under **User Management > User Roles** to keep policy administration in one central location.

- **Device Management > CCA Servers > Filter > Roles > Bandwidth** This is where you can set bandwidth management per role. This applies only to in-band deployment. Cisco best practices recommend that any policy modifications to any defined roles should be performed at the global level under **User Management > User Roles** to keep policy administration in one central location.

- **Device Management > CCA Servers > Filters > Clean Access > Certified Devices** Devices added in this page are exempted from NAC authentication and posture assessment for that specific NAS. Cisco best practices recommend that adding any exempt devices should be performed at the global level.

- **Device Management > CCA Servers > Filter > Clean Access > Add Floating Device**   This is where you can add floating devices that enforce NAC authentication and assessment on a per-session basis for a specific NAS. These devices typically refer to routers, VPN concentrators, or firewall devices that have multiple PCs sitting behind them. Cisco best practices recommend that adding any floating devices should be performed at the global level. See Figure 7-30.

Figure 7-30 *Local Floating Devices Added Within a Specific NAS*

- **Device Management > CCA Servers > Filter > Fallback**   This is useful when deploying NAS across WAN links to remote sites. This failsafe feature starting in 4.1.0 allows the NAS to allow all, block all, or ignore new connections when NAS loses connectivity to NAM due to WAN failure. Setting **Ignore** means that no new connections are allowed to pass through the NAS during the WAN failure. See Figure 7-31.

- **Device Management > CCA Servers > Advanced > Managed Subnet**   This is used mostly during L2 deployments. Managed subnets are used anytime NAS's untrusted interface is responsible for specific user VLANs or subnets. NAS creates an Address Resolution Protocol (ARP) entry for that subnet in order to properly communicate within that subnet space. See Figure 7-32.

- **Device Management > CCA Servers > Advanced > VLAN Mapping**   This is for L2 virtual gateway central NAS deployments only. This feature *must* be configured and enabled for L2 virtual gateway central deployments or there will be unexpected spanning tree behaviors on the network due to network loops. Cisco best practices recommend that VLAN mapping be configured prior to connecting the NAS untrusted

Ethernet1 interface on the network to prevent loops. See Figure 7-33 for sample configuration.

Figure 7-31 *NAS Fallback Configuration for Remote Sites Across the WAN*

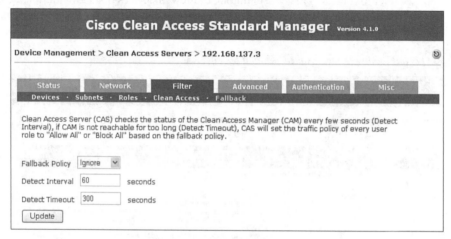

Figure 7-32 *Multiple User VLANs and Subnets Created as Managed Subnets*

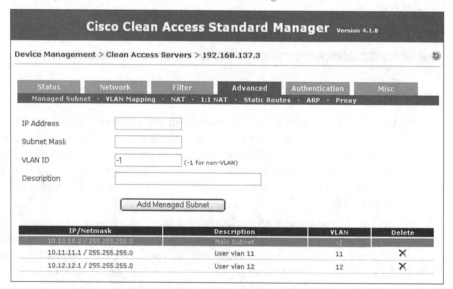

- **Device Management > CCA Servers > Advanced > NAT** This is where you set NAT session timers. Cisco best practices recommend that any NAT functionality within the NAS should be deployed only in lab environments and not production.

- **Device Management > CCA Servers > Advanced > 1:1 NAT** This is where you set one-to-one NAT configuration. Cisco best practices recommend that any NAT functionality within NAS should be deployed only in lab environments and not production.

Figure 7-33 *VLAN Mapping Requirement for L2 Virtual Gateway Central Deployment*

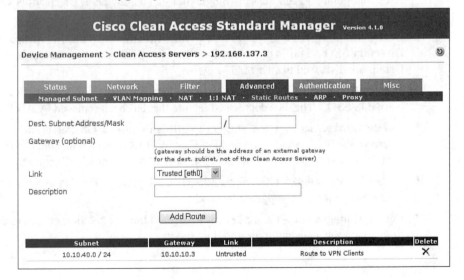

- **Device Management > CCA Servers > Advanced > Static Routes**   This is used for all L3 deployments. Because NAS does not support routing protocols, status routes must be configured for network reachability. This feature is not used for L2 deployments. See Figure 7-34.

Figure 7-34 *Static Routes Configured for L3 Deployments*

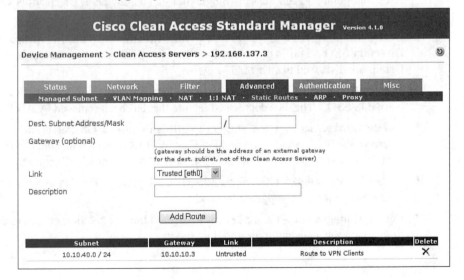

- **Device Management > CCA Servers > Advanced > ARP** This is where you create an ARP entry in the NAS.

- **Device Management > CCA Servers > Advanced > Proxy** Here you specify proxy server IP/port when NAS is deployed in an HTTP/HTTPS proxy environment. This setting redirects user HTTP requests to the proxy server.

- **Device Management > CCA Servers > Authentication > Login Page** This is where you set the local NAS login page that can override the global user login page when enabled. See Figure 7-35.

Figure 7-35 *Local NAS Login Pages Created for Windows, Mac OS, and Linux*

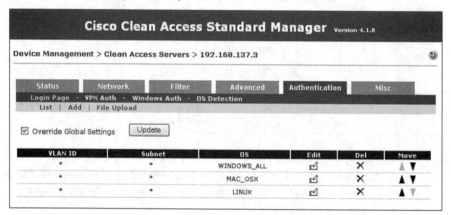

- **Device Management > CCA Servers > Authentication > VPN Auth** This is the NAS configuration page for VPN Single Sign-On deployment. Details of NAS VPN deployment are discussed in Chapter 11.

- **Device Management > CCA Servers > Authentication > Windows Auth > Active Directory SSO** This is the Active Directory Single Sign-On configuration page. Details are discussed in Chapter 11.

- **Device Management > CCA Servers > Authentication > Windows Auth > NetBIOS SSO** This is a deprecated feature that has been replaced by AD SSO.

- **Device Management > CCA Servers > Authentication > OS Detection** This is where you set the OS detection method used by NAS to detect the client's OS. The default method is to examine the HTTP header of the client HTTP request packet.

- **Device Management > CCA Servers > Misc > Update** This is the NAS software upgrade page including upgrade history.

- **Device Management > CCA Servers > Misc > Time** This shows the NAS current time, time zone, date and time, and time server.

NOTE	The NAS and NAM time and clock difference must be less than 5 minutes. If it is more than 5 minutes, clients might not be able to log in successfully.

- **Device Management > CCA Servers > Misc > Heartbeat Timer**   This shows the NAS heartbeat timer.

Adding Additional NAS Appliances

Now that NAM and the first NAS have been configured, they can be added to the network. Both NAM and NAS should be ping-able on the network. NAM will manage the NAS or multiple NAS appliances. Figure 7-12 shows how to add the first NAS. If you need to add more NAS appliances to the network, you can do so by following the explanation accompanying Figure 7-12.

Step 1   Select **Device Management > CCA Servers**.

Step 2   Select the **New Server** tab. Enter the appropriate new NAS information.

Summary

This chapter discussed the basics of the Cisco NAC appliance solution. Three key NAC components—NAM, NAS, and NAC agent—were covered. Details about NAM and NAS software installation were provided to assist with initial configuration and setup. NAM, which is the central administration server for monitoring and configuring NAS appliances, is the brain of the NAC solution because it defines and dictates which user roles and access policies to enforce. NAS, which is the workhorse of NAC, performs all user authentication requests, posture assessments, and PC remediation processes. The NAC agent, when installed on PCs, can gather all necessary information regarding the software application and version levels running to determine whether a PC is in compliance with corporate software policy.

Different NAS deployment scenarios were also discussed. NAS can be deployed in In-Band mode or Out-of-Band mode depending on your network architecture. Three NAS types were explained: Virtual Gateway, Real-IP, and NAT Gateway. Cisco best practices recommend that NAT Gateway should be deployed only in a lab environment and not in a production network.

Global settings and local settings were reviewed. Global settings are parameters defined within NAM and applied to all deployed NAS appliances. Local settings are specific parameters within each NAS that can override the global settings defined by NAM. Each NAS can be configured within the NAM GUI or via direct HTTPS access to that NAS.

This chapter covers the following topics:

- Configuring User Roles
- Configuring Role Assignment
- Configuring Authentication
- Configuring and Creating Traffic Policies
- Customizing User Pages and Guest Access

CHAPTER 8

The Building Blocks: Roles, Authentication, Traffic Policies, and User Pages

It is important that you understand how to configure the various authentication mechanisms and role assignment mechanisms to best apply various policies in your NAC Appliance deployment. After they are applied, you will be able to control authenticated and guest access using various traffic-filtering and bandwidth control mechanisms.

Configuring User Roles

User roles are an extremely important concept that you must completely understand before attempting to deploy Cisco NAC Appliance. Roles are used by NAC Appliance Manager in the same way that groups are used by Microsoft Active Directory (AD). They allow you to group settings that will be applied to user sessions. The settings that can be applied to the various user roles created in NAC Appliance Manager can allow for the control of traffic policies, VLAN assignment, session duration, vulnerability assessment, bandwidth restrictions, and other NAC policies.

When preparing for a NAC Appliance implementation, it is important that the administrator makes proper decisions regarding how users are grouped into user roles. The roles define the posture assessment checks that will be run on a host. In turn, the outcome of the assessment determines the privileges the host and user are given on the network. Because of this, it is critical that user roles be utilized appropriately. Proper role assignment and structure is critical to the success of any NAC Appliance deployment. NAC Appliance has two types of user roles: custom roles and built-in roles.

Creating Custom Roles

The base installation of NAC Appliance Manager includes three default roles: Unauthenticated, Temporary, and Quarantine. These three roles provide a starting framework for your NAC Appliance testing and implementation. When you are ready to begin deeper configuration of NAC roles and policies, you will most likely need to create custom roles to provide the top-level role groupings for application of various configuration parameters and policies.

To configure a custom role, you must first log in to the NAC Appliance Manager as an administrator. Then complete the following steps:

Step 1 Select **User Roles** from the navigation options on the left of the screen.

Step 2 Select **New Role** from the newly presented top navigation bar, as shown in Figure 8-1.

Figure 8-1 **New Role** *Option on the User Roles User Management Screen*

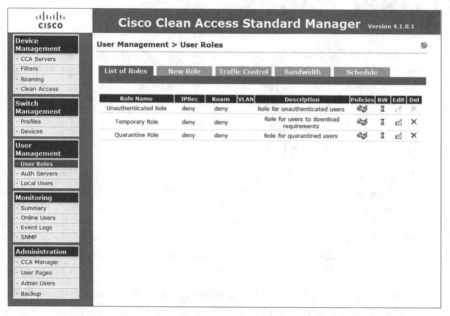

Step 3 Configure a role named "Test Role" with a simple description, as shown in Figure 8-2.

Step 4 Verify that the role type is **Normal Login Role**.

Step 5 Click the **Create Role** button, also displayed in Figure 8-2.

In addition to the required fundamental steps in the preceding list, several other configuration options are available on the role configuration page displayed in Figure 8-2. Those options are as follows:

- **Disable This Role** If this check box is enabled, this role will be unavailable for use. It can be re-enabled by clearing the check box and saving the changes.
- **Role Name** A text field that contains the name of the role as displayed throughout the other configuration pages as a selectable role.
- **Role Description** A text field that contains a description of this role and its purpose.

Figure 8-2 *Custom Role Configuration Screen*

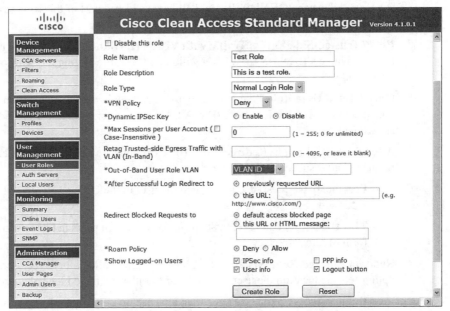

- **Role Type**   This selection box contains the options **Normal Login Role** and **Quarantine Role**:

  — **Normal Login Role**   This is assigned after successful authentication occurs. This role requires that all scans and Clean Access Agent requirements have been met successfully.

  — **Quarantine Role**   This role is assigned when NAC Appliance Network Scanning finds a vulnerability on the system. You will need to create an additional role of this type only if the default Quarantine role alone is not sufficient for your specific deployment.

- **VPN Policy**   This option is no longer recommended. If configured, this option makes the use of IPsec, Layer Two Tunnel Protocol (L2TP), and Point-to-Point Tunneling Protocol (PPTP) encryption by the client: **Deny**, **Option**, or **Enforced (Allowed)**.

- **Dynamic IPsec Key**   This option is no longer recommended. However, if enabled, the system provides users with a one-time key for their IPsec client after they successfully log in.

- **Max Sessions per User Account**—This option allows you to limit the number of concurrent sessions for which these user credentials can be used, from 1 to 255 or unlimited. You can also select the **Case-Insensitive** check box in order to not differentiate case-sensitive names in the session count (for example, JohnUser, Johnuser, johnuser, JOHNUSER could all be considered part of the same session count or separate session counts).

- **Retag Trusted-Side Egress Traffic with VLAN (In-Band)** If you configure this text box with a VLAN ID, the VLAN will retag the traffic exiting the NAS on the trusted side.

- **Out-of-Band User Role VLAN**—For out-of-band deployments, this option allows you to set the trusted-side VLAN ID or VLAN name after authentication and assessment.

- **After Successful Login Redirect To** You can configure a page for the user to be redirected after successful authentication:

  — **Previously Requested URL**—Send the user to the URL originally requested

  — **This URL**—Send the user to the page you define for users in this role in the form of http://*url_here*

- **Redirect Blocked Requests To** If a Block IP traffic policy blocks the user, this option sets the location the user is redirected to rather than the blocked address:

  — **Default Access Blocked Page**—Send the user to the default blocked access page

  — **This URL or HTML Message**—Send the user to the page you define for users in this role, in the form of http://*url_here*

- **Roam Policy** You can set whether this role allows IPsec, L2TP, and PPTP roaming. This feature is no longer recommended and has been deprecated.

- **Show Logged-On Users** If the user using this role is a web user, this option allows you to define which information is presented to the user on the logout page, such as **IPsec Info** (key), **PPP Info**, **User Info**, and **Logout Button**.

Depending on the type of role you are creating, you will utilize various settings on the role configuration page. When the role is created, you can use it throughout the NAC Appliance as well as edit it if required.

Editing or Deleting a Custom Role

After a role is created, you are allowed to return to the role configuration page to edit the role as necessary. In the **User Management** section of the user roles page, you will see a list of available roles for your deployment, which includes the default and custom roles configured. Next to each role name are several options and icons. Selecting the icon in the **Edit** column corresponding to the role you want to modify returns you to the role configuration page.

In addition, should you want to remove a role, you can select the corresponding icon in the **Del** column of the user roles listing page.

NOTE   Any user configured for a role that has been deleted will not be able to access the network. However, after the role is deleted, all current user sessions will remain active. To clear these sessions and allow the user to reconnect using another active role, you must use the **Kick User** option on the view online users page.

Configuring Role Assignment

After you have created roles for use in your deployment, you have to appropriately configure role assignment. This can occur in the following ways:

- Create a local user account and assign a role
- Assign by associated VLAN
- Assign by MAC and IP address
- Assign by subnet
- Use external authentication source attributes

Any of these assignment methods can be used to ensure that a user or system is appropriately placed into the correct role.

Creating a Local User and Assigning a Role

You have the ability to create local user accounts on the NAC Appliance Manager when necessary. It is not the recommended user-store and should typically be used only during testing and for guest accounts due to scale and other factors, such as local users' inability to change their passwords.

To create a local user and assign a role, perform the following steps:

Step 1   Select **Local Users** from the navigation options on the left of the screen located under the User Management section.

Step 2   Select **New Local User** from the newly presented top navigation bar shown in Figure 8-3.

Figure 8-3 **New Local User** *Option on the Local Users User Management Screen*

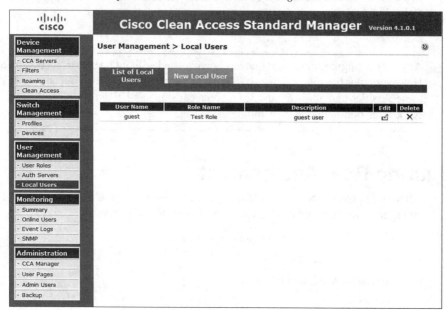

Step 3 Provide a username for this user.

Step 4 Provide and confirm a password.

Step 5 Provide a description for the user account.

Step 6 Select the appropriate available role from the drop-down box.

Step 7 Verify that all fields are correctly configured as in Figure 8-4, and then click the **Create User** button.

When the previous steps are completed, you will be returned to the Local Users listing page. You should see the newly created account listed there among any other accounts that reside locally. As with roles, you can edit or delete this account by selecting the associated icons on the listing page.

Figure 8-4 *Local User Configuration Screen and Role Assignment*

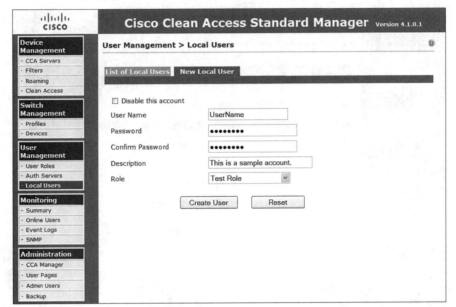

Assigning a Role by VLAN

When attempting to assign a user role, another option is to utilize the user VLAN ID. To create this sort of mapping, you are required to utilize an external authentication server. After you select the authentication server for which you want to add the VLAN ID-to-role mapping, you must select the appropriate **Mapping** icon associated with that authentication server. The list of authentication servers and the **Mapping** icon are displayed in Figure 8-5.

After you click the **Mapping** icon for the provider you selected, use the following steps to configure VLAN ID-to-role mapping:

Step 1   Select the **Add Mapping Rule** link on the right side of the screen, as displayed in Figure 8-6.

Figure 8-5 *Authentication Servers and* **Mapping** *Icon*

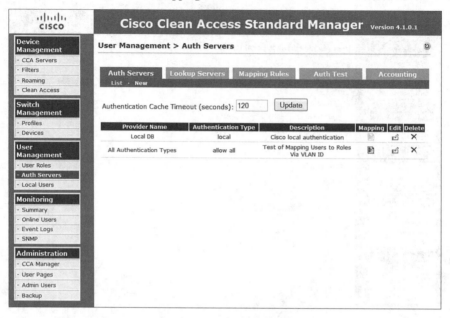

Figure 8-6 **Add Mapping Rule** *Link*

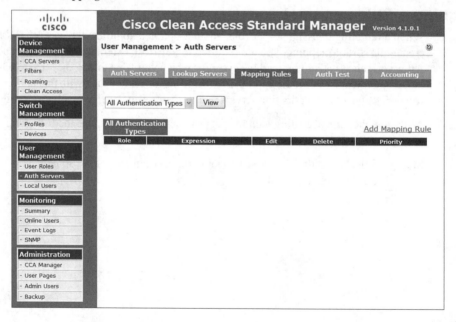

Step 2   On the form that presents itself, verify that **Condition Type** is set to **VLAN ID**.

Step 3   To create a matching condition based on VLAN ID, select an **Operator** of **Equals** or **Belongs To**. When using **Equals**, you are allowed to specify a single VLAN ID (for example, 134). If using **Belongs To**, you are allowed to enter multiple VLAN IDs separated by commas and, if necessary, include ranges using hyphens (for example, 7, 34, 134, 160-165, 182). For this example, you will use a range as displayed in Figure 8-7.

Figure 8-7   *Create VLAN ID Matching Conditions Using the* **Belongs To** *Option*

Step 4   When configuration is complete, click **Add Condition**.

Note   It is possible to create a complex mapping that requires the matching of multiple conditions in the list for a full match and role mapping to occur.

Step 5   Verify that your matching condition is added to the list of conditions. You will notice that this condition can be edited or deleted.

Step 6   Now you can complete the role mapping by completing the top portion of the form.

Step 7 Select the role name to which the matching VLAN IDs should be mapped.

Step 8 Select a priority, if necessary. This influences the order in which mapping rules are matched.

Step 9 Enter a description for this mapping condition.

Step 10 Verify the configuration of the role mapping, as displayed in Figure 8-8.

Figure 8-8 *Role Mapping Configuration Parameters*

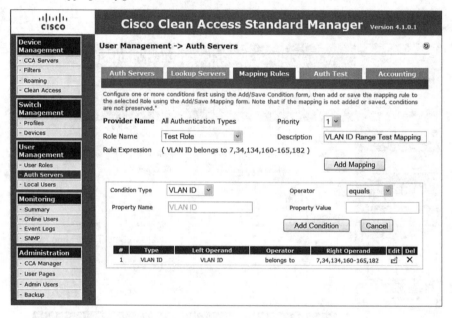

Step 11 Click the **Add Mapping** button.

NOTE   Mapping rules are processed from the top of the list downward. After a match occurs, the user role is mapped and no further processing of the list occurs.

When the previous steps are complete, verify the expression on the mapping rules page. You can create as many mapping rules as necessary. The resulting mapping rule list is displayed in Figure 8-9.

Figure 8-9   *Resulting Mapping Rules List*

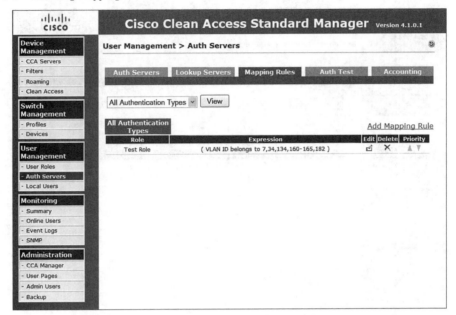

Assigning a Role by MAC and IP Address

Occasionally you will want to define a filter that allows certain MAC addresses and possibly the corresponding IP address to be assigned a user role based on that information alone. This sort of filter can be created at either the global level in NAC Appliance Manager or at the local level in a single NAC Appliance Server. Global policies are automatically distributed to every managed NAS, but if there is a conflicting local policy, the local policy prevails.

To configure a global filter for role assignment in NAM, navigate to **Device Management** and then select **Filters**. On the Filters page, follow these steps to create any necessary filters:

Step 1   On the **Device Management > Filters** page, as displayed in Figure 8-10, select **New** under the **Devices** tab.

Figure 8-10 *Filters Menu Options Available on NAM*

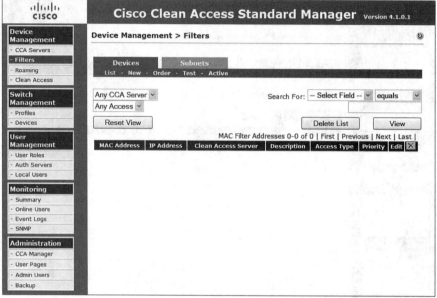

Step 2 In the **MAC Address/IP Address Description (Per Entry)** text box, you need to enter each necessary entry or pattern as necessary, placing each one on its own line using the following rules of entry:

— Format each line as *MAC/IP DESCRIPTION*.

— *MAC* and *DESCRIPTION* are required.

— *IP* is not required.

— Wildcarding of *MAC* is supported. You can use '*' for a wide match or '-' as a range of MACs.

— The *DESCRIPTION* field cannot have any spaces.

Step 3 Provide a description in the **Description (All Entries)** text box.

Step 4 Select the access type necessary for role mapping, as follows:

— **ROLE** Bypasses authentication and assessment and simply provides a role mapping

— **CHECK** Bypasses authentication but applies posture assessment prior to assigning role mapping

Step 5 Select the appropriate user role you want to map to this filter.

Step 6 Verify the configuration as displayed in Figures 8-11 and 8-12, and then click the **Add** button.

Figure 8-11 *Device Filter Role Mapping Configuration (Part 1)*

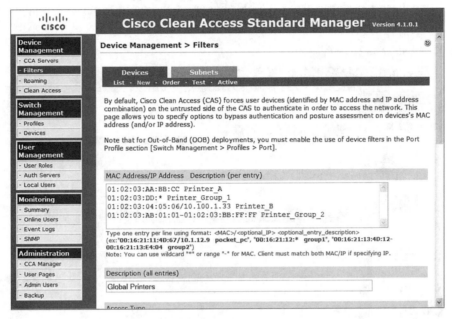

Figure 8-12 *Device Filter Role Mapping Configuration (Part 2)*

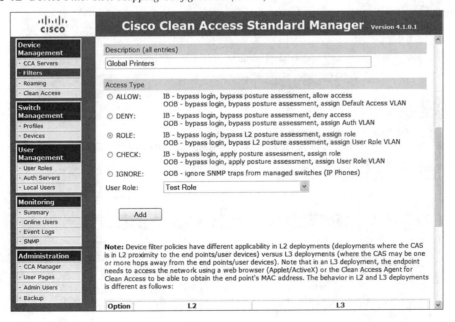

When configuration is completed, the MAC/IP address combinations from the configuration page display in a table, as shown in Figure 8-13. You can now edit or delete these entries line by line and view the filter list as it is applied at the global level or per NAS by changing the upper-left drop-down select box and clicking the **View** button. After applying a local mapping on a NAS, you can see the locally configured mapping filter in the list on NAM, as shown in Figure 8-14.

Figure 8-13 *Resulting Mapping Rules List*

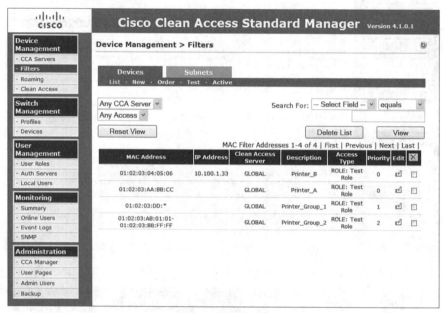

Figure 8-14 *Mapping Filter with Local NAS Filter Inserted on NAM View*

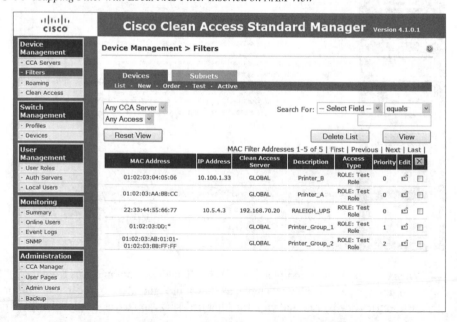

NOTE	Configuring a local mapping in NAS uses the same process as in NAM. Simply navigate to the NAS in question and select the **Filter** tab, **Devices**, and then **New**.

Assigning a Role by Subnet

An alternative method to assigning a role by MAC or IP address is to assign it by subnet of the device. On the NAM, under Device Management, select the **Filters** option and proceed as follows:

Step 1   Select the **Subnets** tab.

Step 2   Enter the classless interdomain routing block you want to match, such as 10.5.30.0/24.

Step 3   Provide a description.

Step 4   Select **Use Role:** and then select the role you want to use from the drop-down selection box.

Step 5   Verify the configuration, as in Figure 8-15, and then click the **Add** button.

Figure 8-15   *Configuration of a Subnet Rule Mapping on NAM*

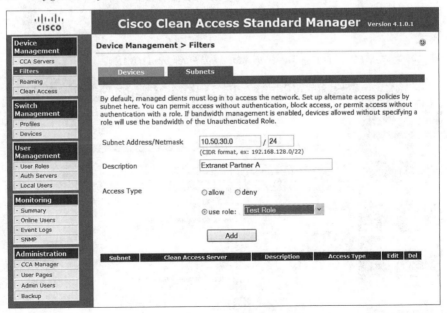

The completed configuration places the newly created rule at the bottom of the subnet filter configuration page as displayed in Figure 8-16. As with many of the other options, this option can also be configured at the local level of each NAS. The configuration on the NAS is identical to the process just described and is located on the NAS configuration page under the **Filter** tab and **Subnets** option. After configuring them, you can see the list of global and local subnet filters on the Subnet Filter configuration page, as displayed in Figure 8-17.

Figure 8-16 *Subnet Rule Mapping Listing Page*

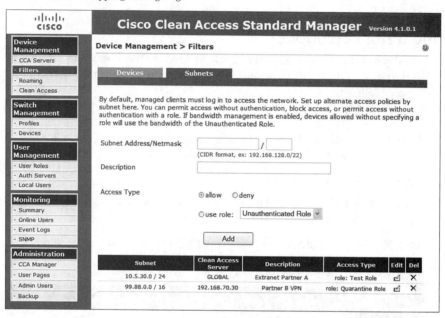

Figure 8-17 *Subnet Rule Mapping List Page with Additional Filter from a NAS*

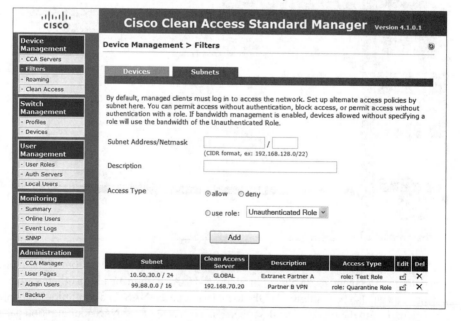

Assigning a Role by External Authentication Source Attributes

Although you have covered a few very simple role mapping methods up to this point, the most complex and comprehensive for role mapping is using an external authentication source's extended attributes. As an example, RADIUS provides to NAM some extremely detailed attributes that you can use for granular role assignment, including NAS IP address and Cisco avpair matching as well as role mapping based on the Lightweight Directory Access Protocol (LDAP). Another example external authenticator is a Cisco VPN for Single Sign-On. Options include but are not limited to Framed_IP_Address, NAS_IP_Address, User_Name, and Framed_Protocol. Configuration of this mapping is identical to VLAN ID mapping covered earlier in this chapter except that you select the **Attribute** option rather than **VLAN ID** from the drop-down selection on the appropriate mapping, as displayed in Figure 8-18.

Figure 8-18 *Attribute Mapping*

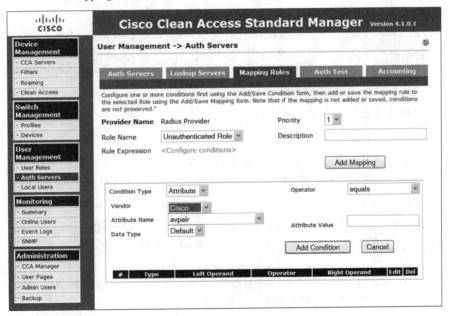

Role Mapping Summary

There are several ways to map roles to various pieces of information available to NAS and NAM from the user device and authentication session. It is important that you plan your mapping options according to what you have available in your network so that you can effectively produce the desired outcome.

Configuring Authentication

The previous section briefly touched on creating local users as a means of testing access. This section continues that discussion of authentication to NAC Appliances in relation to administrative accounts and also for users authenticating to external data sources.

Creating Admin Users and Groups

Administrators requiring access to the NAC Appliance configuration and reporting options must be created on the NAC Appliance Manager server. The admin accounts can belong to three default admin groups: Read-Only, Add-Edit, and Full-Control. In addition, you can create custom groups with special permissions as necessary for your environment.

Creating an Admin Group

To create an admin group that more adequately matches your internal support roles in your organization, you will need to open the **Admin Users** option of the Administration Section on the NAC Appliance Manager. Select the **Admin Groups** tab and then follow these steps:

Step 1   Under the **Admin Groups** tab, click **New**.

Step 2   Provide a group name.

Step 3   Provide a description.

Step 4   Set the default access level for all NAS servers and individual NAS servers. The options for each are **Read Only** or **Local Admin**.

Step 5   Set the default and per-module access levels for each module listed.

Step 6   Verify the configuration as shown in Figure 8-19, and then click **Create Group** at the bottom of the configuration page.

After it is created, the list will be displayed in the admin group list, as shown in Figure 8-20. From there, you can edit and delete other custom groups as necessary. You cannot, however, remove the three default groups.

Figure 8-19 *Admin Group Configuration*

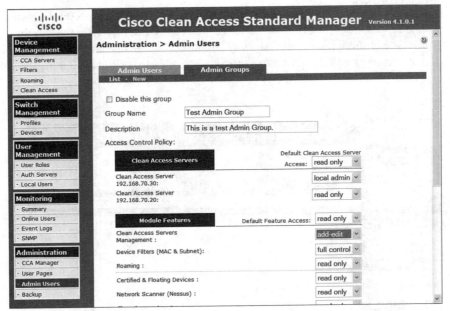

Figure 8-20 *Admin Group List*

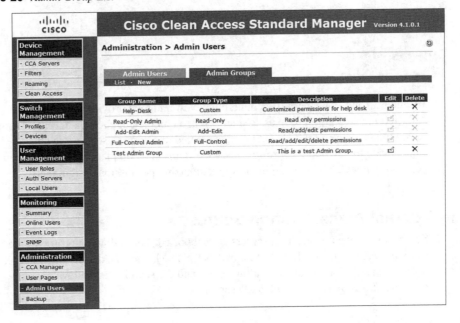

Creating an Admin User

To allow additional administrators of the NAC deployment to access the necessary systems and reports, they must have an account created on NAM. Navigating to **Admin Users** in the Administration section presents the admin users page displayed in Figure 8-21. This page presents options to list active sessions, provide a list of administrators, and create new admin accounts.

Figure 8-21 *Admin Users List*

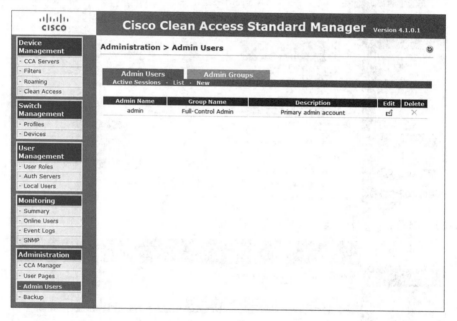

To create an additional admin account, click **New** and then provide a username, password, description, and admin group assignment. When completed, click the **Create Admin** button to create the admin user. After it is created, the admin user will be able to authenticate to NAM and appropriate NAS systems and complete all configuration possible as allowed by the admin group membership permission assignments.

Adding External Authentication Sources

Several external authentication servers are supported. The following protocols are supported: Kerberos, RADIUS, Windows NT NTLM, and LDAP. The next section shows how to add a RADIUS authentication server, and the section that follows that gives an example of how to add an LDAP/AD server.

Adding a RADIUS External Authentication Source

To add a new external authentication provider, you must navigate to the **Auth Servers** menu option under the User Management section. There you will see a list of currently configured authentication providers. Use the following steps to add a RADIUS provider:

Step 1 Under the **Auth Servers** tab, click **New**.

Step 2 From the **Authentication Type** drop-down, select **Radius**.

Step 3 Enter a provider name that will be advertised to the users as a possible authentication mechanism.

Step 4 Provide the server name where the RADIUS server resides.

Step 5 Enter the server port to be used for RADIUS communication.

Step 6 Select the RADIUS type.

Step 7 Enter the timeout in seconds for RADIUS authentications.

Step 8 Enter the default role for anyone using this provider.

Step 9 Enter the RADIUS server's shared secret.

Step 10 Enter the NAS identifier or NAS IP address.

Step 11 Enter the NAS port and NAS port type if necessary.

Step 12 If you are using RADIUS failover, select the **Enable Failover** check box and then provide the failover peer IP.

Step 13 If you need to accept empty attributes, you have to select the final check box.

Step 14 Provide a description.

Step 15 Verify that the configuration is accurate, as in Figure 8-22, and then click **Add Server** to complete the configuration.

Figure 8-22 *Configuration of a RADIUS Authentication Provider*

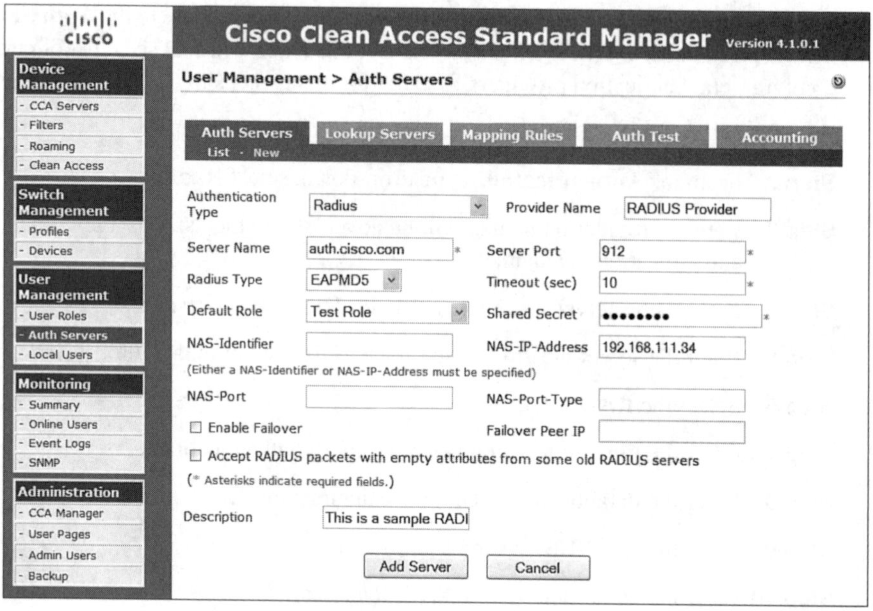

Adding an LDAP/AD External Authentication Source

To add an external authentication mechanism for LDAP/AD, you should select LDAP for the authentication type as the following steps illustrate:

Step 1   Under the **Auth Servers** tab, click **New**.

Step 2   In the **Authentication Type** drop-down, select **LDAP**.

Step 3   Enter a provider name that will be advertised to the users as a possible authentication mechanism.

Step 4   Enter the server URL in the form of ldap://*url*.

Step 5   Select a server version from the **Server Version** drop-down list, which provides the following options: **Auto**, **Version 2**, and **Version 3**.

Step 6   Enter the LDAP Admin ID (Full DN) if the LDAP directory is secured.

Step 7   Enter the associated admin password if the LDAP directory is secured.

Step 8   Enter the search base context in LDAP for searching for the user accounts.

Step 9   Enter a search filter that will match only user accounts. Both UID
and SAMACCOUNTNAME are common, but verify with your
particular deployment.

Step 10   Select the appropriate referral option.

Step 11   Select the appropriate option for **DerefLink** to possibly dereference
object aliases if they are returned.

Step 12   Select the appropriate option for **DerefAlias**.

Step 13   Select **None** or **SSL** from the **Security Type** drop-down list.

Step 14   Select the default role to be assigned to any user authenticating using the
authentication provider.

Step 15   Provide a description.

Step 16   Verify that the configuration is accurate, as in Figure 8-23, and then click
Add Server to complete the configuration.

Figure 8-23   *Configuration of an LDAP/AD Authentication Provider*

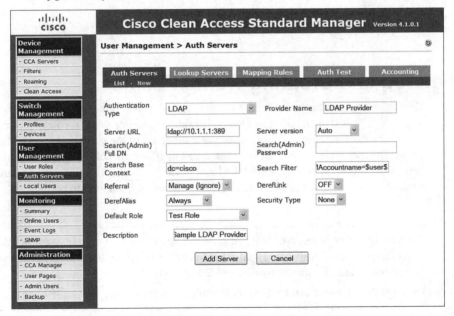

When the configuration of a provider is complete, you can begin to provide role mapping
based on the information the authentication provider returns. To see the list of
configured authentication providers, simply navigate to the auth servers list page displayed
in Figure 8-24.

Figure 8-24 *Auth Server List Page*

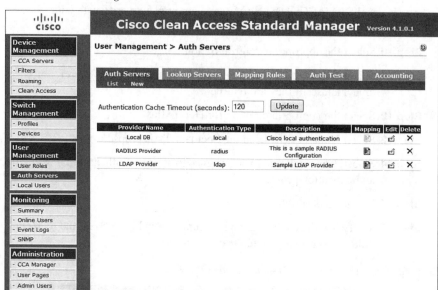

Configuring and Creating Traffic Policies

After a system is authenticated and posture assessed, it will quite possibly be allowed on the network. Based on the results of the authenticated users or systems role assignment and the current status or ultimate outcome of the assessment of the system, it is very likely that the administrator will want to enforce some sort of IP access policy to limit the system's view of the trusted networks behind the local NAS. To accomplish this, you can use a combination of IP-based policies, host-based policies, and bandwidth policies.

NOTE   The Real IP Gateway mode of NAC Appliance Server will pass only IPv4 traffic (IPv6 in an upcoming release of software); all other traffic types will be blocked. Systems Network Architecture traffic forwarding will be added in a future release.

Virtual Gateway mode can be used for passing other protocols, such as IPX.

Although each of these control mechanisms can be configured on the NAM as a global scope, each can also be configured on each NAS as part of a local scope. For brevity, you will configure only global policies in the following sections of this chapter.

NOTE   By default, all access from the trusted network to the untrusted network is allowed, whereas all untrusted-to-trusted network traffic is denied. Policies in either direction can be applied per role outside of the default configurations.

IP-Based Traffic Control Policy

IP-based traffic control policies take into account the following information: ports, protocol, and IP addressing. To see a list of currently configured IP-based traffic control policies by role, navigate to **User Roles**, and then **Traffic Control**, and finally select **IP** from the subtab.

NOTE   IP-based traffic control policies do *not* perform stateful inspection. The IP policies are stateless in nature—very similar to an access control list on a Cisco IOS router.

Follow the remaining steps to configure a sample IP-based policy:

Step 1   Next to the appropriate role, select **Add Policy**.

Step 2   Set the priority of this policy. The lower the number, the sooner it is evaluated against the rest of the multiline resulting policy.

Step 3   Select **Allow** or **Block** as the action type.

Step 4   Select **Enabled** or **Disabled** to enforce or prevent enforcement of this rule.

Step 5   Select a category of **All Traffic**, **IP**, or **IP Fragment**. By default, the NAS prevents IP fragments to prevent certain denial of service attacks. So, if they are needed, you will have to create an allow policy for them to traverse NAS. If you select **IP** here, you are presented with more granular form response requirements relating to the protocol and IP information.

Step 6   Select the protocol and protocol number. Options are **Custom**, **TCP**, **UDP**, **ICMP**, **ESP**, and **AH**.

Step 7   Enter the untrusted (IP/Mask:Port) fields, which can be wildcarded as necessary.

Step 8   Enter the trusted (IP/Mask:Port) fields, which can be wildcarded as necessary.

Step 9   Provide a description.

Step 10   After you verify the configuration as correct, as in Figure 8-25, click **Add Policy** to complete the configuration.

Figure 8-25 *Configuration of an IP-Based Policy*

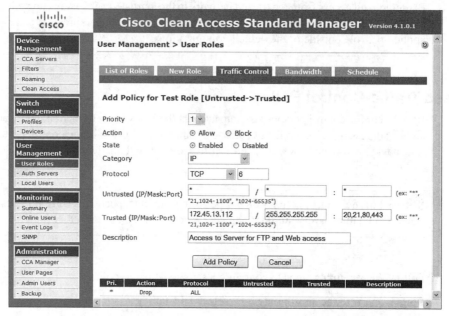

After you add all the necessary IP-based policies required for a particular role, you can view the policy list on the traffic control IP page, as displayed in Figure 8-26. This page also allows you to reprioritize, delete, edit, and enable and disable per rule as necessary.

Figure 8-26 *IP-Based Traffic Control Policy per Role Listing Page*

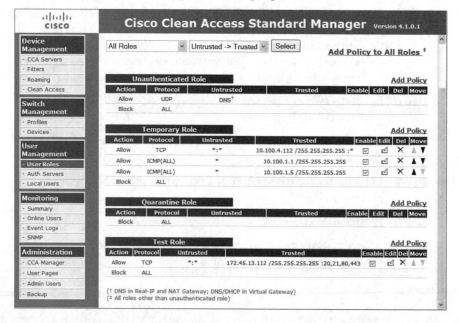

Host-Based Traffic Control Policy

Host-based traffic control policies take into account Domain Name System (DNS) name information when allowing or preventing access. This type of policy allows you to configure access to a particular destination DNS name, which could be resolved to a number of IP addresses if the system happens to be load balanced. This feature is also very helpful for controlling access to DNS-resolved hosts that might have many returned IP addresses or that change over time, such as http://www.windowsupdate.com. Additionally, you can allow access to a partial match of the hostname, which will allow access to an entire domain or parts of the domain by name alone. Prior to adding host-based policies for a given role, you should configure the trusted DNS server for that role. This permits only responses from that trusted server to be allowed via this host-based policy. The following steps will configure a sample host-based policy:

Step 1   On the traffic control host page, navigate to the role you want to configure or select the role from the drop-down list, and click the **Select** button.

Step 2   Enter an allowed hostname or partial hostname, such as **cisco.com**.

Step 3   Select the matching parameter for this host from the following options: **Equals**, **Ends**, **Begins**, or **Contains**.

Step 4   Provide a description.

Step 5   Enable or disable the rule.

Step 6   After verifying it as correct, as in Figure 8-27, click **Add** to complete the configuration.

Figure 8-27   *Configuration of a Host-Based Policy*

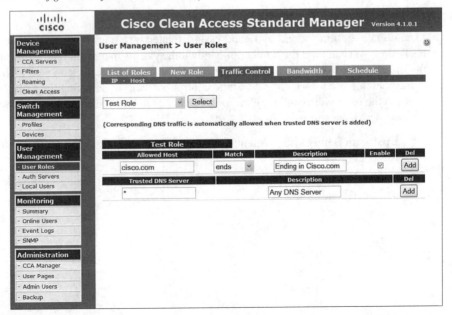

After you add all the necessary host-based policies required for a particular role, you can view the policy list on the traffic control host page, as displayed in Figure 8-28. This page also allows you to delete, add, and enable and disable per rule as necessary.

Figure 8-28 *Host-Based Traffic Control Policy per Role Listing Page*

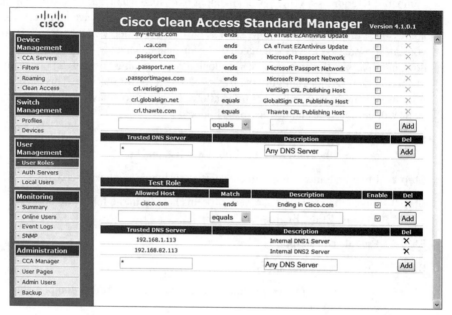

Bandwidth Policies

In addition to limiting access by IP addressing, related information, and hostname resolution, you can limit the number of bandwidth systems in a given role. After selecting the **Bandwidth** tab on the User Roles page, you can select the **Edit** icon next to the corresponding role for which you want to control bandwidth. Selecting the **Edit** icon presents the bandwidth configuration form for that role. You can control the following options, which are shown in Figure 8-29:

- **Upstream Bandwidth**   Amount of bandwidth in kbps. Using **–1** provides unlimited bandwidth.

- **Downstream Bandwidth**   Amount of bandwidth in kbps. Using **–1** provides unlimited bandwidth.

- **Burstable Traffic**   A multiplier from 1 to 10. Multiplying this number by the bandwidth determines the burst traffic.
- **Shared Mode**   Select whether this is for all users in the role or per user.
- **Description**   Provide a description for the bandwidth policy.

Figure 8-29 *Configuration of a Bandwidth Policy*

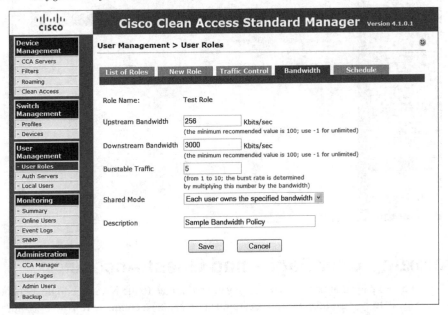

On completion of the configuration steps, the newly created policy will be listed, as displayed in Figure 8-30, among the other bandwidth policies. It is important to note that, by default, NAS does not have bandwidth controls enabled. So, even if a policy is configured on NAM, it will not be enforced until it is enabled on the appropriate NAS.

Figure 8-30 *Viewing the Currently Defined Bandwidth Policies*

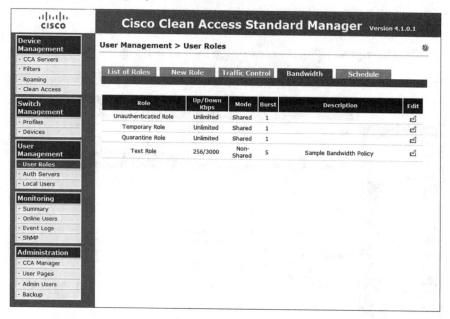

Customizing User Pages and Guest Access

The web page that users see when they are redirected to the NAS web login authentication page is fully customizable. The customization can be a complete rewrite or require only simple editing via the form-based tool provided on the configuration pages. These user pages can also include a guest access option that is relatively simple to configure. If the guest access option is too difficult to manage or not granular enough from a user-tracking perspective, Cisco has provided a web API that allows you to introduce your own scripts capable of creating guest user accounts as necessary.

Login Pages

Configuring and customizing the login pages is a simple process. To start this process, navigate to **User Pages** from the Administration section. There the **Login Page** tab displays a list of available login pages. Following the next several steps will allow you to customize your own distinct login page.

Step 1 On the **Login Page** tab of the User Pages menu, click **Add**.

Step 2 Specify the VLAN ID and the subnet information as necessary to ensure systems on the specified networks will receive this particular login page.

Step 3   Select a specific operating system, if necessary. OS determination is derived from the HTTP GET request, which pulls the login page from the NAS.

Step 4   After you verify it as correct, click **Add** to complete the initial configuration.

Step 5   You may now reorder the login pages to ensure that your page will be delivered by using the **Move** option.

Step 6   When you are ready to continue with the customization, click the associated **Edit** icon.

Step 7   Select **Page Type** from the following: **Frameless**, **Frame-Based**, and **Small-Screen Frameless**. The **Frame-Based** page type allows you to add your own logo and other custom content to the page.

Step 8   Provide a description.

Step 9   Select the web-client method from the drop-down list.

Step 10   Select the configuration check boxes as necessary. These allow for detecting the MAC address and OS as well as renewing IP addresses when necessary.

Step 11   Verify the General Login Page configuration as displayed in Figure 8-31, and then click **Update** to save the changes.

Figure 8-31   *Login Page General Tab Configuration*

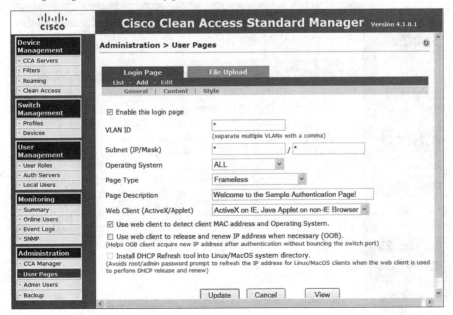

Step 12 Select the **Content** tab.

Step 13 Select the title as well as the image to display on the login page. Images can be uploaded from the **File Upload** tab.

Step 14 Provide labels for username, password, login, and provider. In addition, select which options are to display.

Step 15 Select the default authentication provider.

Step 16 Select the available providers.

Step 17 Enter simple instructions for the user in the form of a text string.

Step 18 Enable or disable guest access.

Step 19 Allow or do not allow the user to install the certificate authority (CA) certificate.

Step 20 Allow or do not allow the user to access the help section.

Step 21 Define the CA certificate to present to the user from the drop-down list.

Step 22 Provide the help section test instructions.

Step 23 Verify the configuration, as in Figure 8-32, and then click **Update** to save the configuration to this point.

Figure 8-32 *Login Page Content Tab Configuration*

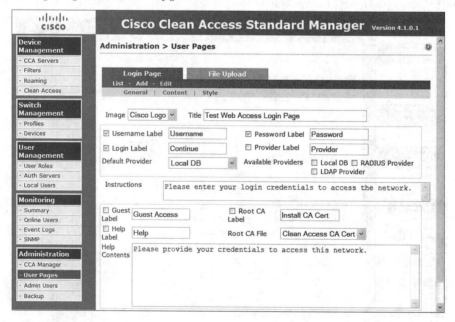

Step 24 Select the **Style** tab.

Step 25 Configure the various color options.

Step 26 Configure the various style-sheet options (Cascading Style Sheets) if necessary.

Step 27 Verify the configuration as displayed in Figure 8-33, and then click **Update** to complete the configuration.

Figure 8-33 *Login Page Style Tab Configuration*

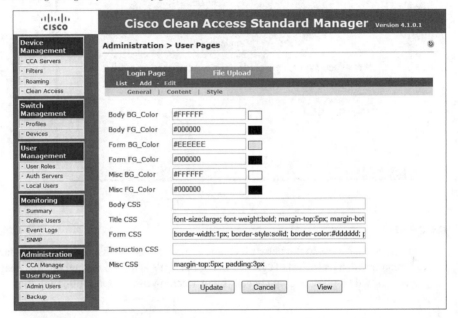

Step 28 After completing the configuration, you can select the **View** option at the bottom of the configuration pages to see how your changes have affected the login page. This page is shown in Figure 8-34.

In addition to the previous customization steps, if you had selected frame-based pages, you could continue to configure the content for the right frame, which is blank until configured. Selecting the right-frame option allows you to copy-paste or manually enter the HTML for this frame. You could also enter a properly formatted URL (http://*url* or https://*nam_ip_address*/upload/*file_name*.htm if the file has been uploaded rather than hosted externally). If you are hosting a file externally for this frame, you must ensure that the file is reachable by the host using IP- or host-based traffic control policies. If the URL rather than the IP is being referenced, the URL or IP must be allowed in the Unauthenticated role for the access to be successful.

Figure 8-34 *Completed Customized Login Page*

Guest Access

Enabling guest access to the network can be a simple task. At installation, a guest account was created with a password of 'guest'. Using the skills acquired throughout this chapter, you can provide a guest account access by proceeding through the following high-level tasks:

Step 1   Add a new guest role for the guest account.

Step 2   Associate the guest user account to the guest role.

Step 3   Configure limiting traffic and bandwidth policies for the guest role.

Step 4   Enable the **Guest Access** button on the login page.

Completing these simple tasks will enable guest access to your network very quickly and securely.

API for Guest Access

Cisco has additionally provided a web-based API that supports Secure Sockets Layer–based POST requests to complete certain tasks. In relation to guest access, this API can be used to create specific user accounts that are applied to a role that is granted only guest access as well as deleting guest access users. The web API is accessible via the NAM at https://*nam_address*/admin/cisco_api.jsp.

When using the API for configuring guest accounts and when writing API access scripts, it is recommended that you refer to the current API guide and sample code at Cisco.com and in the NAC Appliance Manager documentation. Because the Cisco Technical Assistance Center does not support or troubleshoot user scripts, it is important that you work with a developer familiar with accessing web-based API functions.

Summary

Understanding how to effectively configure authentication mechanisms, user roles, and traffic policies is a requirement for any NAC Appliance deployment. All the functionality presented in this chapter should be well planned in advance, and all preparation possible should be taken. Your deployment will be much smoother when the pre-planning related to IP- and host-based access, guest access, login page configuration, and role assignment is closely tied to your implementation goals.

This chapter covers the following topics:

- Understanding Cisco NAC Appliance Setup
- Cisco Clean Access Agent
- Agent Policy Enforcement
- Network Scanning

Host Posture Validation and Remediation: Cisco Clean Access Agent and Network Scanner

After you have implemented the Cisco NAC Appliance architecture appropriately in your environment and configured the necessary roles and role assignments, you will be able to configure agent policy enforcement. This configuration includes various checks, rules, and requirements as well as various scanning policies. After agent policies are configured, you will be able to ensure that systems connecting to your network will be required to authenticate, be interrogated, and comply with your policies prior to gaining access to the network.

Understanding Cisco NAC Appliance Setup

When setting up the Cisco NAC Appliance for policy enforcement, you will typically proceed through a few steps to complete the configuration process. Here is a list of high-level steps that will be explained further throughout this chapter.

Step 1 Obtain and install updates on the NAC Appliance Manager (NAM).

Step 2 Enable and enforce the use of the Cisco Clean Access (CCA) Agent and scanning per role and operating system.

Step 3 Manage the certified list and exemptions.

Step 4 Configure role-based policies such as access and bandwidth restrictions as discussed in Chapter 8, "The Building Blocks: Roles, Authentication, Traffic Policies, and User Pages."

Step 5 Configure network scanning, agent scanning, or a combination of both mechanisms.

Step 6 Install the necessary Nessus plug-ins as required for your scanning needs.

Step 7 Configure agent scanning rules and requirements.

Step 8 Test the configuration and verify that all mechanisms are fully functioning as expected.

Step 9 Continue to fine-tune the configuration as well as the certified list and any additional exemptions.

Now that you have a process to follow, the chapter proceeds by explaining each major step and providing configuration guidance throughout the remaining sections of this chapter.

Cisco NAC Appliance Updates

Prior to configuring your policy requirements, be certain that you have the most up-to-date checks, rules, and software updates available from the Cisco NAC Appliance Updates Server. You can view the current versions and numbers of each updated object by navigating the NAC Appliance Manager menu under **Device Management > Clean Access** and then selecting the **Updates** tab. A sample **Updates** tab screen is displayed in Figure 9-1.

Figure 9-1 *Updates Tab Screen as Displayed on the NAC Appliance Manager*

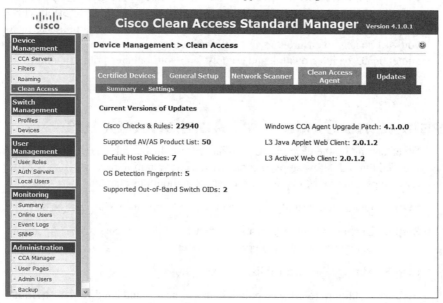

To ensure that you are always up to date with the most current software and policy components, you must set up automatic updating. Automatic updating is configured via the **Device Management > Clean Access > Updates > Settings** menu option as displayed in Figure 9-2.

The following is the list of configurable update options:

- **Automatically Check for Updates Starting From** Checking this option and providing a starting time and a repeat time in hours will allow NAM to automatically begin downloading updates at that time and repeat future checks at the specified interval.

Figure 9-2 *Configuring Automatic Update Retrieval*

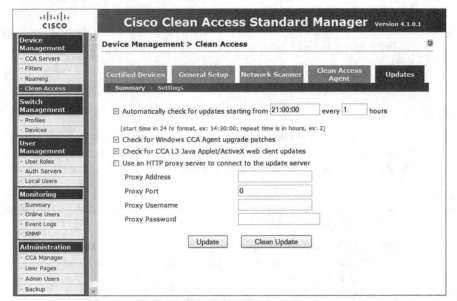

- **Check for Windows CCA Agent Upgrade Patches**   Selecting this option ensures that the automatic retrieval process will look for software updates for the CCA agent.

- **Check for CCA L3 Java Applet/ActiveX Web Client Updates**   Selecting this option downloads and updates to the Java and ActiveX clients.

- **Use an HTTP Proxy Server to Connect to the Update Server**   Selecting this option and then configuring the proxy address, proxy port, proxy username, and proxy password will allow the NAC Appliance Manager to pull the updates if it is behind a proxy.

- **Update button**   Clicking this button will schedule automatic updates as configured on the form as well as immediately checking for updates.

- **Clean Updates**   Clicking this button will allow you to remove all unsupported and invalid checks and rules installed by Cisco. You will want to verify your rules and requirements after performing this task to ensure that nothing you had been using was removed.

After you have completed the configuration of the automatic update retrieval process and performed an update, you can continue with the configuration by proceeding to the **General Setup** tab.

General Setup

Now that you have successfully retrieved the most recent updates from Cisco, you can continue the configuration by selecting the **General Setup** tab on the NAC Appliance menu. From here you can configure the web login parameters and the agent login parameters.

Web Login

The web login page of the **General Setup** tab provides the ability to configure how users authenticating via the web login page will be processed and what options they will have and be able to see on this page. The configuration options, as displayed in Figure 9-3, are as follows:

- **User Role**   Select the appropriate user role from the drop-down selection tool to choose what role to apply.

- **Operating System**   Select the operating system from the drop-down list to ensure that only users with the desired operating system are allowed to use web login. By default, **ALL** is selected.

- **Show Network Scanner User Agreement Page to Web Login Users**   Selecting this option presents users with an agreement page that they must accept to continue on the network. This page is presented after both authentication and scanning occurs.

- **Enable Pop-Up Scan Vulnerability Reports from User Agreement Page** Selecting this check box enables web login users to see the results of their scan after completion.

- **Require Users to Be Certified at Every Web Login**   Checking this box forces network scanning on every login. By default, scanning occurs on only the first login until the system's MAC address is cleared from the certified devices list.

- **Exempt Certified Devices from Web Login Requirement by Adding to MAC Filters**   This check box, when selected, causes the MAC of the system (after first authentication and certification) to be added to the authentication pass-through list so that they will not require authentication at next login.

- **Block/Quarantine Users with Vulnerabilities in Role**   Selecting this check box and then selecting the **Quarantine Role** option from the associated drop-down will cause the user to be placed in quarantine for 4 minutes so that the vulnerability can be addressed prior to attempting reauthentication and recertification. If **Block Access** is selected instead of **Quarantine Role**, the user will be denied access and will be presented with the blocked access page. The blocked access page dialog box becomes available for configuration after this option is selected. The quarantine time is definable and is 4 minutes by default.

Figure 9-3 *Web Login Configuration on the* **General Setup** *Tab*

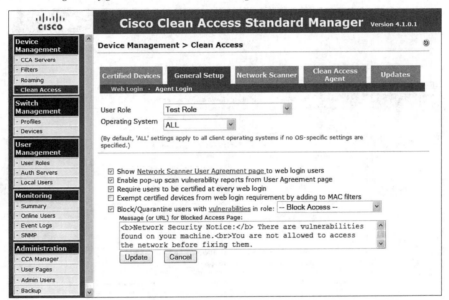

On completion of the form configuration as necessary, clicking the **Update** button commits the changes.

Agent Login

The Agent Login page of the **General Setup** tab provides the ability to configure how users authenticating via the CCA Agent will be processed and what options they will have and be able to see on this page. Figure 9-4 shows the configuration options.

The following explains the options on this page:

- **User Role**   Select the appropriate user role from the drop-down selection tool to choose what role to apply.

- **Operating System**   Select the operating system from the drop-down to ensure that only users with the desired operating system are allowed to use web login. By default, **ALL** is selected.

- **Require Use of Clean Access Agent**   Selecting this option redirects users accessing the web login page to the download page for the CCA Agent software and enforces the use of this agent while disallowing the use of web login for users in the selected OS and user role. The text box below this selection is the dialog box that will be presented to the user required to install the CCA Agent. You can configure this dialog box as necessary.

Figure 9-4 *Agent Login Configuration on the General Setup Tab*

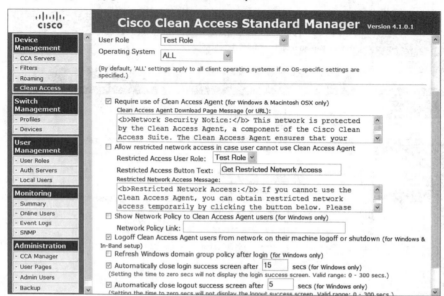

- **Allow Restricted Network Access in Case User Cannot Use Clean Access Agent**   Selecting this check box allows the users some level of access to the network if they bypass the installation of the required CCA Agent. This provides users who are unable to install the agent on the local system, due to permissions issues, the ability to access the network until the installation can be performed. Selecting this option provides a configurable message to the user and allows the administrator to assign the role that this user will be placed into and therefore inherit access limitations.

- **Show Network Policy to Clean Access Agent Users**   Checking this box presents to users the selected web page that they are required to accept before proceeding. You can host this link externally as http://*url* or locally by uploading the page to NAM as https://*nam_ip_address*/upload/filename.htm.

- **Logoff Clean Access Agent Users from Network on Their Machine Logoff or Shutdown**   This check box, when selected, automatically performs a NAC Appliance logoff forcing a reauthentication upon the next Windows login. This is applicable only for in-band deployments.

- **Refresh Windows Domain Group Policy After Login**   Selecting this check box ensures that a Windows Group Policy Object update occurs on the system running the CCA Agent at login.

- **Automatically Close Login Success Screen After**   This option allows the automatic closing of the login success screen after a definable number of seconds. Setting the number to zero seconds prevents the screen from appearing at all.

- **Automatically Close Logout Success Screen After**   This option allows the automatic closing of the logout success screen after a definable number of seconds. Setting the number to zero seconds prevents the screen from appearing at all.

On completion of the form configuration as necessary, clicking the **Update** button commits the changes.

Certified Devices

After configuring the authentication options for your users, you may begin to think about the other devices in your network that might not be able to run the agent but will require access to the network through the NAC Appliance. Devices you might consider are printers and video conference systems as well as select other user-based systems. The **Certified Devices** tab on the NAC Appliance menu allows you to configure the exemptions for these devices. Additionally, you can view the currently certified devices list among other options in the following discussion.

Certified List

The **Certified List** option (see Figure 9-5) on the Certified Devices menu allows the administrator to view and search for the devices that have been granted access to the network.

Figure 9-5   *Certified List of Devices*

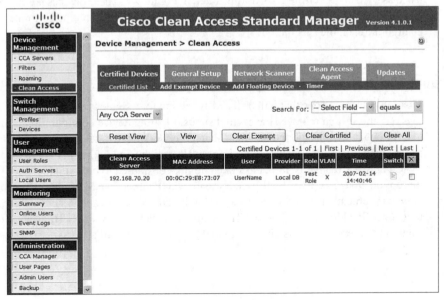

This list is filterable by NAS or globally if desired. The list includes the following information:

- NAS enforcing the policy
- MAC address of the system
- User authenticated
- Authentication provider
- Role
- VLAN
- Time
- Switch to which the system is connected

There is also an option per device to kick the user and remove it from the list. In addition to kicking a single user, the administrator can use the various buttons on the page to clear all exempt systems, clear the certified systems, or clear all systems.

Add Exempt Device

The devices in your network that are not capable of authenticating and posturing can be added as exempt devices. The Add Exempt Device page allows you to add MAC addresses of devices that are not required to meet the NAC Appliance requirements. The configuration of such devices is shown in Figure 9-6. After exempt devices are configured, they will be listed as such in the certified list, as illustrated in Figure 9-7. These devices are exempt from all NAS servers. If you want to locally exempt a system, you should perform the same configuration on the specific NAS.

Add Floating Device

Floating devices are one that will be listed as exempt for a single user session. After the user logs out, the system removes the exempt status. Floating device configuration is also used to ensure that systems hidden behind a shared network device, such as a router, virtual private network (VPN) concentrator, or firewall, which would normally share the same MAC address from the NAS perspective, are not considered to be a single device. Using this option, you can opt to identify each session via IP rather than MAC and ensure that each system is authenticated and scanned accordingly. This requires each system to be translated to its own IP address. Port Address Translation and Network Address Translation are not supported unless the user is always granted the same unique IP address.

Figure 9-6 *Configuring Exempt Devices*

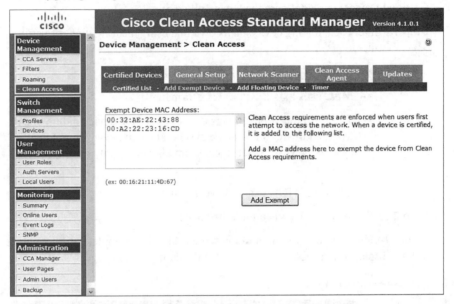

Figure 9-7 *Certified List Including Exempt Devices*

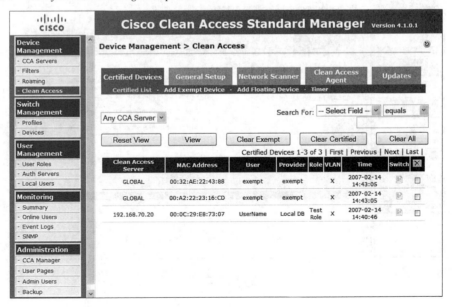

To configure floating devices, simply navigate to the **Add Floating Device** option under Certified Devices and configure the list as follows:

Step 1 Enter each floating device on its own line using the following formatting rules:

— Format must be MAC TYPE DESCRIPTION.

— MAC uses xx:xx:xx:xx:xx:xx format.

— TYPE is ether 1 or 0. 1 sets the system as the device hiding other MAC addresses and lets the system know to never exempt the system by MAC. 0 sets the system as exempt only for the current session.

— DESCRIPTION cannot have any spaces.

Step 2 Click **Add Device** to commit the changes.

Figure 9-8 shows a sample configuration screen. After it is complete, the floating device list will be displayed in a table at the bottom of the configuration page.

Figure 9-8 *Creating Floating Devices*

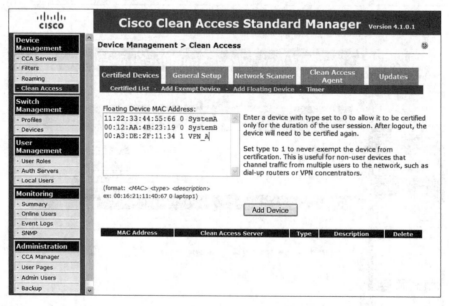

Timer

If desired, you can configure automatically occurring processes that will clear the certified device list as necessary without manual interaction. To configure this setting, navigate to the **Timers** option of the **Certified Devices** tab. Initially you are presented with a list of any configured timers. To create a new timer, select the **New** option and proceed as follows:

Step 1   Provide a timer name.

Step 2   Provide a description.

Step 3   Select **Enable This Timer** to make sure that this automated process will run.

Step 4   Select **Keep Online Users** to ensure that you do not drop any currently active users if necessary.

Step 5   Provide a start date and time for the automated process.

Step 6   Provide a recurrence interval in days to allow the job to run every day as necessary.

Step 7   Define the criteria for the job:

— Select all or a specific NAS.

— Select the role that should be matched or all user roles.

— Select the type of authentication provider that was used for the session.

— Provide a minimum number of days the system in question has been certified or enter **0** to consider all systems.

Step 8   Select one of the following methods:

— **Clear All Matching Certified Devices**.

— **Clear the Oldest** *number* **Matching Certified Devices Only**, where *number* is definable.

— **Clear the Oldest** *number* **Certified Devices Every** *minutes* **Minutes Until All Matching Devices Are Cleared**. This option repeatedly clears a certain definable number of devices every definable number of minutes until the list is cleared according to the matching parameters configured.

Step 9   Click **Add** to commit the actions.

Figure 9-9 shows a sample timer configuration screen. After it is completed, the floating device list will be displayed in the list option under the Timer menu.

Figure 9-9   *Creating a Timer*

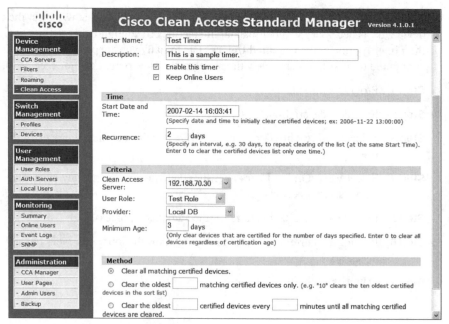

Cisco Clean Access Agent

Cisco Clean Access Agent is required for the most robust level of interrogation and interaction the NAC Appliance can enforce. Clean Access Agent allows the system to collect vulnerability assessment data and provides remediation options to the interrogated system as defined by centrally configured policies. Clean Access Agent is available for Windows systems, and its use can be enforced, as illustrated earlier in this chapter, by configuring the agent login configuration page. The user is prompted to download and install Clean Access Agent to be granted network access. Prior to granting access, Clean Access Agent can look for installed software, registry keys, files, processes and services. In addition, it can require the update of several antivirus and antispyware packages as well as perform various other installations and provide guidance to the user in remediating other issues manually if necessary.

Agent Installation Process

Each NAS will obtain the latest copy of Cisco Clean Access Agent from NAM when it becomes available. The users required to use Clean Access Agent are asked on initial install to download and install the agent. In addition, if desired, Clean Access Agent can be distributed via any number of other methods, such as login script, manual installation, or software distribution systems such as BigFix or Microsoft System Management Server (SMS). After installation, Clean Access Agent can automatically receive and install updates as configured centrally by the NAC Appliance administrator.

Sample Agent Installation

Now you will examine the user-side experience relating to installing Cisco Clean Access Agent.

Step 1 The user attempts to access a website via a web browser. Any other application connection attempt will result in a failed connection until web authentication occurs because the system has not yet been granted access.

Step 2 The web browser displays a message, shown in Figure 9-10, that the user is about to be redirected to the network authentication page.

Figure 9-10 *Redirection to the Web Authentication Page User Message*

Step 3 The browser automatically displays the web login page from the local NAS and requires the user to authenticate and click **Continue**, as displayed in Figure 9-11.

Figure 9-11 *Web Login Page*

Step 4 The web login occurs as configured. Figure 9-12 illustrates the network security notice page with the included button to download Clean Access Agent, which has been configured as a requirement for this deployment.

Step 5 On clicking the Agent download button, the user is prompted to run or save Clean Access Agent downloaded from the local NAS, as illustrated in Figure 9-13.

Figure 9-12 *Network Security Notice and Cisco Clean Access Agent Download Button*

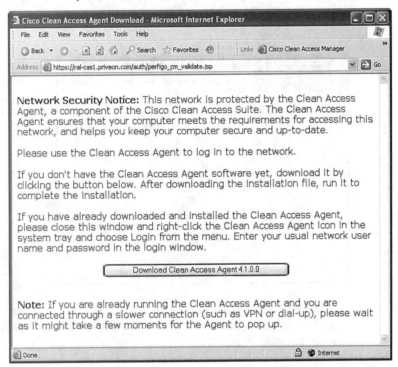

Figure 9-13 *Downloading the Clean Access Agent Locally*

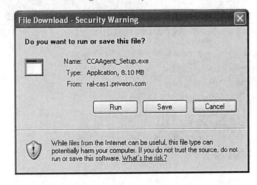

Step 6 On running the installer, the user continues through the installer's steps, as illustrated in Figure 9-14.

Figure 9-14 *Installing Clean Access Agent*

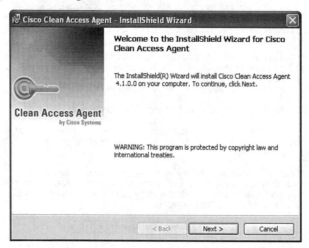

Step 7 After installing Clean Access Agent, the system will start the agent application and prompt the user to authenticate using this mechanism, as shown in Figure 9-15.

Figure 9-15 *Authenticating with the Agent*

Step 8 After successful authentication and interrogation, the user is granted access and notified via Clean Access Agent, as displayed in Figure 9-16.

Figure 9-16 *Successful Authentication Notification from Clean Access Agent*

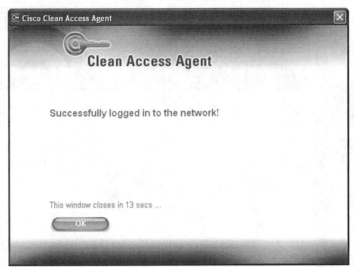

The system and user are now successfully authenticated and postured, which allows NAC Appliance to apply the necessary access restrictions and permissions centrally defined for that user, system, and operating system. If you like, you can view the system in the certified devices list as viewed on the specific NAS or NAM.

Agent Distribution

After Clean Access Agent is deployed, you can force the users to automatically upgrade to the latest version. Additionally, you can upload the necessary patches to NAM when necessary. To perform these tasks, you must navigate to **Device Management > Clean Access > Clean Access Agent > Distribution**. From here, you can configure the distribution using the following options as displayed in Figure 9-17:

- **Current Clean Access Agent Patch Is a Mandatory Upgrade**   Selecting this option and clicking the **Update** button forces the user to upgrade Clean Access Agent. Not selecting this check box offers the upgrade as optional and allows the user to defer installation to a later time.

- **Do Not Offer Current Clean Access Agent Patch to Users for Upgrade**   This option allows you to retain your current agent version deployment and not offer the agent upgrade to any users.

- **Clean Access Agent Setup/Patch to Upload**   Browsing to the patch allows you to manually upload a Clean Access Agent installer in the form of setup.tar.gz or upgrade.tar.gz.

Figure 9-17 *Configuring Agent Distribution*

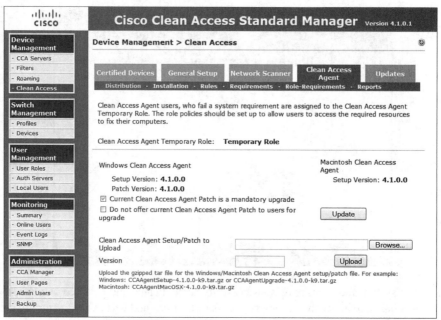

- **Version** This retains the same version information here for the manual upload.
- **Upload button** This uploads the file that was located using the browse function previously.

Other important information pertinent to the Clean Access Agent distribution methodology is configured under the **Installation** option below the **Clean Access Agent** tab. On this page, shown in Figure 9-18, you can configure the following related agent installer configuration information:

- **Discovery Host** This by default is the NAM DNS name or IP address. This must be configured as a reachable IP on the trusted side of each NAS. This is the address Cisco Clean Access Agent uses to attempt to discover the NAS in a Layer 3 deployment. This is also the address that NAS monitors for destination traffic to identify Cisco Clean Access Agent systems. Although this is typically set to the NAM address, it can be changed to any routable and reachable trusted side address to limit the exposure the NAM has to actual client communication.

- **Direct Installation Options** When the installer is invoked by the NAC Appliance authentication mechanisms, the following options for the installer can be set:

    — **No UI** No user input is required. This is a silent install.

Figure 9-18 *Installation Options for the Agent Installer as Well as the Agent Download Options*

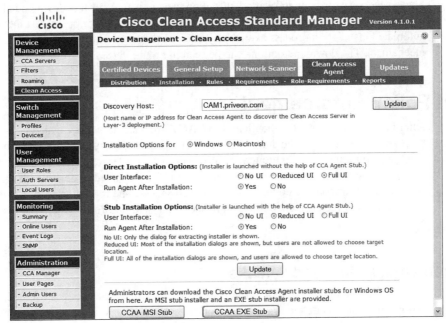

— **Reduced UI**   The user can see the installation, but it requires no user input or selections.

— **Full UI**   The user is required to interact with the installer to complete the installation.

- **Run Agent After Installation**   Choose Yes or No.

- **Stub Installation Options**   When the installer is executed via a stub installer as downloaded for installation by a third-party software distribution system, you can configure how much interaction is required by the end user. The same options that were available to the direct installer are also configurable for the stub installer. Using the stub Clean Access Agent allows a domain administrator to install Clean Access Agent such that on connection to the network, the necessary permissions are granted to the full Clean Access Agent.

Alternative Agent Installation Methods

Another alternative to installing Clean Access Agent via the web authentication page is to distribute it through your typical software delivery mechanism, such as login scripts, BigFix, or Microsoft SMS. To retrieve the installer files from NAM, you must navigate to the **Installation** option under the **Clean Access Agent** tab. At the bottom of this configuration page, you can download either the CCAA MSI Stub or the CCAA EXE Stub file as necessary for your software distribution mechanism. After it is downloaded, your software distribution system administrator has to appropriately script and test the automated installation process as with any other package currently distributed via this mechanism. The download options can be seen in Figure 9-18.

Agent Policy Enforcement

After Clean Access Agent authenticates to NAC Appliance, it is interrogated using mechanisms available to the current Clean Access Agent. The system will either have to meet the requirements or be brought into compliance in order to access the network. If the system does not meet requirements, access will be prevented or degraded if the administrator has configured the system for such access. The following sections cover the configuration of requirements, rules, and checks that will interrogate and remediate the end-user's system.

Requirements, Rules, and Checks

You must map requirements, rules, and checks to implement the necessary remediation actions that you will define for your network-attached systems. Requirements implement decisions (remediation actions) as a result of what you determine systems must have to be considered compliant. Rules are mapped to a requirement in order to define the necessary guidelines that must be met to in turn meet the requirement. Checks are single parameters that must exist for custom rules to be met, such as the existence of a registry key or process.

Creating and Enforcing a Requirement

The following seven types of definable requirements are available:

- File Distribution
- Link Distribution
- Local Check
- AV Definition Update
- AS Definition Update
- Windows Update
- Launch Program

The seven options define what outcome will occur when a requirement is not met. After the necessary configuration between rules and requirements is defined, the administrator can assign the requirement to a specific normal login user role. At this point, on authentication, users are placed into the Temporary role until they meet the requirements tied to their specific normal login role.

A common requirement configured in a customer environment is an antivirus update. The following list steps through the necessary process to create that requirement:

Step 1 Before proceeding, you must ensure that your current antivirus product is supported by navigating to the **Clean Access Agent > Rules > AV/AS Support Info** page. You can select your specific antivirus vendor from the drop-down list and verify that your currently deployed antivirus is supported, as illustrated in Figure 9-19. After you verify that it is supported, you can continue with your configuration steps.

Figure 9-19 *Antivirus and Antispyware Support Verification*

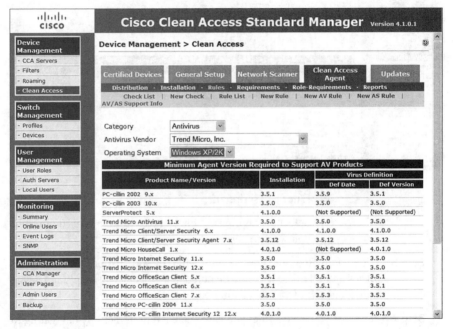

Step 2 Prior to creating the requirement, you have to create the necessary rules that are the building blocks of the requirement. Remaining on the Rules page, select the **New AV Rule** option. All the substeps listed here are displayed in Figure 9-20 for configuring this specific antivirus rule.

    (a) Enter a rule name, such as **Trend_Micro_AV_Definition**.

    (b) Select **Trend Micro, Inc.** from the **Antivirus Vendor** drop-down list.

    (c) Select **Virus Definition** from the **Type** drop-down list.

    (d) Select the appropriate OS.

Figure 9-20 *New Antivirus Rule Configuration*

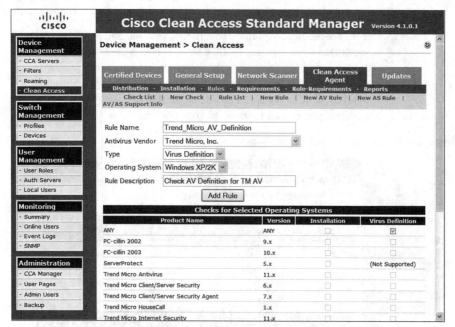

(e) Enter a description.

(f) Select the appropriate check boxes for the virus definitions you want to verify.

Step 3 After adding the rule, you are returned to the rule list page that contains all configured rules. It should be noted that you can edit, copy, and delete individual rules from this listing page.

Step 4 Now that you have a rule, you can create a requirement by navigating to the **Requirements** option under the **Clean Access Agent** tab. Select **New Requirement**. The substeps configured here for the new requirement are displayed in Figure 9-21.

(a) Select **AV Definition Update** from the **Requirement Type** drop-down list.

(b) Select the appropriate enforcement type:

- **Mandatory**   The client absolutely must comply with this requirement to proceed on the network.

- **Optional**   The user can bypass this requirement or comply as desired.

Figure 9-21 *New Antivirus Requirement Configuration*

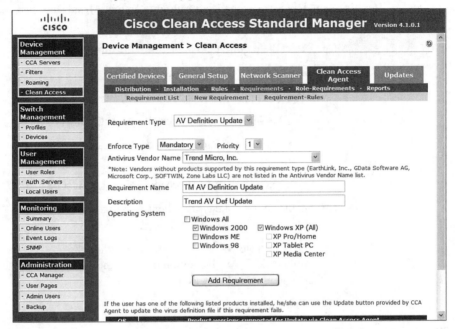

- **Audit**   The requirement is checked, but the user is not notified of either a pass or fail outcome. The system reports the results back for administrative review.

(c) Select the priority. The priority is where in the order of requirement enforcement the requirement is placed. Failure at any point causes the system to fail the requirements check.

(d) Select the appropriate antivirus vendor name from the list.

(e) Provide a requirement name.

(f) Provide a description.

(g) Select the operating systems on which the requirement should be evaluated.

(h) Click the **Add Requirement** button.

Step 5   After completion of that page, you are returned to the requirement list page where you can reorder, edit, and delete individual requirements.

Step 6   You can now associate the rules with your new requirement. Navigate to **Requirement-Rules** under the **Requirements** option. All substeps here are displayed in Figure 9-22.

(a) Select the requirement name from the drop-down list.

(b) Select the appropriate operating system.

(c) Select the appropriate option for **Requirement Met If**:

  • **All Selected Rules Succeed**   All rules must be met.

  • **Any Selected Rule Succeeds**   At least one rule must be met.

  • **No Selected Rule Succeeds**   No rules must be met.

(d) Set the number of days the client antivirus definition can be older than what NAM lists as current.

(e) Select the rule you created earlier regarding the Trend_Micro_AV_Definition or select the appropriate pr_rule provided by Cisco.

(f) Click the **Update** button to commit the mapping.

Figure 9-22 *Requirement-Rules Mapping*

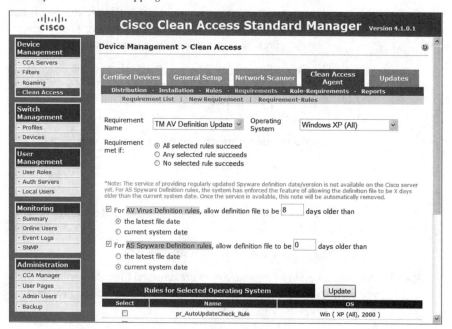

Step 7   Now that you have configured the requirement that relies on the mapped rules, you must choose to enforce the requirement on the chosen role. Navigate to **Role-Requirements** to configure this requirement assignment. The configuration of the following substeps is displayed in Figure 9-23.

(a)   Select the type of role you want to apply to the requirements as either **Normal Login Role** or **Quarantine Role**.

(b)   Select the User role to map the requirement.

(c)   Check the boxes in front of the requirement or requirements you want to map to this role.

(d)   Click the **Update** button to commit the change.

Figure 9-23   *Role-Requirement Mapping*

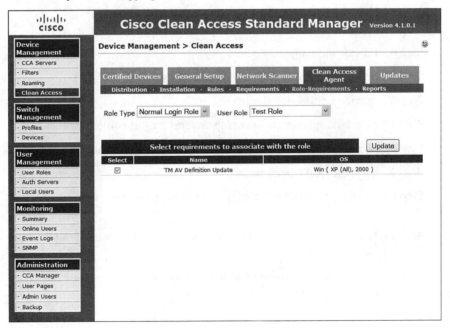

NOTE   You might notice many of the rules and checks are prefaced with *pr_* and *pc_*. pr_ indicates a Cisco-deployed preconfigured rule, and pc_ indicates a Cisco-deployed preconfigured check.

Many requirement types, rules, and checks are preconfigured and automatically updated by Cisco in addition to the unlimited number of configurations you can make yourself. Becoming familiar with the configuration of custom rules will provide you with extremely granular control over the policy you want to enforce.

Creating Checks

Checks are logic that allows the Cisco Clean Access Agent to verify that a registry key, file, service, or application exists and, if pertinent, whether it is running or not running. To create a new check, you simply navigate to the **New Check** option under the **Rules** menu option. You will now configure a simple application check to verify that ftpserv.exe is running on the system you are interrogating. The following steps are illustrated in Figure 9-24.

Step 1 Select **Application Check** from the **Check Category** drop-down list.

Step 2 Leave the default and only option of **Application Status** for this check type.

Step 3 Name the check.

Step 4 Provide the application name.

Step 5 Select **Running** in the **Operator** drop-down list.

Step 6 Provide a check description.

Step 7 Select the appropriate operating systems for this particular check.

Step 8 Select **Automatically Create Rule Based on This Check**.

Step 9 Click the **Add Check** button.

Step 10 Navigate to the **Check List** menu option and scroll to the bottom to see your check.

Step 11 Navigate to the **Rule List** menu option and scroll to the bottom to locate the created rule.

Step 12 Select **Edit Rule** to better understand the creation of the new rule. This rule is displayed in Figure 9-25.

Figure 9-24 *Creating an Application Check for ftpserv.exe*

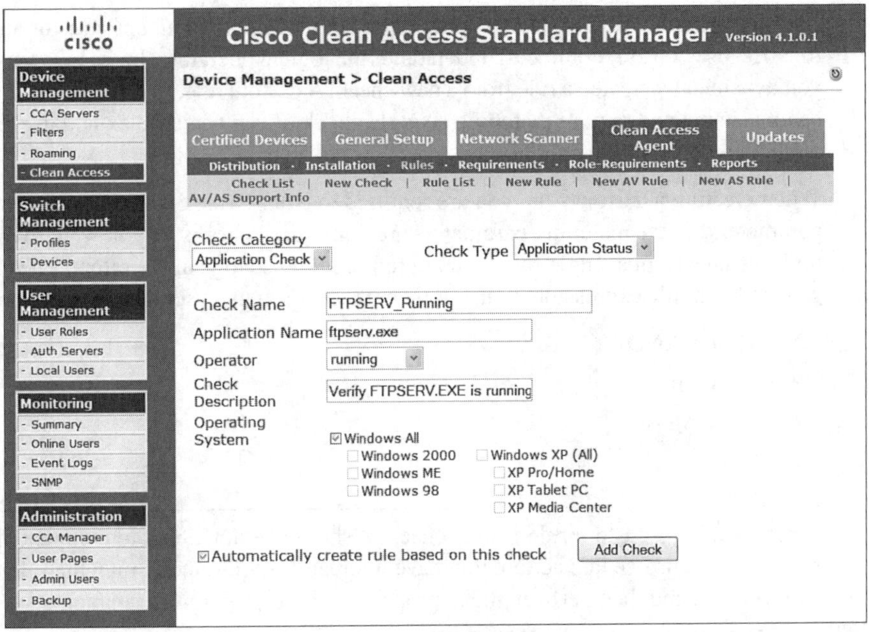

Figure 9-25 *Dynamically Created Rule for ftpserv.exe Running*

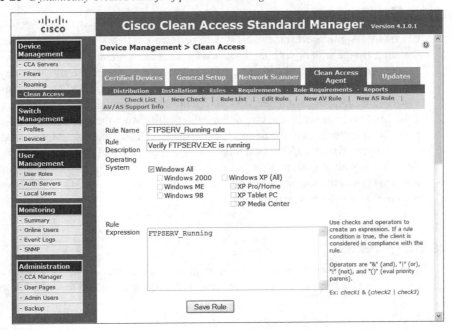

Creating a Custom Rule

Creating a custom rule is slightly more complex than creating an antivirus or antispyware rule because you are required to understand rule logical operators. In the previous example, you dynamically created a rule from a new check. A custom rule, as displayed in Figure 9-25, can be simple and require matching a single check or can be complex and use logical application of multiple checks.

When creating a custom rule, you are required to enter a rule expression as the matching parameters. These matching parameters are configured checks. If you want to evaluate multiple checks in a single rule, you are required to use logical operators. The checks are grouped in a rule expression by using parentheses. You can use the following operators:

- "&" for AND
- "|" for OR
- "!" for NOT

NOTE   When creating a custom rule from a check, it should be noted that to complete the steps necessary to enforce this action, you have to create a requirement, map the rule to that requirement, and then perform the appropriate role-to-requirement mapping.

Network Scanning

Cisco NAC Appliance has the capability to perform a network scan using the Nessus scanning engine with or without the Cisco Clean Access Agent installed on the system to be scanned. The scans and updates are manual processes, and the results will vary depending on other security products and personal firewalls installed on the scanned system. On completion of a network scan of the system attempting access to the network, NAC Appliance can notify the user of the vulnerability, warn the user with a user agreement page, block the user from the network, or assign the Quarantine role. Many Nessus scans (plug-ins) are available today from http://www.nessus.org, including virus and worm detection as well as detecting the presence of network applications such as instant messengers and file-sharing applications. To use scanning, you must load the Nessus plug-ins and then configure scanning.

Nessus Plug-Ins

Nessus plug-ins must be downloaded from http://www.nessus.org due to a licensing requirement by Tenable, the owner of Nessus. After you download the plug-ins, you must rename them plugins.tar.gz before uploading. If you are uploading a single plug-in, it must be named myplugin.nasl. Perform the following steps in Figure 9-26 to complete a Nessus plug-in upload.

Step 1 Navigate to **Clean Access > Network Scanner > Plugin Updates**.

Step 2 Browse to the plug-in file (which is named plugins.tar.gz), and then click the **Upload** button.

Figure 9-26 *Uploading Nessus Plug-Ins*

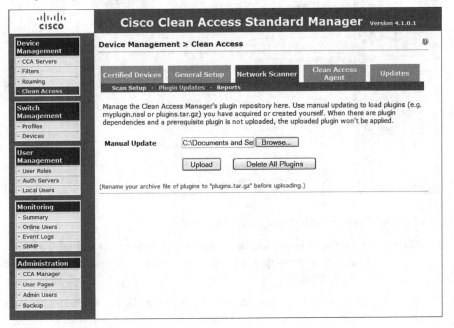

When this is completed, you can continue to configure scanning on your NAC Appliance.

Scanning Setup

Now that you have loaded Nessus plug-ins into your NAM, you can configure scanning to occur from the NAS systems as desired. To select the plug-ins you want to use per user role and operating system, as shown in Figure 9-27, perform the following steps:

Step 1 Navigate to **Clean Access > Network Scanner > Plugins**.

Step 2 Select the user role to configure scanning.

Figure 9-27 *Configuring Network Scanning by User Role and Operating System*

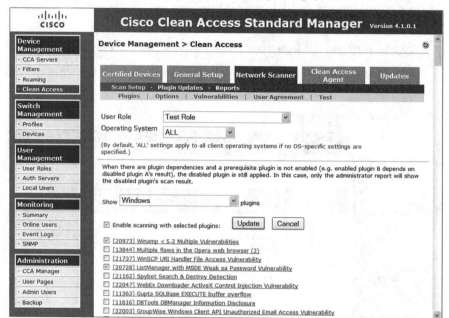

Step 3   Select the associated operating system.

Step 4   In the **Show** drop-down box, select the plug-in group you want to view.
After a plug-in group is selected, the bottom of the page will display the
available plug-ins.

Step 5   Select the plug-ins you want to enable as well as any dependent plug-ins
required for other selected plug-ins.

Step 6   Select the check box next to **Enable Scanning with Select Plugins**.

Step 7   Click the **Update** button.

If you are using the more complex plug-ins that can employ some additional configuration,
you can navigate to the **Options** menu to perform additional configuration as required.
Figure 9-28 shows a sample configuration option.

Figure 9-28 *Configuring Advanced Scanning Configuration Options*

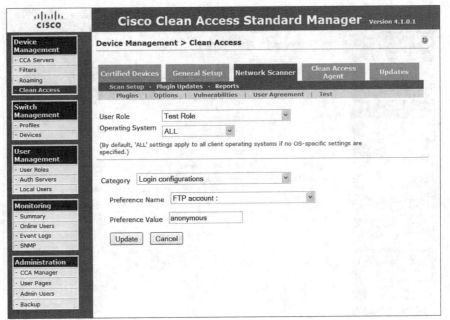

Vulnerability Handling

When NAS scans a system and locates a vulnerability as a result, it can warn the user, block access, or assign the Quarantine role. This is all configured per scanning plug-in on the **Vulnerabilities** menu. The following configuration for a single plug-in is shown in Figure 9-29.

Step 1   Navigate to **Network Scanner > Scan Setup > Vulnerabilities**.

Step 2   Select the plug-in you want to configure.

Step 3   Select **—NEVER—, HOLE, HOLE,WARN,** or **HOLE,WARN,INFO** from the drop-down menu to identify the Nessus scan result that should be returned as a matching parameter from the resulting scan.

Step 4   Click the **Edit** icon next to the particular plug-in. Doing so presents additional configuration options.

Step 5   Enter the instruction, which is the test field that will be presented to users.

Step 6   Enter a link, which is the URL that can assist users in remediating their system.

Step 7   Click the **Update** button to continue.

Figure 9-29 *Configuring Vulnerability Handling per Plug-In*

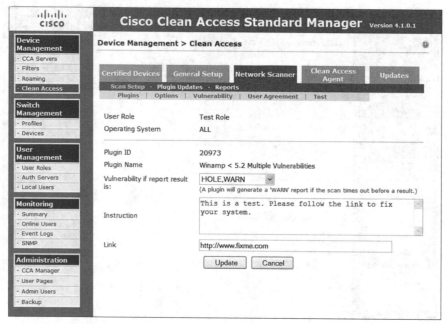

After completing the plug-in vulnerability handling, you return to the Vulnerabilities page, which will show your configuration, as seen in Figure 9-30.

Figure 9-30 *Vulnerabilities List Page*

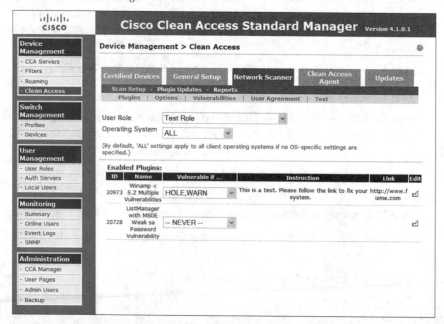

User Agreement Configuration

You can also configure a user agreement page that will be presented to the users so that they can be certified for network access. They are required to agree to this text before proceeding. Figure 9-31 illustrates the simple configuration of this page, which includes role-specific and OS-specific information, an informational message to present to the user, the acknowledgment instructions, and the labels for accepting or declining the user agreement.

Figure 9-31 *User Agreement Page for Network Scanning*

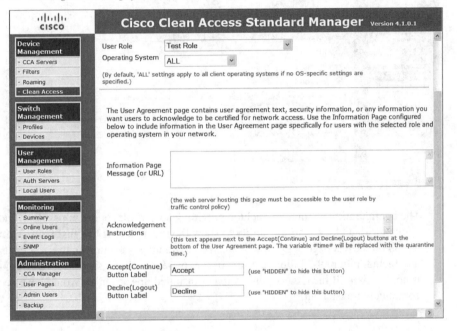

Testing the Scanning Setup

After you have completed the configuration of network scanning, you can test the configuration from the **Test** menu item. Figure 9-32 illustrates the configuration parameters and testing results of the plug-ins you configured.

Figure 9-32 *Testing Scanning in Your Network*

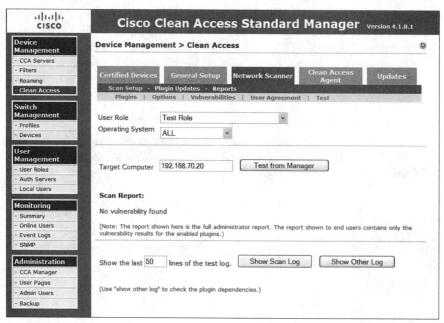

The configuration parameters include providing a user role, operating system, and target computer IP address, and the ability to show the log. Clicking the **Test from Manager** button on the test page begins the scan. While scanning is occurring, the user experience is unaffected. Figure 9-33 illustrates the user experience when using the CCA Agent, which is not required. If the CCA Agent were not installed, the scanning would have been completely transparent.

Figure 9-33 *Scanning User Experience While Using the CCA Agent*

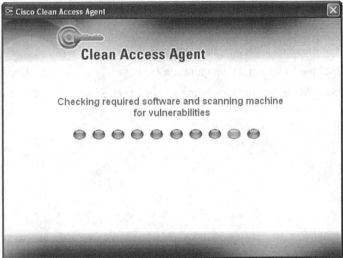

Summary

Configuring the Cisco Clean Access Agent can be a complex task, but the granular requirements can make for an extremely secure and up-to-date computing environment. Properly configuring your NAC Appliance is extremely important, but when it is completed, you can rest assured that your corporate-controlled assets (as well as uncontrolled assets such as contractor systems) will be brought into compliance before they can access critical systems.

This chapter covers the following topics:

- Out-of-Band Overview and Design
- Sample Design and Configuration for Layer 2 Out-of-Band Deployment
- Sample Design and Configuration for Layer 3 Out-of-Band Deployment

CHAPTER 10

Configuring Out-of-Band

This chapter covers the configuration of the Out-of-Band (OOB) mode in both Layer 2 (where users are Layer 2 adjacent to NAC Appliance Server) and Layer 3 (where users are one or more hops away from NAC Appliance Server) scenarios. For detailed information explaining what OOB is and how it compares to In-Band (IB) mode, see Chapter 4, "Making Sense of All the Cisco NAC Appliance Design Options," earlier in this book. This book does not include a chapter on configuring In-Band mode. The main reason for this is that if you know how to configure OOB mode, you also know how to configure IB mode. To configure IB mode, you follow almost the same steps you would to configure OOB mode, but you leave out the switch and VLAN configuration steps.

Out-of-Band Overview and Design

When planning for an Out-of-Band mode deployment, keep in mind that the following factors will affect the design.

User Access Method

Today, NAC Appliance supports Out-of-Band mode only for users on a wired LAN. Wireless and virtual private network (VPN) users must use In-Band mode.

Switch Support

NAC Appliance Out-of-Band mode works with only Cisco Catalyst switches. NAC Appliance In-Band mode supports most Cisco switches. A complete compatibility matrix of supported switches is at

> http://www.cisco.com/univercd/cc/td/doc/product/vpn/ciscosec/cca/cca40/switch.htm

Central Deployment Mode or Edge Deployment Mode

Here the terms *central* and *edge deployment* refer to the physical configuration of NAC Appliance Server. Central Deployment mode means that both the trusted interface and the untrusted interface of NAC Appliance Server (NAS) are plugged in to the same physical switch. Edge Deployment mode means that the interfaces are plugged in to two separate switches. Out-of-band deployments use Central Deployment mode. This is because in an out-of-band deployment, NAC Appliance Servers are almost always placed at the distribution or core layer and not at the edge of the network.

Layer 2 or Layer 3

If NAC Appliance Server is placed such that end users are Layer 2 adjacent to it, configure NAC Appliance Server to be in Layer 2 Out-of-Band (L2OOB) mode.

If NAC Appliance Server is placed such that the end users are one or more hops away from it, configure NAC Appliance Server to be in Layer 3 Out-of-Band (L3OOB) mode.

Gateway Mode for NAC Appliance Server

NAC Appliance Server can be configured in Virtual Gateway mode or Real-IP Gateway mode. Most L2OOB deployments will be in Virtual Gateway mode because this mode requires relatively fewer configuration changes as compared to Real-IP Gateway mode.

In Virtual Gateway mode, the IP address configured on the untrusted port of NAC Appliance Server is of no practical use. Remember that, in Virtual Gateway mode, NAC Appliance Server is acting as a Layer 2 transparent bridge and therefore has only one management IP. The IP address configured on the trusted port of NAC Appliance Server is used as the management IP. Therefore, the untrusted port IP address cannot be used for any practical purposes.

In Real-IP Gateway mode, NAC Appliance Server acts as a Layer 3 device (router); therefore, both the trusted and untrusted port IP addresses are usable. Most L3OOB deployments will be in Real-IP Gateway mode. This is because in L3OOB, you must have a usable IP address on the untrusted port. This will become clearer when the L3OOB designs are discussed later in this chapter.

Table 10-1 lists the compatibility matrix for the switches with the type of gateway mode.

Table 10-1   *Gateway Mode Switch Compatibility Matrix*

L2 or L3 Switch	Virtual Gateway Mode		Real-IP Mode
	Central Deployment	Edge Deployment	Central or Edge Deployment
6500	Yes	Yes	Yes
4500	Yes	Yes	Yes
3750/3560 (L3 switch)	Yes with 12.2(25)SEE and higher	Yes	Yes
3550 (L3 switch)	No*	Yes	Yes
3750/3560 (L2 switch)	Yes	Yes	Yes
3550 (L2 switch)	Yes	Yes	Yes
2950/2960	Yes	Yes	Yes

*Due to Cisco IOS switch caveat CSCsb62432

Note that the information in Table 10-1 is independent of IB or OOB mode. The one red flag in Table 10-1 is that a NAC Appliance Server in Central Deployment mode, connected to a Catalyst 3550 switch (as a Layer 3 switch), cannot be configured in Virtual Gateway mode. This is due to Cisco IOS switch caveat CSCsb62432 (http://www.cisco.com/cgi-bin/Support/Bugtool/onebug.pl?bugid=CSCsb62432). Note that user registration or a service contract is required to access some Cisco.com resources.

Simple Network Management Protocol Trap to Trigger the NAC Process

A switch can be configured to generate a linkup or MAC-notification trap to detect that a new user has connected to the switch port. The choice of using linkup or MAC-notification depends on the switch and the code that the switch is running. If you have a choice, you should always use MAC-notification. It is a more efficient and flexible trap.

Other factors that determine the best trap to use are whether you have IP phones and whether user machines are going to connect to the network from behind those IP phones. When a user connects to the network in this scenario, no new linkup is detected; as a result, you have to rely on MAC notifications to detect whether a new user has connected to the network from behind an IP phone.

Port-Based VLAN Assignment or User Role–Based VLAN Assignment

If you use port-based VLAN assignment in Out-of-Band mode, the untrusted VLAN and the trusted VLAN for a particular port are static. When a user connects to that port, the user moves to a preconfigured untrusted VLAN. After the user authenticates and remediates, the user moves to a trusted VLAN that is also preconfigured for that port.

If you use user role–based VLAN assignment, the untrusted VLAN for a particular port is static. However, after the user is authenticated and remediated, the trusted VLAN that the user moves to depends on the role to which the user belongs. This is dynamically determined based on the user's user role.

Sample Design and Configuration for Layer 2 Out-of-Band Deployment

For this Layer 2 Out-of-Band mode example, consider the topology in Figure 10-1.

Figure 10-1 *Sample Network Topology*

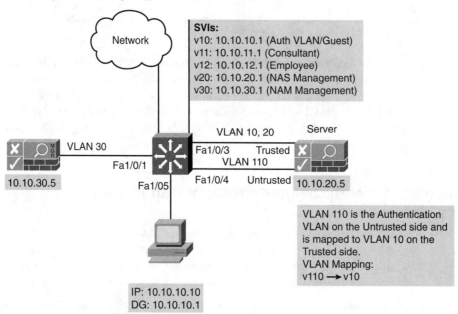

The user PC, NAC Appliance Manager, and NAC Appliance Server are connected to a Catalyst 3750 switch. NAC Appliance Server is configured in Virtual Gateway Central Deployment mode.

NAC Appliance Manager (NAM) is on VLAN 30 and has an IP address (10.10.30.5 /24). NAC Appliance Server management is on VLAN 20 and has an IP address (10.10.20.5 /24).

NOTE   In Virtual Gateway mode, the NAC Appliance Server management IP has to be on a different subnet than the NAC Appliance Manager. This is because when NAS has to initiate packets while in Virtual Gateway mode, it always sends them out of the untrusted port (except for packets destined for its default gateway or a subnet other than the NAC Appliance Server management subnet). NAC Appliance Manager always resides on the trusted network. Therefore, to talk to NAC Appliance Manager, NAC Appliance Server has to send packets out of the trusted port, which necessitates that NAC Appliance Manager resides on a subnet different from that of NAC Appliance Server.

In this design, you will use user role–based VLAN assignment. There are three user VLANs:

- VLAN 10 (Guest)
- VLAN 11 (Consultant)
- VLAN 12 (Employee)

Based on who connects to a switch port, you want to move the user to one of the VLANs in the preceding list. The VLANs have access control lists (ACLs) associated with their switch virtual interfaces (SVIs) to restrict network access appropriately for those user roles. It is important to note that these ACLs are not managed or controlled by NAC Appliance, and they are applied within the Cisco switches themselves as VLAN ACLs. Now that you have a good idea of the design principles, the remainder of this section shows how to configure a Layer 2 out-of-band deployment.

Step 1: Configuring the Switch

The Catalyst 3750 switch is being used as a Layer 3 switch running code 12.2(25)SEE. (See Figure 10-1.)

Configuring VLAN Trunking Protocol and VLANs

One of the first things you will do is configure your switches to support the OOB deployment. Example 10-1 shows how you would configure the VLANs on the switch shown in Figure 10-1 of the sample network.

Example 10-1 *Switch Configuration for OOB Deployment*

```
vtp domain cisco
vtp mode transparent
ip routing
!
vlan 10
 name guest
!
vlan 11
 name consultant
!
vlan 12
 name employee
!
vlan 20
 name NAS_mgmt
!
vlan 30
 name NAM_mgmt
!
vlan 110
 name untrusted_vlan
!
vlan 998-999
 !
```

Configuring SVIs

The next step is to configure the Layer 3 interfaces (SVIs) on the switch. Example 10-2 shows the SVI configurations for the sample network (see Figure 10-1). Note that all these SVIs reside only on the trusted side of NAC Appliance Server. For a client on VLAN 110 (the untrusted side) to reach them, it is forced to go through NAC Appliance Server. The other SVIs are used as default gateways for the different user access VLANs. Remember that after a client is considered clean, its switch port dynamically reconfigures and the client moves to its access VLAN. At this point, NAC Appliance is no longer in the client s traffic path. In this example, the access VLAN is determined by the client s user role; Employee is VLAN 12, for example.

Example 10-2 *Switch SVI Configuration*

```
interface Vlan10
 ip address 10.10.10.1 255.255.255.0
!
interface Vlan11
 ip address 10.10.11.1 255.255.255.0
!
interface Vlan12
 ip address 10.10.12.1 255.255.255.0
!
```

Example 10-2 *Switch SVI Configuration (Continued)*

```
interface Vlan20
 ip address 10.10.20.1 255.255.255.0
!
interface Vlan30
 ip address 10.10.30.1 255.255.255.0
!
```

Notice that you did not configure an SVI for VLAN 110. This is necessary to force VLAN 110 traffic through NAC Appliance Server as the only way out of VLAN 110.

Configuring the Switch as a DHCP Server

NAC Appliance Server running in Virtual Gateway mode cannot act as the DHCP server for its untrusted-side networks. NAC Appliance Server functionality is disabled when running in this mode. Therefore, you must provide a DHCP server. Many organizations use the DHCP server functionality built into most Cisco switches. However, any DHCP server will work.

If NAC Appliance Server is running in Real-IP Gateway mode, using the built-in DHCP server functionality of NAC Appliance Server is recommended. In the sample network (see Figure 10-1), NAC Appliance Server is in Virtual Gateway mode. Example 10-3 shows how to configure a Cisco switch to act as a DHCP server. Remember that VLAN 110 (auth VLAN) is mapped to VLAN 10 on the trusted side. The switch is configured to act as the DHCP server for the auth VLAN 10 and the access VLANs 11 and 12.

Example 10-3 *Cisco Switch DHCP Server Configuration*

```
ip dhcp excluded-address 10.10.10.1
ip dhcp excluded-address 10.10.10.254
ip dhcp excluded-address 10.10.11.1
ip dhcp excluded-address 10.10.11.254
ip dhcp excluded-address 10.10.12.1
ip dhcp excluded-address 10.10.12.254
!
ip dhcp pool vlan10
   network 10.10.10.0 255.255.255.0
   default-router 10.10.10.1
dns-server 192.168.35.2
domain-name  cisco.com
!
ip dhcp pool vlan11
   network 10.10.11.0 255.255.255.0
   default-router 10.10.11.1
dns-server 192.168.35.2
domain-name  cisco.com
```

continues

Example 10-3 *Cisco Switch DHCP Server Configuration (Continued)*

```
!
ip dhcp pool vlan12
   network 10.10.12.0 255.255.255.0
   default-router 10.10.12.1
dns-server 192.168.35.2
domain-name  cisco.com
!
```

Configuring Fa1/0/1—The Interface Connecting the NAC Appliance Manager eth0 Port

Next you must configure the switch port that the eth0 interface of NAC Appliance Manager plugs into. The eth0 interface of NAC Appliance Manager resides on a VLAN on the trusted side. If NAC Appliance Server is running in Virtual Gateway mode, its VLAN must not be the same as the VLAN of NAC Appliance Server management. In the sample network topology (see Figure 10-1), the NAC Appliance Manager eth0 interface connects to the switch's Fa1/0/1 and resides in VLAN 30. Example 10-4 shows this switch configuration.

Example 10-4 *Cisco Switch Configuration of the NAC Appliance Manager eth0 Port*

```
interface FastEthernet1/0/1
 description  Manager eth0
 switchport access vlan 30
 switchport mode access
 spanning-tree portfast
```

Configuring Fa1/0/3—The Interface Connecting the Trusted Port (eth0) of NAC Appliance Server

The switch port that the eth0 interface plugs into will be configured as a trunk link forwarding traffic for the mapped authentication VLANs and the NAC Appliance Server management VLAN. The trunk's native VLAN should be set to something that is not used anywhere else in the network, essentially making it a black hole. Example 10-5 shows the switch configuration for the sample topology (see Figure 10-1). In the sample topology, VLAN 10 is the mapped authentication VLAN, and VLAN 20 is the NAC Appliance Server management VLAN.

Example 10-5 *Cisco Switch Configuration for the NAC Appliance Server eth0 Post*

```
interface FastEthernet1/0/3
 switchport trunk encapsulation dot1q
 switchport trunk native vlan 998
 switchport trunk allowed vlan 10,20
 switchport mode trunk
```

Configuring Fa1/0/4—The Interface Connecting the Untrusted Port (eth1) of NAC Appliance Server

The switch port that the eth1 interface plugs into will be configured as a trunk link forwarding traffic for the authentication VLAN on the untrusted side. Example 10-6 shows the switch configuration based on the sample network topology.

Example 10-6 *Cisco Switch Configuration for the NAC Appliance Server eth0 Port*

```
interface FastEthernet1/0/4
 switchport trunk encapsulation dot1q
 switchport trunk native vlan 999
 switchport trunk allowed vlan 110
 switchport mode trunk
```

When configuring the switch port connecting the trusted and untrusted ports of the NAC Appliance Server, please note the following:

- Always ensure that no common VLANs are being forwarded between the trusted and untrusted ports. A common VLAN between the ports can cause a Layer 2 loop to occur.

- Configure different black hole native VLANs for the untrusted and trusted ports. Make sure that these VLANs are not used for user traffic. Prune these black hole native VLANs from the other trunk ports throughout your network. The goal is to not propagate these VLANs beyond the switch they are configured on.

- Allow the relevant VLANs to be forwarded only on the trunk trusted and untrusted ports. Prune the remaining VLANs off from these ports.

Configuring Fa1/0/5—The Interface Connecting the Host

A best practice is to assign all client switch ports to an initial VLAN equal to the auth VLAN for that switch. In the sample topology, the auth VLAN is VLAN 110. Example 10-7 shows the switch configuration for this.

Example 10-7 *Cisco Switch Configuration for Client Switch Ports*

```
interface FastEthernet1/0/5
 switchport access vlan 110
 switchport mode access
 spanning-tree portfast
```

Configuring Simple Network Management Protocol

The switch and NAC Appliance communicate via Simple Network Management Protocol (SNMP). For this to work, the switch must be set up for SNMP. Example 10-8 configures the switch with SNMP MAC-notification traps and linkdown traps. The MAC-notification trap detects a new user on the network and triggers the NAC process. The linkdown trap detects that the user is disconnected from the network. The read-only community string *public* is used with an access list *10*, which allows access only by NAC Appliance Manager. The read-write community string *private* is used with access list *10*. It is always a security best practice to configure an access list on SNMP communities to protect against unwanted access. The switch is configured to send these traps to NAC Appliance Manager at 10.10.30.5. Example 10-8 shows the configuration of SNMPv2c, but NAC Appliance supports v1 and v3 as well.

Example 10-8 *Cisco Switch SNMP Configuration*

```
snmp-server community public RO 10
snmp-server community private RW 10
snmp-server enable traps snmp linkdown
snmp-server enable traps MAC-Notification
snmp-server host 10.10.30.5 version 2c public
access-list 10 permit ip 10.10.30.5
```

Step 2: Configuring NAC Appliance Manager

Now that the network is configured, move on to configuring NAC Appliance Manager. On NAC Appliance Manager, you have to do some basic configuration using the configuration script. From the NAC Appliance Manager command-line interface (CLI), you must type in **service perfigo config**. Before NAC Appliance Manager has an IP address configured, you can access the CLI either by attaching a monitor and keyboard or by using a serial cable to port 1. The serial speed and setup is 38400, N, 8, 1. Example 10-9 shows the configuration setup script.

Example 10-9 *Configuring NAM via CLI*

```
Fedora Core release 4 (Stentz)
Kernel 2.6.11-perfigo on an i686

cam login: root
Password:
[root@cam ~]# service perfigo config

Welcome to the Cisco Clean Access Manager quick configuration utility.

Note that you need to be root to execute this utility.

The utility will now ask you a series of configuration questions.
Please answer them carefully.

Cisco Clean Access Manager, (C) 2006 Cisco Systems, Inc.

Configuring the network interface:

Please enter the IP address for the interface eth0 [10.2.0.15]: 10.10.30.5
You entered 10.10.30.5. Is this correct? (y/n)? [y]
```

Example 10-9   *Configuring NAM via CLI (Continued)*

```
Please enter the netmask for the interface eth0 [255.255.255.0]:
You entered 255.255.255.0. Is this correct? (y/n)? [y]

Please enter the IP address for the default gateway [10.2.0.1]: 10.10.30.1
You entered 10.10.30.1. Is this correct? (y/n)? [y]

Please enter the hostname [cam1]: nam
You entered nam. Is this correct? (y/n)? [y]

Please enter the IP address for the name server: [192.168.10.1]: 10.10.30.6
You entered 10.10.30.6. Is this correct? (y/n)? [y]

Would you like to change shared secret? (y/n)? [y]
Please remember to configure the Clean Access Server with the same string. Please
   enter the shared secret between Clean Access Server
You entered: cisco123
Is this correct? (y/n)? [y]

>>> Configuring date and time:

The timezone is currently set to:America/Los_Angeles
Would you like to change this setting? (y/n)? [y] n

Current date and time hh:mm:ss mm/dd/yy [01:01:01 01/01/07]: 01:20:00 01/01/07
You entered 01:20:00 01/01/07 Is this correct? (y/n)? [y]
Mon Jan 01 01:20:00 PST 2007

You must generate a valid SSL certificate in order to use the Clean Access Manager's
   secure web console.
Please answer the following questions correctly.
Information for a new SSL certificate:
Enter fully qualified domain name or IP: 10.10.30.5
Enter organization unit name: nacapp
Enter organization name: cisco
Enter city name: san jose
Enter state code: ca
Enter 2 letter country code: us


You entered the following:
Domain: 10.10.30.5
Organization unit: nacapp
Organization name: cisco
City name: san jose
State code: ca
Country code: us
Is this correct? (y/n)? [y]
Generating SSL Certificate...
CA signing: /root/.tomcat.csr -> /root/.tomcat.crt:
CA verifying: /root/.tomcat.crt <-> CA cert
```

continues

Example 10-9 *Configuring NAM via CLI (Continued)*

```
/root/.tomcat.crt: OK
Done

For security reasons, it is highly recommended that you change the default passwords
   for the root user.
User: root
Changing password for user root.
New UNIX password:
Retype new UNIX password:
passwd: all authentication tokens updated successfully.

Changes require a RESTART of Clean Access Manager.
Configuration is complete.
[root@cam1 ~]# service perfigo reboot
```

Step 3: Configuring NAC Appliance Server

On NAC Appliance Server, you have to do some basic configuration using the configuration
script. From the NAC Appliance Server CLI, you must type in **service perfigo config**.
Example 10-10 shows the configuration setup script.

Example 10-10 *Configuring NAS via CLI*

```
[root@cas ~]# service perfigo config

Welcome to the Cisco Clean Access Server quick configuration utility.

Note that you need to be root to execute this utility.

The utility will now ask you a series of configuration questions.
Please answer them carefully.

Cisco Clean Access Server, (C) 2006 Cisco Systems, Inc.

Configuring the network interfaces:

Please enter the IP address for the interface eth0 [10.2.0.15]: 10.10.20.5
You entered 10.10.20.5. Is this correct? (y/n)? [y]

Please enter the netmask for the interface eth0 [255.255.255.0]:
You entered 255.255.255.0. Is this correct? (y/n)? [y]

Please enter the IP address for the default gateway [10.2.0.1]: 10.10.20.1
You entered 10.10.20.1. Is this correct? (y/n)? [y]

[Vlan Id Passthrough] for packets from eth0 to eth1 is disabled.
Would you like to enable it? (y/n)? [n]

[Management Vlan Tagging] for egress packets of eth0 is disabled.
Would you like to enable it? (y/n)? [n]
```

Example 10-10 *Configuring NAS via CLI (Continued)*

```
Please enter the IP address for the untrusted interface eth1 [10.2.0.15]: 10.10.20.5
You entered 10.10.20.5. Is this correct? (y/n)? [y]

Please enter the netmask for the interface eth1 [255.255.255.0]:
You entered 255.255.255.0. Is this correct? (y/n)? [y]

Please enter the IP address for the default gateway [10.2.0.1]: 10.10.20.1
You entered 10.10.20.1. Is this correct? (y/n)? [y]

[Vlan Id Passthrough] for packets from eth1 to eth0 is disabled.
Would you like to enable it? (y/n)? [n]

[Management Vlan Tagging] for egress packets of eth1 is disabled.
Would you like to enable it? (y/n)? [n]

Please enter the hostname [cas1]: nas
You entered NAS1. Is this correct? (y/n)? [y]

Please enter the IP address for the name server: [192.168.10.1]: 10.10.30.6
You entered 10.10.30.6. Is this correct? (y/n)? [y]

Would you like to change shared secret? (y/n)? [y]
Please enter the shared secret: cisco123
You entered: cisco123
Is this correct? (y/n)? [y]

>>> Configuring date and time:


The timezone is currently set to:America/Los_Angeles
Would you like to change this setting? (y/n)? [y] n

Current date and time hh:mm:ss mm/dd/yy [01:01:01 01/01/07]: 01:40:00 01/01/07
You entered 01:40:00 01/01/07 Is this correct? (y/n)? [y]
Mon Jan 01 01:40:00 PST 2007

You must generate a valid SSL certificate in order to use the Clean Access Server's
  secure web console.
Please answer the following questions correctly.
Information for a new SSL certificate:
Enter fully qualified domain name or IP: 10.10.20.5
Enter organization unit name: nacapp
Enter organization name: cisco
Enter city name: san jose
Enter state code: ca
Enter 2 letter country code: us

You entered the following:
Domain: 10.10.20.5
Organization unit: nacapp
Organization name: cisco
```

continues

Example 10-10 *Configuring NAS via CLI (Continued)*

```
City name: san jose
State code: ca
Country code: us
Is this correct? (y/n)? [y]
Generating SSL Certificate...
CA signing: /root/.tomcat.csr -> /root/.tomcat.crt:
CA verifying: /root/.tomcat.crt <-> CA cert
/root/.tomcat.crt: OK
Done

For security reasons, it is highly recommended that you change the default password
   for the root user.
User: root
Changing password for user root.
New UNIX password:
Retype new UNIX password:
passwd: all authentication tokens updated successfully.


Would you like to change the default password for the web console admin user
   password? (y/n)? [y]
Please enter an appropriately secure password for the web console admin user.

New password for web console admin:
Confirm new password for web console admin:
Web console admin password changed successfully.

Configuration is complete.
[root@cas1 ~]# service perfigo reboot
```

Step 4: Logging In to NAC Appliance Manager

Open a browser and connect to NAM through an SSL connection. Type in the IP of the
NAM (https://10.10.30.5) and enter username: **admin** and password: **cisco123**. Figure 10-2
shows a sample screen shot of the NAC Appliance Manager login screen.

Figure 10-2 *NAC Appliance Manager Login Screen*

You can view the network configuration of NAM at **Administration > CCA Manager**. Figure 10-3 shows the network configuration page of NAC Appliance Manager in this sample topology (see Figure 10-1).

Figure 10-3 *Manager Network Configuration Page*

Step 5: Adding NAC Appliance Server to NAC Appliance Manager

You can add NAC Appliance Server by going to **Device Management > CCA Servers > New Server**. Figure 10-4 shows the add new server page.

Figure 10-4 *Add New Server Page*

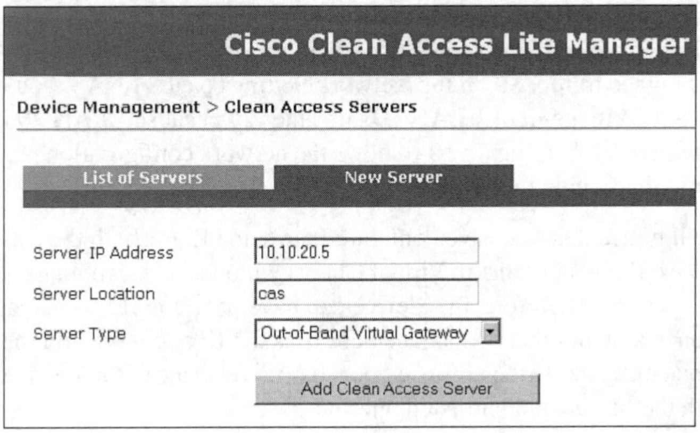

Figure 10-5 shows that NAC Appliance Server has been added in OOB Virtual Gateway mode.

Figure 10-5 *List of Servers Page*

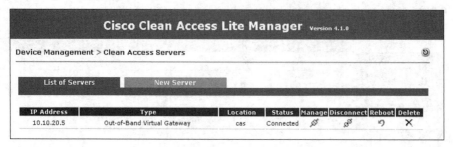

Step 6: Editing Network Settings on NAC Appliance Server

Go to **Device Management > CCA Servers > Manage > Network > IP.** You will see a check box for **Set Management VLAN ID**. This is usually a source of a lot of confusion. By default, this option is not enabled. With this option disabled, when the NAC Appliance Server is initiating traffic and sending out of the trusted port, it sends the packets untagged. Therefore, when those packets reach the switch, it determines that the packets were received on the native VLAN and forwards them in that VLAN toward the destination. If this option is enabled and a VLAN ID is entered, when NAC Appliance initiates traffic, it sends the packets tagged with that VLAN ID. When the switch receives those packets, it determines them to be in that tagged VLAN. Therefore, as long as the configurations on the switch and NAC Appliance Server match, you are okay. If there is a mismatch between these configurations, you could blackhole your NAS traffic and be unable to manage NAS from NAM.

In this example, the NAS trusted port (eth0) is connected to Fa1/0/3, which is an 802.1q trunk link. Therefore, the switch expects to receive traffic from the NAS management as 802.1q-tagged traffic. So, in the Network Settings page of NAS, you should enable the option **Set Management VLAN ID** and enter **20** because VLAN 20 is the NAS management VLAN. Figure 10-6 shows the network configuration page of NAC Appliance Server in the sample topology.

You will notice that you have configured the same IP for both the trusted and untrusted interfaces. Remember that in Virtual Gateway mode, NAC Appliance Server acts as a pure Layer 2 device. Therefore, this device can have only one IP: its management IP. NAC Appliance assumes that its management IP is the IP configured on the trusted port. The IP that you configure on the untrusted port has no relevance. You must configure the same IP on both the trusted and untrusted interfaces.

Figure 10-6 *Server Network Configuration Page*

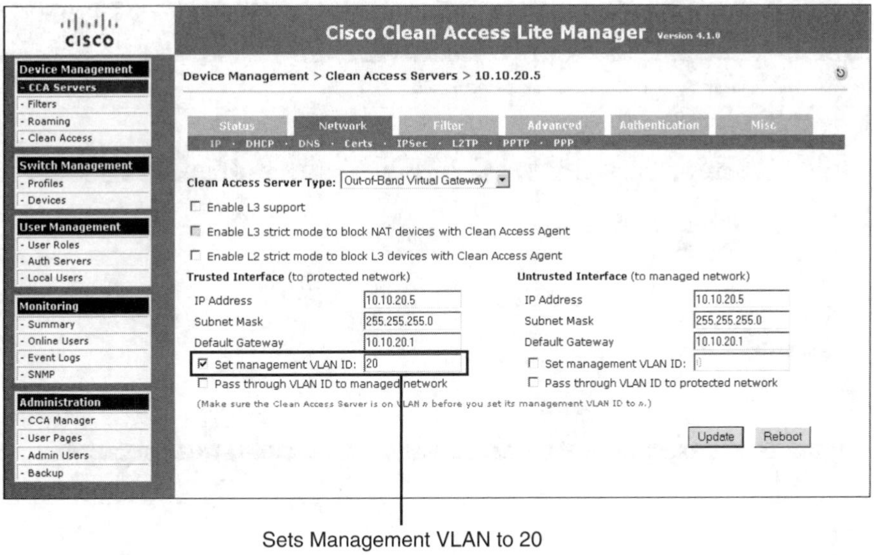

Sets Management VLAN to 20

Step 7: Configuring VLAN Mapping

In OOB Virtual Gateway mode Central deployment, you want the user traffic on the untrusted VLAN to go through NAC Appliance Server before hitting the user's default gateway. The untrusted VLAN is also called the *authentication VLAN* (*auth VLAN* for short) in OOB mode. To achieve this traffic flow, NAC Appliance Server performs VLAN mapping. You configure VLAN mapping on NAC Appliance Server such that the untrusted VLAN is mapped to a trusted VLAN. This allows users on the untrusted side to reach their default gateway on the trusted side through NAC Appliance Server. NAC Appliance Server is bridging the two VLANs.

Of course, before users are bridged, they are stopped by NAC Appliance Server for authentication and posture assessment. By default, the one exception is that the users' DNS and DHCP requests are let through prior to authentication. In this example, traffic from untrusted VLAN 110 is mapped to trusted VLAN 10 (see Figure 10-1). Figure 10-7 shows the VLAN mapping configuration page found by navigating to **Device Management > Clean Access Servers > 10.10.20.5 > Advanced > VLAN Mapping**.

Enable VLAN mapping and click the **Update** button. Configure the untrusted VLAN to be VLAN 110 and the trusted VLAN to be VLAN 10. After you enable and configure VLAN mapping, you can enable interface Fa1/0/4 also. When VLAN mapping is configured, NAC Appliance Server drops all Layer 2 control traffic, including bridge protocol data units, Cisco Discovery Protocol, and so on.

Figure 10-7 *VLAN Mapping Configuration Page*

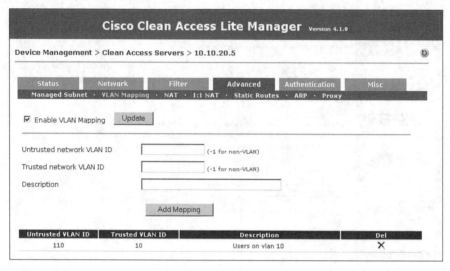

Step 8: Configuring Managed Subnets

It is extremely important to understand the concept of *Managed Subnets* when NAC Appliance Server is configured to be in Virtual Gateway mode. Figure 10-8 shows the sample network topology.

Figure 10-8 *Sample Network Topology*

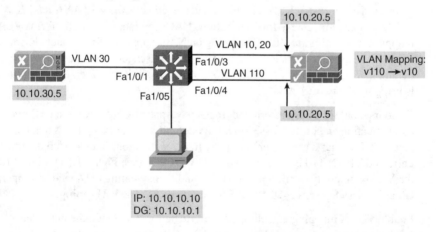

The untrusted interface IP is of no relevance. When the user connects to the network and moves to the untrusted VLAN, the NAC Appliance Agent on the user's machine starts sending discovery packets to the IP address of NAC Appliance Manager. On their way to NAC Appliance Manager, the packets pass through and are intercepted by NAC Appliance Server. NAC Appliance Server has to respond to these packets, but to be able to do so, it must have an Address Resolution Protocol (ARP) entry for the sending client. Therefore, it has to send out an ARP request first. However, it cannot use the untrusted interface's IP as the source for the ARP request. In addition, NAC Appliance Server has to send the ARP request out the correct untrusted VLAN.

This is achieved by configuring managed subnets on NAC Appliance Server. Think of managed subnets as you would think of subinterfaces on routers. Figure 10-9 shows a sample managed subnet configuration page.

Figure 10-9 *Managed Subnet Page*

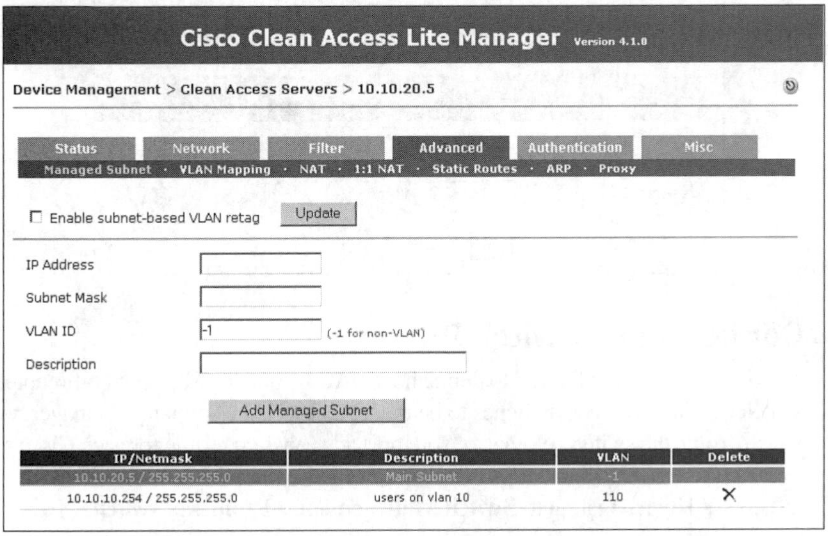

In this example, users on the untrusted network will be on VLAN 110. Because VLAN 110 is mapped to VLAN 10 on the trusted network, the users on VLAN 110 will actually get an IP address from the DHCP server on VLAN 10. The managed subnet that you configure here will be in the VLAN 10 subnet scope; however, it will have a VLAN ID of VLAN 110 because you want the ARP request to go out the untrusted side VLAN 110.

The term managed subnet is a little misleading. It really should be *managed subnet interface*. When you configure a managed subnet, make sure that you configure an IP address and not a subnet address. This is so that the ARP request that the NAC Appliance Server sends out has a valid source IP address. In this example, managed subnet 110 has an IP address of 10.10.10.254. You can see from Figure 10-9 that VLAN –1, which is the management VLAN 20, has an IP address of 10.10.20.5. –1 is a variable that maps to the VLAN configured on the eth0 trusted interface. All managed subnet IP addresses must be excluded from your DHCP server's address scopes.

Step 9: Configuring a Switch Group

This step is optional. A preconfigured Default group is already present. When you add switches to be managed by NAC Appliance Manager, they are added to the Default group.

You can configure additional groups and then add the switches to a particular group. By doing so, when you list the switches, you can list them by group. This step is useful if you have a large number of switches to be managed by NAC Appliance. In this example, you will configure a group called cat3750. This is done by navigating to **Switch Management > Profiles > Group**, as shown in Figure 10-10.

Figure 10-10 *Adding a Switch Group*

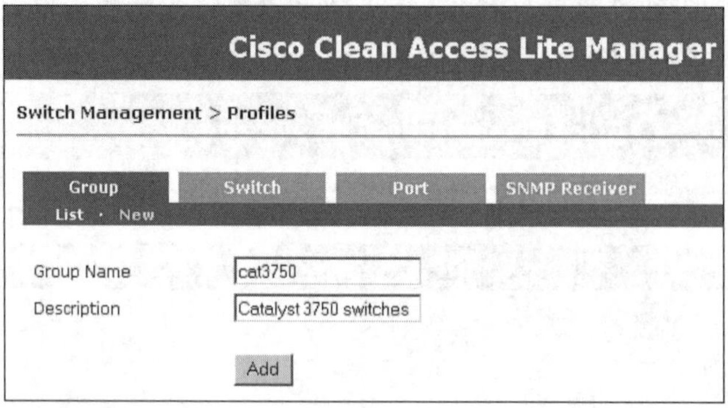

Step 10: Configuring a Switch Profile

A switch profile is configured to define how NAC Appliance Manager communicates with the switches. When you add switches to be managed by NAC Appliance Manager, you configure which profile the switch belongs to. You must add a switch profile for each Cisco switch model you want to support. Figure 10-11 shows a profile for the sample switch, a 3750. This page can be accessed by navigating to **Switch Management > Profiles > Switch > New**.

Figure 10-11 *Creating Switch Profiles*

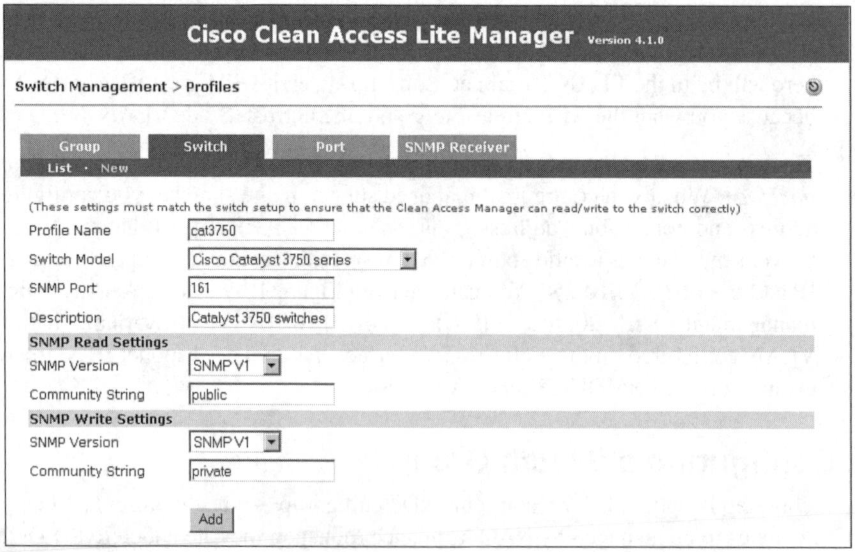

Make sure that you configure the switch model, SNMP port, and the SNMP read/write community strings to match the configuration on the switch.

Step 11: Configuring a Port Profile

A port profile is applied to a port to determine whether and how the port is controlled by NAC Appliance. You can configure the authentication VLAN, the default access VLAN, and the VLAN assignment method using a port profile. In the configuration shown in Figure 10-12, for the **Access VLAN** field, **User Role VLAN** has been chosen from the drop-down menu. This means that when a user is authenticated and healthy, the VLAN to which the user is moved will be decided by user role. The page shown in Figure 10-12 can be accessed by navigating to **Switch Management > Profiles > Port > New**.

Figure 10-12 *Port Profile Configuration Page*

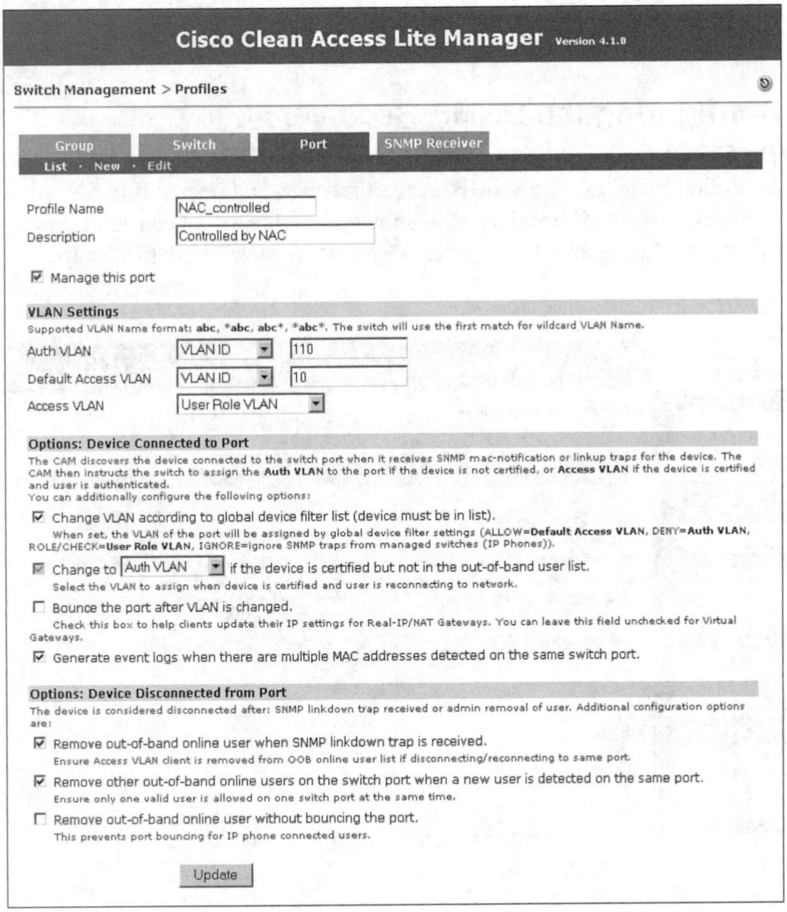

The **Generate Event Logs When There Are Multiple MAC Addresses Detected on the Same Switch Port** option has been enabled so that you will know whether an end user has connected a hub or an unmanaged switch behind the NAC-controlled switch.

The **Remove Out-of-Band Online User When SNMP Linkdown Trap Is Received** option has been enabled so that if the user machine disconnects from the switch port, the user will be logged off from NAC Appliance.

If a user connects his machine from behind an IP phone, when that user disconnects, the switch will not detect a linkdown, and therefore will not log the user off from NAC Appliance. The **Remove Other Out-of-Band Online Users on the Switch Port When a New User Is Detected on the Same Port** option has been enabled so that if a new user is detected on a port, NAC Appliance will automatically log off the old user.

If your clients will be plugged into IP phones, you must check the **Remove Out-of-Band Online User Without Bouncing the Port** option. This ensures that the IP phone is not disconnected every time a host disconnects.

Step 12: Configuring the SNMP Receiver

The SNMP receiver configuration must match the SNMP configuration on the NAC-controlled switches. The SNMP receiver receives and responds to SNMP traps sent by switches. The SNMP receiver page shown in Figure 10-13 can be accessed by navigating to **Switch Management > Profiles > SNMP Receiver > SNMP Trap**.

Figure 10-13 *SNMP Receiver Configuration Page*

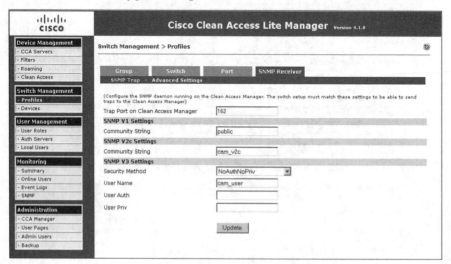

Advanced settings with which you can tweak different timers are also available. They are accessed by navigating to **Switch Management > Profiles > SNMP Receiver > Advanced Settings**. Tweaking the timers is not usually required unless there is unexpected latency in the switch and the NAC Appliance Manager communication. Figure 10-14 shows the advanced settings configuration page.

Figure 10-14 *SNMP Receiver Advanced Settings*

Step 13: Adding a Switch to NAC Appliance Manager

Now you need to add the individual switches. To do this, navigate to **Switch Management > Devices > Switches > New**. Choose the appropriate switch profile and switch group. Most of the time it is best to set the default port profile to **Uncontrolled**. This instructs NAC Appliance not to control any switch port until told to. Finally, type in the IP address of the switch and click **Add**. Figure 10-15 shows the addition of the sample switch.

Figure 10-15 *Adding a Switch to NAC Appliance*

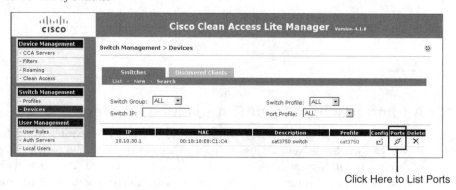

Step 14: Configuring Ports to Be Managed by NAC

To configure the control of switch ports, click the **Ports** icon, shown in Figure 10-16, for the switch.

Figure 10-16 *List of Switches*

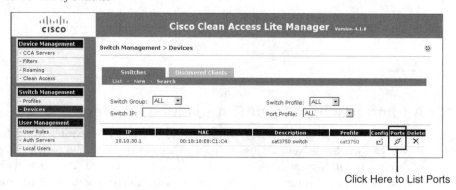

As shown in Figure 10-17, clicking the **Ports** icon lists all the ports available on that switch and the configuration of each.

Figure 10-17 *Ports List*

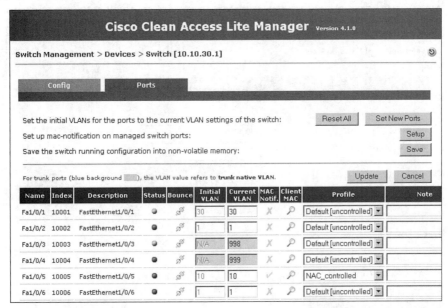

Because the user PC is connected on Fa1/0/5, change the profile for port Fa1/0/5 to the **NAC_controlled** port profile and click **Update**. When you click the **Update** button, NAC Appliance Manager adds the command **snmp trap mac-notification added** to the Fa1/0/5 interface configuration. This configuration change is made to the running configuration of the switch.

Step 15: Configuring User Roles

You will configure three user roles: Guest, Consultant, and Employee. In the user role page, you will also configure the OOB user role VLAN—this is the VLAN that the switch port will be assigned to when a user belonging to that user role completes the NAC process. Note that the configuration of any IPsec, VPN, or roaming parameters is not relevant anymore. These are deprecated features soon to be removed from the solution. Figure 10-18 shows the user role creation for Guest.

Figure 10-18 *New User Role Configuration Page—Guest*

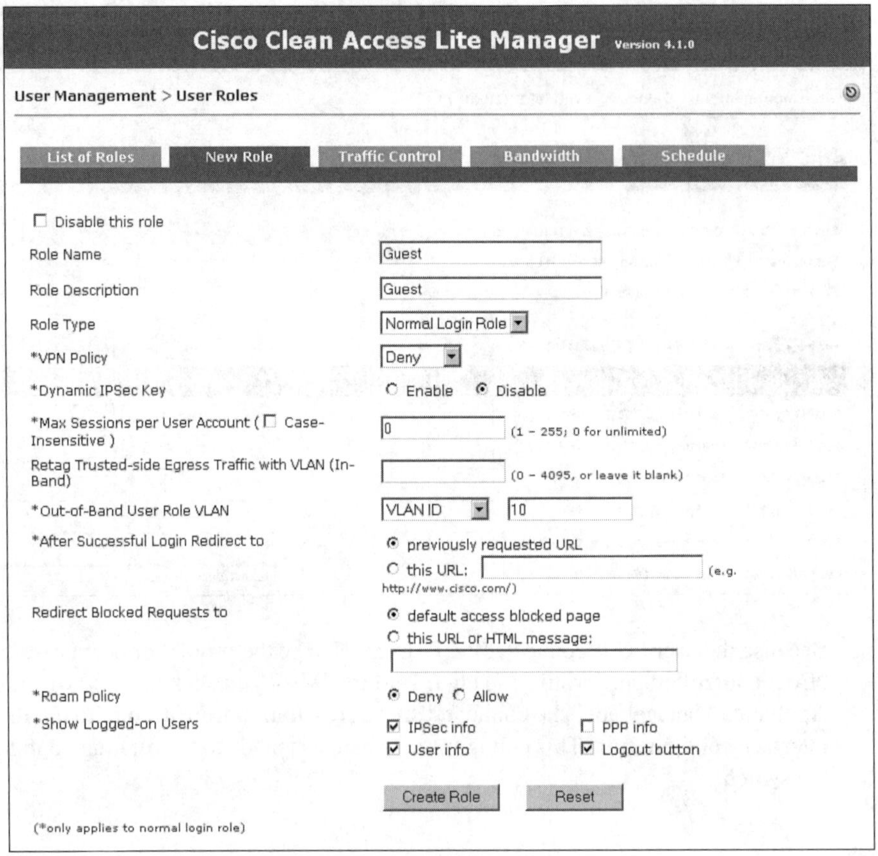

Figure 10-19 shows the user role creation for Consultant.

Figure 10-19 *New User Role Configuration Page—Consultant*

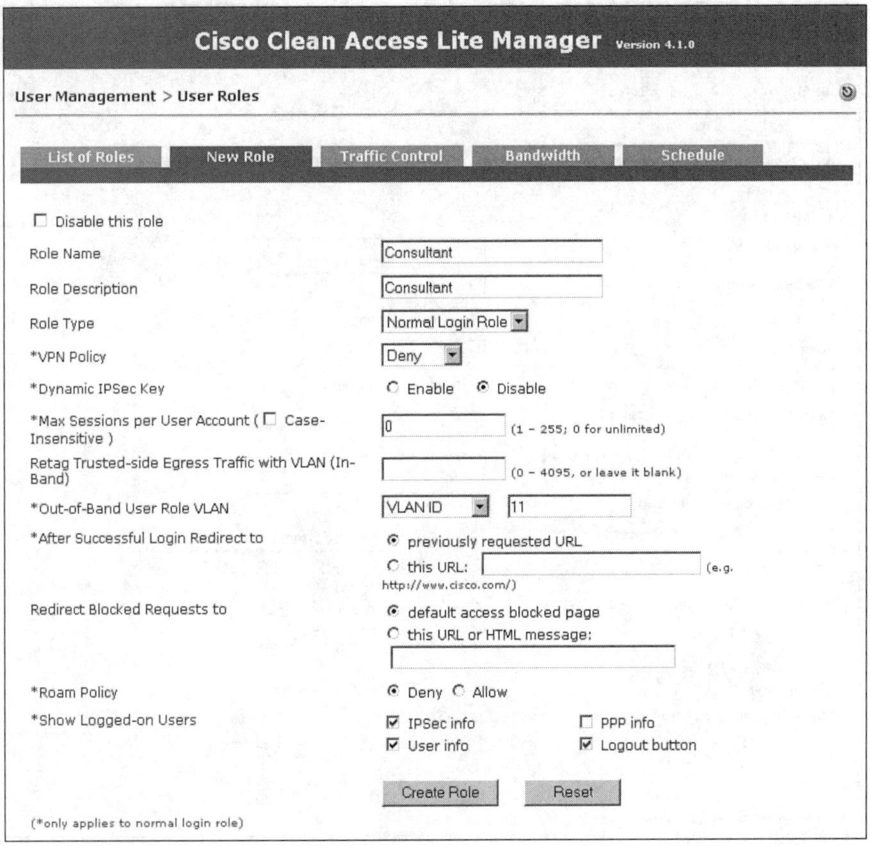

Figure 10-20 shows the user role creation for Employee.

Figure 10-20 *New User Role Configuration Page—Employee*

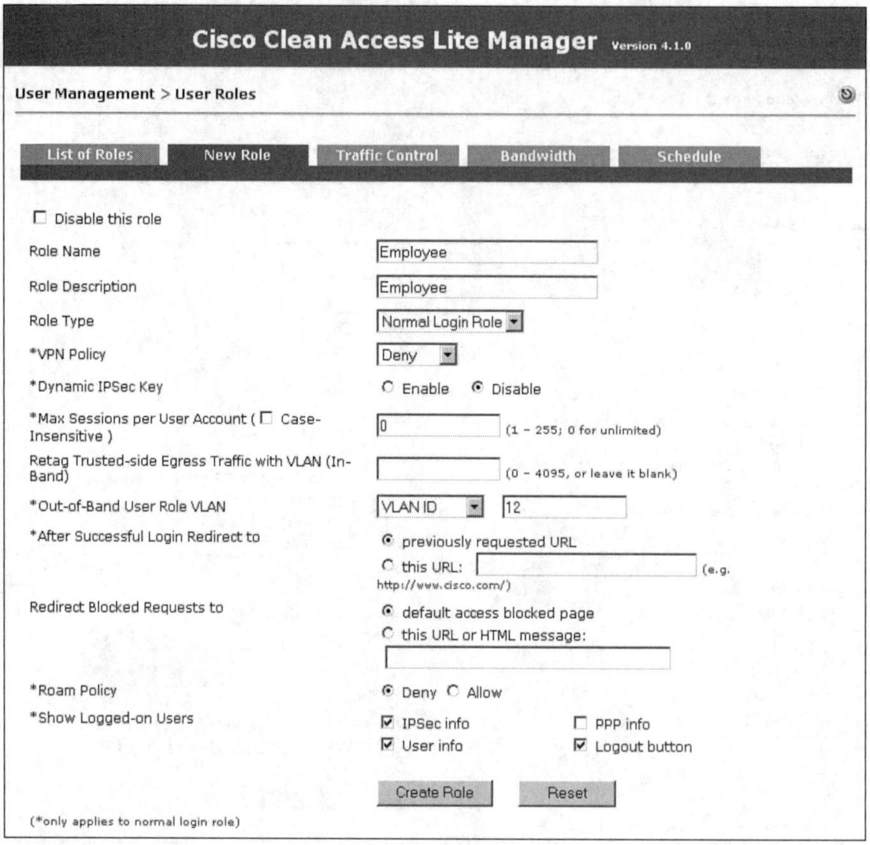

Figure 10-21 shows all the user roles.

Figure 10-21 *List of Roles Page*

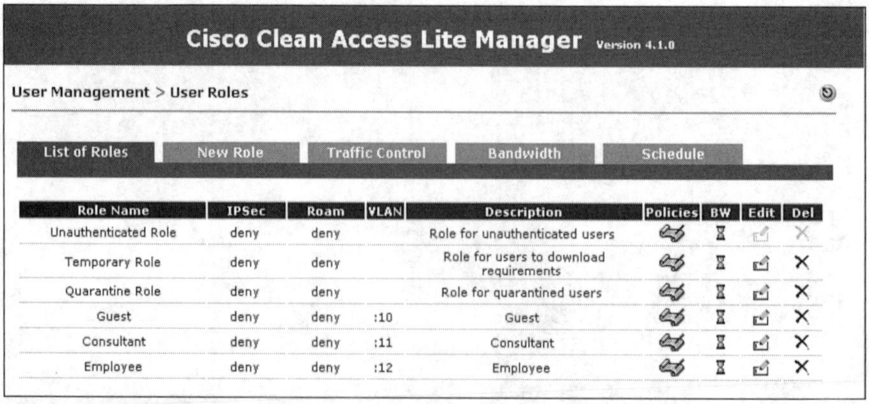

Step 16: Configuring User Authentication on the Local Database

Add two local users to the NAC Appliance local database. One will be an employee and the second will be a consultant. These local user accounts will be used for testing purposes. In a production environment, you should configure an LDAP, Kerberos, or RADIUS server instead. Local users should generally be used only for testing and guest access. Figure 10-22 shows creation of a consultant user who is a member of the Consultant role.

Figure 10-22 *New Local User Configuration Page—Consultant*

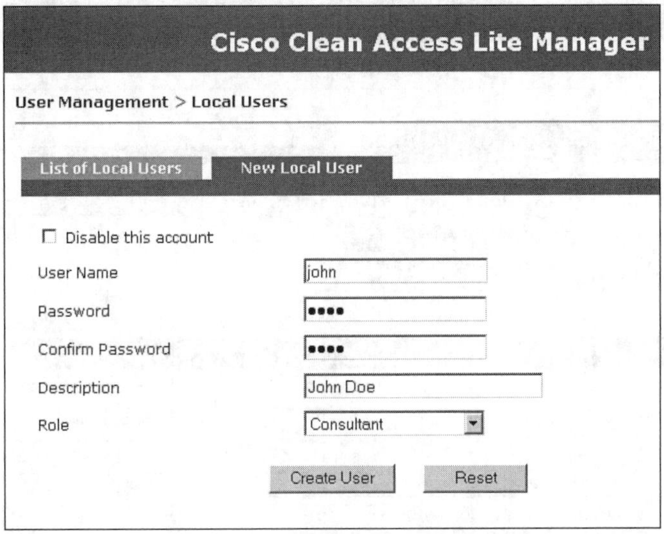

Figure 10-23 shows creation of an employee user who is a member of the Employee role.

Figure 10-23 *New Local User Configuration Page—Employee*

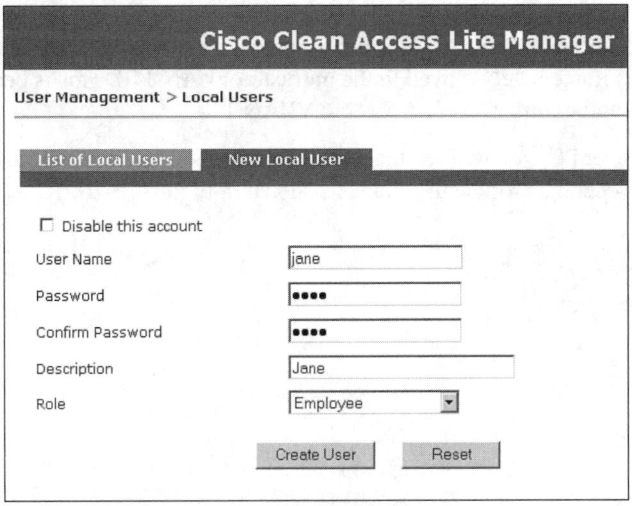

Step 17: Testing Whether OOB and User Role–Based VLAN Assignment Works

If you go to **Switch Management > Device > Switches > List > 10.10.30.1 > Ports**, you will see that interface Fa1/0/5, the client port, is currently on VLAN 10. This is shown in Figure 10-24.

Figure 10-24 *List of Ports*

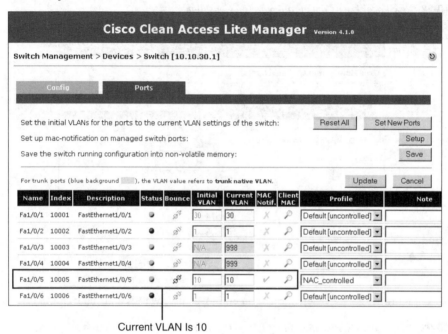

Current VLAN Is 10

Now go ahead and connect a laptop to interface Fa1/0/5. You see in Figure 10-25 that the port was immediately moved to the untrusted VLAN 110. This is because that port profile had the auth (untrusted) VLAN set to VLAN 110.

On the user PC, you will see that NAC Appliance Agent has popped up. Go ahead and put in the credentials for the user jane, as shown in Figure 10-26.

Figure 10-25 *List of Ports After Client Linkup*

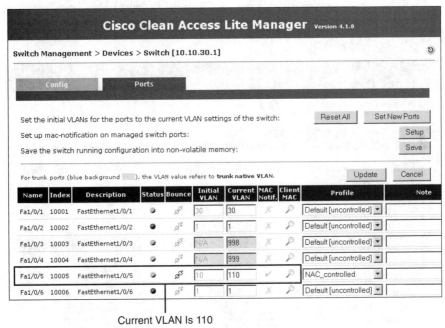

Current VLAN Is 110

Figure 10-26 *Clean Access Agent Authentication Popup*

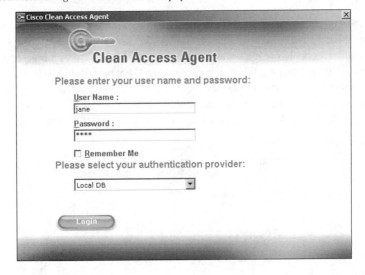

After you click **Login**, NAC Appliance determines that the user jane belongs to the Employee user role. NAC Appliance looks at the OOB user role VLAN configured under the Employee user role and moves the user's switch port Fa1/0/5 to VLAN 12.

See Chapter 6, "Building a Cisco NAC Appliance Host Security Policy," for more information about user roles. Figure 10-27 shows the port Fa1/0/5 now in the access VLAN 12, as determined by the user role.

Figure 10-27 *Port List—Access VLAN*

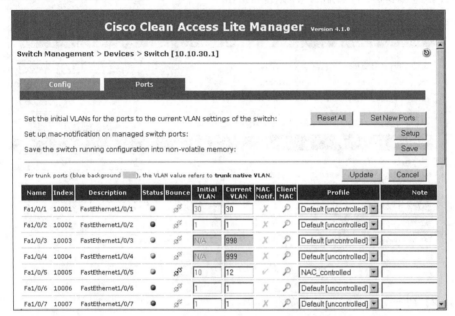

Name	Index	Description	Status	Bounce	Initial VLAN	Current VLAN	MAC Notif.	Client MAC	Profile	Note
Fa1/0/1	10001	FastEthernet1/0/1	●		30	30	X	🔎	Default [uncontrolled]	
Fa1/0/2	10002	FastEthernet1/0/2	●		1	1	X	🔎	Default [uncontrolled]	
Fa1/0/3	10003	FastEthernet1/0/3	●		N/A	998	X	🔎	Default [uncontrolled]	
Fa1/0/4	10004	FastEthernet1/0/4	●		N/A	999	X	🔎	Default [uncontrolled]	
Fa1/0/5	10005	FastEthernet1/0/5	●		10	12	✓	🔎	NAC_controlled	
Fa1/0/6	10006	FastEthernet1/0/6	●		1	1	X	🔎	Default [uncontrolled]	
Fa1/0/7	10007	FastEthernet1/0/7	●		1	1	X	🔎	Default [uncontrolled]	

Because you changed the VLAN of the user from VLAN 110 to VLAN 12 in this process, the subnet for the user also changed. Previously the user received an IP address from the VLAN 10 subnet scope. However, because the user is in VLAN 12 now, it must refresh its IP address. This can be done by configuring port bouncing. However, doing so is not recommended and not possible if you have IP phones. Instead, use the DHCP release/renew functionality built into Clean Access Agent and the web login applet. As a result, during the login process, you will see the Clean Access Agent screens shown in Figure 10-28 and Figure 10-29.

Figure 10-28 *IP Refresh Dialog Box*

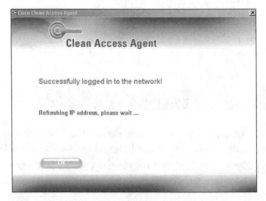

Figure 10-29 *IP Refresh Successful Dialog Box*

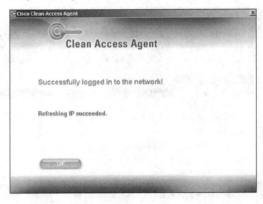

The user will show up in the Online User list shown in Figure 10-30. This list is accessed by navigating to **Monitoring > Online Users > Out-of-Band**. If the OOB user is in quarantine, it shows up in the In-Band user list until it passes certification.

Figure 10-30 *OOB Online Users List*

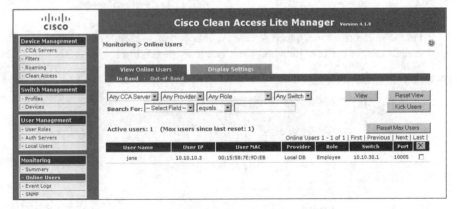

Now if the user disconnects from the switch port, NAC Appliance removes the user from the online user list. NAC Appliance knows that the user disconnected because the switch is configured to send a linkdown SNMP trap to NAC Appliance Manager. Note that the port remains in VLAN 12. The port's VLAN does not change again until NAC Appliance Manager receives a linkup or MAC-notification trap on that port from the switch.

Another user, John, now connects to the same user port. The port immediately moves to the auth (untrusted) VLAN 110, as shown in Figure 10-31.

Figure 10-31 *Switch Ports List—Untrusted*

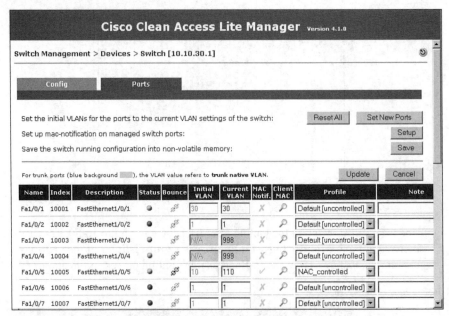

On the user's machine, Clean Access Agent pops up asking for authentication. Put in the credentials for the user john and click **Login** as shown in Figure 10-32.

Figure 10-32 *Clean Access Agent Login*

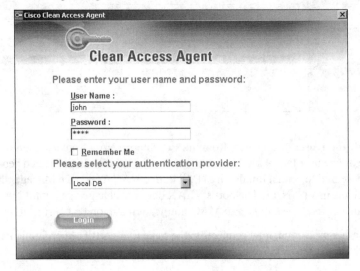

After the user is authenticated, NAC Appliance Manager determines that this user is a consultant and moves the user to VLAN 11. This is shown in the ports list of Figure 10-33 for the interface FastEthernet1/0/5. The Consultant user role is configured to use VLAN 11.

Figure 10-33 *Switch Ports List—Consultant Role*

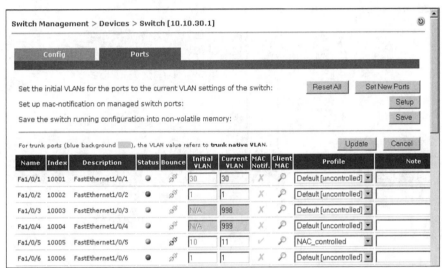

The user shows up in the online user list as a Consultant, as shown in Figure 10-34.

Figure 10-34 *Online User List—Consultant*

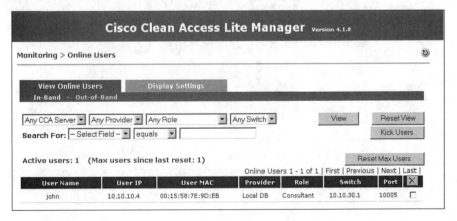

Sample Design and Configuration for Layer 3 Out-of-Band Deployment

For Layer 3 out-of-band deployment, consider the topology in Figure 10-35.

Figure 10-35 *Sample Layer 3 OOB Network Topology*

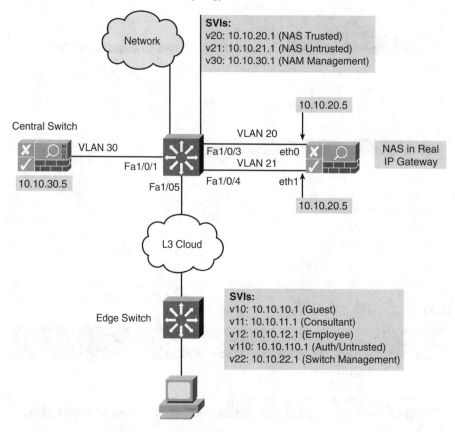

NOTE   Figure 10-35 is the basis for this example and is referred to several times throughout the following text. It will be helpful to bookmark this page or note the page number for easy reference as you read through this example.

You can see from the topology in Figure 10-35 that NAC Appliance Server is connected to the central switch. There is a network cloud between the central and edge switch. This cloud could be just a routed campus network, or it could be a WAN connection. The main point in this scenario is that the users are multiple routing hops away from NAC Appliance Server; therefore, it is Layer 3 OOB mode. In this example, the clients are no longer Layer 2 adjacent to NAC Appliance Server they are now Layer 3 adjacent to it.

With Out-of-Band mode, the goal is to move the user to the untrusted VLAN when that user connects to the network. While the user is in the untrusted VLAN, you want to be able to carry out authentication, posture assessment, and remediation for the user. When the user is in the untrusted VLAN, NAC Appliance Server acts as the enforcement device and communicates with NAC Appliance agent for user authentication, posture assessment, and remediation.

In Out-of-Band mode, NAC Appliance Server has to be able to determine the IP and MAC addresses of the user. When the user is Layer 2 adjacent to NAC Appliance Server (L2OOB) and the user's packets reach NAC Appliance Server, NAS can determine the source IP and MAC addresses of the user from those packets. When the user is one or more hops away from NAC Appliance Server, previous hop routers overwrite the source MAC address of the packets reaching NAS. As a result, NAC Appliance Server is unable to determine the MAC address of the user from the packets.

NAC Appliance Agent from release 4.0.0.0 onward sends the information regarding the user's MAC address and IP to NAC Appliance Server. For users who don't have NAC Appliance Agent, the web login page can be configured to use ActiveX or Java applet controls to get the same information from the user's device.

Chapter 4 explains the various traffic control methods for Layer 3 OOB. In the following example, you will see how to configure Layer 3 OOB using ACLs. As shown in the topology, NAC Appliance Server is configured to be in Real IP Gateway mode. This makes NAC Appliance Server into a router and requires that the untrusted port (eth1) of NAC Appliance Server has a unique IP address and subnet. The following sections form a step-by-step method for configuring Layer 3 OOB deployments using ACLs.

Step 1: Configuring the Switches

The sample topology (see Figure 10-35) has a central switch and an edge switch, both of which are Catalyst 3750 series switches running code 12.2 (25) SEE or later.

Configuring the Central Switch

The first step is configuring the central switch. You have to complete the following configuration steps at a minimum:

- Configure Virtual LAN Trunking Protocol (VTP) and VLANs
- Configure SVIs
- Configure the ports that NAC Appliance Manager and NAC Appliance Server connect to

After these steps are completed, you might have to configure additional interfaces and features if doing so is necessary for your environment.

Configuring VTP and VLANs

It is a best practice campus design not to enable VTP Server mode on switches. You should instead set VTP to Transparent mode, which effectively disables VTP operation. The **ip routing** command allows the switch to act as a router as well. Example 10-11 shows the VTP and VLAN central switch configuration as it pertains to the sample network topology.

Example 10-11 *Central Switch VTP and VLAN Configuration*

```
vtp domain cisco
vtp mode transparent
ip routing
!
vlan 20
 name NAS_Trusted
!
vlan 21
 name NAS_Untrusted
!
vlan 30
 name NAM_mgmt
!
```

Configuring SVIs

Next configure the switch virtual interfaces on the central switch. An SVI is a Layer 3 virtual interface that is mapped to a VLAN for routing traffic through a switch. Example 10-12 shows the central switch configuration for SVIs in the sample topology (see Figure 10-35).

Example 10-12 *Central Switch SVI Configuration*

```
interface Vlan20
 ip address 10.10.20.1 255.255.255.0
description Server Trusted
!
interface Vlan21
 ip address 10.10.21.1 255.255.255.0
description Server Untrusted
!
interface Vlan30
 ip address 10.10.30.1 255.255.255.0
description Manager eth0
!
```

Configuring Fa1/0/1—The Interface Connecting NAC Appliance Manager

Configure this interface to be an access port in VLAN 30. The Central switch configuration is shown in Example 10-13.

Example 10-13 *Switch Configuration of Manager port*

```
interface FastEthernet1/0/1
description Manager
 switchport access vlan 30
 switchport mode access
 spanning-tree portfast
!
```

Configuring Fa1/0/1—The Interface Connecting the Trusted Port of NAC Appliance Server

Configure this NAC Appliance Server interface, eth0, as an access port in VLAN 20. Example 10-14 shows the switch configuration.

Example 10-14 *Switch Configuration of Trusted Server Port*

```
interface FastEthernet1/0/3
description Server Trusted eth0
 switchport access vlan 20
 switchport mode access
spanning-tree portfast
!
```

Configuring Fa1/0/4—The Interface Connecting the Untrusted Port of NAC Appliance Server

Configure this interface, eth1, as an access port in VLAN 21, as shown in Example 10-15.

Example 10-15 *Switch Configuration of Untrusted Server Port*

```
interface FastEthernet1/0/4
description Server Untrusted eth1
 switchport access vlan 21
 switchport mode access
spanning-tree portfast
!
```

Configuring the Edge Switch

Next configure the edge switch. You have to complete the following configuration steps at a minimum:

- Configure VTP and VLANs.
- Configure ACLs on the switch for added security and traffic control.

- Configure SVIs.
- Configure a DHCP server; in this sample case, you are using the switch as the DHCP server.
- Configure the client ports.
- Configure SNMP on the switch.

After these steps are completed, you might have to configure additional interfaces and features if doing so is necessary for your environment.

Configuring VTP and VLANs

Using VTP is not recommended, and you accomplish this by setting it to Transparent mode. You enable IP routing by using the **ip routing** command. Example 10-16 shows the switch configuration for VTP and VLANs as it pertains to the sample network topology (see Figure 10-35).

Example 10-16 *Edge Switch VTP and VLAN Configuration*

```
vtp domain cisco
vtp mode transparent
ip routing
!
vlan 10
 name guest
!
vlan 11
 name consultant
!
vlan 12
 name employee
!
vlan 110
 name untrusted
!
vlan 22
 name switch_mgmt
!
```

Configuring Access Control Lists

In this design, the enforcement piece has moved from NAC Appliance Server to the edge switch. You will configure ACLs on the authentication/untrusted VLAN so as to allow traffic to NAC Appliance Server, remediation servers, DHCP server, Active Directory server (if using AD SSO), and any other resources required for remediation purposes. When the user is in the untrusted VLAN, NAC Appliance Agent starts sending discovery packets that will be allowed by the ACL. After NAC Appliance Server gets the NAC Appliance

Agent discovery packets, it will know that there is a new host connected to the network. It can then prompt the user for authentication and posture assessment.

For posture remediation, NAC Appliance Agent facilitates remediation by directing the user to go to the remediation resources. Access to these resources has been allowed by the ACLs. So, a user goes through the complete NAC process while in the untrusted VLAN. The ACLs block access to anything else on the network, thus preventing noncompliant users from getting access to other network resources. Example 10-17 shows a sample of the access list that you will configure for the untrusted VLAN 110.

Example 10-17 *Untrusted VLAN 110 ACL*

```
ip access-list 100 permit ip any host 10.10.21.5
ip access-list 100 permit udp any any eq domain
ip access-list 100 permit tcp any any eq domain
ip access-list 100 permit udp any any eq 67
ip access-list 100 permit udp any any eq 68
ip access-list 100 permit ip any host [wsus,av,etc]
```

Host 10.10.21.5 is NAC Appliance Server. This ACL allows the NAC Appliance Agent discovery packets to reach NAS. Remaining ACLs allow DNS (domain), DHCP (port 67), and access to the WSUS server, antivirus server, and other remediation resources.

In addition to the ACL on the untrusted VLAN, you have to configure an ACL on the trusted VLANs. This is because NAC Appliance Agent is going to send discovery packets every 5 seconds, continuously. So, even when the user is moved to the trusted access VLAN, NAC Appliance Agent continues to send the discovery packets. You want to prevent those packets from reaching NAC Appliance Server. To do so, configure the following ACL on the trusted VLANs:

```
access-list 101 deny ip any host 10.10.21.5
access-list 101 permit ip any any
```

This access list will block any traffic from reaching NAC Appliance Server when the user is on the trusted VLAN. You can optionally add to the preceding ACL to further control client traffic. For example, you might create an ACL, specific to consultants, which allows them only limited access to your network. You would then apply this ACL to the consultant VLAN 11.

Configuring SVIs

Example 10-18 shows the switch configuration of the Layer 3 SVI interfaces. Notice the command **ip access-group 100 in** or **ip access-group 101 in** on the SVI interfaces. This command applies to the SVI an access list that can limit the access of clients. You can find the access list definitions in the "Configuring Access Control Lists" section.

Example 10-18 *Edge Switch SVI Configuration*

```
interface Vlan10
description Guest
  ip address 10.10.10.1 255.255.255.0
  ip access-group 101 in
!
interface Vlan11
description Consultant
  ip address 10.10.11.1 255.255.255.0
  ip access-group 101 in
!
interface Vlan12
description Employee
  ip address 10.10.12.1 255.255.255.0
  ip access-group 101 in
!
interface Vlan110
description Untrusted
  ip address 10.10.110.1 255.255.255.0
  ip access-group 100 in
!
interface Vlan22
description Switch Management
  ip address 10.10.22.2 255.255.255.0
!
```

Configuring the Switch as a DHCP Server

Almost every network needs a DHCP server. In the sample topology (see Figure 10-35),
you will configure the switch to act as the DHCP server. The switch is configured to act as
the DHCP server for the user VLANs 10, 11, and 12, and the untrusted VLAN 110.
Example 10-19 shows the edge switch DHCP configuration.

Example 10-19 *Edge Switch DHCP Server Configuration*

```
ip dhcp excluded-address 10.10.10.1
ip dhcp excluded-address 10.10.10.254
ip dhcp excluded-address 10.10.11.1
ip dhcp excluded-address 10.10.11.254
ip dhcp excluded-address 10.10.12.1
ip dhcp excluded-address 10.10.12.254
ip dhcp excluded-address 10.10.110.1
ip dhcp excluded-address 10.10.110.254

!
ip dhcp pool vlan10
   network 10.10.10.0 255.255.255.0
   default-router 10.10.10.1
dns-server 192.168.35.2
domain-name  cisco.com

!
```

Example 10-19 *Edge Switch DHCP Server Configuration (Continued)*

```
ip dhcp pool vlan11
    network 10.10.11.0 255.255.255.0
    default-router 10.10.11.1
dns-server 192.168.35.2
domain-name  cisco.com
!
ip dhcp pool vlan12
    network 10.10.12.0 255.255.255.0
    default-router 10.10.12.1
dns-server 192.168.35.2
domain-name  cisco.com
!
ip dhcp pool vlan110
    network 10.10.110.0 255.255.255.0
    default-router 10.10.110.1
dns-server 192.168.35.2
domain-name  cisco.com
!
```

Configuring Fa1/0/5—The Interface Connecting the Host

Configuration of the client ports is straightforward; they just need to be set up as access ports. In the sample topology, the client port Fa1/0/5 is configured to be an access port in VLAN 10, as shown in Example 10-20.

Example 10-20 *Edge Switch Configuration— Client Port*

```
interface FastEthernet1/0/5
description client port
 switchport access vlan 10
 switchport mode access
 spanning-tree portfast
!
```

Configuring SNMP

The switch must be configured with SNMP MAC-notification traps and linkdown traps. The MAC-notification trap is used to detect a new user on the network and to trigger the NAC process. The linkdown trap is used to detect that the user disconnected from the network. Example 10-21 shows the necessary SNMP configuration on the edge switch. An access list 10 is applied to the SNMP configuration to increase security. This allows only NAC Appliance Manager to speak SNMP with the switch.

Example 10-21 *Edge Switch SNMP Configuration*

```
snmp-server community public RO 10
snmp-server community private RW 10
snmp-server enable traps snmp linkdown
snmp-server enable traps MAC-Notification
snmp-server host 10.10.30.5 snmpv2c public
access-list 10 permit ip 10.10.30.5
```

Step 2: Configuring NAC Appliance Manager

On NAC Appliance Manager, you have to do some basic configuration using the configuration script. From the NAC Appliance Manager CLI, you must type in **service perfigo config**. Initially, you can access the CLI by putting a keyboard and monitor on NAC Appliance Manager or via the serial port (38400bps). After NAC Appliance Manager has an IP address, the CLI can be accessed via SSH. Example 10-22 shows the configuration setup script.

Example 10-22 *Running the Configuration Script on the Manager*

```
Fedora Core release 4 (Stentz)
Kernel 2.6.11-perfigo on an i686

cam login: root
Password:
[root@cam ~]# service perfigo config

Welcome to the Cisco Clean Access Manager quick configuration utility.

Note that you need to be root to execute this utility.

The utility will now ask you a series of configuration questions.
Please answer them carefully.

Cisco Clean Access Manager, (C) 2006 Cisco Systems, Inc.

Configuring the network interface:

Please enter the IP address for the interface eth0 [10.2.0.15]: 10.10.30.5
You entered 10.10.30.5. Is this correct? (y/n)? [y]

Please enter the netmask for the interface eth0 [255.255.255.0]:
You entered 255.255.255.0. Is this correct? (y/n)? [y]

Please enter the IP address for the default gateway [10.2.0.1]: 10.10.30.1
You entered 10.10.30.1. Is this correct? (y/n)? [y]

Please enter the hostname [cam1]: nam
You entered nam. Is this correct? (y/n)? [y]

Please enter the IP address for the name server: [192.168.10.1]: 10.10.30.6
You entered 10.10.30.6. Is this correct? (y/n)? [y]

Would you like to change shared secret? (y/n)? [y]
Please remember to configure the Clean Access Server with the same string.
  Please enter the shared secret between Clean Access Server
You entered: cisco123
Is this correct? (y/n)? [y]

>>> Configuring date and time:
```

Example 10-22 *Running the Configuration Script on the Manager (Continued)*

```
The timezone is currently set to:America/Los_Angeles
Would you like to change this setting? (y/n)? [y] n

Current date and time hh:mm:ss mm/dd/yy [01:01:01 01/01/07]: 01:20:00 01/01/07
You entered 01:20:00 01/01/07 Is this correct? (y/n)? [y]
Mon Jan 01 01:20:00 PST 2007

You must generate a valid SSL certificate in order to use the Clean Access Manager's
  secure web console.
Please answer the following questions correctly.
Information for a new SSL certificate:
Enter fully qualified domain name or IP: 10.10.30.5
Enter organization unit name: nacapp
Enter organization name: cisco
Enter city name: san jose
Enter state code: ca
Enter 2 letter country code: us


You entered the following:
Domain: 10.10.30.5
Organization unit: nacapp
Organization name: cisco
City name: san jose
State code: ca
Country code: us
Is this correct? (y/n)? [y]
Generating SSL Certificate...
CA signing: /root/.tomcat.csr -> /root/.tomcat.crt:
CA verifying: /root/.tomcat.crt <-> CA cert
/root/.tomcat.crt: OK
Done

For security reasons, it is highly recommended that you change the default passwords
  for the root user.
User: root
Changing password for user root.
New UNIX password:
Retype new UNIX password:
passwd: all authentication tokens updated successfully.

Changes require a RESTART of Clean Access Manager.
Configuration is complete.
[root@cam1 ~]# service perfigo reboot
```

Step 3: Configuring NAC Appliance Server

On NAC Appliance Server, you must again perform some basic configuration using the configuration script. From the NAC Appliance Server CLI, type in **service perfigo config**. Initially, you can access the CLI by putting a keyboard and monitor on NAC Appliance

Manager or via the serial port (38400bps). After NAC Appliance Server has an IP address, the CLI can be accessed via SSH. Example 10-23 shows the configuration setup script.

Example 10-23 *Configuring the NAS via CLI*

```
[root@cas ~]# service perfigo config

Welcome to the Cisco Clean Access Server quick configuration utility.

Note that you need to be root to execute this utility.

The utility will now ask you a series of configuration questions.
Please answer them carefully.

Cisco Clean Access Server, (C) 2006 Cisco Systems, Inc.

Configuring the network interfaces:

Please enter the IP address for the interface eth0 [10.2.0.15]: 10.10.20.5
You entered 10.10.20.5. Is this correct? (y/n)? [y]

Please enter the netmask for the interface eth0 [255.255.255.0]:
You entered 255.255.255.0. Is this correct? (y/n)? [y]

Please enter the IP address for the default gateway [10.2.0.1]: 10.10.20.1
You entered 10.10.20.1. Is this correct? (y/n)? [y]

[Vlan Id Passthrough] for packets from eth0 to eth1 is disabled.
Would you like to enable it? (y/n)? [n]

[Management Vlan Tagging] for egress packets of eth0 is disabled.
Would you like to enable it? (y/n)? [n]

Please enter the IP address for the untrusted interface eth1 [10.2.0.15]: 10.10.21.5
You entered 10.10.20.5. Is this correct? (y/n)? [y]

Please enter the netmask for the interface eth1 [255.255.255.0]:
You entered 255.255.255.0. Is this correct? (y/n)? [y]

Please enter the IP address for the default gateway [10.2.0.1]: 10.10.21.1
You entered 10.10.20.1. Is this correct? (y/n)? [y]

[Vlan Id Passthrough] for packets from eth1 to eth0 is disabled.
Would you like to enable it? (y/n)? [n]

[Management Vlan Tagging] for egress packets of eth1 is disabled.
Would you like to enable it? (y/n)? [n]

Please enter the hostname [cas1]: l3oobnas
You entered NAS1. Is this correct? (y/n)? [y]

Please enter the IP address for the name server: [192.168.10.1]: 10.10.30.6
You entered 10.10.30.6. Is this correct? (y/n)? [y]
```

Example 10-23 *Configuring the NAS via CLI (Continued)*

```
Would you like to change shared secret? (y/n)? [y]
Please enter the shared secret: cisco123
You entered: cisco123
Is this correct? (y/n)? [y]

>>> Configuring date and time:


The timezone is currently set to:America/Los_Angeles
Would you like to change this setting? (y/n)? [y] n

Current date and time hh:mm:ss mm/dd/yy [01:01:01 01/02/07]: 01:55:00 01/01/07
You entered 01:55:00 01/02/07. Is this correct? (y/n)? [y]
Tues Jan 02 01:55:00 PST 2007


You must generate a valid SSL certificate in order to use the Clean Access Server's
   secure web console.
Please answer the following questions correctly.
Information for a new SSL certificate:
Enter fully qualified domain name or IP: 10.10.20.5
Enter organization unit name: nacapp
Enter organization name: cisco
Enter city name: san jose
Enter state code: ca
Enter 2 letter country code: us


You entered the following:
Domain: 10.10.20.5
Organization unit: nacapp
Organization name: cisco
City name: san jose
State code: ca
Country code: us
Is this correct? (y/n)? [y]
Generating SSL Certificate...
CA signing: /root/.tomcat.csr -> /root/.tomcat.crt:
CA verifying: /root/.tomcat.crt <-> CA cert
/root/.tomcat.crt: OK
Done


For security reasons, it is highly recommended that you change the default password
   for the root user.
User: root
Changing password for user root.
New UNIX password:
Retype new UNIX password:
passwd: all authentication tokens updated successfully.
```

continues

Example 10-23 *Configuring the NAS via CLI (Continued)*

```
Would you like to change the default password for the web console admin user
   password? (y/n)? [y]
Please enter an appropriately secure password for the web console admin user.

New password for web console admin:
Confirm new password for web console admin:
Web console admin password changed successfully.

Configuration is complete.
[root@cas1 ~]# service perfigo reboot
```

Step 4: Logging In to NAC Appliance Manager

Open a browser and connect to NAM through a SSL connection. Type in the IP or domain name of the NAM (https://10.10.30.5). The default username is *admin*, and the default password is *cisco123*.

You can view the NAM configuration at **Administration > CCA Manager**, as shown in Figure 10-36.

Figure 10-36 *NAC Appliance Manager Configuration Page*

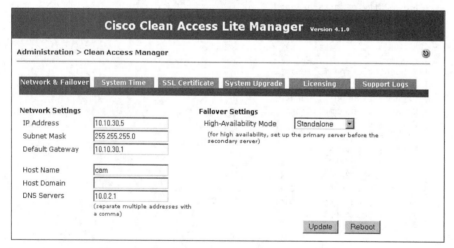

Step 5: Adding NAC Appliance Server to NAC Appliance Manager

You can add NAC Appliance Server by going to **Device Management > CCA Servers > New Server**, as shown in Figure 10-37. In the sample topology (see Figure 10-35), NAC Appliance Server is of type **Out-of-Band Real-IP Gateway**. Be sure to select the proper server type from the drop-down menu.

Figure 10-37 *New Server Configuration Page*

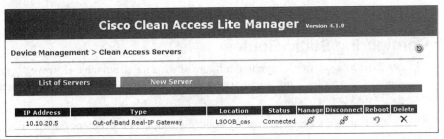

Figure 10-38 shows that NAC Appliance Server has been added in OOB Real-IP Gateway mode, and its status is connected.

Figure 10-38 *Server List*

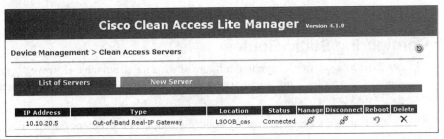

Step 6: Editing Network Settings on NAC Appliance Server

In Figure 10-39, notice that **Set Management VLAN ID** is not enabled. This is because the switch ports to which NAC Appliance Server is connected are access ports, not 802.1q trunk ports. Therefore, you don't want NAS to tag any packets. In addition, the check box next to **Enable L3 Support** is checked. This allows NAC Appliance Server to communicate with clients that are Layer 2 adjacent or multiple routing hops away.

Figure 10-39 *Server Network Configuration Page*

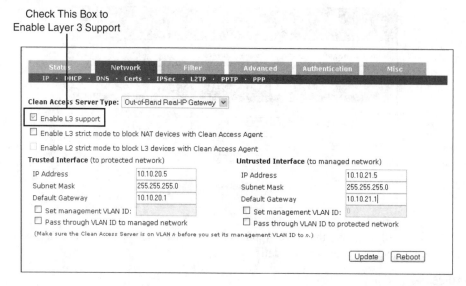

Step 7: Configuring Static Routes

In this example, you don't have to configure any managed subnets. However, you will configure static routes. This is one difference between a Layer 2 OOB deployment and a Layer 3 OOB deployment.

Think of managed subnets as directly connected subnets for routers. So, for user subnets directly connected to NAC Appliance Server, you configure managed subnets.

NAC Appliance Server does not support routing protocols. Therefore, for user subnets that are one or more hops away from NAC Appliance Server, you have to configure static routes. NAC Appliance Server communicates with the user device when the user is in the untrusted VLAN. So, you will configure static routes for the subnets associated with the untrusted VLANs, as shown in Figure 10-40. In this example, VLAN 110 (10.10.110.0/24) is the untrusted VLAN.

Figure 10-40 *Adding a Static Route on NAC Appliance Server*

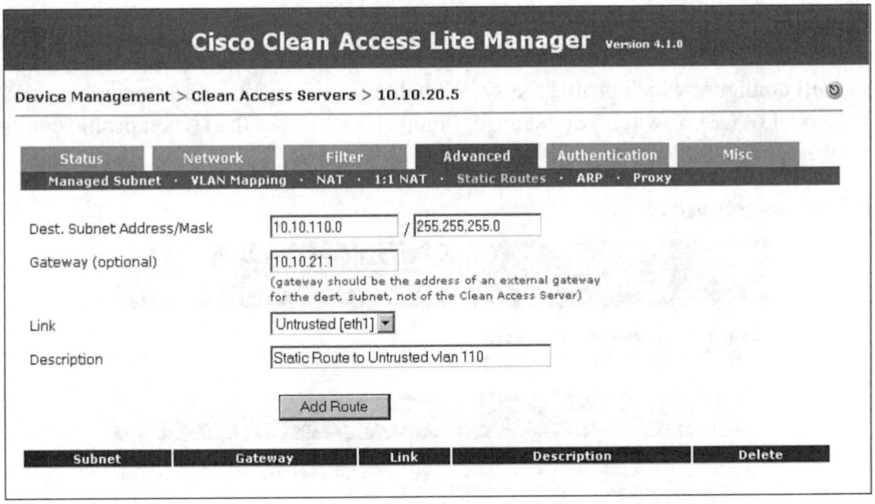

Step 8: Configuring a Switch Group

This step is optional. A preconfigured Default group is already present. When you add switches to be managed by the NAC Appliance Manager, they are added to the Default group. You can configure additional groups and then add the switches in a particular group. By doing this, when you list the switches, you can list them by group. This step is useful if you have a large number of switches to be managed by NAC Appliance. In this example, you will configure a group called cat3750, as shown in Figure 10-41.

Figure 10-41 *Adding a Switch Group*

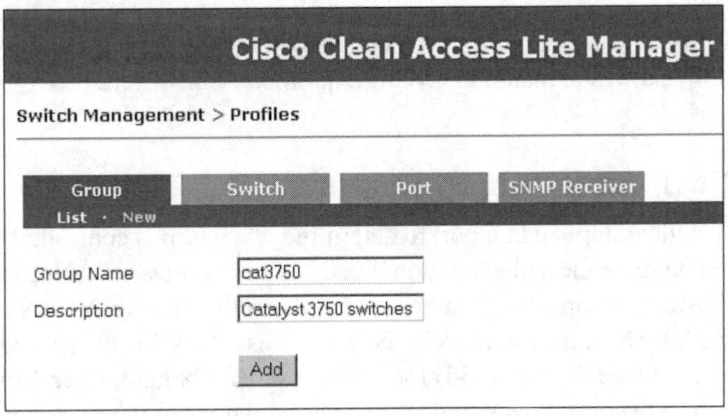

Step 9: Configuring a Switch Profile

A switch profile is configured to define how NAC Appliance Manager communicates with the switches. When you add the switches to be managed by NAC Appliance Manager, you will configure which profile the switch belongs to. You must add a switch profile for each model of Cisco switch you manage. Figure 10-42 shows the switch profile configuration page.

Figure 10-42 *Adding a Switch Profile*

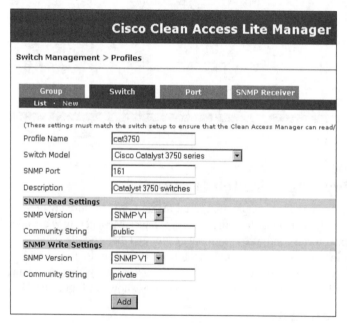

Make sure that you configure the switch model, the SNMP port, and the SNMP read/write community strings to match the configuration on each switch.

Step 10: Configuring a Port Profile

A port profile is applied to a port to determine whether it is controlled by NAC Appliance. You can configure the authentication VLAN, default access VLAN, and VLAN assignment method using port profiles. Remember that the authentication VLAN is the same as the untrusted VLAN or quarantine VLAN. The access VLAN is the trusted side VLAN. In the configuration (see Figure 10-35) for the **Access VLAN** field, **User Role VLAN** has been chosen from the drop-down menu. This means that when the user is authenticated and healthy, the VLAN to which the user is moved is determined by user role. Figure 10-43 shows the port profile configuration page.

Figure 10-43 *Port Profile Configuration Page*

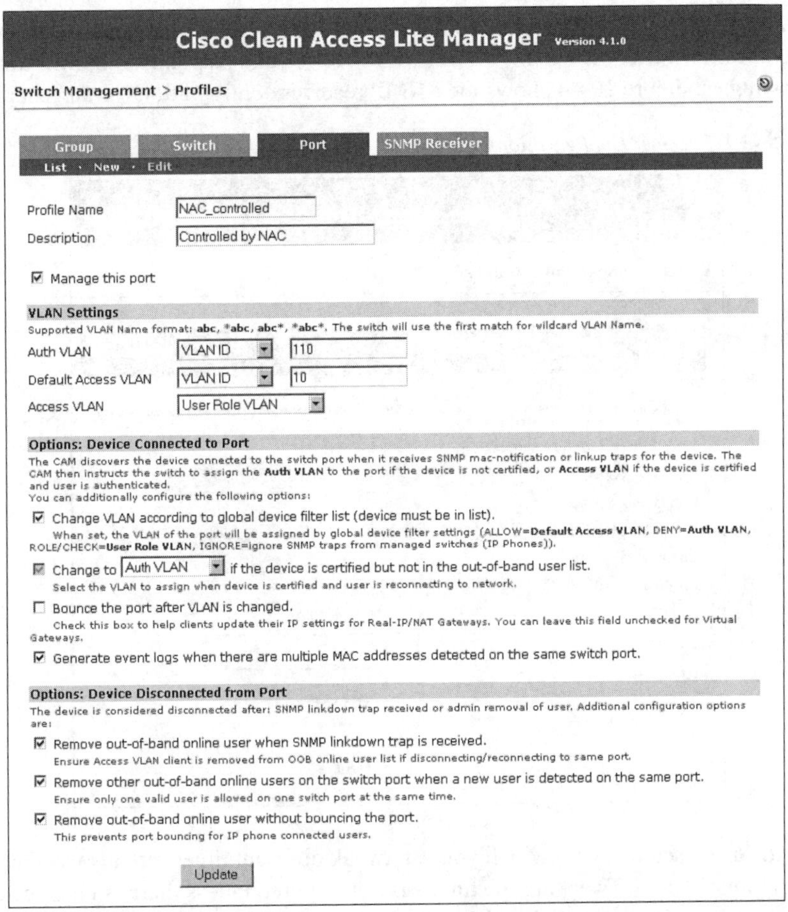

The **Generate Event Logs When There Are Multiple MAC Addresses Detected on the Same Switch Port** option is enabled so that you will know if an end user has connected a hub or an unmanaged switch behind the NAC-controlled switch.

The **Remove Out-of-Band Online User When SNMP Linkdown Trap Is Received** option is enabled so that if the user machine is disconnected from the switch port, the user will be logged off from NAC Appliance.

In a scenario in which a user connects his machine from behind an IP phone, when the user disconnects, the switch will not detect a linkdown and therefore will not log off the user from NAC Appliance. The **Remove Other Out-of-Band Online Users on the Switch Port When a New User Is Detected on the Same Port** option is enabled so that if a new user is detected on a port, NAC Appliance will automatically log off the old user. In addition, the **Remove Out-of-Band Online User Without Bouncing the Port** option is checked. This is required if clients will be behind IP phones.

Step 11: Configuring the SNMP Receiver

The SNMP receiver configuration must match the SNMP configuration on the NAC-controlled switches. The SNMP receiver receives and responds to SNMP traps sent by switches. Figure 10-44 shows the SNMP receiver configuration for the sample topology.

Figure 10-44 *SNMP Receiver Configuration Page*

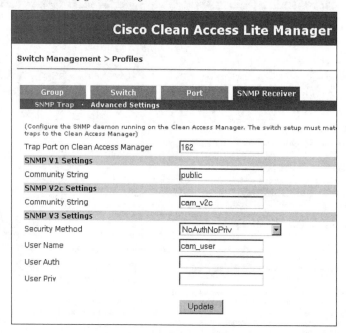

Advanced settings with which you can tweak different timers are also available, as shown in Figure 10-45. Tweaking the timers is not required unless there is unexpected latency in the switch and the NAC Appliance Manager communication.

Step 12: Adding the Switch to NAC Appliance Manager

For NAC Appliance to manage a switch, the switch must first be added (see Figure 10-46). This page can be found by navigating to Switch Management > Devices > New.

Figure 10-45 *SNMP Receiver Advanced Settings*

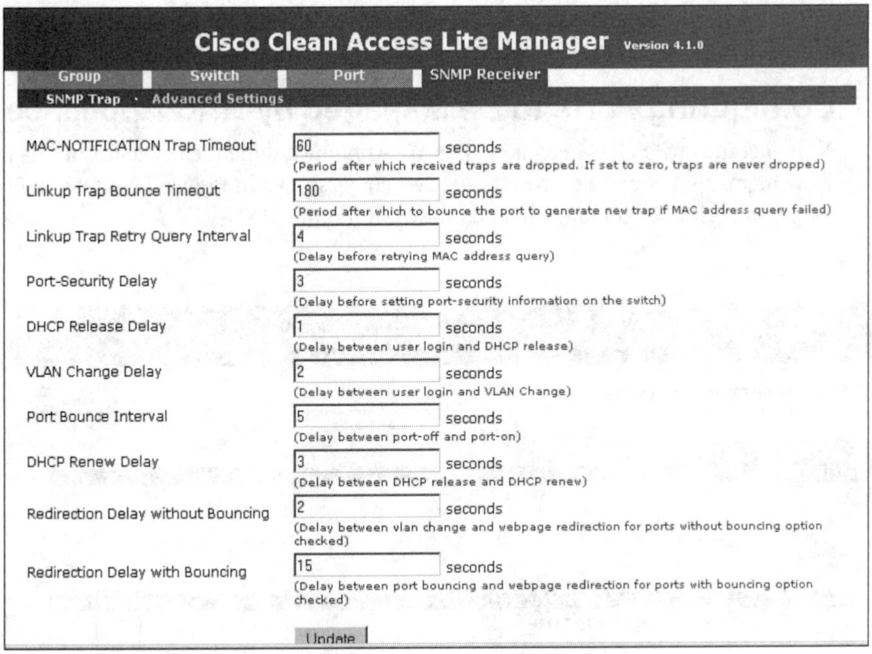

Figure 10-46 *Add a New Switch Configuration Page*

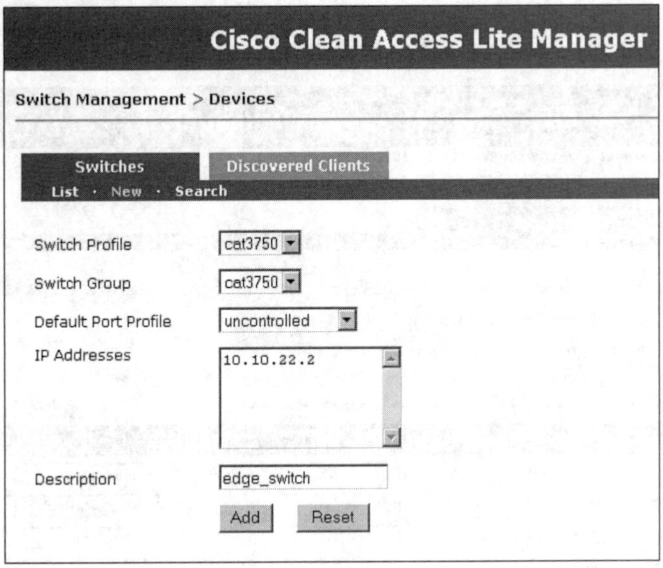

You must choose the appropriate switch profile and switch group. Make sure that you choose **Default Port Profile** as **Uncontrolled**. Put in the IP address of the switch and click **Add**.

Step 13: Configuring Ports to Be Managed by NAC Appliance

Now that the switch has been added, NAC Appliance dynamically learns all its ports. To view them, click the **Ports** icon for the switch, as shown in Figure 10-47. Doing so lists all the ports available on that switch, as shown in Figure 10-48.

Figure 10-47 *Switches List*

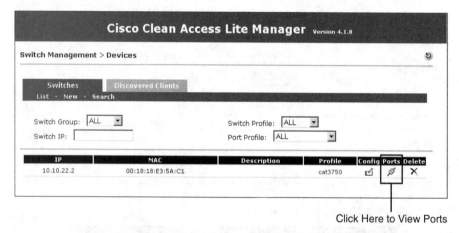

Click Here to View Ports

Figure 10-48 *Port List*

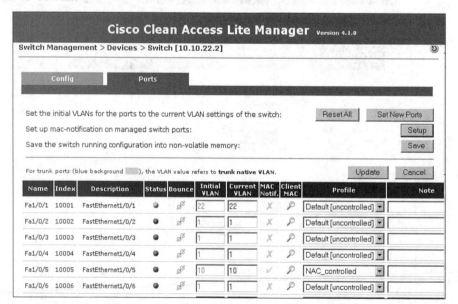

Because the user PC is connected on Fa1/0/5, change the profile for port Fa1/0/5 to the **NAC_controlled** port profile and click **Update**. When you click the **Setup** button, NAC Appliance Manager adds the command **snmp trap mac-notification added** to the Fa1/0/5 interface configuration. This configuration change is made to the running configuration of the switch. To save it to the startup-config, click the **Save** button.

Step 14: Configuring User Roles

For the sample topology, you will configure three user roles: Guest, Consultant, and Employee. In the user role page, you will define the OOB user role VLAN. This is the VLAN to which the switch port will be assigned when a user belonging to the user role completes the NAC process. See Figure 10-35 for a list of these VLAN assignments. Remember that all references to roaming, IPsec, and VPN on the user role configuration page should be ignored because they are deprecated features. Figure 10-49 shows the user role creation for Guest.

Figure 10-49 *Adding a User Role—Guest*

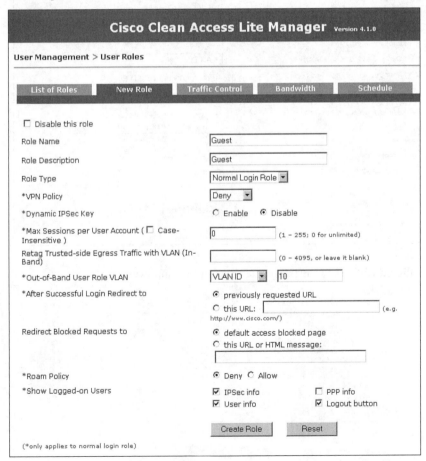

Figure 10-50 shows the user role creation for Consultant.

Figure 10-50 *Adding a User Role—Consultant*

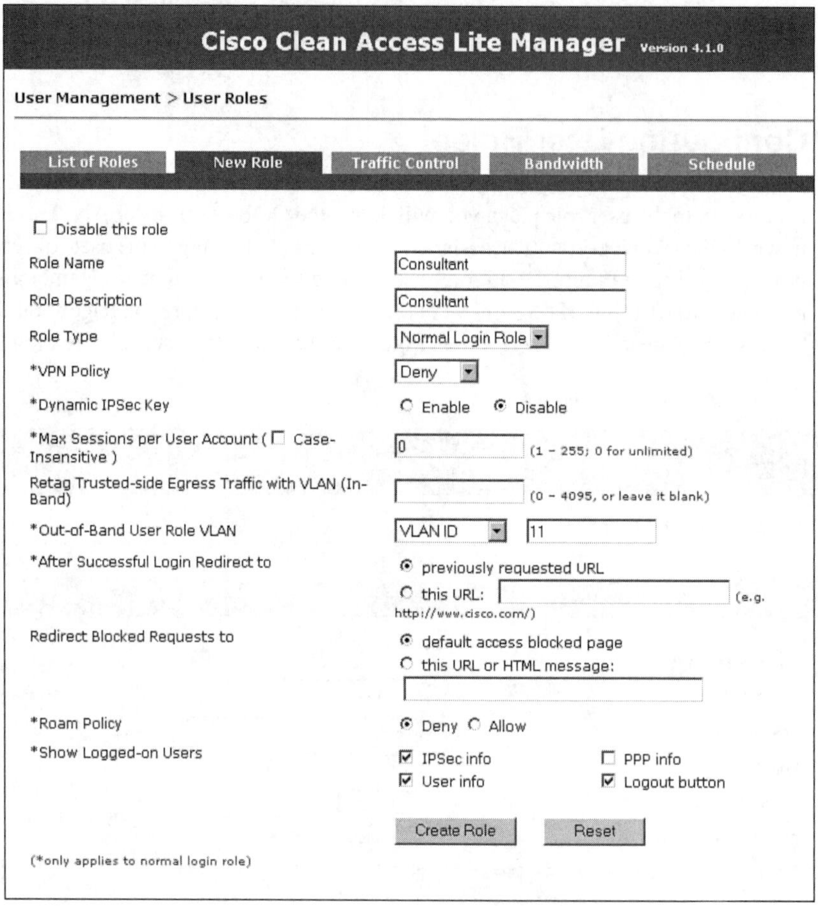

Figure 10-51 shows the user role creation for Employee.

Figure 10-51 *Adding a User Role—Employee*

Cisco Clean Access Lite Manager Version 4.1.0

User Management > User Roles

| List of Roles | New Role | Traffic Control | Bandwidth | Schedule |

☐ Disable this role

Role Name	Employee
Role Description	Employee
Role Type	Normal Login Role ▾
*VPN Policy	Deny ▾
*Dynamic IPSec Key	○ Enable ⦿ Disable
*Max Sessions per User Account (☐ Case-Insensitive)	0 (1 – 255; 0 for unlimited)
Retag Trusted-side Egress Traffic with VLAN (In-Band)	(0 – 4095, or leave it blank)
*Out-of-Band User Role VLAN	VLAN ID ▾ 12
*After Successful Login Redirect to	⦿ previously requested URL ○ this URL: (e.g. http://www.cisco.com/)
Redirect Blocked Requests to	⦿ default access blocked page ○ this URL or HTML message:
*Roam Policy	⦿ Deny ○ Allow
*Show Logged-on Users	☑ IPSec info ☐ PPP info ☑ User info ☑ Logout button

Create Role   Reset

(*only applies to normal login role)

Figure 10-52 shows all the user roles.

Figure 10-52 *User Role List*

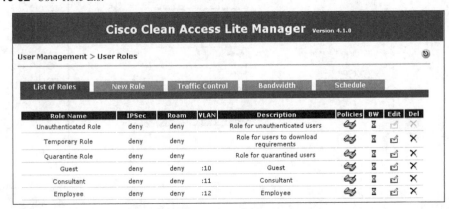

Cisco Clean Access Lite Manager Version 4.1.0

User Management > User Roles

| List of Roles | New Role | Traffic Control | Bandwidth | Schedule |

Role Name	IPSec	Roam	VLAN	Description	Policies	BW	Edit	Del
Unauthenticated Role	deny	deny		Role for unauthenticated users	⬙	⌧	⧠	✕
Temporary Role	deny	deny		Role for users to download requirements	⬙	⌧	⧠	✕
Quarantine Role	deny	deny		Role for quarantine users	⬙	⌧	⧠	✕
Guest	deny	deny	:10	Guest	⬙	⌧	⧠	✕
Consultant	deny	deny	:11	Consultant	⬙	⌧	⧠	✕
Employee	deny	deny	:12	Employee	⬙	⌧	⧠	✕

Step 15: Configuring User Authentication on the Local Database

Add two local users to the NAC Appliance local database: an employee and a consultant. These local user accounts will be used for testing purposes. In a production environment, you should configure an LDAP, Kerberos, or RADIUS server instead of a local user database. Local users should generally be used only for testing and guest access. Figure 10-53 shows the creation of a Consultant user.

Figure 10-53 *Adding a Local User—Consultant*

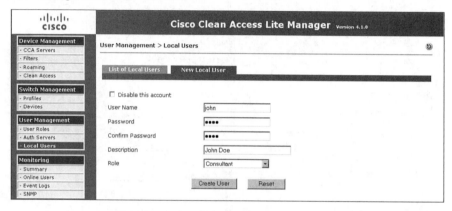

Figure 10-54 shows the creation of an Employee user.

Figure 10-54 *Adding a Local User—Employee*

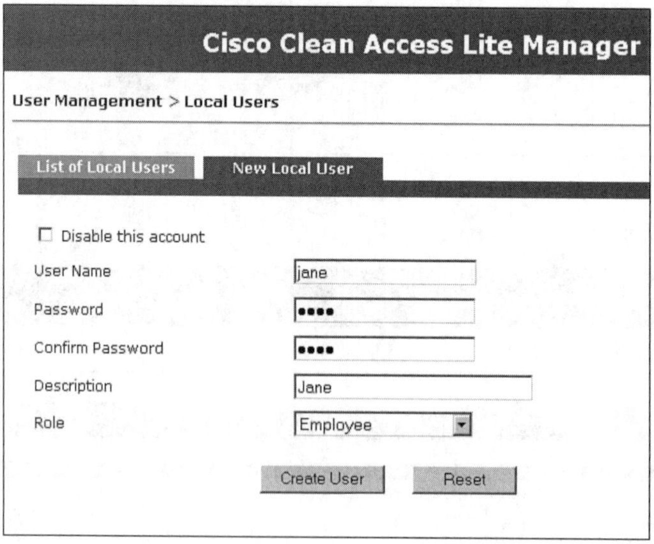

Step 16: Changing the Discovery Host

NAC Appliance Agent sends discovery packets to discover the NAC Appliance Server so that it can start communicating with it and begin the NAC process. These packets are sent on UDP port 8905 and 8906.

NAC Appliance Server listens on the UDP ports 8905 and 8906. So, when it receives packets from NAC Appliance Agent on these ports, it knows that a new host has connected to the network and instructs NAC Appliance Agent to pop up and challenge the user for authentication. The NAC Appliance Server doesn't forward these packets out on the trusted network.

The packets on UDP 8905 are sent to the default gateway of the user device. Therefore, if a NAC Appliance Server is Layer 2 adjacent to the user, the NAC Appliance Agent packets will reach NAS.

NAC Appliance Agent sends the discovery packets on port 8905 to the discovery host configured on NAC Appliance Manager. By default, the discovery host is the IP address of NAM. This is because NAM always exists on the trusted network, and for a user on the untrusted network to reach a host on the trusted network, it has to go through NAS and therefore will discover NAS.

In this design, you are not forcing all user traffic to reach NAC Appliance Server. Adding a technology such as policy-based routing, virtual routing and forwarding, or generic routing encapsulation would force traffic through NAC Appliance Server. You are using VLAN ACLs that do not force traffic back to NAC Appliance Server, but only restrict where it can go. Therefore, you must change the discovery host from NAC Appliance Manager (the default) to be the untrusted port IP of NAC Appliance Server, as shown in Figure 10-55. Doing so ensures that the NAC Appliance Agent discovery packets will reach NAC Appliance Server.

Figure 10-55 *Changing Discovery Host*

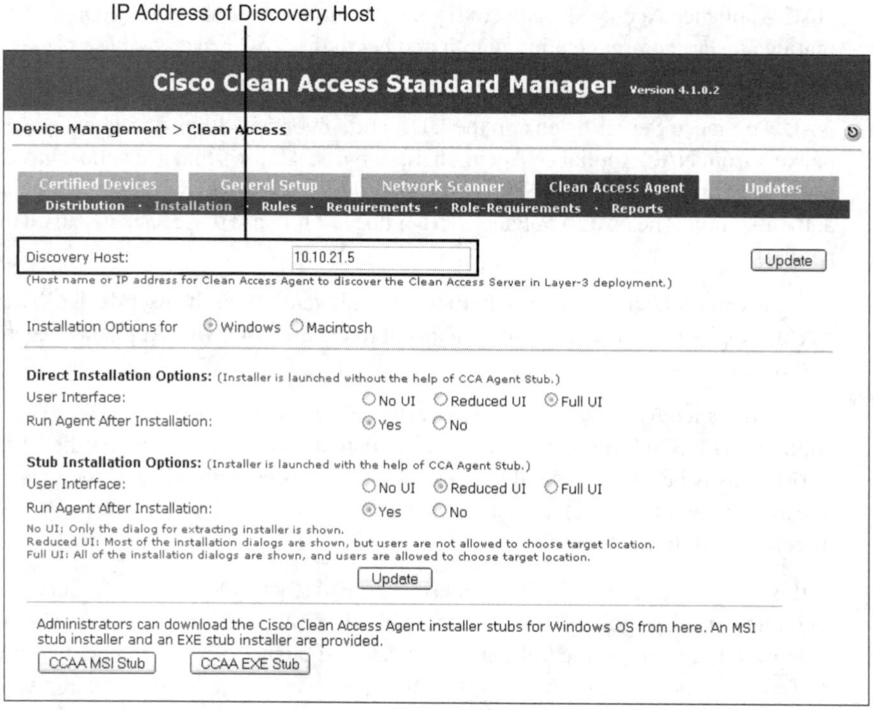

IP Address of Discovery Host

Step 17: Configuring the Web Login Page

You have to configure the web login page for users who don't use NAC Appliance Agent. The Login Page edit screen is shown in Figure 10-56.

This design uses ActiveX and Java applet controls for the following two purposes:

* To obtain the MAC address of the user device. This is required for OOB Layer 3 mode to operate. The client's MAC address is used to find the switch port the client is connected to.

* To trigger an IP release/renew when the user is moved from the untrusted VLAN to the trusted VLAN.

Be sure to enable the web client and check or enable each of the options below it.

Figure 10-56 *Login Page Edit Screen*

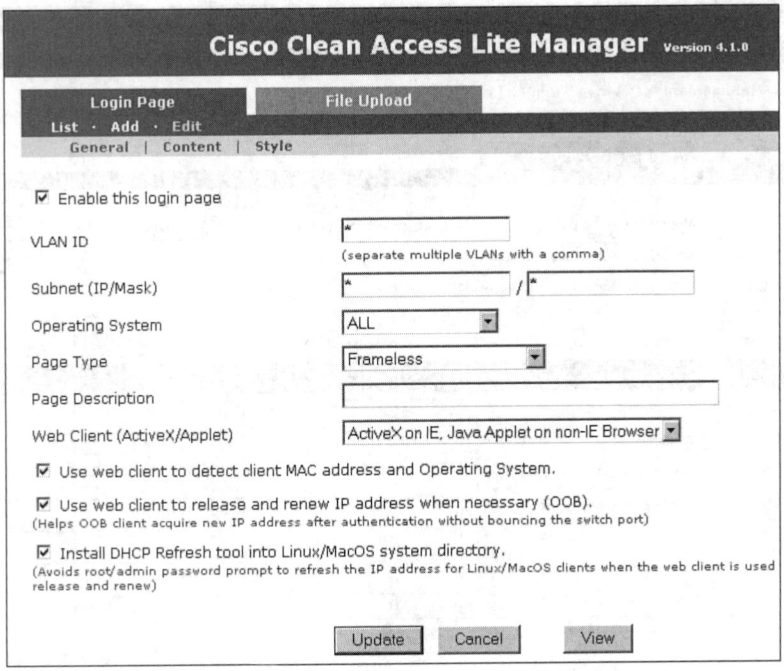

Step 18: Testing Whether OOB and User Role–Based VLAN Assignment Works

If you navigate to **Switch Management > Device > Switches > List > 10.10.30.1 > Ports**, you will see that interface Fa1/0/5 is not connected and is currently on VLAN 10 (Initial VLAN). This is shown in Figure 10-57.

Now connect a laptop to interface Fa1/0/5. You will see that the port was immediately moved to the untrusted VLAN 110. This was triggered by the switch sending an SNMP MAC-notification trap to NAC Appliance Manager. The port was moved to VLAN 110 because the port profile had the auth (untrusted) VLAN set to VLAN 110. See Figure 10-58 for details.

Figure 10-57 *Ports List—Before Connection*

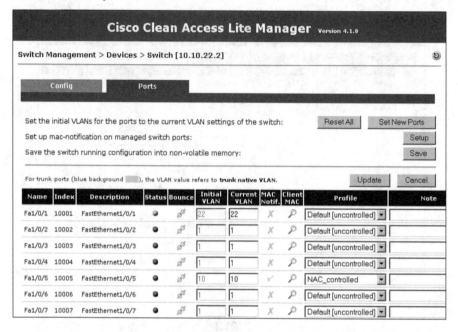

Figure 10-58 *Ports List—After Connection*

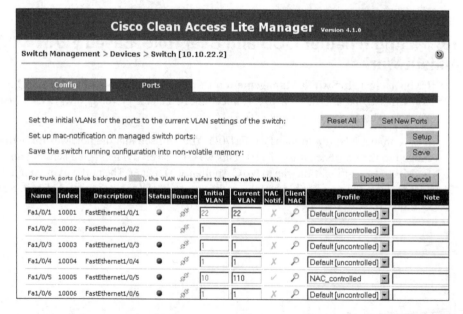

On the user PC, you will see that NAC Appliance Agent has popped up. Put in the credentials for the user jane, as shown in Figure 10-59.

Figure 10-59   *Clean Access Agent Authentication Popup*

When you click **Login**, NAC Appliance determines that the user jane belongs to the Employee user role. NAC Appliance looks at the OOB user role VLAN configured under the Employee user role and moves the user's switch port, Fa1/0/5, to VLAN 12. This is shown in Figure 10-60.

Figure 10-60   *Ports List—After Authentication*

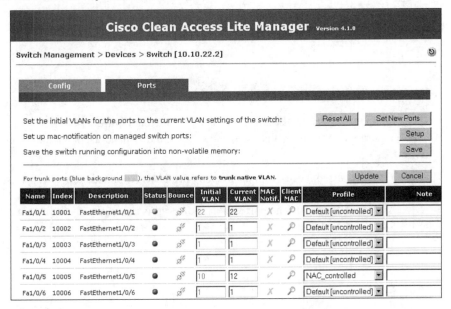

Because you changed the VLAN of the user from VLAN 110 to VLAN 12 in this process, you will also trigger a DHCP release/renew on the user's machine. As a result, during the login process, you will see the NAC Appliance agent screens shown in Figure 10-61 and Figure 10-62.

Figure 10-61 *Agent Refreshing IP*

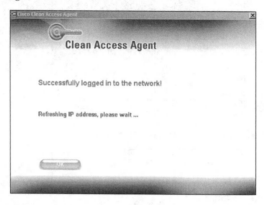

Figure 10-62 *Agent Refreshing IP Successful*

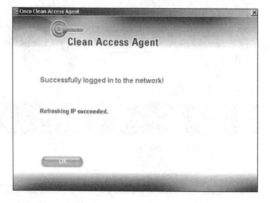

The user appears in the OOB online user list, as shown in Figure 10-63. If the user is put in the Temporary role for remediation, it shows up in the in-band users list until it becomes clean.

Now if the user disconnects from the switch port, NAC Appliance removes the user from the online users list. This is triggered by the switch sending an SNMP linkdown trap to NAC Appliance Manager. The port VLAN, however, is not changed—it remains in VLAN 12.

Figure 10-63 *Online Users List—OOB*

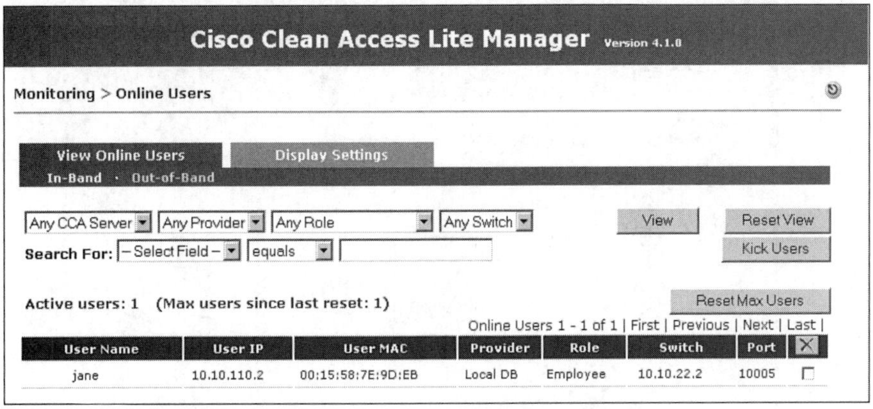

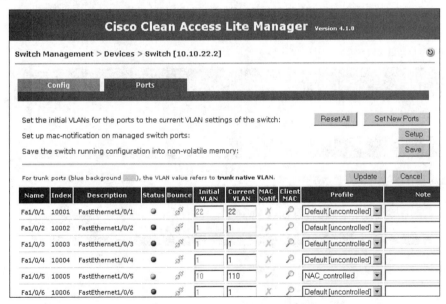

Now another user, John, connects to the same switch port. The switch sends a new SNMP MAC-notification trap to NAC Appliance Manager. The port will immediately move to the auth (untrusted) VLAN 110, as shown in Figure 10-64, so that the new user can log in.

Figure 10-64 *Ports List—Next User*

Name	Index	Description	Status	Bounce	Initial VLAN	Current VLAN	MAC Notif.	Client MAC	Profile	Note
Fa1/0/1	10001	FastEthernet1/0/1	●	⚙	22	22	✗	🔍	Default [uncontrolled] ▾	
Fa1/0/2	10002	FastEthernet1/0/2	●	⚙	1	1	✗	🔍	Default [uncontrolled] ▾	
Fa1/0/3	10003	FastEthernet1/0/3	●	⚙	1	1	✗	🔍	Default [uncontrolled] ▾	
Fa1/0/4	10004	FastEthernet1/0/4	●	⚙	1	1	✗	🔍	Default [uncontrolled] ▾	
Fa1/0/5	10005	FastEthernet1/0/5	●	⚙	10	110	✓	🔍	NAC_controlled ▾	
Fa1/0/6	10006	FastEthernet1/0/6	●	⚙	1	1	✗	🔍	Default [uncontrolled] ▾	

On the user's machine, Clean Access Agent pops up, as shown in Figure 10-65. Put in the credentials for the user John and click **Login**.

Figure 10-65 *Clean Access Agent Authentication Popup*

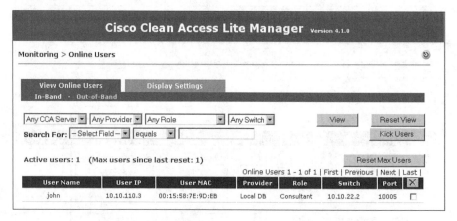

After the user is authenticated, NAC Appliance Manager determines that this user is a consultant and moves the user to VLAN 11, which is the VLAN configured for the OOB user role VLAN for the Guest role. The user shows up in the out-of-band online user list as a Consultant, as shown in Figure 10-66.

Figure 10-66 *Online Users List—OOB*

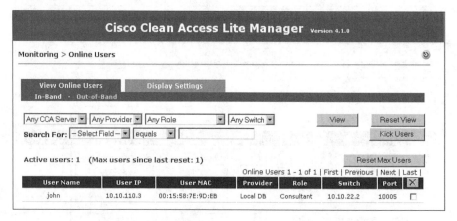

Additional Out-of-Band Considerations

Here is a list of other considerations worth noting in regard to the sample setup you just ran through:

- The previous steps covered a scenario in which users have NAC Appliance Agent and the agent is able to discover NAC Appliance Server.

Users who don't have NAC Appliance Agent have to be given a URL to which they can go for authentication. That URL should resolve to the untrusted port IP of NAC Appliance Server. Therefore, guest users who want to get network access can be given a URL, for example: http:// hotspot.cisco.com/. You can put an entry into the DNS server to make this DNS name resolve to 10.10.21.5, which is the untrusted port IP of the NAS.

- If you want to perform NAC Appliance Server load balancing in a Layer 3 OOB environment, you have several choices:

  — Use a server load-balancing device, such as a Cisco ACE module.

  — Use a discovery host IP address that points to a client that is reachable only by going through the servers. Then configure the network to load balance this address via routing.

  — Use DNS round-robin to load balance the servers. Be careful with this method because it might not deal well with failures, depending on your environment. To use it, you can configure the DNS host name to resolve to the different servers and make the DNS server load balance between them. If you are using NAC Appliance Agent, you can configure the discovery host to be a DNS name instead of an IP, make the DNS server resolve that DNS name to the different servers, and load balance between them.

- In Out-of-Band mode, use SNMP traps to trigger the NAC process and SNMP sets to change the VLAN on the switch port. If configuring out-of-band in a Layer 3 environment, you must ensure that the network is reliable and will not drop the SNMP packets. You should consider this factor if you deploy Layer 3 OOB for remote sites where the SNMP traffic might traverse an unreliable or congested WAN link. You might consider prioritizing SNMP traffic on the WAN link using QoS mechanisms. Doing so will help ensure good SNMP communication between the switches at the remote site and NAC Appliance Manager at the central site. A future release of NAC Appliance will use SNMP informs to help with this issue.

Summary

In this chapter, you examined how to configure NAC Appliance using the Out-of Band deployment mode. You covered several of the design considerations for OOB as well as how it works. Two detailed, step-by-step OOB sample setups were given. The first setup used OOB with Layer 2 client adjacency, whereas the second setup used OOB with Layer 3 client adjacency. Each example provided instructions on how to configure each of the relevant devices in the solution. This includes the Cisco switches, routers, NAC Appliance Manager and NAC Appliance Server, and VLAN access lists where appropriate. These sample configurations are intended as guides to help you build your own NAC Appliance OOB solution that fits your environment.

This chapter covers the following topics:

- Active Directory Single Sign-On Overview
- Supported Devices for AD SSO
- Basic AD SSO Configuration Steps
- Configuring Single Sign-On for Windows AD
- Configuring Single Sign-On for VPN
- Configuring Single Sign-On for Cisco Wireless LAN Controller

CHAPTER 11

Configuring Single Sign-On

This chapter covers how to configure Single Sign-On (SSO) for the following deployments. Step-by-step screen shots and explanations of each deployment are provided. For details of the benefits that SSO provides, review the single sign-on material in Chapter 5, "Advanced Cisco NAC Appliance Design Topics."

- Active Directory Single Sign-On (AD SSO)
- Cisco Virtual Private Network (VPN) SSO
- Cisco Wireless SSO

Active Directory Single Sign-On Overview

Prior to NAC Appliance 4.0, a typical Windows user running NAC Agent would have to manually log in via the NAC Agent prompt to gain access to the network. The NAC Agent login is an additional login step to the Ctrl-Alt-Delete login process that all Windows users go through when booting up their machine. Many users complained that the extra login was a hassle and inconvenient.

Starting with 4.0, that extra login step for Windows users logging in to the domain has been removed. Windows users simply enter their login name and password as they normally do when booting into their Windows desktop via Ctrl-Alt-Delete, and NAC Agent takes care of the rest. NAC Agent takes the user's login credentials and automatically passes that info to NAC Appliance for authentication. After being successfully authenticated and posture assessed, the user is mapped to an assigned role and granted the appropriate network access.

Supported Devices for AD SSO

Single Sign-On in a LAN is supported only in a Windows environment with Active Directory (AD) deployed. AD SSO requires NAC Agent to be installed for SSO to work. NAC Agent leverages the cached Windows login credentials and Kerberos ticket from the host PC and uses them for authentication without additional user login. Table 11-1 shows OS support for Active Directory SSO.

Table 11-1 *Operating System Support for Active Directory SSO*

AD Servers	Host Computers
Windows 2000 Server Service SP 4	Windows 2000 SP4
Windows 2003 Enterprise SP 1	Windows XP (Home/Pro) SP 1, SP 2, or later
Windows 2003 Enterprise R2	
Windows 2003 Standard Service Pack 1	Vista Basic, Premium, Business, Ultimate, and Enterprise

Basic AD SSO Configuration Steps

Before configuring AD SSO, you should have a good understanding of the AD domain structure. The following are several items that you will need to prepare:

- Windows 2000 or Windows 2003 Server installation CD. This CD is required to install the support tools needed for the **ktpass** command. The **ktpass** command is required to be run on the AD server or domain controller that the NAS is logging in.

- The fully qualified domain name (FQDN) of the AD server that the NAS logs in to.

- NAC Appliance Server (NAS) and NAC Appliance Manager (NAM) must be able to resolve the FQDN of the AD server.

A summary of the configuration steps is as follows:

Step 1 In NAM, add the NAS to be managed.

Step 2 In NAM, add the AD server as AD SSO Auth Server.

Step 3 Configure traffic policies and ports in unauthenticated role for AD authentication.

Step 4 In NAS, configure the AD server settings. This includes the NAS user account and FQDN settings of the AD server.

Step 5 In the AD server, add the NAS user account that NAS will use to log in to the AD server.

Step 6 In the AD server, run the **ktpass** command to configure encryption parameters to support Linux OS of the NAS.

Step 7 In the NAS, enable the Agent-Based Windows Single-Sign-On service.

Step 8   (Optional) Enable Group Policy Object (GPO) updates.

Step 9   (Optional) Add a Lightweight Directory Access Protocol (LDAP) lookup server for AD SSO if mapping users to multiple roles is required after authentication.

Step 10   Make sure that the current time in the NAM, NAS, and AD server are all in sync.

Configuring Single Sign-On for Windows AD

This section provides a step-by-step configuration example of how to configure AD SSO. The example chosen here is a Layer 2 Out-Of-Band (OOB) Real-IP deployment. This model is used because most high-speed LAN deployments will be OOB for performance reasons. In addition, Real-IP has the capability to provide a /30 or 30-bit mask address that will quarantine an infected end host before accessing the network. Note that most enterprise networks already have a DHCP infrastructure in place. Therefore, it is strictly optional for customers if they would like to use the 30-bit mask functionality in NAS. Figure 11-1 shows the topology of this Layer 2 OOB Real-IP example.

Figure 11-1   *Layer 2 OOB Real-IP NAS Deployment*

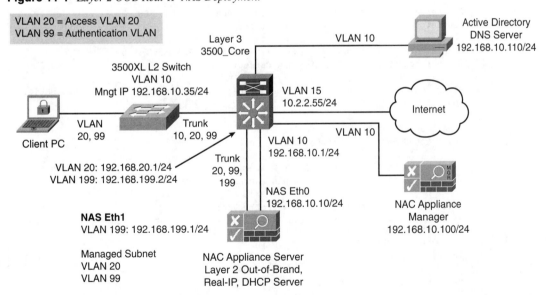

NAM Configuration

From the command-line interface (CLI) of NAM, use the **service perfigo config** command to set up the NAM IP info. The CCA software used is version 4.1.0. Example 11-1 shows the configuration setup script.

Example 11-1 *Configuring NAM via CLI*

```
Fedora Core release 4 (Stentz)
Kernel 2.6.11-perfigo on an i686

cam1 login: root
Password:
[root@cam1 ~]# service perfigo config

Welcome to the Cisco Clean Access Manager quick configuration utility.

Note that you need to be root to execute this utility.

The utility will now ask you a series of configuration questions.
Please answer them carefully.

Cisco Clean Access Manager, (C) 2006 Cisco Systems, Inc.

Configuring the network interface:

Please enter the IP address for the interface eth0 [192.168.137.3]: 192.168.10.100
You entered 192.168.10.100. Is this correct? (y/n)? [y]

Please enter the netmask for the interface eth0 [255.255.255.0]:
You entered 255.255.255.0. Is this correct? (y/n)? [y]

Please enter the IP address for the default gateway [192.168.137.1]: 192.168.10.1
You entered 192.168.10.1. Is this correct? (y/n)? [y]

Please enter the hostname [cam1]: NAM1
You entered NAM1. Is this correct? (y/n)? [y]

Please enter the IP address for the name server: [192.168.100.100]: 192.168.10.110
You entered 192.168.10.110. Is this correct? (y/n)? [y]

Would you like to change shared secret? (y/n)? [y]
Please remember to configure the Clean Access Server with the same string. Please
enter the shared secret between Clean Access Server
You entered: cisco123
Is this correct? (y/n)? [y]

>>> Configuring date and time:

The timezone is currently set to:America/Los_Angeles
Would you like to change this setting? (y/n)? [y] n

Current date and time hh:mm:ss mm/dd/yy [23:20:08 12/17/06]: 15:20:00 12/17/06
You entered 15:20:00 12/17/06. Is this correct? (y/n)? [y]
Sun Dec 17 15:20:00 PST 2006
```

Example 11-1 *Configuring NAM via CLI (Continued)*

```
You must generate a valid SSL certificate in order to use the Clean Access Manager's
secure web console.
Please answer the following questions correctly.
Information for a new SSL certificate:
Enter fully qualified domain name or IP: NAM1.selab.net
Enter organization unit name: cisco
Enter organization name: cisco
Enter city name: san jose
Enter state code: ca
Enter 2 letter country code: us


You entered the following:
Domain: NAM1.selab.net
Organization unit: cisco
Organization name: cisco
City name: san jose
State code: ca
Country code: us
Is this correct? (y/n)? [y]
Generating SSL Certificate...
CA signing: /root/.tomcat.csr -> /root/.tomcat.crt:
CA verifying: /root/.tomcat.crt <-> CA cert
/root/.tomcat.crt: OK
Done

For security reasons, it is highly recommended that you change the default passwords
for the root user.
User: root
Changing password for user root.
New UNIX password:
Retype new UNIX password:
passwd: all authentication tokens updated successfully.

Changes require a RESTART of Clean Access Manager.
Configuration is complete.
[root@cam1 ~]# service perfigo reboot
```

NAS Configuration

From the CLI of the NAS appliance, use the **service perfigo config** command to set up the NAS IP info. Example 11-2 shows how to configure NAS via CLI.

Example 11-2 *Configuring NAS via Configuration and Setup Script*

```
[root@cas1 ~]# service perfigo config

Welcome to the Cisco Clean Access Server quick configuration utility.

Note that you need to be root to execute this utility.

The utility will now ask you a series of configuration questions.
Please answer them carefully.

Cisco Clean Access Server, (C) 2006 Cisco Systems, Inc.

Configuring the network interfaces:

Please enter the IP address for the interface eth0 [10.1.110.2]: 192.168.10.10
You entered 192.168.10.10. Is this correct? (y/n)? [y]

Please enter the netmask for the interface eth0 [255.255.255.0]:
You entered 255.255.255.0. Is this correct? (y/n)? [y]

Please enter the IP address for the default gateway [10.1.110.1]: 192.168.10.1
You entered 192.168.10.1. Is this correct? (y/n)? [y]

[Vlan Id Passthrough] for packets from eth0 to eth1 is disabled.
Would you like to enable it? (y/n)? [n]

[Management Vlan Tagging] for egress packets of eth0 is disabled.
Would you like to enable it? (y/n)? [n]

Please enter the IP address for the untrusted interface eth1 [10.1.111.2]:
192.168.199.1
You entered 192.168.99.1. Is this correct? (y/n)? [y]

Please enter the netmask for the interface eth1 [255.255.255.0]:
You entered 255.255.255.0. Is this correct? (y/n)? [y]

Please enter the IP address for the default gateway [10.1.111.1]: 192.168.199.2
You entered 192.168.10.1. Is this correct? (y/n)? [y]

[Vlan Id Passthrough] for packets from eth1 to eth0 is disabled.
Would you like to enable it? (y/n)? [n]

[Management Vlan Tagging] for egress packets of eth1 is disabled.
Would you like to enable it? (y/n)? [n]

Please enter the hostname [cas1]: NAS1
You entered NAS1. Is this correct? (y/n)? [y]

Please enter the IP address for the name server: [10.1.112.105]: 192.168.10.110
You entered 192.168.10.110. Is this correct? (y/n)? [y]

Would you like to change shared secret? (y/n)? [y]
Please enter the shared secret: cisco123
```

Example 11-2 *Configuring NAS via Configuration and Setup Script (Continued)*

```
You entered: cisco123
Is this correct? (y/n)? [y]

>>> Configuring date and time:


The timezone is currently set to:America/Los_Angeles
Would you like to change this setting? (y/n)? [y] n

Current date and time hh:mm:ss mm/dd/yy [15:39:15 12/17/06]:
You entered 15:39:15 12/17/06. Is this correct? (y/n)? [y]
Sun Dec 17 15:39:15 PST 2006

You must generate a valid SSL certificate in order to use the Clean Access Server's
secure web console.
Please answer the following questions correctly.
Information for a new SSL certificate:
Enter fully qualified domain name or IP: NAS1.selab.net
Enter organization unit name: cisco
Enter organization name: cisco
Enter city name: san jose
Enter state code: ca
Enter 2 letter country code: us


You entered the following:
Domain: NAS1.selab.net
Organization unit: cisco
Organization name: cisco
City name: san jose
State code: ca
Country code: us
Is this correct? (y/n)? [y]
Generating SSL Certificate...
CA signing: /root/.tomcat.csr -> /root/.tomcat.crt:
CA verifying: /root/.tomcat.crt <-> CA cert
/root/.tomcat.crt: OK
Done

For security reasons, it is highly recommended that you change the default password
for the root user.
User: root
Changing password for user root.
New UNIX password:
Retype new UNIX password:
passwd: all authentication tokens updated successfully.


Would you like to change the default password for the web console admin user
password? (y/n)? [y]
Please enter an appropriately secure password for the web console admin user.
```

continues

Example 11-2 *Configuring NAS via Configuration and Setup Script (Continued)*

```
New password for web console admin:
Confirm new password for web console admin:
Web console admin password changed successfully.

Configuration is complete.
[root@cas1 ~]# service perfigo reboot
```

Layer 3 3550 Core Switch Configuration

Example 11-3 shows the working configuration in the Layer 3 3550 core switch using Cisco IOS Software Release 12.2(25)SEE2.

Example 11-3 *3550 Core Switch Configuration*

```
hostname 3550_core
!
vtp domain cisco
vtp mode transparent
!
vlan 10
 name ManagementVlan10
!
vlan 15
 name Internet
!
vlan 20
 name AccessVlan20
!
vlan 99
 name AuthenticationVlan99
!
vlan 1004
 bridge 1
!
vlan 1005
 bridge 1
!
!
interface FastEthernet0/1
 description Active Director/DNS
 switchport access vlan 10
 switchport mode access
 spanning-tree portfast
!
interface FastEthernet0/2
 description Link to Internet
 switchport access vlan 15
 switchport mode access
 spanning-tree portfast
!
```

Example 11-3 *3550 Core Switch Configuration (Continued)*

```
interface FastEthernet0/3
 description NAM
 switchport access vlan 10
 switchport mode access
 spanning-tree portfast
!
interface FastEthernet0/4
 description NAS Eth0 Trusted
 switchport access vlan 10
 switchport mode access
 spanning-tree portfast
!
interface FastEthernet0/5
 description NAS Eth1 Untrusted
 switchport trunk encapsulation dot1q
 switchport trunk native vlan 10
 switchport trunk allowed vlan 20,99,199
 switchport mode trunk
!
!
!<Omit... to save paper>
!
!
interface FastEthernet0/24
 description Link to edge 3500 XL L2 switch
 switchport trunk encapsulation dot1q
 switchport trunk native vlan 10
 switchport trunk allowed vlan 10,20,99
 switchport mode trunk
!
interface Vlan10
 description User Vlan 10
 ip address 192.168.10.1 255.255.255.0
!
interface Vlan15
 description Internet link
 ip address 10.2.2.55 255.255.255.0
!
interface Vlan20
 description User Access Vlan 20
 ip address 192.168.20.1 255.255.255.0
 shutdown
!
interface Vlan199
 description Link to NAS Eth1 Real-IP
 ip address 192.168.199.2 255.255.255.0
!
ip classless
ip route 0.0.0.0 0.0.0.0 10.2.2.1
ip route 192.168.99.0 255.255.255.0 192.168.10.10
```

continues

Example 11-3 *3550 Core Switch Configuration (Continued)*

```
ip http server
ip http secure-server
!
!
snmp-server group cam_user v3 auth notify *tv.00000001.00000000.00000020.000000000F
snmp-server group cam_group v3 auth write v1default notify v1default
snmp-server group 3550_group v3 auth write v1default
snmp-server community cisco123 RO
snmp-server location SELab
snmp-server contact Jerry Lin
snmp-server enable traps snmp linkdown
snmp-server enable traps mac-notification
!
line con 0
 exec-timeout 0 0
 length 0
line vty 0 4
 exec-timeout 0 0
 password cisco
 login
line vty 5 15
 password cisco
 login
!
mac-address-table notification interval 0
mac-address-table notification
end
```

3500XL Edge Layer 2 Switch Configuration

Example 11-4 shows the 3500XL edge Layer 2 switch configuration using software version c3500XL-c3h2s-mz.120-5.3.WC.1.bin. Note that the 3500XL switches have been designated End-Of-Life by Cisco. Although the 3500XL switch is still supported by NAM and NAS, Cisco best practices recommend that customers deploy active Cisco LAN switches that are not on the End-Of-Sale or End-Of-Life list. The current switches support many popular enhanced security features, such as SNMP Version 3. For the simplicity of this example, the 3500XL is used with SNMP Version 1.

Example 11-4 *3500XL Edge Layer 2 Switch Output*

```
interface FastEthernet0/1
 switchport access vlan 99
 spanning-tree portfast
!
interface FastEthernet0/2
 switchport access vlan 99
 spanning-tree portfast
!
interface FastEthernet0/3
 switchport access vlan 99
 spanning-tree portfast
```

Example 11-4 *3500XL Edge Layer 2 Switch Output (Continued)*

```
!
!
interface FastEthernet0/23
 switchport access vlan 99
 spanning-tree portfast
!
interface FastEthernet0/24
 description Trunk to core 3550 L3 switch
 switchport trunk encapsulation dot1q
 switchport trunk native vlan 10
 switchport trunk allowed vlan 1,10,20,99,1002-1005
 switchport mode trunk
!
interface VLAN1
 no ip address
 no ip directed-broadcast
 no ip route-cache
 shutdown
!
interface VLAN10
 ip address 192.168.10.35 255.255.255.0
 no ip directed-broadcast
 no ip route-cache
!
ip default-gateway 192.168.10.1
logging trap debugging
snmp-server engineID local 000000090200000628F8F8C0
snmp-server community cisco123 RW
snmp-server enable traps snmp authentication linkdown linkup coldstart
snmp-server host 192.168.10.100 trap cisco123  snmp
!
line con 0
 exec-timeout 0 0
 length 0
 transport input none
 stopbits 1
line vty 0 4
 password cisco123
 login
!
end
```

Active Directory or Domain Controller Configuration

The AD server in this deployment is a Windows 2003 Server Enterprise Edition with Service Pack 1. The AD server's FQDN is win2003-ad-ca.selab.net. The computer name of the AD server is "win2003-ad-ca". The domain name is "selab.net". Figure 11-2 shows the FQDN of the AD server win2003-ad-ca.selab.net.

Figure 11-2 *FQDN of the AD Server*

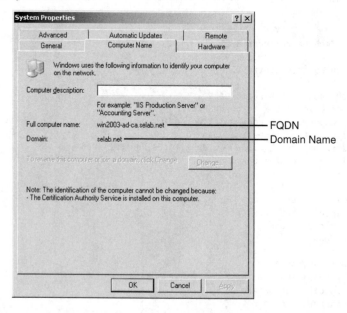

This AD server is also the DNS server for this sample deployment.

Beginning Overall Setup

In any NAC deployment, a single NAM (primary) or a pair of NAMs (active and standby) can manage up to 40 NAS appliances. This means that nearly all the NAS configurations can be performed within the NAM GUI. But first, NAS has to be added to NAM. The following steps detail how to add NAS to the NAM:

Step 1   Go to **Device Management > CCA Servers > New Server**.

Step 2   Enter the server IP of the NAS: **192.168.10.10**.

Step 3   Enter the server location: **SE Lab**.

Step 4   Select the server type **Out-Of-Band Real-IP Gateway**.

Step 5   Click **Add Clean Access Server**. Figure 11-3 shows NAS as status Connected after being added successfully.

Figure 11-3 displays the Clean Access Server (NAS) added to the NAM.

Figure 11-3 *OOB Real-IP NAS Added*

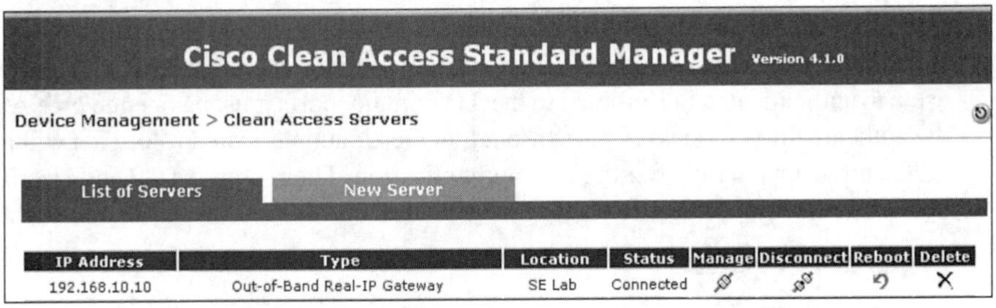

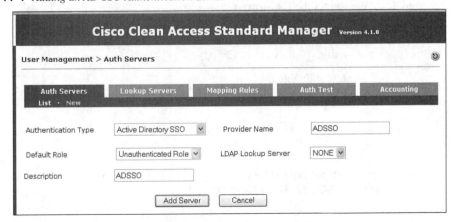

Adding an AD Server as an AD SSO Auth Server

The following steps show how to add an AD server in NAS as an AD SSO authentication server:

Step 1   In NAM, go to **User Management > Auth Servers > New**.

Step 2   Select the authentication type **Active Directory SSO**.

Step 3   Enter the provider name **ADSSO**.

Step 4   Leave the default role as **Unauthenticated Role**. This is the default user assigned role unless it is overridden by the **LDAP Lookup Server** field.

Step 5   For now, leave the LDAP lookup server as **NONE**. This step will be created later.

Step 6   In the **Description** field, enter **ADSSO**.

Step 7   Click **Add Server**.

Figure 11-4 shows the addition of an AD SSO authentication server.

Figure 11-4 *Adding an AD SSO Authentication Server*

Configuring Traffic Policies and Ports in the Unauthenticated Role for AD Authentication

By default, NAS permits only DNS and DHCP traffic in the Unauthenticated role. For AD users to authenticate via Kerberos to the AD domain, ports must be opened on NAS to allow the authentication process to pass through in the Unauthenticated role. This will also allow GPO and scripts to run after the user authentication. The required TCP and User Datagram Protocol (UDP) ports are listed next.

Required TCP ports:

- TCP 88 (Kerberos)
- TCP 135 (remote-procedure call [RPC])
- TCP 389 (LDAP) or TCP 535 (LDAP with Secure Sockets Layer [SSL])
- TCP 1025 (RPC), nonstandard
- TCP 1026 (RPC), nonstandard

Alternative UDP ports:

If you do not know whether the AD server is using Kerberos, open the following UDP ports as well:

- UDP 88 (Kerberos)
- UDP 389 (LDAP) or UDP 636 (LDAP with SSL)
- Internet Control Message Protocol (ICMP)

To configure the ports, do the following:

Step 1 Go to **User Management > User Roles > List of Roles > Policies(icon)_[Unauthenticated role]**.

Step 2 Make sure that the screen shows **Unauthenticated Role, Untrusted->Trusted**. Click **Add Policy**.

Step 3 Make sure of the following settings:

    — Priority = 1

    — Action = Allow

    — State = Enabled

    — Category = IP

    — Protocol = TCP,6

    — Untrusted (IP/Mask:Port) = */*,*

Step 4 Change **Trusted(IP/Mask:Port)** to AD server: **192.168.10.110/ 255.255.255.255, 88,135,389,1025,1026**.

Step 5 Enter an optional description: **User AD authentication policy**.

Step 6 Click **Add Policy**.

Step 7 Repeat the preceding steps for the alternative UDP ports and ICMP.

Figure 11-5 shows the user AD authentication policy in Unauthenticated role. Only the TCP traffic policy is shown. The UDP traffic policy should be added by an administrator.

Figure 11-5 *TCP Traffic Policy Added for AD Authentication During Unauthenticated Role*

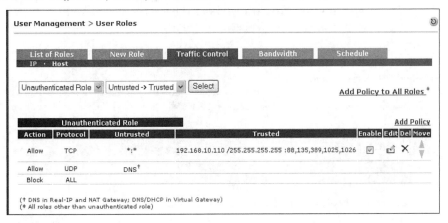

Configuring AD SSO Settings in NAS

To configure AD SSO Settings in NAS, do the following:

Step 1 Go to **Device Management > CCA Servers > List of Servers > Manage(icon)_192.168.10.10**.

Step 2 Select **Authentication > Windows Auth > Active Directory SSO**.

Step 3 **Account for CAS**: For smaller networks where a single Active Directory server is deployed, click the **Single Active Directory Server** option. For large enterprise networks where multiple AD servers are deployed, click the **Domain (All Active Directory Servers)** option. For this simple example, the single AD server option is selected. The multiple Active Directory server option is available only in NAC Appliance software 4.1.1 and higher.

Step 4 **Active Directory Server (FQDN): win2003-ad-ca.selab.net**. This is the full computer name of the AD server.

Step 5 **Active Directory Domain: SELAB.NET**. *The domain name here must be in all capital letters.*

Step 6   **Account Name for CAS: ccasso**. This is the user account name for NAS in AD.

Step 7   **Account Password for CAS: Cisco123**. Password policy is subject to Active Directory password policy. The Plain password cisco123 would not work. AD requires at least one capital letter.

Step 8   **Active Directory SSO Auth Server: ADSSO**.

Step 9   Click **Update**. *Do not check* the **Enable Agent-Based Windows Single Sign-On with Active Directory (Kerberos)** check box yet. The NAS user account has not yet been created in AD.

Figure 11-6 shows how to configure Active Directory SSO settings in NAS.

Figure 11-6 *Single AD Server Configuration*

Configuring the AD Server and Running the **ktpass** Command

The following is how to prepare and configure the AD server for AD SSO:

Step 1   Create the NAS user account in AD.

Step 2   Install the support tools from the Windows 2003 Server CD.

Step 3   Run the **ktpass.exe** command.

Creating the NAS User Account in AD

Use the following steps to create the NAS user account in the AD server:

Step 1 In the AD server, go to **Start > Administrative Tools > Active Directory Users and Computers**.

Step 2 Go to the **Users** folder under the AD domain. In this example, the AD domain is **selab.net**.

Step 3 Right-click **Users > New > User**.

Step 4 Enter the user account name for NAS. In this example, the NAS user account is "ccasso." Click **Next** after entering the ccasso user credential. Figure 11-7 shows the creation of the NAS user account in AD.

Figure 11-7 *Creating the NAS User Account in AD*

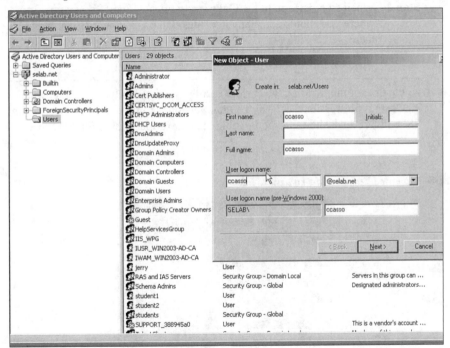

Step 5 At the password screen, enter a password acceptable by AD. The sample password used is Cisco123. Also, click on **Password Never Expires**. (This is common practice for service accounts only.) If you choose to allow AD to expire the NAS user password, you must go back into the NAS and change the AD SSO account password when AD expires the account. Click **Next** when complete.

Step 6 Review the NAS user logon name and password expiration period. If okay, click **Finish**. You should see the ccasso account successfully created in AD.

Installing the Support Tools from the Windows 2003 Server CD

To install the support tools from the Windows 2003 Server CD, do the following:

Step 1 Within your Windows 2003 Server CD, go to the D:\SUPPORT\TOOLS directory. You should see the SUPTOOLS.MSI installer package. Double-click it to start the installation process.

Step 2 Follow the typical Windows installation process and click **Finish** when complete.

Step 3 When complete, go to the C:\Program Files\Support Tools directory, where you should see many new files. ktpass.exe (~80kB) should be there.

CAUTION At the time of this writing, the current verified version of ktpass.exe that works with NAC AD SSO is file version 5.2.3790.0. Other versions of ktpass failed to work with NAC AD SSO. Figure 11-8 shows the compatible ktpass.exe file version for AD SSO.

Figure 11-8 *Supported Version of the ktpass.exe File*

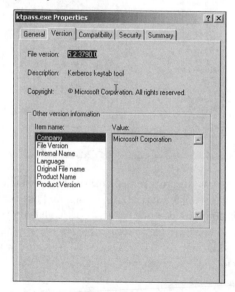

Running the **ktpass.exe** Command

The ktpass.exe file is required because NAC Appliance uses a Linux OS. Linux uses Data Encryption Standard (DES) encryption, whereas Microsoft Active Directory uses RC4 encryption for Kerberos. For NAC appliance to communicate to MS AD in Kerberos, both have to agree on a common encryption format. Running the **ktpass.exe** command on the AD domain controller changes the NAS user account to use DES-only encryption.

In addition, every domain controller that the NAS communicates with must run the **ktpass.exe** command. This applies to multiple controllers used by multiple NAS server under a single domain. The NAS user account will be replicated to other multiple controllers, but the map user functionality will have to be modified on each domain controller. Therefore, the **ktpass.exe** command has to be run on each domain controller defined on NAS. Keep the following in mind:

- **ktpass.exe** *must* be run in a DOS window. Open a DOS window. Change the directory to the Support Tools directory using **cd\program files\support tools**.

- The **ktpass.exe** command line is rather lengthy. Please execute with caution and accuracy because typos are *very common*.

The **ktpass.exe** command syntax is as follows:

```
ktpass.exe -princ NASusername/Full_AD_DomainName@AD_DOMAIN -mapuser NASusername
 -pass NASpassword -out c:\NASusername.keytab -ptype KRB5_NT_PRINCIPAL +DesOnly
```

In this case:

- *NASusername* (this is the NAS user account name): **ccasso**

- *NASpassword*: **Cisco123**

- *Full_AD_DomainName* (case sensitive): **win2003-ad-ca.selab.net**

- *AD_DOMAIN* (*must be all capitals*): **SELAB.NET**

Example 11-5 shows a sample **ktpass.exe** execution.

Example 11-5 *Sample* **ktpass.exe** *Command Run*

```
C:\Program Files\Support Tools>ktpass.exe -princ ccasso/win2003-ad-
ca.selab.net@SELAB.NET -mapuser ccasso -pass Cisco123 -out c:\ccasso.keytab -ptype
KRB5_NT_PRINCIPAL +DesOnly
Targeting domain controller: win2003-ad-ca.selab.net
Successfully mapped ccasso/win2003-ad-ca.selab.net to ccasso.
Key created.
Output keytab to c:\ccasso.keytab:
Keytab version: 0x502
keysize 67 ccasso/win2003-ad-ca.selab.net@SELAB.NET ptype 1 (KRB5_NT_PRINCIPAL)
vno 3 etype 0x3 (DES-CBC-MD5) keylength 8 (0x91cec19e40f4e3dc)
Account ccasso has been set for DES-only encryption.
```

NOTE   It is highly recommended that the **ktpass.exe** output be saved for support and troubleshooting purposes with Cisco Technical Assistance Center when needed.

Enabling Agent-Based Windows AD SSO

Now that the AD server has been configured, you need to enable the Agent-based Windows SSO service in the NAS by doing the following:

Step 1   Go to **Device Management > CCA Servers > Manage** icon > **NAS_IP > Authentication > Windows Auth > Active Directory SSO**.

Step 2   Click the **Enable Agent-Based Windows Single Sign-On with Active Directory (Kerberos)** check box.

Step 3   Click **Update**. If there have not been any typos or misconfigurations along the way, the AD SSO service on the NAS should start within 3–5 seconds. The **Enable Agent-Based Windows Single Sign-On with Active Directory (Kerberos)** check box should remain checked. If there is a misconfiguration somewhere, you will see an error message in red print above the check box.

Step 4   To verify that the AD SSO service has indeed started, go to **Device Management > CCA Servers > Manage** icon [NAS_IP] > **Status**. The Active Directory SSO module status should say **Started**. See Figure 11-9 to verify the AD SSO service starting.

Figure 11-9   *Verify That the AD SSO Service Has Started*

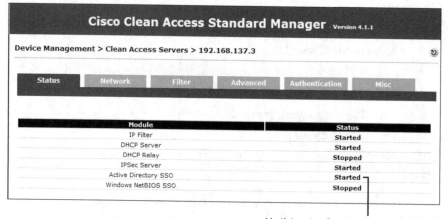

Verifying the Starting of the AD SSO Service

Enabling GPO Updates

Starting with NAC software 4.1.0, NAC Agent (4.1.0) can retrigger a GPO update after an AD user has signed in to the network. This is helpful in ensuring that all AD domain users inherit the appropriate user policies as defined by the AD administrator. For example, the administrator can create a policy that prevents the users from changing their desktop wallpaper. With the 4.1.0 release, NAC Agent executes the **gpupdate** command to retrigger the Group Policy update after login and prevent users from changing their desktop wallpaper.

To trigger the GPO update, do the following:

Step 1   Go to **Device Management > Clean Access > General Setup > Agent Login**.

Step 2   Select the appropriate user role, such as employee/faculty or student, to which this GPO update should apply. Outside guests or temporary visitors most likely would not participate in Active Directory.

Step 3   Select **All** for the operating system.

Step 4   Check the box **Refresh Windows Domain Group Policy After Login (for Windows Only)**. Click **Update**. See Figure 11-10 on enabling GPO Update.

Figure 11-10   *Enabling Windows Domain Group Policy Update After User Login*

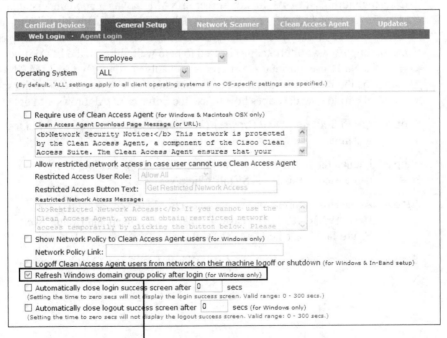

Enabling GPO Update

(Optional) Adding LDAP Lookup Server to Map Users to Multiple Roles

If you plan to map AD SSO users to multiple user roles, you will have to configure a secondary LDAP Lookup server in the NAM. For example:

- User student1 should be mapped to a Students user role with limited network access.
- User employee1 should be mapped to an Employee role with full network access.
- User visitor1 should be mapped to a Visitors role with only http/https network access.

NAM will map the user logging in based on the AD attributes and the mapping rules created. However, if only basic AD SSO without multiple role assignment is required, it is not necessary to configure an LDAP lookup server. For this test network, three roles are created to map users to specific roles after successful authentication.

LDAP Browser (Not Required but Very Helpful)

Before configuring an LDAP lookup server in NAM, having a good understanding of Active Directory and LDAP tree structure is helpful. To assist with this learning, an LDAP directory browser is *highly* recommended. For this exercise, a free LDAP browser from Softerra (http://www.softerra.com/) is used to help walk through the LDAP tree and correctly identify user attributes. Softerra is probably not the only free LDAP browser available on the Internet. You can use any other tool you choose to achieve the same goal. For now, the following describes how to use the Softerra LDAP browser to get started:

Step 1 Install Softerra LDAP Browser (Version 2.6) on your laptop or desktop machine.

Step 2 Launch the LDAP browser and click **File > New Profile**. The profile name used in this lab is **SElab**. Click **Next**.

Step 3 At the Host Information screen, enter the AD server IP (in this case, **Host: 192.168.10.110**). Leave all other fields at the default value. See Figure 11-11 on entering AD/LDAP server IP address. Click **Next**.

Step 4 Click **Yes** when prompted "Base DN is not specified. Continue anyway?"

Figure 11-11 *Using an LDAP Browser to Access AD Domain Structure*

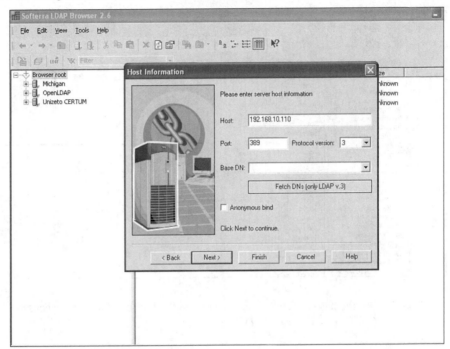

Step 5 At the credentials screen, enter the User DN (**ccasso**) and Password
(**Cisco123**). This is the NAS user account created earlier in AD. Click
Next.

Step 6 At the LDAP Settings window, delete the default parameter in the **Filter**
field. Leave everything else at the default. Click **Finish**.

Step 7 When prompted with the Password Dialog window, enter **Cisco123**.
Click **OK**.

Step 8 Allow the free LDAP Browser to walk through the LDAP tree over a few
minutes. The LDAP structure slowly expands in the browser. Expand the
SElab domain controller and click **CN=Users > CN=ccasso**. See
Figure 11-12 for the user ccasso LDAP structure.

Figure 11-12 *LDAP Structure Info for User ccasso*

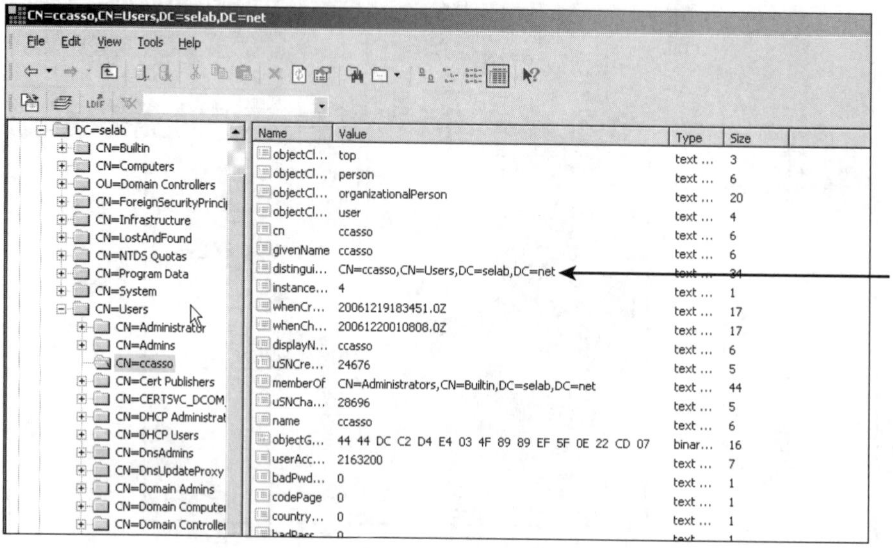

Step 9 See the base context for user ccasso in the **Value** column: **CN=ccasso, CN=Users, DC=selab, DC=net**.

Configuring LDAP Lookup Server in NAM

After the LDAP structure info has been acquired for user ccasso, you can enter the user into the LDAP lookup server in NAM. The configured info is how NAS will access AD for user account lookups:

Step 1 Go to **User Management > Auth Servers > Lookup Servers > New**. Enter the information that follows.

— **Server URL: ldap://192.168.10.110:389**

— **Search(Admin)Full DN: CN=ccasso, CN=Users, DC=selab, DC=net**. This info is taken from the LDAP browser for NAS user account ccasso.

— **Search Base Context: CN=Users, DC=SELAB, DC=NET**. This is the base context (root of the LDAP tree) to begin a search for the users. *Make sure all DC values are in capital letters.*

— **Referral: Manage (Ignore)**. Sets whether referral entries are managed or returned as handles (Handle(Follow)).

— **DerefAlias: Always** (default).

    — **Description** (optional): **LDAP Lookup for ADSSO**

    — **Provider Name: LDAP Lookup**

    — **Server Version: Auto**

    — **Search(Admin) Password: Cisco123**

    — **Search Filter: sAMAccountName=$user$**

    — **DerefLink: OFF**

    — **Security Type: None**

Step 2   Click **Add Server**. See Figure 11-13 for a screen shot of adding an LDAP Lookup server.

Figure 11-13 *LDAP Lookup Server Configuration for AD SSO*

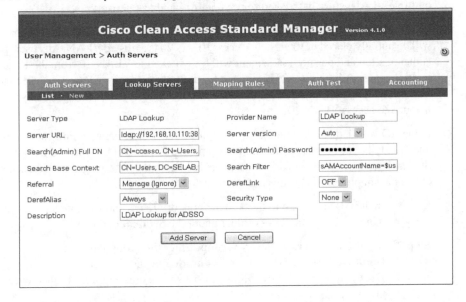

Step 3   Now that the LDAP lookup server has been added, the AD SSO auth server configured earlier (see Figure 11-4) needs to reference the LDAP lookup server for the role mapping. Click **User Management > Auth Servers > Edit[ADSSO]**.

Step 4   Select **LDAP Lookup Server**: **LDAP Lookup**. This LDAP Lookup server will map AD SSO users to their appropriate roles when the mapping rules are matched. This role mapping also overrides the default role of **Unauthenticated Role**.

Step 5   Click **Update Server**.

User Attributes in Active Directory

Active Directory tree structure can be multilevel and quite complex. Therefore, it is important that the NAC Appliance administrator work with the AD server administrators to coordinate the user-role-to-AD-attribute mapping effort. The scope of this book is not to discuss how to correctly configure and deploy AD in an enterprise environment. Therefore, the test lab used in this exercise is simplified to demonstrate the technique of how to map AD user attributes to NAC mapping rules.

Earlier, three user roles (Employee, Students, Visitors) were discussed. These roles are maintained in NAM itself and are referred to by all the NAS Appliances after authenticating users to determine the correct role to assign. To do this, simply go to **NAM > User Management > User Roles > New**. Enter one role name at a time: **Employee, Students**, or **Visitors**. Leave all other fields at their default values. Click **Add** when done with one role. The GUI is fairly intuitive. What these roles mean in the Layer 2 switch world is that multiple VLANs must be created for this out-of-band test network.

In this lab setup, VLAN 99 is the untrusted authentication VLAN. Any users coming online will be initially placed in VLAN 99. Access VLAN 20 is a trusted VLAN. Any users passing authentication and posture assessment will be switched to VLAN 20 from 99. Ideally, multiple access VLANs would be created for multiple user roles. However, to keep this lab network simple, only VLAN 20 is demonstrated. All Employees, Students, and Visitors are mapped to access VLAN 20.

In the AD world, three different groups are most likely to be created. Full-time employees and faculty members would fall into the Employee group. Students would fall into the Students group, and visitors and contractors belong in the Visitors group. Here's how to create the simplified AD groups and users in AD:

Step 1   In the AD server, go to the Active Directory Users and Computers window. Select the **Users** folder under the **Selab.net** domain.

Step 2   Right-click **Users > New > Group**. Enter the group name of **Employee**. Select **Global** for **Group Scope** and **Security** for **Group type**. Click **OK**. Figure 11-14 shows creating the Employee group in AD.

Figure 11-14 *Creating the Employee Group Object in AD*

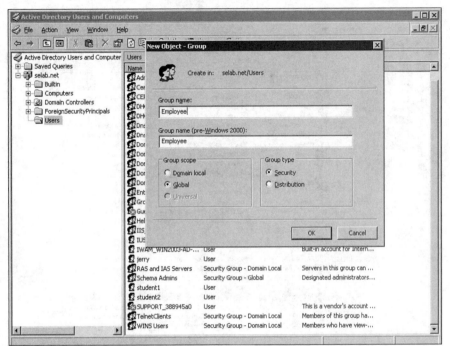

Step 3   The **Employee** global security group should now be created. Repeat the same process to create groups for Students and Visitors. Figure 11-15 shows the three new groups created in AD.

Figure 11-15 *Creating Multiple Group Objects in AD*

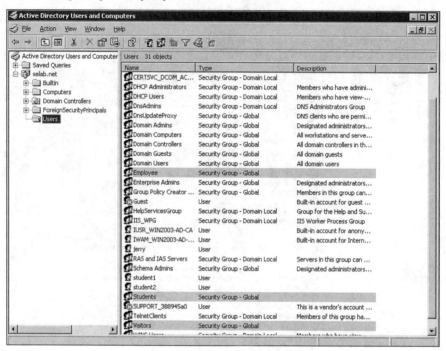

Step 4   Now create users for each group. Right-click **Users > New > user**.
Enter **employee1** name. **First name=employee1, User logon
name=employee1**. Leave other fields blank or at the default value. Click
Next. Figure 11-16 shows adding user employee1.

Figure 11-16 *Creating User employee1 in AD*

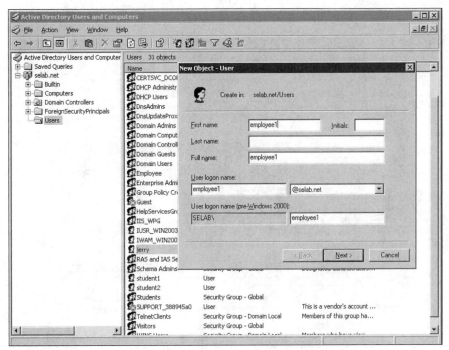

Step 5   Enter a user password and confirm it. This example's password is
Cisco123. **Password Never Expires** is checked for the purposes of this
simplified test lab network. Click **Next**.

Step 6   Click **Finish** after you verify your entries. Repeat the process by adding
the users student1 and visitor1.

Step 7   Next, each user should be assigned to its respective group: Employee1 >
Employee group, student1 > Students, and so on. Right-click user
employee1, select the **Member Of** tab, click **Add**, enter the object name
employee, and click the **Check Names** button. Figure 11-17 shows
assigning user employee1 to group Employee.

Figure 11-17 *Associating a User with the Employee Group*

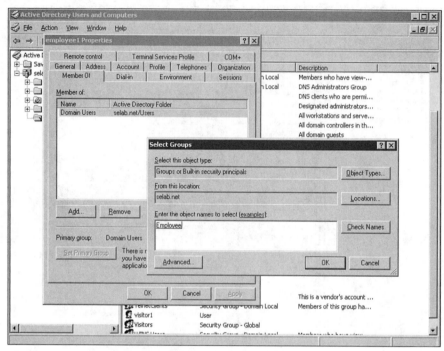

Step 8 The Employee group should be found. Click **OK**. User employee1 should now be a member of the Employee group, so verify its Employee group membership. Click **Apply** and **OK** when verified.

Step 9 Repeat the same process for the users student1 and visitor1.

Step 10 Using the LDAP browser, verify that employee1, student1, and visitor1 are members of their related groups. Notice that **Users > employee1** is **memberOf CN=Employee, CN=Users, DC=selab, DC=net**. The same applies to student1 and visitor1. Figure 11-18 shows employee1 is a member of the CN=Employee group.

Step 11 Go back to NAM. Go to **User Management > Auth Servers > Lookup Server > Mapping** (icon)**[LDAP Lookup]**. Click the **Mapping** icon. Figure 11-19 shows the creation of mapping rules for the LDAP lookup server.

Figure 11-18 *User employee1 Is a Member of the Employee Group*

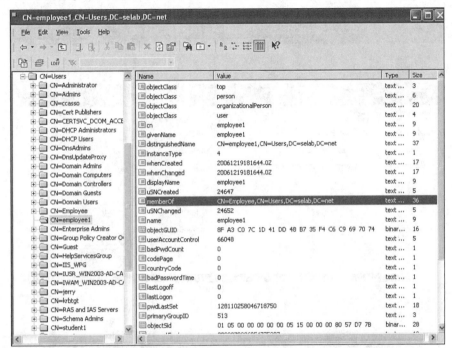

Figure 11-19 *Create Mapping Rules for the LDAP Lookup Server*

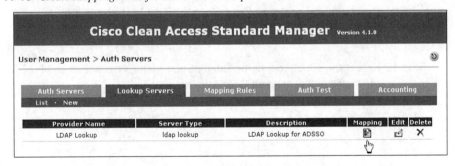

Step 12 Click **Add Mapping Rule** in the upper-right side of the screen.

Step 13 In the bottom half of the screen, select **Condition Type=Attribute**, **Attribute Name=memberOf**, **Operator=contains**, **Attribute Value=Employee**, and click the **Add Condition** button. Figure 11-20 shows the addition of the memberOf attribute for the Employee role.

Figure 11-20 *Defining the memberOf Attribute for the Employee Role*

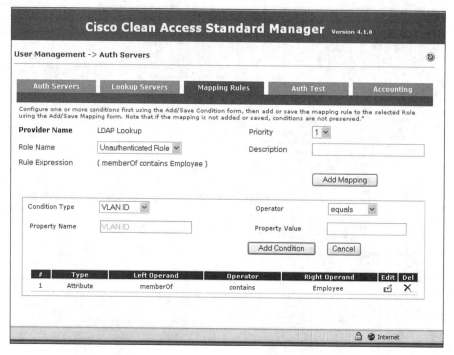

Step 14 Near the top half of the screen, select **Role Name=Employee** and
Description=Employee Role. Click the **Add Mapping** button.
Figure 11-21 shows the mapping of attributes to the Employee
role.

Step 15 Repeat the same process for Students and Visitors roles. Figure 11-22
shows the output after all three roles are mapped.

Figure 11-21 *Associating the memberOf Attribute with the Employee Role*

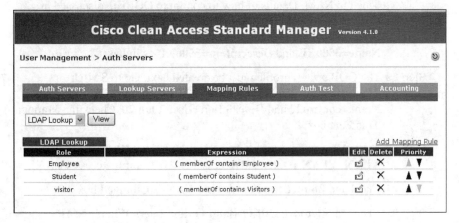

Figure 11-22 *LDAP Lookup Rules for Three Defined Roles*

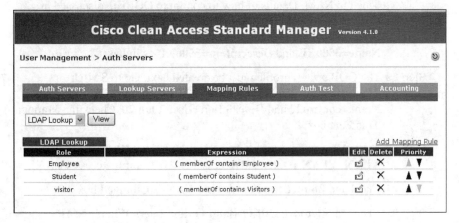

The AD SSO setup process is complete. However, there are other NAC setup tasks to perform before testing AD SSO.

Step 16 Go to **Device Management > Clean Access > General Setup > Agent Login**. Select **Employee** from the **User Role** drop-down menu. Select **All** from the **Operating System** drop-down menu.

Step 17 Check the **Require Use of Clean Access Agent (for Windows & Macintosh OSX Only)** box. Click **Update**. Figure 11-23 shows the NAC Agent general setup.

Figure 11-23 *Checking This Box Requires All Users in the Employee Role and Using Windows and Mac OS X Machines to Have NAC Agent Installed*

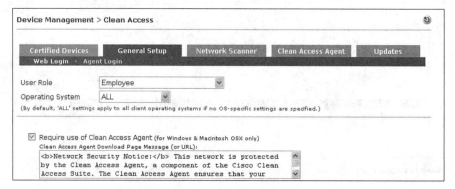

Step 18 Because this is an OOB deployment, the edge 3500XL switch must be added to NAM. Details of how to configure OOB are discussed in Chapter 10, "Configuring Out-of-Band." But here are some instructions. Go to **Switch Management > Profiles > Group > New**. Enter **Group Name=3500XL** and **Description=3500XL switches**. Click **Add**.

Step 19 The OOB switch profile must be created next. Go to **Switch Management > Profiles > Group > New**. Enter **Profile Name=control20** and **Description=User Vlan 20**. Check the **Manage This Port** box.

Step 20 Under VLAN Settings, set **Auth VLAN: VLAN ID:99**, **Default Access VLAN: VLAN ID:20**, and **Access VLAN: Default Access VLAN**.

Step 21 Check the **Bounce the Port After VLAN Is Changed** box.

Step 22 Check the **Remove Out-of-Band Online Users When SNMP Linkdown Trap Is Received** box.

Step 23 Click **Add**.

Step 24 Go to **Profiles > Switch > New**. Enter **Profile Name=3500XL** and select **switch model=Cisco Catalyst 3500XL series, SNMP port=161**, and **SNMP read/write v1 string=cisco123**. Click **Add**.

Step 25 At the **Profile > Group > List** screen, find the 3500XL group name and click the magnifying glass icon under the **Switches** column.

Step 26 Click **Switches > Search**. The switch profile should be **3500XL**. Enter the IP range of **192.168.10.35 – 192.168.10.35**. Click **Search**.

Step 27 After clicking Search, select **Switch Group=3500XL** and **Default Port Profile=control20**. Check the box for the discovered 3500XL switch, 192.168.10.35. Click **Commit**.

Step 28 Go to **Profiles > SNMP Receiver > SNMP Trap**. Enter SNMPv1 settings and **Community String=cisco123**. Leave the other fields at their default value because they are not used. Click **Update**.

Enabling DHCP in NAS

For this sample deployment, NAS is the DHCP server providing a /30 or 30-bit subnet mask for each user in the authentication VLAN 99. The advantage of a 30-bit mask is that an infected host cannot reach any other hosts while in the auth VLAN. The infected host is essentially quarantined. NAS performs a posture assessment of that host and, if certified, the host is switched to the access VLAN 20 with another IP address assigned to access VLAN 20.

In a real-world deployment where a corporate DHCP server is used instead of using NAS as the DHCP server, the access VLAN 20 would not be managed by NAS. Only VLAN 99 would be managed by NAS. But for simplicity in this example, NAS is configured as the corporate DHCP server for VLAN 99 and 20. Therefore, NAS manages both the access VLAN 20 and authentication VLAN 99. The following is an example of setting up a DHCP server in NAS:

Step 1 For this L2 deployment, authentication VLAN 99 and access VLAN 20 must be managed by NAS. Go to **Device Management > CCA Servers > Manage** (icon) **[192.168.10.10] > Advanced > Managed Subnet**. Enter the following:

— **IP address=192.168.199.1**

— **Subnet Mask=255.255.255.0**

— **VLAN ID=99**

— **Description=Auth Vlan 99**

Click **Add Managed Subnet**.

Step 2 Repeat the same process for access VLAN 20.

Step 3 When complete, you will see Figure 11-24, which shows auth VLAN 99 and access VLAN 20 added to the managed subnets. As a reminder, access VLAN 20 is managed by NAS only because NAS is acting as the corporate DHCP server.

Figure 11-24 *VLANs Managed by the NAS*

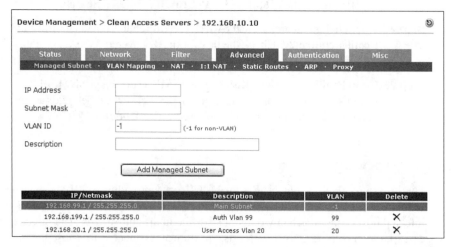

Step 4 Go to **Device Management > CCA Servers > Manage** (icon) **[192.168.10.10] > Network > DHCP**. Choose **DHCP Server** and click the **Select DHCP Type** button. When you select the DHCP server from **None** to **DHCP Server**, NAS will prompt you to reboot.

Step 5 Select the **Auto-Generate** tab and enter the following:

— **Enter Starting IP = 192.168.199.0**

— **Number of Subnets to Generate = 60**

— **General Subnet Size = /30 –1 IP per Subnet**

— **Default Lease Time (Seconds) = 7200**

— **Max Lease Time (Seconds) = 7200**

— **DNS Suffix = selab.net**

— **DNS Servers = 192.168.10.110**

— **WINS Servers = <blank>**

Check the **Restrict This Subnet to VLAN ID** box. Enter **VLAN ID=99**.

Step 6   Click **Generate Subnet List**. You should see a list of 60 /30 subnets.
Click **Commit Subnet**.

Step 7   Now the user access VLAN 20 DHCP scope must also be created. Go
to **Network > DHCP > Subnet List > New**. Figure 11-25 shows adding
in DHCP scope for access VLAN 20. Click **Update** when complete.

Figure 11-25   *Adding in a DHCP Scope for Access VLAN 20*

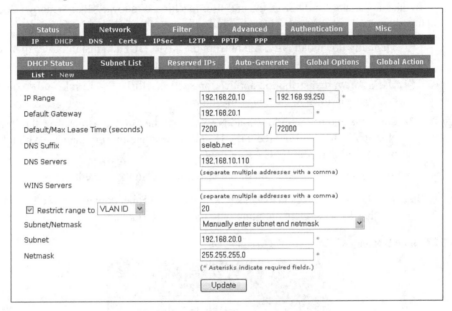

Step 8   When both DHCP scopes are complete, Figure 11-26 shows what you
should see.

Figure 11-26   *DHCP Scopes Generated for VLANs 20 and 99*

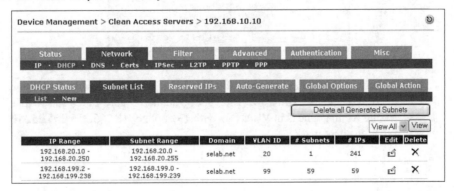

Enabling User Login Pages in NAM

Go to **Administration > User Pages > Login Page**. Click **Add**. Select **Operating System=WINDOWS_ALL**.

NAC Agent Download and Login

To take advantage of AD SSO, the end-user machine Windows XP or Windows 2000 must first download NAC Agent. There are multiple ways to download NAC Agent:

- Manually download NAC Agent from the NAM GUI and install NAC Agent on each end-user machine—not an easily scalable solution.

- Use a software distribution application such as Altiris, PatchLink, and so on, to push NAC Agent down to each user machine.

- Force the end users to download NAC agent when they try to browse the Internet. NAC appliance will intercept the HTTP request and present the user with a login prompt and then the NAC Agent download screen.

The following is a demonstration of the last option from the preceding list:

Step 1   The user first logs in to a machine in the SELAB.net domain. Figure 11-27 shows user student1 logging in to the SELAB domain.

Figure 11-27 *Main Windows XP Login for the User student1*

Step 2   After signing on, verify that the IP address of the Windows XP machine is in VLAN 99 with a 192.168.99.x/30 subnet. Figure 11-28 shows that the XP machine is in VLAN 99 with 192.168.99.18 255.255.255.252 IP and subnet mask.

Figure 11-28 *Verifying Initial User IP Address in Authentication VLAN 99*

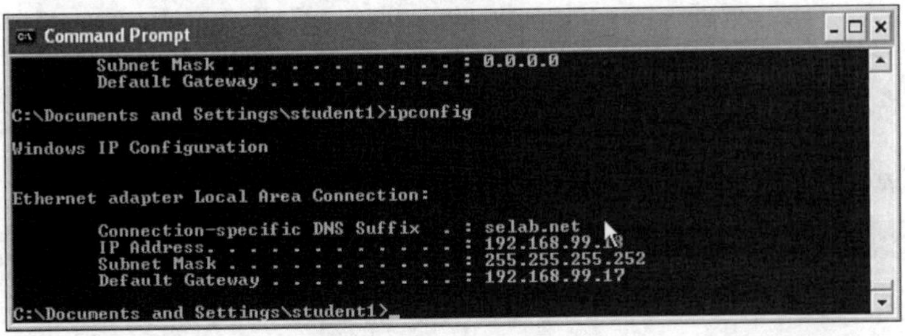

```
 Command Prompt                                              _ □ ×
        Subnet Mask . . . . . . . . . . . : 0.0.0.0
        Default Gateway . . . . . . . . :
C:\Documents and Settings\student1>ipconfig

Windows IP Configuration

Ethernet adapter Local Area Connection:

        Connection-specific DNS Suffix  . : selab.net
        IP Address. . . . . . . . . . . . : 192.168.99.18
        Subnet Mask . . . . . . . . . . . : 255.255.255.252
        Default Gateway . . . . . . . . . : 192.168.99.17

C:\Documents and Settings\student1>
```

Step 3   Launch a browser and try to connect to the NAM. Mostly likely, a security alert will pop up regarding a new security certificate. This is normal because the client has never trusted NAC Appliance's digital certificate. Click **Yes**. As an option, you can click **View Certificate** and install the certificate so that you won't be prompted to accept the NAC certificate again in the future.

Step 4   Next, the user's HTTP request is intercepted and redirected to the NAC authentication page. Another security alert pops up regarding untrusted digital certificates. Click **Yes** to proceed. Figure 11-29 shows the NAC redirect page during initial user login.

Figure 11-29 *Initial Security Alert for an Untrusted Digital Certificate*

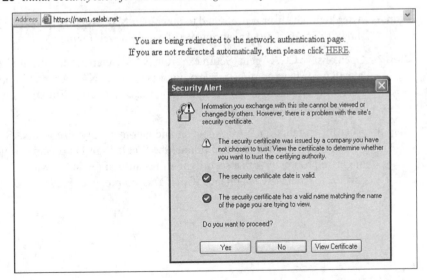

Step 5   Next is the Cisco Clean Access Authentication Login page. Because this lab network was not configured with an LDAP authentication server (for web login), the Guest user account in the NAM local database can be used to log in. A guest user account was already created in the local database. Figure 11-30 shows the NAC web login page.

Figure 11-30 *NAC Web Login Page*

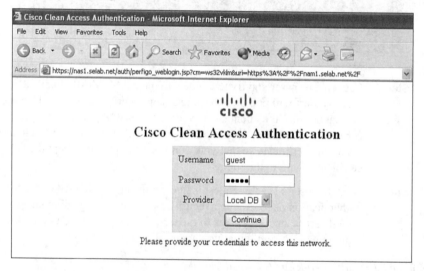

Step 6   After login, the user is prompted to download NAC Agent. Figure 11-31 shows the NAC 4.1.0 Agent download page via web login.

Step 7   Open or save CCAAgent_Setup.exe from NAS1.selab.net and install. Be sure that you have administrative privileges to install NAC Agent. Simply follow the typical Windows installation process and click **Finish** when the installation is complete.

Step 8   After the installation, NAC Agent should automatically discover NAS Appliance on the network and initiate the Single Sign-On process. You might be prompted with a security alert because of the unknown certificate from NAC Appliance. Click **Yes** and proceed. Figure 11-32 shows the AD SSO process.

Figure 11-31 *Web User Being Directed to Download NAC Agent 4.1.0*

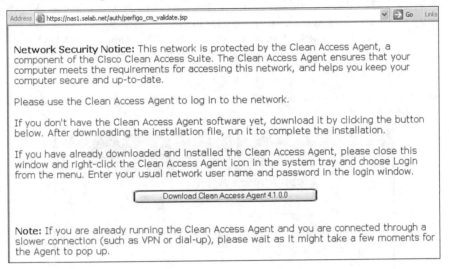

Figure 11-32 *Performing Windows AD SSO Automatic Login*

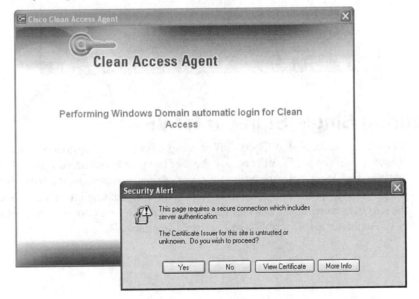

Step 9   Finally, after authentication (and posture assessment, if it is configured), NAM switches the client PC from the auth VLAN 99 to the access VLAN 20. NAC Agent issues a "Refreshing IP . . ." message and the client acquires a new IP address, 192.168.20.x /24, within access VLAN 20. Figure 11-33 shows a successful OOB logon with the new IP in access VLAN 20.

Figure 11-33   *Successful User Login to Access VLAN 20; the User Also Acquires a New IP Address for Access VLAN 20*

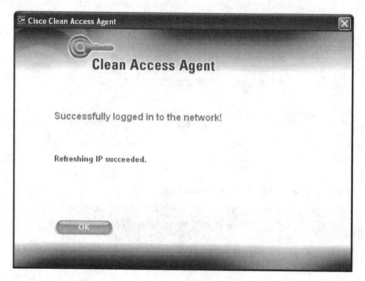

Configuring Single Sign-On for VPN

Single Sign-On for NAC + Cisco VPN provides a similar user login experience to AD SSO. However, in IPsec or SSL VPN access, the user is typically prompted with a VPN username and password login. After the users enter their username and password, NAC Appliance can assign the appropriate user role based on RADIUS accounting information received from the RADIUS authentication server used by the VPN concentrator. Figure 11-34 shows the NAC Appliance and Cisco VPN test network diagram.

Figure 11-34 *Deploying NAC over VPN*

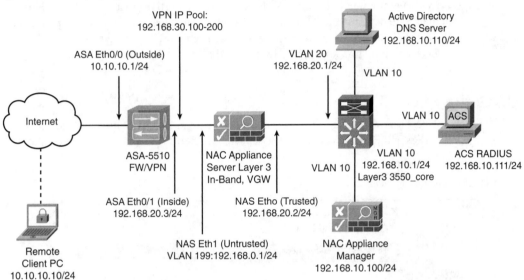

The VPN SSO setup in this test network consists of the following components:

- NAC Manager (4.1.x).

- NAC Server (4.1.x).

- Cisco Access Control Server (ACS) 3.3.

- Cisco Adaptive Security Appliance (ASA) 5510 (7.2.2) with SSLVPN Tunnel Client (sslclient-win-1.1.3.173.pkg). Adaptive Security Device Manager (ASDM) 5.2.2 is used to configure the ASA 5510.

- Remote client PC has NAC Agent installed.

Only In-Band mode supports VPN SSO at the time of this writing.

The following is a high level summary for configuring SSO over Cisco VPN:

Step 1 Configure the RADIUS server (ACS Server). Add users and authentication, authorization, and accounting (AAA) clients (ASA, NAM, and NAS).

Step 2 Set up SSLVPN in the ASA-5510. Add ACS to ASA for RADIUS authentication. Add NAS as the RADIUS accounting server.

Step 3 Configure NAS to support VPN SSO.

The scope of this book is not to show details of how to configure or design Cisco SSLVPN services. Therefore, only the main VPN configuration portions that interact with NAC Appliance are demonstrated. For basic VPN setup reference, see the following Cisco.com URL for a VPN setup example: http://www.cisco.com/en/US/products/ps6120/products_configuration_example09186a008071c428.shtml.

ACS Setup

In this test network, Cisco ACS is used as the back-end RADIUS authentication server. VPN users and RADIUS clients must be added. Figure 11-35 shows the added RADIUS clients.

Figure 11-35 *Added AAA Clients*

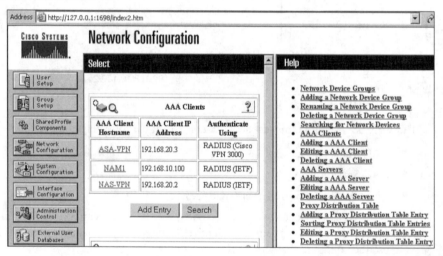

ASA-5510 VPN Setup

Here's a summary of enabling SSLVPN in the ASA appliance. Again, not all the SSLVPN setup steps are shown. ASDM is used to configure ASA.

Step 1 Enable WebVPN for the Outside interface. Figure 11-36 shows enabling WebVPN.

Figure 11-36 *Enabling WebVPN Services on the Outside Interface Using the ASDM GUI*

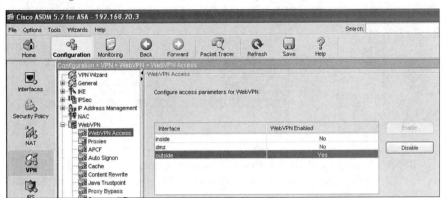

Step 2 Load and enable the SSLVPN tunnel client. Figure 11-37 shows the loading of the SSLVPN tunnel client.

Figure 11-37 *SSLVPN Client Image Must Be Loaded into the ASA Appliance*

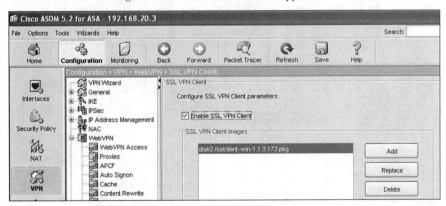

Step 3 Go to the IP address assignment section. Select **Use Internal Address Pools** and create your IP address pools. Figure 11-38 shows the creation of IP address pools.

Figure 11-38 *Creating IP Address Pools for SSLVPN Users*

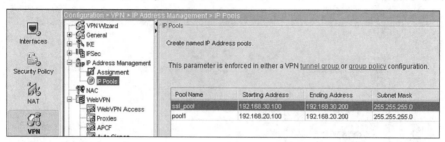

Step 4 Next, go to the AAA server section and create the RADIUS authentication server group. Figure 11-39 shows the creation of the AAA server group.

Figure 11-39 *Creating the AAA Server Group*

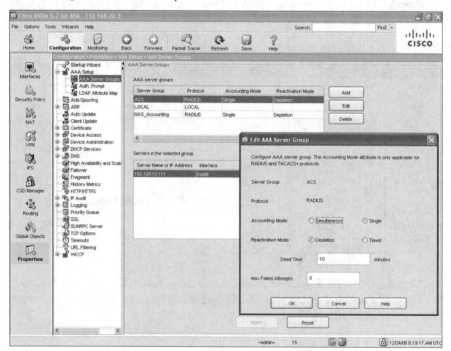

Step 5 Now a RADIUS server (192.168.10.111) must be added to the AAA
server group. Figure 11-40 shows the addition of a RADIUS server.

Figure 11-40 *Defining the RADIUS Server Under the AAA Server Group*

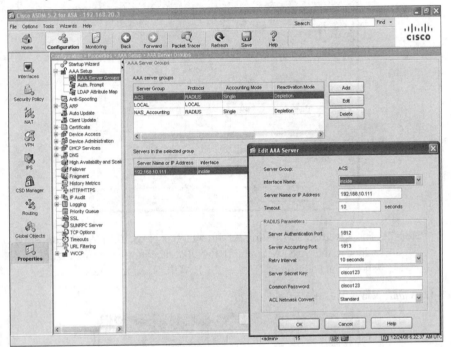

Step 6 Next, a RADIUS accounting server group must be created so that the
ASA VPN concentrator will send the RADIUS accounting start packet to
pass the user role assignment info and to perform Single Sign-On.
Figure 11-41 shows adding a RADIUS accounting group called
NAS_Accounting.

Figure 11-41 *Adding a RADIUS Accounting Group*

Step 7 The RADIUS accounting server, which is NAS 192.168.20.2, must be added to the NAS_Accounting RADIUS accounting group. Figure 11-42 shows the addition of NAS as the RADIUS accounting server.

Figure 11-42 *Adding NAS as the RADIUS Accounting Server*

Step 8 The WebVPN tunnel policy must select the NAS_Accounting group. Figure 11-43 shows the selection of the NAS_Accounting group.

Figure 11-43 *Associating the NAS_Accounting Group to the WebVPN Tunnel Policy*

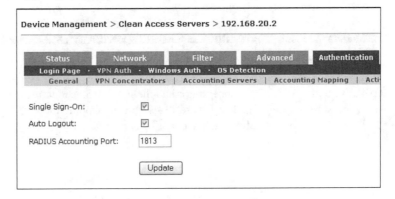

Configuring NAS to Support VPN SSO

After the user authenticates to the concentrator, it sends a RADIUS accounting start packet to NAS. NAS then completes the SSO process with NAC Agent and adds that host to the certified device list. The same process applies when a user terminates a VPN tunnel. The concentrator sends a RADIUS accounting stop packet to NAS, and NAS removes that user from the certified device list.

The final step is to enable VPN SSO capabilities within NAS. Follow these steps to do so:

Step 1 Go to the NAS-VPN appliance from the NAM GUI and select the **Authentication > VPN Auth > General** page. Set **Single Sign-On**, **Auto Logout**. Set **RADIUS Accounting port: 1813** and click **Update**. Figure 11-44 shows the configuration of the SSO and RADIUS accounting port.

Figure 11-44 *Configuring VPN SSO in NAS*

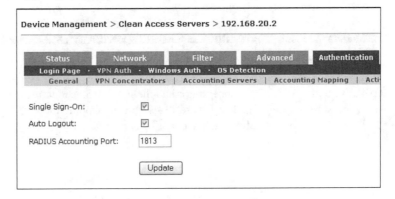

Step 2 Go to the **Authentication > VPN Auth > VPN Concentrator** page. Add the ASA-5510 VPN concentrator. See Figure 11-45.

Figure 11-45 *Adding the ASA Appliance as a VPN Concentrator*

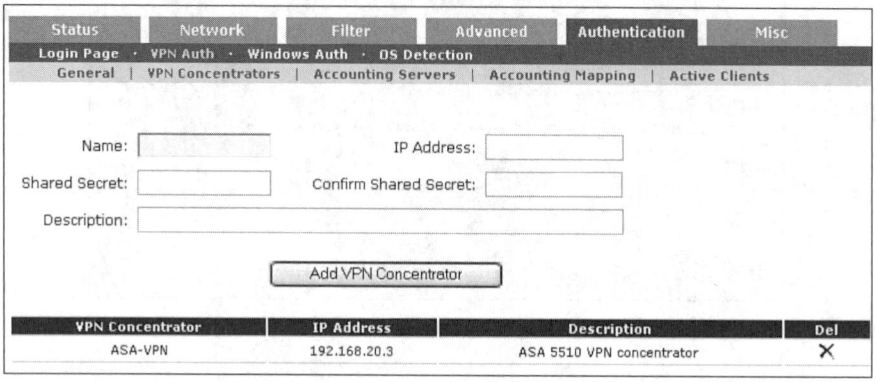

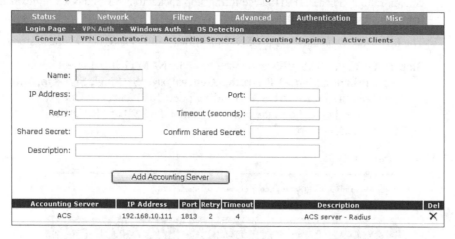

Step 3 Go to the **Authentication > VPN Auth > Accounting Servers** page. Add the ACS server as the RADIUS accounting server. See Figure 11-46.

Figure 11-46 *Adding the ACS Server as the RADIUS Accounting Server*

Step 4 Next, the ASA VPN concentrator and the RADIUS accounting server must be mapped together. Figure 11-47 shows mapping the VPN concentrator to the RADIUS accounting server.

Figure 11-47 *Mapping the ASA VPN Concentrator to the ACS Accounting Server*

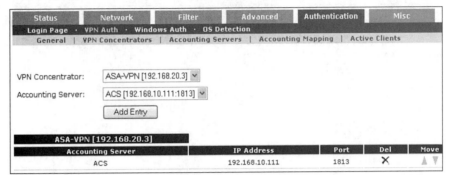

Step 5 Go back to the User **Management > Auth Servers** page. Now the Cisco VPN SSO authentication server must be added. Assign **Default Role=Employee** for now to permit full network access for all authenticated VPN users. Add **Description**: **Remote VPN support**.

Step 6 With the Cisco VPN SSO server created, mapping rules must be created to assign the appropriate user roles based on RADIUS accounting the vendor-specific attribute value 25. Go to **Auth Servers > List > Cisco VPN > Mapping** (icon).

Step 7 To create the mapping rule for the Employee user role, vendor attribute 25 [Class] must be added. The property value or right operand value **Employee** is the keyword used to match against the vendor-specific attribute 25 [Class] value sent inside the RADIUS accounting packet from the accounting server. Figure 11-48 shows creating the Employee mapping rule. This value is mapped to the Employee role.

Figure 11-48 *Vendor Attribute 25 [Class] Mapping for the Employee Role*

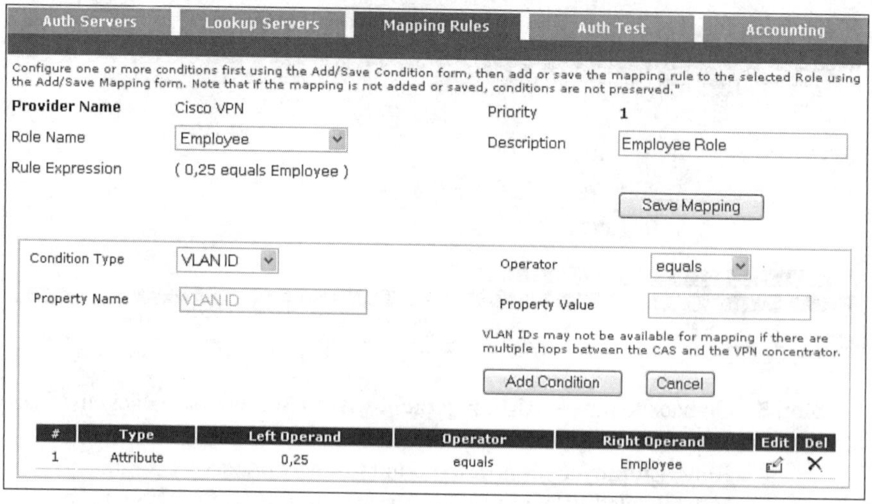

Step 8 You can repeat the previous step to create another mapping rule for the Student role. After you have successfully done so, a summary of the Cisco VPN mapping rules will appear.

Step 9 The final step is to return to the ACS RADIUS server and assign the correct vendor-specific attribute 25 [Class] values for each user. In this test network, user1 is part of Group 1 Employee. In ACS, go to **Group Setup > Group:Employee > Edit Settings**, and make sure that the **[025] Class** box is checked and the keyword value is **Employee**. Figure 11-49 shows the RADIUS vendor-specific attribute [025] Class value setting.

Step 10 Finally, if all configurations are accurate and valid, you should see that when VPN clients connect to the VPN concentrator, they will automatically sign in to NAC without an additional username and password login. You can view the active VPN clients within NAS by going to **Device Management > CCA Servers > Manage[192.168.20.2] > Authentication > VPN Auth > Active Clients**. See Figure 11-50.

Figure 11-49 *RADIUS Vendor-Specific Attribute Setting of Attribute [25] Class in ACS*

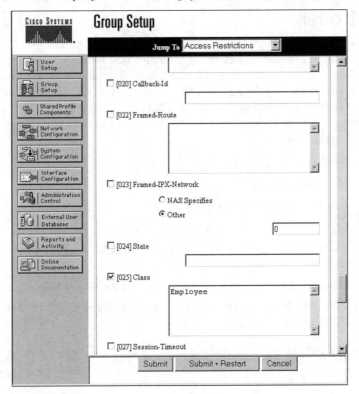

Figure 11-50 *View the Active NAC-VPN Clients*

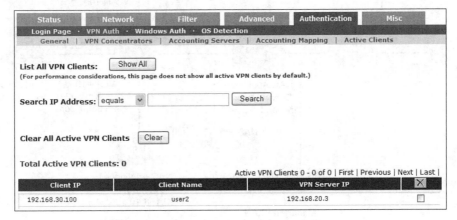

Configuring Single Sign-On for Cisco Wireless LAN Controller

Configuring Single Sign-On for Cisco Wireless LAN Controller (WLC, from Airespace acquisition) is similar to configuring SSO for Cisco VPN SSO. From the NAS and NAM perspectives, WLC functions as if it were a VPN concentrator. In fact, adding WLC through the NAM GUI is done by adding a VPN concentrator logically. WLC communicates with NAM through RADIUS accounting, and NAM assigns user roles based on default rules or mapping rules you create. The WLC SSO setup in this test network consists of the following components:

- NAC Manager (4.1.x).

- NAC Server (4.1.x).

- Cisco Access Control Server (ACS) 3.3.

- Cisco Wireless LAN Controller (4.0.179.11).

- Cisco AP 1200 access point with Lightweight Access Point Protocol (LWAPP) support.

- Wireless client PC has NAC Agent installed for WLC SSO.

Like VPN SSO, WLC SSO is supported only in In-Band mode. See Figure 11-51 for the WLC SSO network diagram.

Figure 11-51 *Wireless LAN Controller SSO Network*

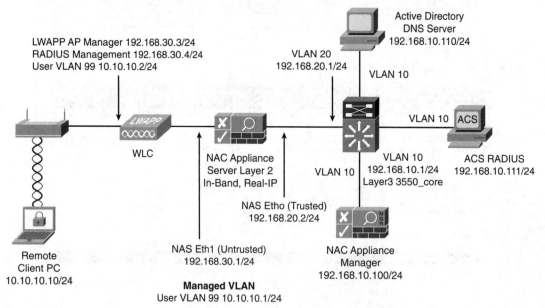

The following is a high-level summary for configuring single sign-on for Cisco Wireless LAN Controller:

Step 1   Configure the RADIUS server (ACS Server). Add users and AAA clients (ASA, NAM, and NAS).

Step 2   Set up WLC wireless settings. Add ACS to WLC for RADIUS authentication. Add NAS as RADIUS accounting server.

Step 3   Configure NAS to support VPN SSO for WLC. WLC is added to NAS as a floating device if the WLC is deployed as a router hop.

ACS Server Setup

The configuration of the ACS server is nearly identical to the VPN SSO setup. Users are added in the same way. Simply add WLC as a RADIUS client.

WLC Setup

The goal of this chapter is not to teach you how to configure and deploy Wireless LAN Controller. Therefore, only relevant screenshots are shown in the following steps:

Step 1   Figure 11-52 shows the basic IP address and software version of WLC.

Figure 11-52 *WLC Software and IP Summary*

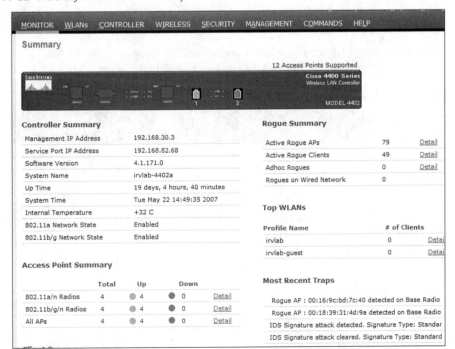

Step 2 Under the **Controller > General** menu, LWAPP transport mode must be enabled for Layer 3. In addition, enter a mobility domain name. A sample domain name used is irvlab. Figure 11-53 shows enabling LWAPP Transport Mode in Layer 3.

Figure 11-53 *WLC General Controller Setting for Layer 3*

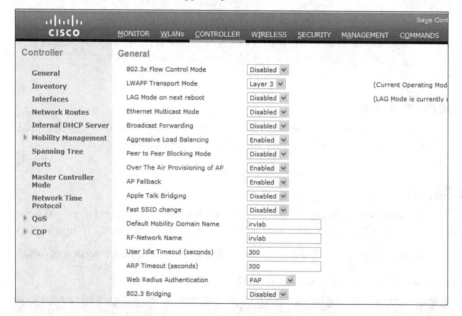

Step 3 Go to **Controller > Interfaces** and add in the user traffic VLAN information. Figure 11-54 shows the added interfaces.

Figure 11-54 *WLC Interface Summary*

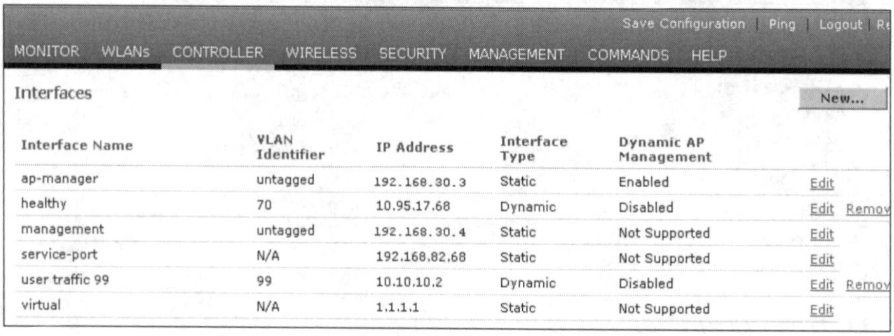

Interface Name	VLAN Identifier	IP Address	Interface Type	Dynamic AP Management		
ap-manager	untagged	192.168.30.3	Static	Enabled	Edit	
healthy	70	10.95.17.68	Dynamic	Disabled	Edit	Remov
management	untagged	192.168.30.4	Static	Not Supported	Edit	
service-port	N/A	192.168.82.68	Static	Not Supported	Edit	
user traffic 99	99	10.10.10.2	Dynamic	Disabled	Edit	Remov
virtual	N/A	1.1.1.1	Static	Not Supported	Edit	

Step 4   Next, the RADIUS authentication server must be added. Go to **Security > AAA > RADIUS Authentication**. Click **New** to add the ACS server. Figure 11-55 shows the added RADIUS authentication server.

Figure 11-55 *Adding a RADIUS Authentication Server in WLC*

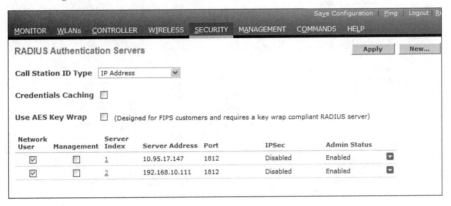

Step 5   The RADIUS accounting server must be added next. Click the **Radius Accounting** link and then click **New**. Figure 11-56 shows the added RADIUS accounting server.

Figure 11-56 *Adding a RADIUS Accounting Server in WLC*

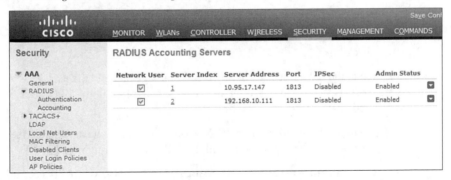

Step 6   Go to the **WLANs** menu and find the irvlab WLAN SSID. Click **irvlab SSID** and make sure the WLAN status is Enabled. In addition, make sure that the correct RADIUS authentication and accounting servers are selected on the **AAA Servers** tab. See Figure 11-57 for a summary.

Figure 11-57 *AAA Servers Used in WLC*

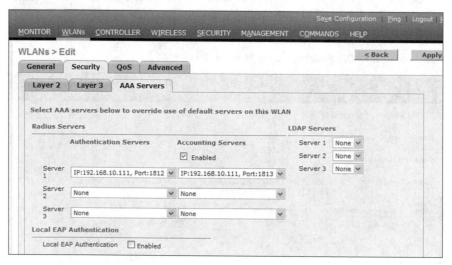

NAM/NAS Setup

With the ACS and WLC components configured, the next step is to add WLC into NAS. Adding WLC into NAS is similar to adding a VPN concentrator, as shown in the following steps:

Step 1 Go to the NAM GUI and manage the NAS used for the WLC. NAS in this setup is a Real-IP gateway. Make sure to check the **Enable L3 Support** check box.

Step 2 Go to the **Advanced > Managed Subnet** page and add the user VLAN 99. This step is similar to the managed subnet setup in the VPN SSO section.

Step 3 Go to the **Authentication > VPN Auth > General** page and enable the **Single Sign-On** boxes along with RADIUS Accounting port 1813.

Step 4 Go to the **Authentication > VPN Auth > VPN Concentrators** page. Add the WLC unit as a VPN concentrator.

Step 5 Go to the **Authentication > VPN Auth > Accounting Servers** page. Add the NAS server (not the ACS server) as the RADIUS accounting server.

Step 6 Go to the **Authentication > VPN Auth > Accounting Mapping** page. The WLC entry must be mapped to the ACS accounting server. Click **Add Entry**.

Step 7 WLC must be added as an authentication server. Go to the **User Management > Auth Servers > New** page. Add WLC as a Cisco VPN SSO authentication type. The default role can be **Allow All**. Allow All is a created role that has full network access. This role assigns all authenticated wireless users full network access.

Note	For this simple test network, we assigned all authenticated users with the Allow All role. If more granular roles are desired, mapping rules can be created for the WLC auth server using the same procedure described in the earlier section on Cisco VPN SSO.

Step 8 Monitoring the wireless controller users is performed by viewing the **User Management > Online Users > In-Band** page. Successfully authenticated users will appear under the provider Cisco VPN.

Summary

This chapter provided an overview of AD SSO as well as step-by-step configuration details. Today, customers who have invested in Active Directory can take advantage of LAN SSO for the Windows 2000, XP, and Vista operating systems when NAC Agent is installed. Without NAC agent, there is no AD SSO benefit.

For AD SSO to work, the administrator must pay special attention to configuration details within the NAS and AD server itself. To assist with AD/LDAP structure configuration, free LDAP browser tools are available if needed. A sample LDAP browser was provided in this chapter. By mapping AD user attributes to roles within the NAS, users can be placed in the appropriate role with the appropriate network access policy.

SSO extends beyond the LAN to VPN and wireless services. Both VPN and WLC SSO are configured and deployed in a similar fashion. The NAC agent is required in both VPN and WLC SSO implementations.

This chapter covers the following topics:

- High Availability on NAC Appliance Manager
- High Availability on NAC Appliance Server
- Example of a High Availability Configuration for NAC Appliance Manager and Server

CHAPTER 12

Configuring High Availability

This chapter explains how NAC Appliance Manager and NAC Appliance Server work in a failover mode. You will learn how to configure high availability (HA) and what happens if one of the NAC Appliance Managers or NAC Appliance Servers fails.

High Availability on NAC Appliance Manager

NAC Appliance Manager is the brains behind the Cisco NAC Appliance solution. All configuration is done on NAC Appliance Manager, and it pushes the relevant configurations to all NAC Appliance Servers. NAC Appliance Manager essentially controls the NAC solution at your site. As a result, it is extremely important that you protect your NAC solution from a single point of failure.

NAC Appliance Manager can be configured in High Availability mode, which means there are two NAC Appliance Managers acting in an active-standby configuration. The entire configuration on NAC Appliance Manager is stored in a database. The standby NAC Appliance Manager synchronizes its database with the database on the active NAC Appliance Manager. Any changes made to the configuration on the active NAC Appliance Manager are immediately pushed to the standby NAC Appliance Manager.

The active and standby NAC Appliance Managers share a virtual IP; however, they don't share a virtual MAC. The active and standby NAC Appliance Managers exchange heartbeat packets every 2 seconds on User Datagram Protocol (UDP) port 694. These heartbeat packets can be sent in one of the following ways:

- Over a serial link
- Over the eth1 interface
- Over both the serial link and the eth1 interface

The standby NAC Appliance Manager monitors the heartbeat packets, and if the heartbeat timer expires, it determines that the active NAC Appliance Manager is no longer up and failover occurs. The standby NAC Appliance Manager moves to Active status, taking up the functioning of the active NAC Appliance Manager. The heartbeat timer, as of the 4.1 release, is set to 15 seconds by default and is not configurable. However, this timer will become a configurable option in one of the future releases to provide more flexibility to customers. If the heartbeat packets are sent over both the serial link and the eth1 interface, the heartbeat packets on both links have to fail for the failover to occur. If the standby NAC Appliance Manager detects missed heartbeats on the serial link while heartbeats on the eth1 interface are fine, no failover occurs. The same condition exists if heartbeats on the eth1 interface fail, but the serial link heartbeats are fine.

As you might have noticed by now, the heartbeat packet exchange mechanism protects you from a box failure or a failure of the eth1 interface link. However, it doesn't provide protection if the eth0 interface fails.

For protection against eth0 interface failure, NAC Appliance Manager has High Availability failover using link failure detection. On the active and standby NAC Appliance Managers, configure an IP address that is external to both NAC Appliance Managers and exists on the trusted part of the network. Both NAC Appliance Managers will ping this external IP address every 2 seconds using the eth0 interface. The status of the pings is exchanged between the two NAC Appliance Managers using the heartbeat packets. If the active NAC Appliance Manager detects that it hasn't received a response to three ping packets, it communicates a ping failed status to the standby NAC Appliance Manager using the heartbeat packets. If the standby NAC Appliance Manager has a successful ping status, it determines that there is a problem with the active NAC Appliance Manager's eth0 interface and failover occurs. If both the active and standby NAC Appliance Managers are unable to ping the external IP address, no failover occurs. To avoid a single point of failure, be sure to choose an external IP that is highly available. Hot Standby Router Protocol (HSRP) virtual addresses are good choices for this external IP selection.

Now that you know about the high availability options, your next question might be what the best method is to configure High Availability mode on NAC Appliance Manager. This depends on the topology of the network and where the NAC Appliance Managers are placed.

As an example, assume that you have a collapsed core/distribution layer with two switches configured with HSRP, and all the access switches are dual-homed to the core/distribution switches. Each NAC Appliance Manager is connected to one of the core switches. Make sure that NAC Appliance Manager fails over if any one of the following conditions arises:

- Active Manager fails
- eth0 link of active Manager fails
- Core 1 switch fails

The following is how you design a High Availability solution for NAC Appliance Manager in this situation:

- Use both the serial link and the eth1 interface for the heartbeat packets.
- Use eth0 link failure detection based failover.

- The external IP address to be used for the eth0 link failure detection will be the HSRP address on the core switch configured for the NAC Appliance Manager's management VLAN.

The active and standby NAC Appliance Managers will send Internet Control Message Protocol (ICMP) echo ping packets out of the eth0 interface to the core switch HSRP address. The status of these pings will be sent via the heartbeat packets on both the serial link and the eth1 link.

If the active NAC Appliance Manager fails, no heartbeat packets will be sent on either the serial or eth1 link. As a result, the standby NAC Appliance Manager transitions to Active status after the heartbeat timer expires.

If the eth0 link of the active NAC Appliance Manager fails, the active NAC Appliance Manager will communicate this ping failed status to the standby NAC Appliance Manager. The standby NAC Appliance Manager will check whether it is able to ping the external IP address. If it is successful, the standby NAC Appliance Manager will instruct the currently active NAC Appliance Manager to go into Standby status, and the former standby NAC Appliance Manager transitions to Active status.

If the Core 1 switch fails, the Core 2 switch becomes the HSRP active switch. Pings from the eth0 interface will fail, and the heartbeat over the eth1 link will also fail. The serial link will remain up, however. The eth0 ping failed status will be communicated to the standby NAC Appliance Manager. The standby NAC Appliance Manager will have a ping success status because it will be able to get a response to its ping packets from the core 2 switch. This causes the currently active NAC Appliance Manager to go into Standby status and the standby NAC Appliance Manager becomes the active NAC Appliance Manager. If the core 1 switch comes back up, the NAC Appliance Managers will not fail back because both NAC Appliance Managers have been exchanging heartbeat packets over the serial link, and each knows the other's status correctly.

In certain situations where NAC Appliance Managers are placed at a long distance from each other, it might not be possible to use a serial link for the heartbeat packets. Instead, the NAC Appliance Managers share their heartbeat messages over a single VLAN. In such a situation, the failover behavior remains the same if the active NAC Appliance Manager fails or the eth0 link fails. However, if the core 1 switch fails in this scenario, there is no heartbeat exchange between the two NAC Appliance Managers. The standby NAC Appliance Manager successfully transitions to Active status, but the NAC Appliance Manager connected to the core 1 switch has no way of knowing that the standby NAC Appliance Manager has become active, so it remains in Active status also.

Because the core 1 switch is down, the NAC Appliance Manager connected to Core 1 will not be able to communicate to any devices on the network. However, when the core 1 switch comes back up, the two NAC Appliance Managers will be in Active-Active status. They will be able to exchange heartbeat packets, and the NAC Appliance Manager connected to the core 1 switch will instruct the NAC Appliance Manager connected to the core 2 switch to go into Standby status. Consequently, a failover will occur again when the core 1 switch comes back up if no serial link is used for failover. To protect against this active-active scenario, build in a healthy amount of network-level resiliency and fault tolerance between the two NAC Appliance Managers.

High Availability on NAC Appliance Server

NAC Appliance Server is the policy enforcement firewall of the Cisco NAC Appliance solution. To provide protection against a single point of failure, NAC Appliance Server can be configured in High Availability mode.

The High Availability solution for NAC Appliance Server is similar to that of NAC Appliance Manager. The two servers act in active-standby configuration. They share virtual IPs called *service IPs*, but they don't share virtual MACs. The servers share a service IP on the trusted-side eth0 and the untrusted-side eth1. Like NAC Appliance Manager, the NAC Appliance Server service IPs are shared IPs that the external network uses to address the NAC Appliance Server pair. All server certificates should use the service IP or a domain name that resolves to the service IP. In addition, NAM communications should be directed to the service IP of the trusted-side eth0.

The active NAC Appliance Server carries out the Network Admission Control (NAC) process and maintains state information regarding the user device, login status, and DHCP leases if NAC Appliance Server is acting as the DHCP server. This information is synchronized with the standby NAC Appliance server. The standby NAC Appliance Server does not pass end-user packets between its eth0 and eth1 interfaces. Because most of the configuration data for NAC Appliance Server is stored on NAC Appliance Manager, when a failover occurs, NAC Appliance Manager pushes the configuration to the newly active NAC Appliance Server. The only configuration changes not automatically synchronized between NAC Appliance Servers are network configuration changes. Any network changes performed on the primary NAC Appliance Server have to be manually changed on the secondary NAC Appliance Server through its direct access web GUI (http://*eth0_IP_Server*/admin). This includes default gateway, Secure Sockets Layer (SSL) certificates, system time, time zone, DHCP server, Domain Name System (DNS), and service IP.

Initially, one NAC Appliance Server is configured to be the primary (active) and the other the secondary (standby). However, this status is not permanent. When a failover occurs, the secondary NAC Appliance Server assumes the primary (active) role and remains there until another failover event occurs. When the previously failed primary NAC Appliance Server is brought back online, it checks to see whether its peer is active. If so, the reactivated NAC Appliance Server assumes the standby role until another failover event occurs.

NAC Appliance Servers exchange heartbeat packets every 2 seconds on UDP port 694 and can be sent in one of the following ways:

- Over a serial link
- Over the eth0 link
- Over a separate dedicated Ethernet interface, eth2
- Over both serial and eth0 links
- Over both serial and eth2 links

NOTE   Do not connect the serial null modem cable before fully configuring high availability. Connect the cable only after the HA configuration is complete.

The standby NAC Appliance Server monitors the heartbeat packets. If the heartbeat timer expires, the standby NAC Appliance Server determines that the active NAC Appliance Server is no longer up, and stateful failover occurs. The heartbeat timer is a configurable option for NAC Appliance Server. If the heartbeat packets are sent using the last two options in the previous list, the heartbeat has to fail on both links for failover to occur, similar to NAC Appliance Manager.

Using eth0 for heartbeat purposes is not recommended because the eth0 interface is also used for user traffic, and there is no quality of service for the heartbeat packets if they are sent via the eth0 interface.

NAC Appliance Server also has failover due to eth0 and eth1 link failure detection. You can configure external IP addresses that NAC Appliance Servers will ping via the eth0 and eth1 interfaces. The status of these pings will be communicated via the heartbeat packets. This is similar to NAC Appliance Manager except that NAC Appliance Servers have to ping two external IP addresses: one via the eth0 interface and the other via the eth1 interface.

The external IP address that you choose for the pings via the eth0 interface is simple. Any IP that exists on the trusted part of the network can be used.

The external IP address for pings via the eth1 interface has to be chosen carefully. To ensure that the ping exits the eth1 (untrusted) interface and not the eth0 (trusted) interface, the IP address must be a part of a defined managed subnet. This is because when NAC Appliance Server has to send out a packet, it always looks at the managed subnet section first. If the destination IP of the packet belongs to a subnet managed by NAC Appliance Server, NAC Appliance Server will always send the packet out of the eth1 interface. Therefore, when selecting an external IP for the pings via the eth1 interface, make sure that the external IP belongs to a subnet managed by NAC Appliance Server. To avoid a single point of failure, make sure that the external IPs you choose are highly available. HSRP virtual IPs are good choices.

To demonstrate a high-availability design for NAC Appliance Server, you'll use the same topology that you did for NAC Appliance Manager. There are two core switches, and each NAC Appliance Server is connected to a respective core switch.

CAUTION   For Out-of-Band mode deployments, make sure that port security is *disabled* on all switch ports to which NAC Appliance Manager and NAC Appliance Server are connected. Port security can interfere with NAC Appliance Server HA and DHCP.

The NAC Appliance Servers in this example are configured to be in L2 Real-IP Gateway Central Deployment mode. Make sure that the NAC Appliance Server fails over if any one of the following conditions arises:

- Active NAC Appliance Server fails
- eth0 or eth1 link fails on the active NAC Appliance Server
- Core 1 switch fails

The following are the best practices for configuring high availability for NAC Appliance Server:

- Use both the serial link and the eth2 interface for the heartbeat packets. You can use eth0 for the heartbeat if no eth2 interface is available.
- Use eth0 and eth1 link failure detection–based failover.
- The external IP address used for the eth0 link failure detection will be the HSRP address on the core switches configured for NAC Appliance Manager's management VLAN.
- The external IP address used for the eth1 link failure detection will be the HSRP address on the core switches configured for one of the managed subnets of NAC Appliance Server.

The active and standby NAC Appliance Servers send ICMP echo ping packets out of the eth0 and eth1 interfaces to the core switch HSRP addresses. The status of these pings will be sent via the heartbeat packets on both the serial link and the eth2 link.

If the active NAC Appliance Server fails, no heartbeat packets are sent on either the serial or eth2 link. The standby NAC Appliance Server will transition to Active status when its heartbeat timer expires.

If the eth0 or eth1 link of the active NAC Appliance Server fails, the active NAC Appliance Server communicates that ping failed status to the standby NAC Appliance Server. The standby NAC Appliance Server will check whether it is able to ping the external IP address. If the ping is successful, the standby NAC Appliance Server instructs the currently active NAC Appliance Manager to go into Standby status and standby NAC Appliance Server transitions to Active status.

If the core 1 switch fails, the core 2 switch will become the HSRP active switch. Pings from the eth0 and eth1 interfaces of the active standby NAC Appliance Server will fail, as will the heartbeat over the eth2 link. The serial link will remain up, however. The ping failed status will be communicated to the standby NAC Appliance Server. The standby NAC Appliance Server will have a ping success status because it will be able to get a response to its ping packets from the core 2 switch. This will cause the currently active NAC Appliance Server to go into Standby status, and the standby NAC Appliance Server will become the active NAC Appliance Server. If the core 1 switch comes back up, the NAC Appliance Servers will not fail back because both NAC Appliance Servers have been exchanging heartbeat packets over the serial link, and each knows the other's status correctly.

This also avoids the situation in which both NAC Appliance Servers are in active-active status when the core 1 switch comes back up. With NAC Appliance Servers, if both NAC Appliance Servers become active and they are configured to be in Virtual Gateway mode, a Layer 2 loop will occur in the network. Therefore, in the High Availability design of NAC Appliance Servers, it is important to send the heartbeat packets over the serial link in addition to sending them over the dedicated Ethernet link.

Example of a High Availability Configuration for NAC Appliance Manager and Server

This section explains the design and configuration of a High Availability design for NAC Appliance Manager and NAC Appliance Server. Assume that you have the network topology in Figure 12-1, with the VLANs described in Table 12-1 already defined.

Figure 12-1 *Sample Network Topology*

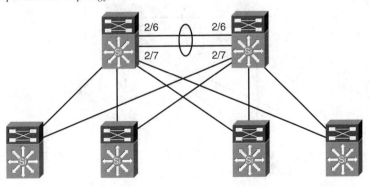

Table 12-1   *VLAN Mapping for Sample Network Topology*

VLAN	Description
VLAN 10	Untrusted VLAN
VLAN 30	Trusted-side VLAN
VLAN 90	NAC Appliance Manager eth1 heartbeat VLAN
VLAN 91	NAC Appliance Server eth2 heartbeat VLAN

This topology is a collapsed core/distribution layer design with the access switches dual homed to the two core switches. The core switches are running HSRP.

Adding NAC Appliance Managers in High Availability Mode

As you see from the diagram in Figure 12-2, both the serial interface and the eth1 interface are used for the heartbeat packets. eth0 link failure–based failover is also being used.

Figure 12-2   *NAC Appliance Manager in HA Mode*

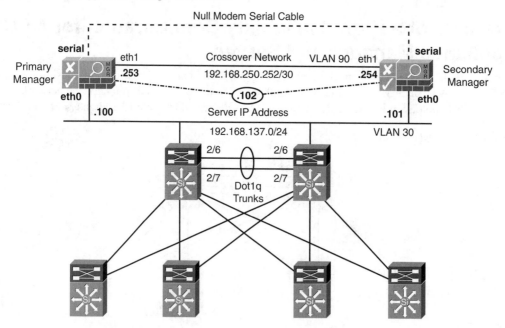

The first step in configuring a high-availability pair is adding or modifying their certificates. The certificates of both the primary and secondary Cisco NAC Appliance Managers must be generated using the service IP address or a domain name that DNS resolves to the service IP address. In a production environment, you will want to use a Certificate Authority–signed certificate. For a test environment, you can generate a temporary self-signed certificate in Cisco NAC Appliance Manager.

Adding a CA-Signed Certificate to the Primary NAC Appliance Manager

Figure 12-3 shows the certificate configuration page. Remember that the imported certificate must use the service IP address or domain name.

Figure 12-3 *CA-Signed Certificate Configuration Page*

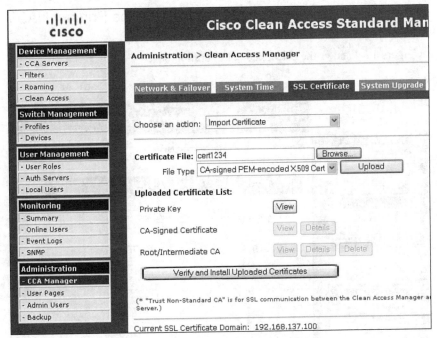

Follow these steps to add a CA-signed certificate to the primary NAC Appliance Manager:

Step 1 On the Primary Cisco NAC Appliance Manager's admin GUI, navigate to **Administration > Clean Access Manager > SSL Certificate**.

Step 2 Select **Import Certificate** from the **Choose an Action** menu.

Step 3 Browse to your certificate file.

Step 4	Leave the file type to the default value: **CA-Signed PEM-encoded X.509 Cert**.
Step 5	Click the **Upload** button.
Step 6	Click **Verify and Install Uploaded Certificates**.
Step 7	Select **Export CSR/PrivateKey/Certificate** from the **Choose an Action** menu.
Step 8	Click **Export** next to **Currently Installed Private Key**.
Step 9	Save this export to your hard disk. Later it will be imported into the secondary NAC Appliance Manager.

Generating a Self-Signed Temporary Certificate on the Primary NAC Appliance Manager

Figure 12-4 shows the certificate configuration page.

Figure 12-4 *Generate Temporary Certificate Configuration Page*

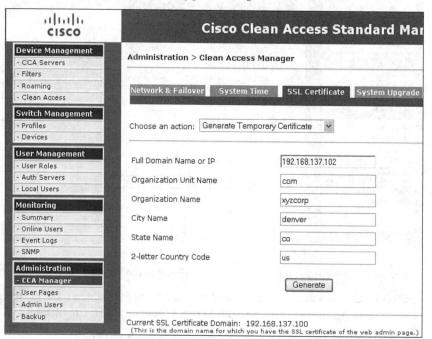

Follow these steps to add a self-signed temporary certificate to the primary Manager. This should be done only for testing purposes.

Step 1   On the Primary Cisco NAC Appliance Manager's admin GUI, navigate to **Administration > Clean Access Manager > SSL Certificate**.

Step 2   Fill in the **Full Domain Name or IP** field with the service IP address of the HA pair.

Step 3   Fill in the rest of the form's fields.

Step 4   Click the **Generate** button.

Step 5   Select **Export CSR/PrivateKey/Certificate** from the **Choose an Action** menu.

Step 6   Click **Export** next to **Currently Installed Private Key**. Save this export to your hard disk. Later it will be imported into the secondary NAC Appliance Manager.

Step 7   Click **Export** next to **Currently Installed Certificate**. Save this export to your hard disk. Later it will be imported into the secondary NAC Appliance Manager.

Adding a Certificate to the Secondary NAC Appliance Manager

Now that the certificate has been added to the primary NAC Appliance Manager, you need to import the private key file and certificate file into the secondary NAC Appliance Manager. The configuration process on the secondary NAC Appliance Manager is the same regardless of whether the primary NAC Appliance Manager used self-signed temporary certificates or Certificate Authority–signed certificates. Use the following steps to configure certificates:

Step 1   On the Secondary Cisco NAC Appliance Manager's admin GUI, navigate to **Administration > Clean Access Manager > SSL Certificate**.

Step 2   Select **Import Certificate** from the **Choose an Action** menu.

Step 3   Browse to the private key file that was exported from the primary NAC Appliance Manager.

Step 4   Choose the file type **Private Key**.

Step 5   Click **Upload**.

Step 6   Select **Import Certificate** from the **Choose an Action** menu.

Step 7   Browse to your Certificate Authority–signed certificate file.

Step 8   Choose the file type **CA-Signed PEM-encoded X.509 Cert**.

Step 9   Click **Upload**.

Step 10 Click **Verify and Install Uploaded Certificates**.

Configuring High Availability for NAC Appliance Managers

Figure 12-5 is a screen shot of the High Availability configuration on the Primary Manager.

Figure 12-5 *Primary NAC Appliance Manager High Availability Configuration*

The following are some of the key configuration steps shown in Figure 12-5:

Step 1   Set the **High-Availability Mode** field to **HA-Primary**. This setting makes this NAC Appliance Manager the primary, but its role is not permanent. If the primary NAC Appliance Manager fails, the standby becomes the new primary. When the original primary NAC Appliance Manager comes back online, it will assume the standby role.

Step 2   Set the service IP address. This allows the failover pair to appear on the network as a single entity. This IP address is shared between the primary and secondary NAC Appliance Managers. NAC Appliance Servers communicate with the NAC Appliance Manager pair using only the single service IP address.

Note	Be sure to generate your SSL certificate using the service IP address or a domain name that resolves to the service IP address. Both the primary and secondary NAC Appliance Managers will have the same certificate loaded.

Step 3 Set the peer host name. It is critical that this exactly matches the host name defined on the standby NAC Appliance Manager. This value is case sensitive.

Step 4 Set the correct COM port to use for the heartbeat serial interface. It is highly recommended that a heartbeat serial interface be configured and connected between the Cisco NAC Appliance pair (a standard serial null modem cable is required). Doing so substantially increases the fault tolerance of the NAC Appliance Manager pair.

Step 5 The **Disable Serial Login** option should be selected only when your NAC Appliance Manager platform has only a single serial port on the motherboard. If you have two serial ports, do not select this option. When you have two ports, the serial login port is always the first tty port, so be sure to attach your heartbeat serial null modem cable to the second serial port.

How to Find Your Serial Port

In most cases, serial port 1 will map to com1/ttyS0 and serial port 2 will map to com2/ttyS1. But in some cases this doesn't happen. In Linux, serial ports are called *tty ports*, and their configuration and status can be found in the /proc/tty/driver/serial file. To figure out where your serial port is, you can issue the commands shown in Figure 12-6. If the tty port shows data terminal ready (DTR) and tx (transmit)/rx (receive) packets, it is an active serial port. As you can see from Figure 12-6, ttyS0 is active and shows DTR, whereas ttyS1 is not active and does not have DTR.

Figure 12-6 *Finding Serial Ports in Linux*

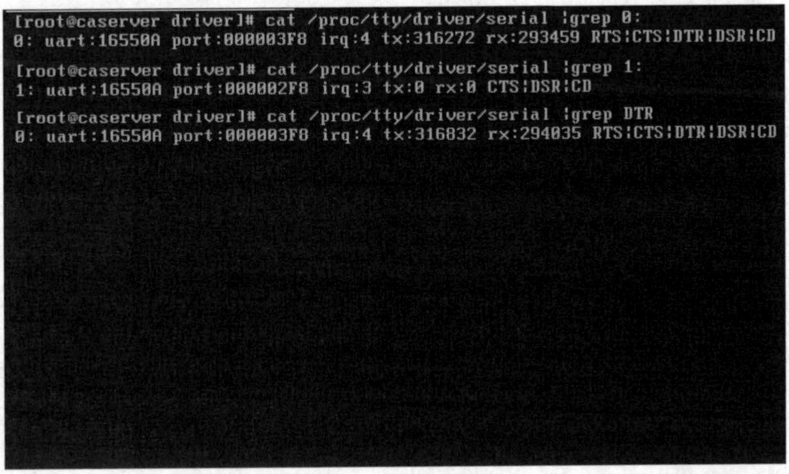

```
[root@caserver driver]# cat /proc/tty/driver/serial |grep 0:
0: uart:16550A port:000003F8 irq:4 tx:316272 rx:293459 RTS:CTS:DTR:DSR:CD

[root@caserver driver]# cat /proc/tty/driver/serial |grep 1:
1: uart:16550A port:000002F8 irq:3 tx:0 rx:0 CTS:DSR:CD

[root@caserver driver]# cat /proc/tty/driver/serial |grep DTR
0: uart:16550A port:000003F8 irq:4 tx:316832 rx:294035 RTS:CTS:DTR:DSR:CD
```

Step 6 Set the network address to be used on the mandatory eth1 crossover network. As you can see, the fourth octet of the address is preset. The primary NAC Appliance Manager's IP address will be x.x.x.253; the secondary's will be x.x.x.254.

Step 7 Click **Update** and then reboot.

To configure the secondary NAC Appliance Manager for high availability, you start by navigating to the GUI of the secondary NAC Appliance Manager: https://*eth0_ip_of_secondary*/admin. Follow the same instructions as you did for the primary NAC Appliance Manager, except set the High Availability mode to **HA-Secondary**. It is extremely important that the host names and the peer host names be consistent between the primary and secondary NAC Appliance Managers because the heartbeat mechanism looks at this information when exchanging heartbeat packets.

Adding NAC Appliance Servers in High Availability Mode

When configuring HA on NAC Appliance Servers, it is recommended that you first configure the primary NAC Appliance Server and test it with clients. After successful testing is done, add the secondary server to the system. Testing with only the primary NAC Appliance Server active first will make it easier to troubleshoot any issues. When you add the secondary NAC Appliance Server to the mix, you know you are adding it to a known good working NAC Appliance configuration. As a result, troubleshooting any issues arising from the addition of the secondary NAC Appliance Server will be isolated to only a few possibilities.

The principal configuration steps for configuring High Availability mode for NAC Appliance Servers are the following:

Step 1 Configure the eth2 interfaces.

Step 2 Configure HA on the primary NAC Appliance Server.

Step 3 Test a client—do not continue until this test is successful.

Step 4 Configure HA on the secondary NAC Appliance Server.

Step 5 Connect the NAC Appliance Servers and test.

Step 6 Optionally, configure DHCP failover.

Step 7 Test failing over the pair.

See Figure 12-7 for a sample HA network topology. As shown in Figure 12-7, the serial interface and the eth2 interfaces are used for heartbeat signals. eth2 will be the heartbeat UDP interface. If you do not have an eth2 interface, you can use the eth0 (trusted-side) interface instead. For the serial heartbeat, you can use any available serial port on NAC Appliance Server. If you have only a single serial port, it can be used, but make sure that you disable serial console login when completing the HA configuration steps. The heartbeat serial ports are connected to each other using a null modem cable.

Figure 12-7 *Sample NAC Appliance Server HA Network Topology*

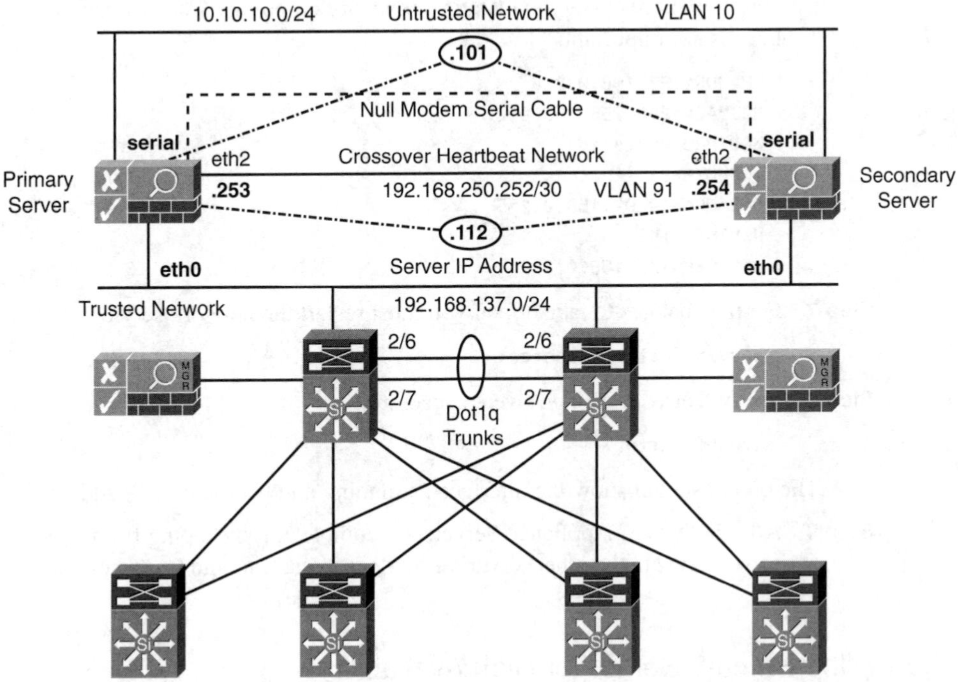

Configuring the eth2 Interfaces

If you are using eth2 as your heartbeat interface, you will have to configure it manually. This will have to be completed on both the primary and secondary NAC Appliance Servers before HA can be configured. To do this, use the following steps:

Step 1 Use Secure Shell (SSH) to connect to NAC Appliance Server's trusted-side interface. Log in as root.

Step 2 Type **cd /etc/sysconfig/network-scripts**.

Step 3 List the directory's contents by typing **ls**.

Step 4 If you do not see a file named ifcfg-eth2, create one by copying ifcfg-eth1 to ifcfg-eth2. Issue the following command:

```
cp ifcfg-eth1 ifcfg-eth2.
```

Step 5   Edit ifcfg-eth2:

```
vi ifcfg-eth2
```

Step 6   Change the file so that it includes only the following information. Change the values as necessary to match your network topology. The order of the lines is not important.

```
IPADDR=192.168.0.253
NETMASK=255.255.255.252
BOOTPROTO=static
ONBOOT=yes
BROADCAST=192.168.0.255
DEVICE=eth2
NETWORK=192.168.0.252
```

Step 7   For the changes to take effect, you must restart the network service:

```
service network restart
```

Step 8   Verify that your changes were successful:

```
ifconfig eth2
```

The output should show the interface as running and list the new IP address.

Step 9   After both NAC Appliance Servers are complete, issue a ping from one server's eth2 to the other server's eth2 IP address. It should be successful.

Configuring the Primary Server for High Availability

The principal configuration steps for configuring high availability on the primary NAC Appliance Server are as follows:

Step 1   Access the primary NAC Appliance Server directly.

Step 2   Configure the network and host information for the primary NAC Appliance Server.

Step 3   Configure HA-Primary Failover.

Step 4   Configure the SSL certificate.

Step 5   Reboot the primary NAC Appliance Server.

Step 6   Add NAC Appliance Server to NAC Appliance Manager by using the service IP.

Step 7   Complete the configuration and test a client through NAC Appliance.

When these steps are complete, continue on to configure the secondary NAC Appliance Server.

Accessing the Primary Server Directly

NAC Appliance Server has a direct access console GUI. You must use this direct access console to complete the High Availability configuration. These configuration pages are reachable by going directly to NAC Appliance Server at https://*eth0_Server_IP*/admin. You must access the primary and secondary NAC Appliance Servers in this way for network and HA setup.

Configuring the Network and Host Information for the Primary Server

Before you can configure the failover piece, you must first complete the network and host configuration. Figure 12-8 shows a sample network configuration page. This page is accessed by navigating to **Administration > Network Settings > IP**.

Figure 12-8   *Primary Server Network Settings*

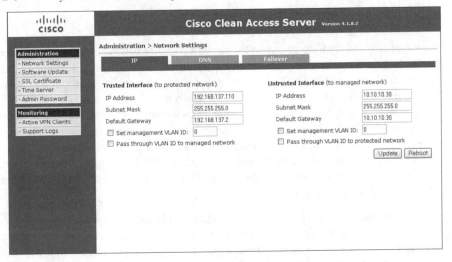

Figure 12-8 is shown as a reference so that you can compare the values shown in the figure to those shown later in the HA configuration pages. Some of the key configuration references shown in Figure 12-8 are as follows:

- Because NAC Appliance Server is in Real-IP Gateway mode, it has two unique IP addresses: one for the trusted interface and one for the untrusted interface. If you were running in Virtual Gateway mode, you would have only one IP address for the whole box. Note that this single IP address would be put on both the trusted and untrusted interfaces and would be used for management traffic.

- The **Set management VLAN ID** option is not checked (disabled). If you were using VLAN trunking, you could check it and assign it to a VLAN, such as VLAN 20. This would instruct NAC Appliance Server that it should respond to only the configured IP address on VLAN 20. This VLAN is typically a dedicated management VLAN. It is checked only on the trusted side of the configuration; this prohibits users on the untrusted side from reaching the NAC Appliance Server management IP address.

Make sure that the NAC Appliance Server is on VLAN *X* before you set its management VLAN to *X*. Otherwise, you will not be able to use the IP to reach NAC Appliance Server after the reboot.

The next step is to set the host name and domain name for the Primary Server. To do this, navigate to **Administration > Network Settings > DNS**. You must fill this page out completely for HA to function. The host name used must be resolvable by DNS or added to the /etc/hosts file of each NAC Appliance Server directly. Record this information for each NAC Appliance Server because it will be needed in the HA configuration.

Now on to the high-availability configuration steps for the primary NAC Appliance Server.

Configuring HA-Primary Failover

When configuring HA, an important piece to consider is what external IPs to choose for the link failure detection–based failover. In Virtual Gateway mode, if NAC Appliance Server initiates traffic destined for an IP that is part of a subnet configured in the managed subnet section, that packet will always be sent out of the eth1 interface except for packets destined for its default gateway. The management subnet of NAC Appliance Server is automatically added to the managed subnet section. Therefore, when you choose the external IP for eth0 link failure detection, it cannot be an IP in the same subnet as NAC Appliance Server (except for the default gateway of NAC Appliance Server). In this scenario, the default gateway address is an HSRP address and is a good choice for the external IP for the eth0 link failure detection.

The external IP for eth1 link failure detection can be any IP that is part of a subnet configured in the managed subnet section. Adding an additional VLAN and subnet in the managed subnet section is recommended. By doing this, you can configure a VLAN switched virtual interface (SVI) on the core switches and use the HSRP address for this new VLAN as the external IP for eth1 link failure detection.

NOTE   Before configuring HA on NAC Appliance Servers, you must remove them from NAC Appliance Manager if they were previously added to the management domain. This is done by navigating to **Device Management > Clean Access Servers > List of Servers** and clicking the **Delete** button next to each NAC Appliance Server.

The High-Availability configuration pages can be accessed only by going to the direct access NAC Appliance Server console located at http://*eth0_IP_address*/admin. The next step in HA setup is to configure failover. Figure 12-9 shows the failover configuration page from the primary NAC Appliance Server in the sample network shown previously in Figure 12-7.

Figure 12-9 *Primary Server Failover Configuration*

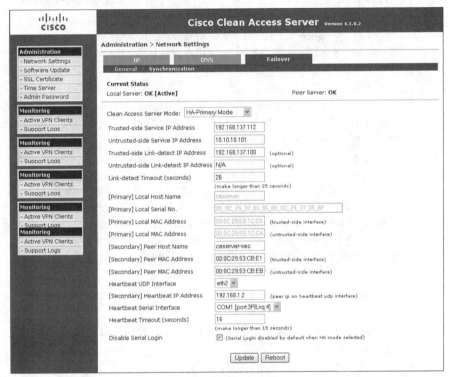

Each field shown in the failover configuration page (see Figure 12-9) is explained in the following list:

- The configuration page shown in Figure 12-9 is accessed by navigating to **Administration > Network Settings > Failover**.

- **Clean Access Server Mode**   Set **Clean Access Server Mode** to **HA-Primary Mode**. This enables all the additional configuration options shown.

- **Trusted-Side Service IP Address**   This is the IP address that is shared between the primary and secondary NAC Appliance Servers. They will communicate to the network using this address.

- **Untrusted-Side Service IP Address**   Set the unique service IP Address. If the server type is set to Virtual Gateway Mode, you would set the untrusted-side service IP address to the same as the trusted-side service IP address.

- **Trusted-Side Link Detect (optional)** The IP address entered here will be pinged by NAC Appliance Server using its trusted-side interface. The primary and secondary NAC Appliance Servers will typically use the same link detect IP address. This is not a requirement, but a best practice. The pings will be sent out every 2 seconds.

- **Untrusted-Side Link Detect (optional)** The IP address entered here will be pinged by NAC Appliance Server using its untrusted-side interface. The primary and secondary NAC Appliance Servers will typically use the same link detect IP address. This is not a requirement, but a best practice. The pings will be sent out every 2 seconds.

- **Link-Detect Timeout (Seconds)** This field must be greater than 25 seconds. When the set timeout expires, the device is considered unreachable. This timeout applies to both trusted and untrusted link detection.

  Link detection for the trusted and untrusted sides is another mechanism, like heartbeat serial and UDP, which NAC Appliance Servers can use to detect failures. NAC Appliance Server pings each configured link detect IP address and counts the number of reachable hosts—that is, the number of hosts that did not time out. The count would be between zero and two hosts alive. If the standby NAC Appliance Server has a higher count, meaning it can reach more hosts, a failover occur. If the count is the same for both the active and standby NAC Appliance Servers, no failover occurs.

- **[Primary] Local Host Name** This field is filled out automatically and cannot be changed here.

- **[Primary] Local Serial Number** This field is filled out automatically and cannot be changed here.

- **[Primary] Local MAC Address (Trusted-Side)** This field is filled out automatically and cannot be changed here.

- **[Primary] Local MAC Address (Untrusted-Side)** This field is filled out automatically and cannot be changed here.

Note　It is a good idea to copy the host name, serial number, and trusted and untrusted MAC addresses of the primary NAC Appliance Server to a text file. These will be needed later when configuring HA on the secondary NAC Appliance Server.

To avoid errors, it is best to copy and paste the required secondary NAC Appliance Server information needed in the following list directly from the direct access console of the secondary NAC Appliance server or from a previously created configuration text file.

- **[Secondary] Peer Host Name**   This must exactly match the host name of the secondary NAC Appliance Server. This information will be found or set in the secondary server under **Administration > Network Settings > DNS > Host Name**.

- **[Secondary] Peer MAC Address (Trusted-Side)**   This must exactly match the MAC address of the eth0 interface of the secondary NAC Application Servers. This value should be copied from the secondary server under **Administration > Network Settings > Failover > [Secondary] Local MAC Address (Trusted-Side)**.

- **[Secondary] Peer MAC Address (Untrusted-Side)**   This must match exactly the MAC address of the eth1 interface of the secondary NAC Appliance Servers. This value should be copied from the secondary server under **Administration > Network Settings > Failover > [Secondary] Local MAC Address (Untrusted-Side)**.

- **Heartbeat UDP Interface**   This defines what interface to send the UDP heartbeat signals across. If available, a dedicated heartbeat interface is recommended (eth2). If not available, use eth0. eth1 should never be used for heartbeats.

- **[Secondary] Heartbeat IP Address**   This is the IP address on the secondary's UDP heartbeat interface.

- **Heartbeat Serial Interface**   Select the COM port to be used to send serial heartbeats across. If you have more than one serial interface on your NAC Appliance Server, using the second interface for heartbeats is recommended. The first interface is reserved for serial login unless disabled in the field following this one.

Caution   Do *not* connect the serial null modem cable until you have completed HA configuration and rebooted both the primary and secondary NAC Appliance Servers. Unpredictable results could occur.

- **Heartbeat Timeout (Seconds)**   This timeout value is used by both the serial and UDP heartbeat methods. The value must be greater than 15 seconds. If this timer expires on the standby server, a failover will occur. The standby NAC Appliance Server will assume the active role. If both serial and UDP heartbeat methods are configured, both must time out before a failover event will occur. A heartbeat message is sent every 2 seconds.

- **Disable Serial Login**   By default this is checked, meaning that you lose the ability to manage your NAC Appliance Server via a direct connect serial cable. If you have more than one serial interface on your server and you configure the serial heartbeat interface to anything other than the first serial port, you can uncheck this value to maintain serial login capabilities.

- **Update**   Click this button now. Clicking this button updates the information on the failover configuration page but does not reboot the NAC Appliance Server.

- **Reboot**   Do *not* click **Reboot** at this point. You will do so later.

Configuring the SSL Certificate of the Primary NAC Appliance Server

A new SSL certificate needs to be generated using the new service IP address just configured in the failover configuration page. To do this, go to the direct console Web GUI of the primary NAC Appliance Server and navigate to **Administration > SSL Certificate**. Perform one of the following procedures depending on whether you will be using a temporary certificate or a Certificate Authority–signed certificate. It is highly recommended that a Certificate Authority–signed certificate be used in a production environment. Without a Certificate Authority–signed certificate, your clients will see the annoying "accept this certificate?" Windows pop-up message each time they log in.

If you use a Certificate Authority–signed certificate, follow these steps:

Step 1   From the **Choose an Action** drop-down menu, choose **Import Certificate**. The page will now look like the one in Figure 12-10.

Figure 12-10 *Server's Import Certificate Authority–Signed Certificate Configuration Page*

Step 2   In the **Certificate** field, browse to your certificate file.

Step 3   The **File Type** menu should show **CA-Signed PEM-encoded x.509 Cert**. Click the **Upload** button to import your certificate file.

Step 4   Click **Verify and Install Uploaded Certificates**.

Step 5   Export the private key file to import it on the secondary NAC Appliance Server later. Choose **Export CSR/Private Key/Certificate** from the **Choose an Action** drop-down menu.

Step 6   Click **Export** next to the **Currently Installed Private Key** option. Save this to your hard drive—it will be imported into the secondary NAC Appliance Server later. Figure 12-11 shows the certificate export page.

Figure 12-11   *Certificate Export Configuration Page*

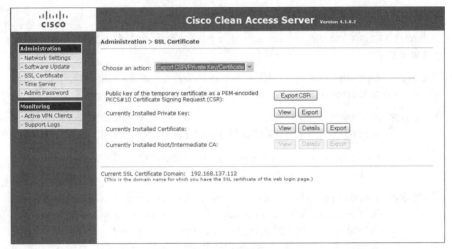

If you use a temporary certificate, follow these steps:

Step 1   From the **Choose an Action** drop-down menu, choose **Generate Temporary Certificate**.

Step 2   Fill out the form completely.

Step 3   Be sure to use the service IP address or a DNS domain name that resolves to the service IP address of the HA pair when filling out the **Full Domain Name** section.

Step 4   Click the **Generate** button.

Step 5   Export the private key file and certificate file to import it on the secondary NAC Appliance Server later. Choose **Export CSR/Private Key/ Certificate** from the **Choose an Action** drop-down menu.

Step 6   Click **Export** next to the **Currently Installed Private Key** option. Save this to your hard drive—it will be imported into the secondary NAC Appliance Server later.

Step 7   Click **Export** next to the **Currently Installed Certificate** option. Save this to your hard drive—it will be imported into the secondary NAC Appliance Server later.

Rebooting the Primary Server

Now reboot the primary NAC Appliance Server by navigating to **Network Settings >
Failover** and clicking the **Reboot** button.

Adding the Primary Server to the Manager

Now you must add the primary server to NAC Appliance Manager. To do so, follow
these steps:

Step 1   Open the Manager GUI (https://*Service_IP_of_Managers*) and navigate
to **Device Management > CCA Servers > New Server**.

Step 2   Add the new NAC Appliance Server to NAC Appliance Manager, being
sure to use the *service IP address* of the HA NAC Appliance Server pair.

Step 3   Click the **Add Clean Access Server** button. This might take a few
minutes to complete.

Step 4   If you are not able to connect, check that you used the *service IP address*
in your primary NAC Appliance Server's certificate file as stated in the
"Configuring the SSL Certificate of the Primary NAC Appliance Server"
section. In addition, you can check the "Troubleshooting HA" section of
this chapter for more assistance.

Step 5   Navigate to **Device Management > Clean Access Servers > List of
Servers**. The IP address of the active NAC Appliance Server is listed in
brackets next to the service IP for the HA pair, as shown in Figure 12-12.
Its status should be Connected. If not, force a connection by clicking the
Manage button. If this works, return to the list of IP address servers—
the status should now say Connected.

Figure 12-12 *List of Servers Showing HA Mode*

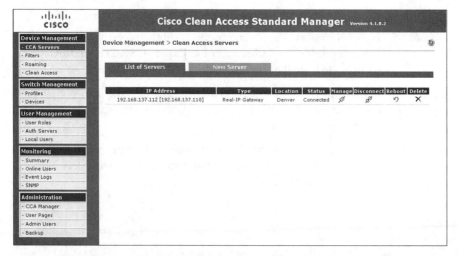

Completing NAC Appliance Configuration and Testing Client Access

Before continuing on to configuring the secondary NAC Appliance Server, stop here and complete a basic NAC Appliance configuration. This will allow you to test client access to ensure that basic client NAC is working before you enable the complexity of full HA with a secondary NAC Appliance Server. Following the configuration steps outlined in Chapter 8, "The Building Blocks: Roles, Authentication, Traffic Policies, and User Pages," earlier in this book will give you a good basic NAC Appliance configuration to use.

After you complete a basic configuration, plug in a client to the untrusted side of the network and test access. When everything works as you expect, move on to the next section.

Configuring the Secondary Server for High Availability

The principal configuration steps for configuring high availability on the Secondary Server are as follows:

Step 1 Access the Secondary Server directly.

Step 2 Configure the network and host information for the secondary NAC Appliance Server.

Step 3 Configure HA-secondary failover.

Step 4 Configure the SSL certificate.

Step 5 Reboot the secondary NAC Appliance Server.

Step 6 Complete the cable connections and DHCP settings.

Step 7 Test NAC Appliance HA.

Accessing the Secondary Server Directly

The NAC Appliance secondary server has a direct access console GUI. You must use this direct access console to complete the high-availability configuration. These configuration pages are reachable by going directly to NAC Appliance Server at https://*eth0_Secondary_Server_IP*/admin. You will have to access the primary and secondary NAC Appliance Servers in this way for network and HA setup.

Configuring the Network and Host Information for the Secondary Server

Before you can configure failover, you must first complete the network and host configuration. Figure 12-13 shows the sample network configuration screen from the secondary NAC Appliance Server.

Figure 12-13 *Secondary Server Network Settings*

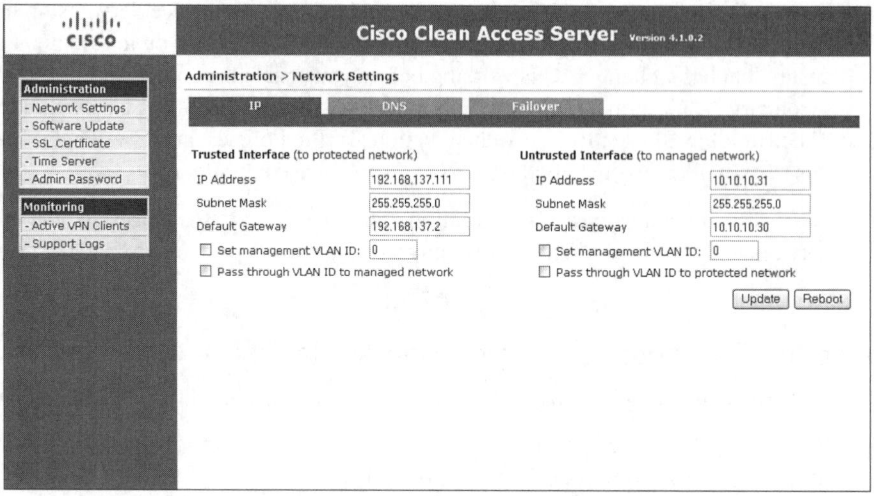

Figure 12-13 is shown as a reference so that you can compare the values shown in the figure to those shown later in the HA configuration pages. Some of the key configuration references shown in Figure 12-13 are the following:

- Because NAC Appliance Server is in Real-IP Gateway mode, it has two unique IP addresses: one for the trusted interface and one for the untrusted interface. If you were running in Virtual Gateway mode, you would have only one IP address for the whole box. Note that this single IP address would be put on both the trusted and untrusted interfaces and would be used for management traffic.

- The **Set Management VLAN ID** is not checked (it is disabled). If you were using VLAN trunking, you could check it and assign it to a VLAN, such as VLAN 20. This would instruct NAC Appliance Server that it should respond only to the configured IP address on VLAN 20. This VLAN is typically a dedicated management VLAN. It is checked only on the trusted side of the configuration, which prohibits users on the untrusted side from reaching the management IP address of NAC Appliance Server.

  Make sure that NAC Appliance Server is on VLAN *X* before you set its management VLAN to *X*. Otherwise, you will not be able to use the IP to reach NAC Appliance Server after the reboot.

The next step is to set the host name and domain name for the secondary NAC Appliance Server. To do this, navigate to **Administration > Network Settings > DNS**. You must fill this page out completely for HA to function. The host name used must be resolvable by DNS or added to the /etc/hosts file of each NAC Appliance Server directly. Record this information for each NAC Appliance Server because it will be needed in the HA configuration.

Configuring HA-Secondary Failover

The HA configuration setup on the secondary NAC Appliance Server is pretty much a mirror copy of the configuration of the HA configuration of the primary NAC Appliance Server. Figure 12-14 shows the HA configuration page of the secondary NAC Appliance Server.

Figure 12-14 *Secondary Server HA Configuration*

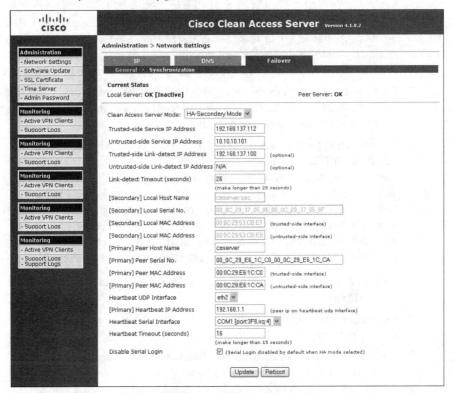

Each field shown in the Failover configuration page of the secondary NAC Appliance Server (see Figure 12-14) is explained in the following list:

- The configuration page shown in Figure 12-14 is accessed by navigating to **Administration > Network Settings > Failover**.

- **Clean Access Server Mode**   Set **Clean Access Server Mode** to **HA-Secondary Mode**. This enables all the additional configuration options shown.

- **Trusted-Side Service IP Address**   This is the IP address that is shared between the primary and secondary NAC Appliance Servers. They will communicate to the network using this address.

- **Untrusted-Side Service IP Address**   Set the service IP for the untrusted side. If your server type is set to Virtual Gateway mode, set the **Untrusted-Side Service IP Address** field value to the same as the trusted-side service IP address.

- **Trusted-Side Link Detect (optional)**   The IP address entered here will be pinged by NAC Appliance Server using its trusted-side interface. The primary and secondary NAC Appliance Servers will typically use the same link detect IP address. This is not a requirement, but a best practice. The pings will be sent out every 2 seconds.

- **Untrusted-Side Link Detect (optional)**   The IP address entered here will be pinged by NAC Appliance Server using its untrusted-side interface. The primary and secondary NAC Appliance Servers typically use the same link detect IP address. This is not a requirement, but a best practice. Pings will be sent out every 2 seconds.

- **Link-Detect Timeout (Seconds)**   This field must be greater than 25 seconds. When the set timeout expires, the device is considered unreachable. This timeout applies to both trusted and untrusted link detection.

  Link detection for the trusted and untrusted sides is another mechanism, like heartbeat serial and UDP, which NAC Appliance Servers can use to detect failures. NAC Appliance Server pings each configured link detect IP address and counts the number of hosts that are reachable—that is, the number of hosts that did not time out. The count would be between zero and two hosts alive. If the standby NAC Appliance Server has a higher count, meaning it can reach more hosts, a failover will occur. If the count is the same for both the active and standby NAC Appliance Servers, no failover occurs.

- **[Secondary] Local Host Name**   This field is filled out automatically and cannot be changed here.

- **[Secondary] Local Serial Number**   This field is filled out automatically and cannot be changed here.

- **[Secondary] Local MAC Address (Trusted-Side)**   This field is filled out automatically and cannot be changed here.

- **[Secondary] Local MAC Address (Untrusted-Side)**   This field is filled out automatically and cannot be changed here.

Note   To avoid errors, it is best to copy and paste the required primary NAC Appliance Server information needed from the following list directly from the direct access console of the primary NAC Appliance Server or from a previously created configuration text file.

- **[Primary] Peer Host Name**   This must exactly match the host name of the primary NAC Appliance Server. This information will be found or set in the primary NAC Appliance Server under **Administration > Network Settings > DNS > Host Name**.

- **[Primary] Peer MAC Address (Trusted-Side)** This must exactly match exactly the MAC address of the eth0 interface of the primary NAC Appliance Server. This value should be copied from the primary NAC Appliance Server under **Administration > Network Settings > Failover > [Primary] Local MAC Address (Trusted-Side)**.

- **[Primary] Peer MAC Address (Untrusted-Side)** This must exactly match exactly the MAC address of the eth1 interface of the primary NAC Appliance Server. This value should be copied from the primary NAC Appliance Server under **Administration > Network Settings > Failover > [Primary] Local MAC Address (Untrusted-Side)**.

- **Heartbeat UDP Interface** This defines what interface to send the UDP heartbeat signals across. If available, a dedicated heartbeat interface is recommended (eth2). If one is not available, use eth0. eth1 should never be used for heartbeats.

- **[Primary] Heartbeat IP Address** This is the IP address on the UDP Heartbeat interface of the primary NAC Appliance Server.

- **Heartbeat Serial Interface** Select the COM port to be used to send serial heartbeats across. If you have more than one serial interface on your NAC Appliance Server, using the second interface for heartbeats is recommended. The first interface is reserved for serial login unless it is disabled in the following setting.

Note Do *not* connect the serial null modem cable until you have completed HA configuration and rebooted both the primary and secondary NAC Appliance Servers. Otherwise, unpredictable results could occur.

- **Heartbeat Timeout (Seconds)** This timeout value is used by both the serial and UDP heartbeat methods. The value must be greater than 15 seconds. If this timer expires on the standby NAC Appliance Server, a failover will occur. The standby NAC Appliance Server will assume the active role. If both serial and UDP heartbeat methods are configured, both must time out before a failover event occurs. A heartbeat message is sent every 2 seconds.

- **Disable Serial Login** This is checked by default, meaning you lose the ability to manage your NAC Appliance Server via a direct connect serial cable. If you have more than one serial interface on your server and you configure the serial heartbeat interface setting to anything other than the first serial port, you can uncheck this value to maintain serial login capabilities.

- **Update** Click this button now. Doing so updates the information on the failover configuration page but does not reboot NAC Appliance Server.

- **Reboot** Do *not* click **Reboot** at this point. You will do so later.

Configuring the Secondary Server's SSL Certificate

To configure the SSL certificate for the secondary NAC Appliance server, go to the direct console web GUI of the secondary NAC Appliance Server and navigate to **Administration > SSL Certificate**. Perform one of the following procedures depending on whether you plan to use a temporary certificate or a Certificate Authority–signed certificate. It is highly recommended that a Certificate Authority–signed certificate be used in a production environment. Without a Certificate Authority–signed certificate, your clients will see the annoying "accept this certificate?" Windows pop-up message each time they log in.

If you use a Certificate Authority–signed certificate, follow these steps:

Step 1 From the **Choose an Action** drop-down menu, select **Import Certificate**, as shown in Figure 12-15.

Figure 12-15 *Importing a Certificate*

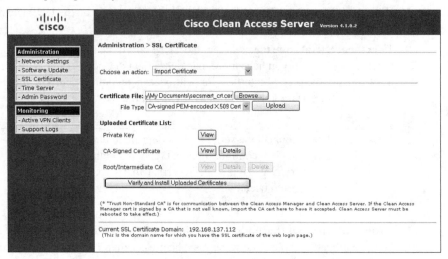

Step 2 Browse to the previously saved private key file exported from the primary NAC Appliance Server.

Step 3 Choose **File Type Private Key** and Click **Upload**.

Step 4 Now import the same certificate file you previously imported into the primary NAC Appliance Server. Browse to the certificate file.

Step 5 Choose **File Type CA-Signed PEM-encoded X.509 Cert** and click the **Upload** button.

Step 6 Click the **Verify and Install Uploaded Certificates** button.

Step 7 Import and install the root or any intermediate certificates as necessary.

If you use a temporary certificate, follow these steps:

Step 1   From the **Choose an Action** drop-down menu, select **Import Certificate**.

Step 2   Browse to the previously saved private key file exported from the primary NAC Appliance Server.

Step 3   Choose **File Type Private Key** and click **Upload**.

Step 4   Now import the same temporary certificate file you previously exported from the primary NAC Appliance Server. Browse to the certificate file.

Step 5   Choose **File Type CA-Signed PEM-encoded X.509 Cert** and click the **Upload** button.

Step 6   Click the **Verify and Install Uploaded Certificates** button. You should see a **Successfully Installed** message toward the top of the web page.

Rebooting the Secondary Server

Reboot the secondary NAC Appliance Server by navigating to **Network Settings > Failover** and clicking the **Reboot** button.

Complete Cable Connections and DHCP Settings

Now you need to hook up the necessary failover cabling and, optionally, replicate any primary server DHCP settings onto the secondary NAC Appliance Server. The DHCP step applies only if you are using the NAC Appliance DHCP server function to serve IP addresses to your untrusted-side clients.

NOTE   The DHCP server configuration settings are replicated between the primary and secondary NAC Appliance Servers, but they are not written to disk—only RAM memory on the secondary NAC Appliance Server. To permanently save the DHCP settings, you must do so manually.

In addition, be sure to follow the configuring DHCP failover steps if you are using the DHCP server functions.

CAUTION   If you remove an HA-pair from NAC Appliance Manager, you will lose all DHCP configurations on both the primary and secondary NAC Appliance Server. The settings will have to be re-added manually and the NAC Appliance Servers rebooted.

Here are the steps to follow for connecting HA cabling:

Step 1 Physically connect the required null modem serial and Ethernet crossover cables that will be used for HA. If you plan to use eth0 as the HA Ethernet card, an additional Ethernet cable will not be necessary.

Step 2 Wait about 45 seconds for the NAC Appliance Servers to link to each other before continuing.

Step 3 To verify that the serial link has come up, use SSH to go to the primary NAC Appliance Server and open the /var/log/messages file. You should see messages similar to those highlighted in Figure 12-16.

Figure 12-16 *Serial Link Log Messages*

```
May 18 23:37:57 caserver gpm[2705]: Started gpm successfully. Entered daemon mode.
May 18 23:37:58 caserver gpm[2705]: *** info [mice.c(1766)]:
May 18 23:37:58 caserver gpm[2705]: imps2: Auto-detected intellimouse PS/2
May 18 23:38:13 caserver kernel: scsi0: Allocated 7 additional CCBs (total now 35)
May 18 23:41:14 caserver kernel: click: starting router thread pid 2830 (d10c0500)
May 18 23:41:39 caserver kernel: Software Watchdog Timer: 0.07 initialized. soft_noboot=0 soft_margin=60 sec (nowayout= 0)
May 18 23:41:59 caserver login(pam_unix)[3082]: session opened for user root by (uid=0)
May 18 23:41:59 caserver  -- root[3082]: ROOT LOGIN ON tty1
May 18 23:42:09 caserver kernel: device eth1 entered promiscuous mode
May 18 23:43:29 caserver kernel: device eth1 left promiscuous mode
May 19 00:43:32 caserver ipsec_setup: ...Openswan IPsec stopped
May 19 00:43:32 caserver ipsec_setup: Stopping Openswan IPsec...
May 19 00:43:32 caserver ipsec_setup: stop ordered, but IPsec does not appear to be running!
May 19 00:43:32 caserver ipsec_setup: doing cleanup anyway...
May 19 00:43:35 caserver ipsec_setup: ...Openswan IPsec stopped
May 19 00:43:35 caserver ipsec_setup: Stopping Openswan IPsec...
May 19 00:43:35 caserver ipsec_setup: stop ordered, but IPsec does not appear to be running!
May 19 00:43:35 caserver ipsec_setup: doing cleanup anyway...
May 18 23:43:37 caserver kernel: klips_info:ipsec_init: KLIPS startup, Openswan KLIPS IPsec stack version: 2.4.4
May 18 23:43:37 caserver kernel: NET: Registered protocol family 15
May 18 23:43:37 caserver kernel: ipsec_tunnel_init_devices: no fake2 device found.
May 18 23:43:37 caserver kernel: klips_info:ipsec_alg_init: KLIPS alg v=0.8.1-0 (EALG_MAX=255, AALG_MAX=251)
May 18 23:43:37 caserver kernel: klips_info:ipsec_alg_init: calling ipsec_alg_static_init()
May 18 23:43:37 caserver kernel: KLIPS cryptoapi interface: alg_type=15 alg_id=12 name=aes keyminbits=128 keymaxbits=256, fou
May 18 23:43:38 caserver kernel: KLIPS cryptoapi interface: alg_type=15 alg_id=253 name=twofish keyminbits=128 keymaxbits=256
May 18 23:43:38 caserver kernel: KLIPS cryptoapi interface: alg_type=15 alg_id=252 name=serpent keyminbits=128 keymaxbits=256
May 18 23:43:38 caserver kernel: KLIPS cryptoapi interface: alg_type=15 alg_id=6 name=cast5 keyminbits=128 keymaxbits=128, fo
May 18 23:43:38 caserver kernel: KLIPS cryptoapi interface: alg_type=15 alg_id=7 name=blowfish keyminbits=96 keymaxbits=448,
May 18 23:43:38 caserver kernel: KLIPS cryptoapi interface: alg_type=15 alg_id=3 name=des3_ede keyminbits=192 keymaxbits=192,
May 18 23:43:38 caserver kernel: KLIPS cryptoapi interface: alg_type=15 alg_id=2 name=des keyminbits=64 keymaxbits=64, found(
May 19 00:43:38 caserver ipsec_setup: KLIPS debug `none'
May 18 23:43:39 caserver kernel:
May 19 00:43:39 caserver ipsec_setup: KLIPS ipsec0 on eth1:0 10.10.10.101/255.255.255.0 broadcast 10.10.10.255
May 19 00:43:40 caserver ipsec_setup: ...Openswan IPsec started
May 19 00:43:40 caserver ipsec_setup: Starting Openswan IPsec 2.4.4...
May 19 00:43:45 caserver ipfail[3268]: info: Link Status update: Link 192.168.137.100/192.168.137.100 now has status dead
May 19 00:43:47 caserver ipfail[3268]: info: Link Status update: Link 192.168.137.100/192.168.137.100 now has status up
May 18 23:43:56 caserver kernel: device eth1 entered promiscuous mode
May 19 00:46:56 caserver ipfail[3268]: info: Link Status update: Link caserver-sec//dev/ttyS0 now has status up
May 19 00:46:56 caserver ipfail[3268]: info: Status update: Node caserver-sec now has status up
May 19 00:46:57 caserver ipfail[3268]: info: Status update: Node caserver-sec now has status active
May 19 00:46:59 caserver ipfail[3268]: info: Asking other side for ping node count.
May 19 00:46:59 caserver ipfail[3268]: info: No giveup timer to abort.
May 19 00:01:02 caserver crond(pam_unix)[4327]: session opened for user root by (uid=0)
May 19 00:01:02 caserver crond(pam_unix)[4327]: session closed for user root
May 19 00:46:30 caserver sshd(pam_unix)[5143]: session opened for user root by root(uid=0)
May 19 01:01:01 caserver crond(pam_unix)[5386]: session opened for user root by (uid=0)
May 19 01:01:02 caserver crond(pam_unix)[5386]: session closed for user root
May 19 01:01:02 caserver kernel: ttyS0: 1 input overrun(s)
May 19 01:06:58 caserver kernel: ttyS0: 1 input overrun(s)
```

Here are the steps to follow for optional DHCP configuration:

Step 1 Shut down the primary NAC Appliance Server. To do this, use SSH to go to the primary NAC Appliance Server as root and issue the **service perfigo stop** command-line interface (CLI) command before issuing the shutdown command or clicking the power button. This will prevent a data corruption of the NAC Appliance files.

Step 2 Navigate to **Device Management > Clean Access Servers > List of Servers**. The IP address of the active NAC Appliance Server is listed in brackets next to the service IP for the HA pair. The active IP address now should match that of the secondary NAC Appliance Server because the primary NAC Appliance Server is off.

Note	To find the active or standby status of a server from the CLI, you can run the fostate.sh shell script. This script can be found in the directory of your last upgrade, such as /store/cca_upgrade-4.1.0.2. To run it, issue the command **./fostate.sh** in the proper directory.

Step 3 Now configure the DHCP server settings on the secondary NAC Appliance Server to mirror what was done previously on the primary NAC Appliance Server. To do this, click the **Manage** icon for the HA pair. Doing so brings up the management pages for the active NAC Appliance Server, which is currently the secondary NAC Appliance Server.

Step 4 Navigate to **Network > DHCP**. Configure the DHCP settings to match those on your primary NAC Appliance Server.

Continue on to test the NAC Appliance HA.

Testing NAC Appliance HA

Finally, you need to test the HA setup to ensure that it works properly. If you are using the DHCP server function, configure DHCP failover before continuing your HA testing. You will need a client machine connected to the untrusted side of the network. In your current setup, the primary NAC Appliance Server has been turned off, and the secondary NAC Appliance Server is currently the active server. Now turn on the primary NAC Appliance Server, and wait for it to completely boot up before continuing. The secondary NAC Appliance Server should still be the active server even after the primary NAC Appliance Server comes online. The primary server will assume the standby server role. Verify this by navigating to **Device Management > CCA Servers > List of Servers**. The secondary NAC Appliance Server's IP address should be listed in brackets.

To test the HA setup, follow these steps:

Step 1 Issue a DHCP release/renew on your client test machine. Ensure that you receive a proper IP address.

Step 2 Log in to NAC Appliance. You should now be logged in via the secondary NAC Appliance Server.

Step 3 Start a continuous ping from the client to a reachable host on the trusted side.

Step 4 Now reboot the secondary NAC Appliance Server. This should force a failover and make the primary NAC Appliance Server become the active NAC Appliance Server. The client will briefly lose connectivity—watch the pings.

Step 5 After about 15 seconds, verify this by navigating to **Device Management > CCA Servers > List of Servers** and periodically refreshing the screen. The IP address of the primary NAC Appliance Server should be listed in brackets.

Step 6   The client's connectivity should be restored in about 16 seconds. Traffic is now going through the primary NAC Appliance Server.

Step 7   To test DHCP failover, issue a DHCP release/renew on the client machine. Check to make sure that you receive a proper IP address.

Step 8   After the secondary NAC Appliance Server reboots and comes back online, it will assume the standby role.

Step 9   You can view the event log on NAC Appliance Manager by navigating to **Monitoring > Event Logs**. You will see messages similar to "HA status alert of Clean Access Server: caserver up."

Setting Up DHCP Failover on NAC Appliance Servers

When using the DHCP Server mode on a NAC Appliance HA pair, you need to configure DHCP failover. Doing so allows for the constant synchronization of DHCP-related information (for example, active leases, lease expirations, and so on) between the primary and secondary NAC Appliance Servers. As a result, when a failover occurs, the new active NAC Appliance Server picks up exactly where the old active NAC Appliance Server left off. DHCP failover works by setting up an SSH-encrypted tunnel between the primary and secondary NAC Appliance Servers. For the SSH tunnel to be established, keys must be exchanged between servers. To complete the DHCP failover setup, follow these steps:

Step 1   Open two web browsers. Point one at the web GUI (https:// IP_primary_Server/admin) of the primary NAC Appliance Server and one at the web GUI of the secondary NAC Appliance Server.

Step 2   On the primary NAC Appliance Server, navigate to **Administration > Network Settings > Failover > Synchronization**.

Step 3   On the secondary NAC Appliance Server, navigate to **Administration > Network Settings > Failover > Synchronization**.

Step 4   Click the **Enable** button on both NAC Appliance Servers. This will generate a client SSH key.

Step 5   Now copy and paste the client and server SSH keys between the primary and secondary NAC Appliance Servers.

Step 6   Click the **Update** button on the secondary NAC Appliance Server.

Step 7   Click the **Update** button on the primary NAC Appliance Server.

Step 8   Reboot both NAC Appliance Servers now. A reboot is required to create the /var/state/dhcp directories and files on both the primary and secondary NAC Appliance Servers.

The SSH tunnel should now be established. Figure 12-17 shows the synchronization page of the primary NAC Appliance Server. Figure 12-18 shows the synchronization page of the secondary NAC Appliance Server.

Figure 12-17 *HA Synchronization Page of the Primary NAC Appliance Server*

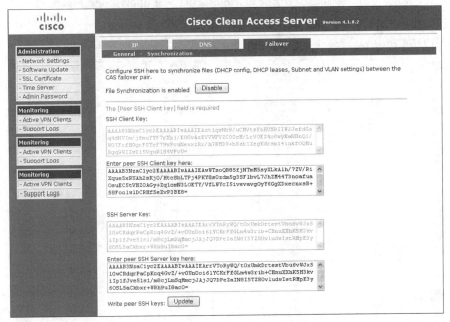

Figure 12-18 *HA Synchronization Page of the Secondary NAC Appliance Server*

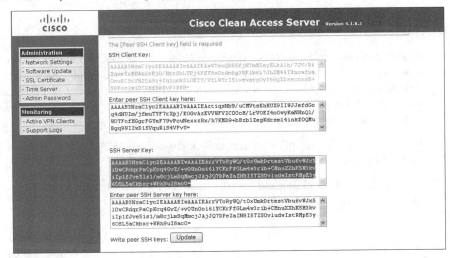

Troubleshooting HA

Most of your troubleshooting will be done using the event log found on the web GUI of the NAC Appliance Manager and the individual log files on the NAC Appliance Servers themselves. To change the level of logging detail on the NAC Appliance Servers and to download the log files, navigate to **Monitoring > Support Logs**. Figure 12-19 highlights the most useful files for HA troubleshooting purposes.

Figure 12-19 *HA Troubleshooting Log Files*

Name	Type	Modified	Size	R...	Packed	Path
netstat.out	OUT File	5/19/2007 2:08 AM	4,736	0%	4,736	system\
ifconfig.out	OUT File	5/19/2007 2:08 AM	5,304	0%	5,304	system\
ha-log	File	5/19/2007 2:08 AM	345,584	0%	345,584	var\log\
dmesg.out	OUT File	5/19/2007 2:08 AM	12,405	0%	12,405	system\
date.out	OUT File	5/19/2007 2:08 AM	29	0%	29	system\
messages	File	5/19/2007 2:06 AM	45,441	0%	45,441	var\log\
secure	File	5/19/2007 1:46 AM	3,470	0%	3,470	var\log\
localhost_access_log.2007-05-19.txt	Text Document	5/19/2007 1:32 AM	1,897	0%	1,897	perfigo\acc...
access_log	File	5/19/2007 1:32 AM	13,830	0%	13,830	perfigo\acc...
env	File	5/19/2007 1:13 AM	1,245	0%	1,245	perfigo\acc...
ha-log.1	1 File	5/19/2007 1:01 AM	106,469	0%	106,469	var\log\
ha-debug	File	5/19/2007 1:01 AM	0	0%	0	var\log\
ha-debug.1	1 File	5/19/2007 12:46 AM	708	0%	708	var\log\
vlan_subnet_retag	File	5/19/2007 12:46 AM	0	0%	0	perfigo\acc...
vlan_map_retag	File	5/19/2007 12:46 AM	0	0%	0	perfigo\acc...
vlan_map	File	5/19/2007 12:46 AM	0	0%	0	perfigo\acc...
subnet	File	5/19/2007 12:46 AM	30	0%	30	perfigo\acc...
routes	File	5/19/2007 12:46 AM	0	0%	0	perfigo\acc...
dhcplog	File	5/19/2007 12:46 AM	7,280	0%	7,280	var\log\
arp	File	5/19/2007 12:46 AM	0	0%	0	perfigo\acc...
loginpage.properties	PROPERTIE...	5/19/2007 12:46 AM	887	0%	887	perfigo\acc...
dhcpd.conf	CONF File	5/19/2007 12:46 AM	228	0%	228	etc\
click-config	File	5/19/2007 12:43 AM	15,547	0%	15,547	perfigo\logs\
perfigo-redirect-log0.log.0	0 File	5/19/2007 12:42 AM	659	0%	659	perfigo\logs\
perfigo-redirect-log0.log.0.lck	LCK File	5/19/2007 12:41 AM	0	0%	0	perfigo\logs\
localhost_log.2007-05-19.txt	Text Document	5/19/2007 12:41 AM	1,832	0%	1,832	perfigo\acc...
catalina.out	OUT File	5/19/2007 12:41 AM	1,316	0%	1,316	perfigo\acc...
error_log	File	5/19/2007 12:41 AM	2,139	0%	2,139	perfigo\acc...
perfigo-log	File	5/19/2007 12:41 AM	4,083	0%	4,083	perfigo\logs\
.gussk	GUSSK File	5/19/2007 12:41 AM	36	0%	36	etc\
nessusd.messages	MESSAGES File	5/19/2007 12:41 AM	65,569	0%	65,569	var\nessus...
localhost_access_log.2007-05-18.txt	Text Document	5/18/2007 8:17 AM	3,184	0%	3,184	perfigo\acc...
perfigo.conf	CONF File	5/18/2007 7:50 AM	384	0%	384	etc\ha.d\
hosts	File	5/18/2007 7:50 AM	64	0%	64	etc\

Summary

This chapter examined how NAC Appliance Manager and NAC Appliance Server High Availability mode works and is configured. Because both NAC Appliance Manager and NAC Appliance Server are critical components of your NAC Appliance solution, designing a high-availability solution for them is strongly recommended. Without high availability enabled, you run the risk of impairing your clients' capability to access the network.

The chapter includes the following recommendations for NAC Appliance Manager in High Availability mode:

- Use both the serial link and the eth1 interface for the heartbeat packets.
- Use eth0 link failure detection–based failover.

- The external IP address used for eth0 link failure detection can be the HSRP address on the core switch configured for the management VLAN of NAC Appliance Manager or some other high-availability IP address.

- Use a Certificate Authority–signed certificate file in a production environment.

The chapter includes the following recommendations for NAC Appliance Server in High Availability mode:

- Use both the serial link and the eth2 interface for the heartbeat packets.

- Use eth0 and possibly eth1 link failure detection-based failover.

- The external IP address used for the eth0 link failure detection can be the HSRP address on the core switches configured for the management VLAN of NAC Appliance Manager or any other highly available IP address on the trusted part of the network.

- The external IP address used for the eth1 link failure detection can be the HSRP address on the core switches configured for one of the managed subnets of NAC Appliance Server or any other highly available IP address on the untrusted part of the network.

- Use a Certificate Authority–signed certificate file in a production environment.

PART V

Cisco NAC Appliance Deployment Best Practices

This chapter covers the following topics:

- Pre-Deployment Phase
- Deployment Plan Overview
- Proof of Concept Phase
- Pilot Phase
- Production Deployment Phases

CHAPTER 13

Deploying Cisco NAC Appliance

This chapter focuses on how to develop a deployment plan for a NAC Appliance solution rollout. This deployment plan focuses on larger-sized deployments, but it can be tailored to fit just about any size environment. It cannot be stressed enough how important it is to have a solid, well thought-out deployment plan in place before you start any rollout of the solution. A good deployment plan should result in a good deployment experience for all involved. In most cases, a NAC Appliance deployment should be broken into four distinct phases:

- Pre-deployment phase
- Proof of concept phase
- Pilot phase
- Production phase

The production phase should be broken into three subphases: initial introduction, host security policy checks with no enforcement, and host security policy enforcement. This phased approach is designed to flush out any host policy issues, configuration mistakes, and design issues before the final production phase. This should result in a more positive experience for the end users and fewer calls to the help desk.

As you are putting together your deployment plan, be sure to keep in mind that the success of a NAC Appliance deployment can be jeopardized as much by negative political sentiment as by having poor technical execution. Therefore, it is critical that the deployment plan include goals, scopes, and success criteria agreed to by those individuals or groups that have political influence over the NAC Appliance implementation.

Figure 13-1 shows the four phases of deployment. The creation of your host security policy should be done prior to deployment.

Figure 13-1 *Phases of Deployment*

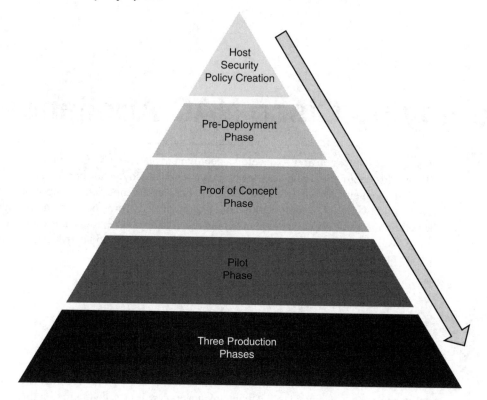

Pre-Deployment Phase

The pre-deployment phase is where you get your hands wrapped around the project as a whole. You will set your overall vision statement and define your NAC Appliance project scope of work. During this phase, you will determine what additional resources are needed, what the overall timeline should look like, and how communication for the project will work. This phase should also include an executive summary and business drivers section. Having these sections well thought out and agreed to by all relevant parties can help later if you run into any political pressure. An outline for the pre-deployment phase might look like this sample:

Pre-Deployment Phase

    1.1 Executive Summary
    1.2 Scope
    1.3 Vision
       1.3.1 NAC Appliance Overview (diagram)
       1.3.2 Host Security Policy Reference

Use this outline as a guideline and adapt it to fit the needs of your environment. The following sections discuss each section of this pre-deployment phase outline.

Executive Summary

The executive summary should be a one-page (or less) nontechnical explanation of the NAC Appliance deployment project. It should provide a quick, easy to understand, summary overview of the deployment project plan as a whole. Here is an example:

> Maintaining a reliable and secure data network is critical to the health of our business. Almost all our business functions in some way rely on the network to complete tasks. In an effort to further secure our network from rogue users, viruses, worms, and other detrimental network activity, we have purchased the Cisco Network Admission Control (NAC) Appliance solution. Additionally, industry and government regulations, such as Payment Card Industry (PCI), the Sarbanes-Oxley (SOX) Act, and the Health Insurance Portability and Accountability Act (HIPAA), are mandating that many of the controls that Cisco NAC Appliance will provide be in place on our network. Cisco NAC Appliance will allow us to control who is allowed on the network, what access rights they will have on our network, and ensure that their PC is running the most up-to-date security software. The following phased deployment plan has been put together to ensure that the rollout of the NAC Appliance solution will not adversely affect users or business processes. The three phases that have been defined are 1. proof of concept, 2. pilot, and 3. production. The production phase has additionally been broken into three separate phases. This phased plan is designed to uncover and remediate any deployment issues before the final production rollout phase is complete.

Scope

This section should define the overall scope of the NAC Appliance deployment project. This should mirror the goals set forth in your host security policy document. Try to keep it short and simple. Additionally, it may include details about the following:

- Number and location of PCs affected

- Departments and user types affected

- Location of the NAC Appliance Servers

- Network diagram showing the final solution

Vision

This section should contain your NAC Appliance Solution vision statement. It should also include details about what you envision the future to be like after NAC Appliance is fully deployed. For example, a future vision might be as follows:

> After deployment, all guest and contract workers will be authenticated, authorized, and posture assessed before they are allowed access to the network.

If necessary, create a bulleted list of all your future visions. After this is done, you can use this section to show others how things will be different and enhanced when NAC Appliance is deployed. Use this section to gain political buy-in and support.

NAC Appliance Overview (Diagram)

It might be advantageous to include a diagram of the way the network will look in the future. This diagram will clearly indicate the positions of the NAC Appliance Servers throughout the network. In most cases, the diagram should be fairly abstract at this point. As your deployment plan matures, you will want to increase the diagram's level of detail accordingly. Use the initial diagram as a guide for developing your deployment plan.

Host Security Policy

It is not necessary to include your host security policy document here. Rather, use this section to indicate that such a document exists, and where and how to obtain it. Indicate that the policies contained within the host security policy document will be enforced using Cisco NAC Appliance. For information on how to create a host security policy document, see Chapter 6, "Building a Cisco NAC Appliance Host Security Policy."

Business Drivers for Deployment

To make informed decisions regarding what the goals and scope of the deployment will be, it is important to understand the business drivers and priorities of the project. NAC Appliance has a multitude of features that you could use. The challenge will be in deciding which features you will enable and at what phase they should be tested and implemented. Typically, these feature decisions are based on the business drivers for the project in the first place. This section should include what those business drivers are. To keep the project within scope, be sure to refer to these drivers often. Here are a couple sample business drivers for NAC Appliance:

- Protect the company's intellectual property by ubiquitously denying access to the network until a user successfully passes authentication and authorization. Only those users who are authorized will be allowed access to sensitive information.

- Decrease business-affecting network and PC outages that are caused by security-related incidents such as virus and worm outbreaks.

Deployment Schedule

A realistic deployment schedule should be included as a part of the pre-deployment plan. Be sure to give realistic estimates of the time it will take to roll out a production NAC deployment. Keep this section brief and high level; detailed deployment schedules for each deployment phase will be included separately in the plan. For this reason, it is sometimes best to complete the detailed schedules before attempting to complete this high-level deployment schedule. The sample time frames below are for example only, and should not be used to judge how long a NAC Appliance deployment takes. In some circumstances, the NAC solution can be set up in a few hours or in a few days—the amount of time you spend in each phase is completely up to you. In some cases, you might even skip some phases in your deployment. Here is a sample high-level deployment schedule with sample time frames.

Deployment Start Date: 6/1/2007

Full Deployment End Date: 9/29/2007

- Testing Phase
  - Start Date: 6/1/2007
  - End Date: 7/1/2007
- Pilot Phase
  - Start Date: 7/2/2007
  - End Date: 8/1/2007
- Production Phase 1: Introduction to User Community
  - Start Date: 8/2/2007
  - End Date: 8/14/2007
- Production Phase 2: Security Checks with No Enforcement
  - Start Date: 8/15/2007
  - End Date: 9/20/2007
- Production Phase 3: Security Checks with Enforcement
  - Start Date: 9/21/2007
  - End Date: 9/29/2007

Resources

This section should list all the human and material resources you will need to complete this project. Be sure to include members of the relevant departments in this process. This helps ensure that what you think is available to you from another department is, in fact, actually available. It is usually a good idea to break down the resources list into the phases of deployment. Use this section to list any currently owned material resources that will need to be reappropriated for this project. Do not list any new purchases; they will be listed in the next section, "New Equipment." For human resources, you need not put specific names of individuals in this section because, where appropriate, they will be included in the plan for the individual phases. Instead, just listing the number of people required, characterize the skill sets and list the departments that people will be needed from. If you will be obtaining outsourced manpower, give approximate hours and cost totals. Table 13-1 shows a short example of a resource requisition list.

Table 13-1 *Sample Resource Requisition List*

	Human Resources	**Number of People Needed**	**Description of the Skill Set Needed**	**Relevant Department for Resource**	**If Resource Is to Be Outsourced, List Vendor and Approximate Hours and Cost Totals**	**Purpose**
Pilot Phase		1	RADIUS expert	IT-Networking	N/A	Needed for configuring VPN SSO
		3	Help desk personnel	IT-Operations	N/A	Needed to support pilot users
	Material Resources	**Quantity of Resource**	**Type of Resource**	**Description of Resource**	**Current Owner of Resource (Department and Location)**	**Purpose**
		6	Hardware	Cisco Catalyst 3750 Switches	IT Denver storage	Replacement of old building A closet hubs
		18	Software	Microsoft Windows 2003 Server	IT Corporate license	Needed for setup of new LDAP Authentication Server

New Equipment

Use this section to list all the new hardware that you will have to purchase to complete your NAC Appliance deployment. This might include new Cisco switches in some areas to support out-of-band (OOB) access or a new web server for remediation purposes. Try to give approximate pricing and total costs here. Remember that this section will be used to obtain the necessary funding amounts and later to create a bill of materials.

Support Plan

Indicate what departments or individuals will be responsible for supporting end-user trouble tickets during the various phases of the NAC Appliance deployment. The assigned support personnel might vary based on the deployment phase. If your support staff will need to be augmented with additional resources, note that here and again in the Resources section.

Communication Plan

Provide an overview of your messaging plan to end users regarding the introduction and use of the NAC Appliance solution. Appendix A, "Sample User Community Deployment Messaging Material," includes sample messaging material you can adapt to fit your environment. You might also include a communication plan for the help desk personnel that will be supporting the solution.

Cisco NAC Appliance Training

Develop a training program or plan for your support and implementation teams as well as for your end users. It is a best practice to appoint someone to project-manage the creation of the training plan. It is critical that these personnel be properly trained on the Cisco NAC Appliance solution before it is deployed. The support and help desk personnel should receive training on how the NAC solution works in your environment, how best to troubleshoot any issues that might come up, and what escalation procedures they should follow if they get stuck or the issue falls outside their department. Additionally, your implementation team must include several persons who have advanced knowledge of how to deploy the solution. This can be done either by outsourcing the whole or a part of your implementation team or by sending your own personnel to training. This might include either onsite or offsite training provided by a Cisco-certified training partner. End users will have to be trained on how to use the new system after it is deployed. As a general rule, this training is delivered to your end users via an e-mail, video on demand, or paper mailer, and it does not require a formal training class.

Deployment Plan Overview

The deployment plan is broken up into three main phases. Each phase has several sections. A sample deployment plan outline follows.

Sample Deployment Plan Outline

1: Proof of Concept Phase

1.1: Determine Goal of the Proof of Concept

1.2: Determine Scope of the Proof of Concept

1.3: Determine Criteria for Success

1.4: Work Assignments

1.5: Document Test Plan and Results

1.6: Post-Deployment Review

2: Pilot Phase

2.1: Determine Goal of the Pilot Phase

2.2: Determine Scope of the Pilot Phase

2.3: Determine Criteria for Success

2.4: Work Assignments

2.5: Document Deployment Plan and Results

2.6: Post-Deployment Review

3: Production Deployment Phases

3.1: Production Deployment Phase 1: Initial Introduction to User Community

3.1.1: Determine Goal of Phase 1

3.1.2: Determine Scope of Phase 1

3.1.3: Determine Criteria for Success

3.1.4: Work Assignments

3.1.5: Document Deployment Plan and Results

3.1.6: Post-Deployment Review

3.2: Production Deployment Phase 2: Implementing Host Security Policy Checks Without Enforcement

3.2.1: Determine Goal of Phase 2

3.2.2: Determine Scope of Phase 2

3.2.3: Determine Criteria for Success

3.2.4: Work Assignments

3.2.5: Document Deployment Plan and Results

3.2.6: Post-Deployment Review

3.3: Production Deployment Phase 3: Host Security Policy Enforcement

3.3.1: Determine Goal of Phase 3

3.3.2: Determine Scope of Phase 3

3.3.3: Determine Criteria for Success

3.3.4: Work Assignments

3.3.5: Document Deployment Plan and Results

3.3.6: Post-Deployment Review

Use this outline as a guideline, and adapt it to fit the needs of your environment. The elements that make up the plan for each phase are the same at a high level. The elements of each phase are described here:

- **Determine and state the goal of each deployment phase**   Be sure to pick a goal that is measurable, attainable, concise, and unique to the phase it represents.

- **Determine and state the scope of each phase**   This section might end up being lengthy. At a minimum, it must state the overall mission of the phase. For example, the scope of the pilot phase might be to authenticate, posture assess, and provide remediation services to all virtual private network (VPN) and guest users connecting to the network at the Colorado location. An overview network diagram should be included as part of the scope. Here is an example of some of the things you might include in the pilot phase scope:

  — Access types to be used, such as OOB, VPN, wireless, and in-band (IB)

  — Users or departments involved

  — Types of workstations involved, such as Windows XP, Mac, and so on

  — Types of checks and requirements for host posture assessment, such as antivirus, antispyware, Windows, network scanner plug-ins, and so on

  — Authentication provider types, such as RADIUS, Active Directory (AD), local, Lightweight Directory Access Protocol (LDAP), and so on

  — User role types and privileges, such as guests, employees, contractors, and so on

  — Use of the Clean Access Agent (CCA) and web login

- **Define the criteria for success of each phase**   Because the definition of success can be different for different people, the key stakeholders must agree on a standard measure of success criteria to be used for each phase. After success criteria are defined and acceptable to the stakeholders, the project manager must periodically report on the phase's status. This will ensure that if you meet these criteria, you can claim a successful deployment with all involved. Part of this process is to decide on what variables will be used in the success criteria. Examples include end-user satisfaction, installation success, roll out of CCA's success, help desk support success, and so on.

- **Work assignments for each phase**   A critical component of ensuring a successful deployment phase is agreeing on and keeping track of who is doing what, where, and when. This is accomplished by creating a detailed work assignment plan. Your work assignments section in each deployment phase should list the following:

  — Individuals and departments involved. Indicate who the project or team lead is.

  — Contact information for all involved.

  — Scope of work to be accomplished by each individual.

— Time frame for the work to be completed. If the time frame is long enough, it is beneficial to create milestone dates along the way.

— If applicable, list the location at which the work will be completed.

- **Document deployment plan and results**   This section will include the detailed deployment plan. This section should make up the majority of the documentation for a phase. After the deployment has been completed, the results should be documented here as well. Keeping track of the results will enable you to adjust your future plans and learn from the successes and failures.

- **Post-deployment review**   After the successful completion of a deployment phase, you should bring together the key stakeholders for a post-deployment review. During this review process, be sure to document the following:

— Overall success of deployment. Did you achieve your success criteria?

— What worked well and what didn't.

— The next steps or phase to be implemented.

— Key stakeholders signing off on the completion of the deployment phase and approving the project's completion or moving forward with subsequent phases.

The remainder of this chapter defines in more detail the purpose of each phase in the sample deployment outline.

Proof of Concept Phase

The proof of concept phase is your testing phase. Use this phase to test the various features available in NAC Appliance. Testing will help you narrow down exactly what features you want to implement in your pilot and production rollouts. Be sure to have your testing environment mimic your real environment as much as possible. This will ensure that your test results will accurately reflect those you will find in your production environment. Use this phase to get comfortable with the NAC Appliance solution; be sure to test out each of the production scenarios you will be confronted with. Of course, document everything along the way. This documentation, especially any troubleshooting methods discovered, will be invaluable to you in subsequent phases of the deployment.

If possible, at the end of your POC phase, it is a good idea to rebuild the POC lab to the exact specifications you will have in your pilot phase. When that is complete, rebuild the POC lab to the specifications of each phase as you progress. In this way, the POC lab can serve as an ongoing testing lab for troubleshooting and verifying viability of any configuration changes and new checks before putting them in production. The value of having a complete testing lab to use cannot be understated.

Pilot Phase

The pilot phase will be the first limited production deployment of the NAC Appliance solution. This is where you apply all the knowledge you gained during the proof of concept phase. The pilot phase plan should use the proof of concept testing as a guide to decide what NAC Appliance features and deployment methods you want to use in your production environment. Subsequently, the pilot phase plan should mirror that production vision as much as possible—just on a much smaller scale. You should aim to keep the pilot phase only as big as it has to be for your team to test all the NAC Appliance features you decided on. Keep your pilot small, focused, and simple. A good pilot phase plan should have the following elements included:

- A network deployment plan should be created. This will lay out all the networking changes that have to be made for the pilot phase rollout.

- A NAC Appliance configuration plan should be created. This plan should include the specific NAC Appliance features, functions, and configuration settings that will be used.

- A representative sampling of users, hosts, and network access types (for example, wireless, VPN, wired, and so on) should be incorporated. It is usually a good idea to include some nonuser devices, such as printers, in your pilot phase.

- A host security policy guide should be used or created for the purposes of deciding what security checks NAC Appliance will enforce.

- A NAC Appliance pilot phase support and help desk team should be created and trained. Be sure to keep your support team in the loop throughout the pilot phase— especially for any moves, adds, or changes to the pilot program. Your pilot phase participants should be educated on how and when to engage the support team.

- A solid fallback plan should be created and shared with the support team and pilot participants, as relevant. This will allow the support team to quickly remove users from the pilot and recover from any business affecting outages. Any fallback plan available directly to end users will allow users to remove themselves from the pilot program in the event of a problem. End users should be instructed to alert the support team as quickly as possible of this condition.

- A comprehensive, ongoing feedback plan should be created and implemented. Feedback is typically collected from all parties involved in the pilot phase. This includes any end users, support personnel, IT staff, and management that are directly or indirectly involved in the pilot.

- A documentation strategy should be created and strictly adhered to. The more comprehensive your pilot phase documentation, the better. This will improve the execution of subsequent deployment phases.

The individuals and departments that you choose to take part in the pilot phase should:

- Be located in a part of the network that makes the installation of the NAC Appliance solution feasible and straightforward.

- Allow you to test all the features and functions that your production phases will require.

- Be willing participants with some free time to dedicate to the pilot and the feedback process.

Here are a few other things you may need to consider when developing your pilot phase plan:

- Consider how to deploy the Clean Access Agent to hosts. This might include using a systems management server system, the built-in web download mechanism, or some other means that allows you to install the agent on the pilot hosts.

- Determine what authentication providers, host checks, host requirements, and user roles will be used in the pilot phase.

- Come up with a common naming convention for checks, rules, and requirement names.

- Determine what the traffic control and bandwidth policies will be for each user role.

Production Deployment Phases

Now that the pilot phase is complete, use the knowledge and experience gathered to decide what your final production deployment should look like. It is possible and likely that your organization will have multiple production deployments. For example, you might have a wireless production phase plan, a VPN production phase plan, and a wired OOB production phase plan. Each production deployment will be done on its own time schedule, and lessons learned from each should be applied to subsequent deployment plans.

The final production deployment should come in three phases:

- **Production Deployment Phase 1**   Initial Introduction to User Community
- **Production Deployment Phase 2**   Implementing Host Security Policy Checks Without Enforcement
- **Production Deployment Phase 3**   Host Security Policy Enforcement

This staged approach allows you to identify and address issues before a final networkwide deployment.

Production Deployment Phase 1: Initial Introduction to User Community

Phase 1 includes the initial introduction of the NAC Appliance solution. This includes both the introduction into the network as well as the introduction to the general user community. During this phase, you will install the NAC Appliance Servers throughout your network environment and make all necessary network modifications. You will also install the Clean Access Agent on end-user hosts.

The NAC Appliance solution should be introduced with a very limited set of features enabled. It is recommended that phase 1 be limited to performing user authentication.

If applicable, a user agreement page can also be added to this phase. No host posture assessment or checking should be included in this phase. This phase is designed to get users comfortable using the Clean Access Agent and web login process of authenticating to the network. It is also designed to minimize the amount of change that users deal with at one time. Given that this phase is heavy on the amount of network changes and the potential downtime involved with implementing NAC Appliance, it is a good idea to limit NAC Appliance to performing only user authentication. As a result, your support personnel and IT staff will have fewer things to support and troubleshoot.

All production deployment phases should include a comprehensive communication plan. This plan will alert end users and support staff to the upcoming changes they will experience. It should also include information on how end users can obtain NAC Appliance support.

Production Deployment Phase 2: Implementing Host Security Policy Checks Without Enforcement

Welcome to production deployment phase 2. During this phase, you will start to implement host posture assessment without enforcement. With the changes on the hosts and in the network completed, it is time to introduce host security policy checking. At this point, your users should be comfortable with the operation of the Clean Access Agent and web login. Any NAC Appliance solution kinks should have been worked out, and your environment should be stable before moving on to phase 2.

The goal of this phase is to gradually start implementing host security checks with remediation options. However, users are not yet forced to comply with or remediate any failed security checks. This will allow your user community to become familiar with the checking and remediation process but still have the flexibility to bypass it if necessary. The IT team can monitor the remediation progress users have made through the reporting mechanisms included in NAC Appliance Manager. This will also give you a way to ensure your remediation services are working as planned without affecting a user's ability to log on to the network.

This phase requires that you decide which security checks to start implementing and set up reliable remediation sources that users will use to self-patch their systems. This might include a Microsoft Windows Server Update Services system or a corporate AV system. In many cases, these remediation solutions will already be installed and ready to go. During this phase, users will be alerted by NAC Appliance that their hosts are not up to date and why. It is then up to the users to follow the remediation steps provided by NAC Appliance. Ideally, most users will start to follow these remediation steps and self-patch their systems. It is important that the security updates related to your first few security checks are easy for users to install and do not require users to reboot their machines after updating. You want the users' first few remediation experiences to be as positive as possible.

It is a good best practice to reach out to a few users who have not successfully remediated their systems up to this point. This research can be used to ensure that there are no endemic reasons users are not patching their systems. It may uncover hidden remediation issues that need to be addressed before you move to enforcement of host checks in phase 3. Before moving to the next phase, which involves moving from optional requirements to enforced requirements, your user community must be alerted to the upcoming enforcement. Common methods for communicating this are via e-mail, websites, message boards, flyers, and mailers. The goal is to alert users to remediate soon because, starting at a certain date, enforcement of checks will be applied. Users have to understand that if they do not remediate prior to enforcement, their network access will be limited until they comply.

Production Deployment Phase 3: Host Security Policy Enforcement

After a majority of users run through remediation and are comfortable with this process, it is safe to move to production deployment phase 3. This phase involves enforcing the previously introduced optional security checks. One of the action items for this phase will be to establish a time frame between when a security check should be moved from optional to enforced and required. This established time frame can then be used going forward for subsequent patch cycles from Microsoft and other vendors. By establishing a common time frame for NAC Appliance enforcement cycles, users will learn this process quicker than if you use time frames that vary considerably patch to patch. Of course, when the security risk of a patch is very high, the enforcement cycle should be shortened accordingly.

A critical component of this phase will be ensuring that the help desk personnel are prepared to support the potential influx of support calls from end users. Given the sheer number of operating system, patch level, and installed application combinations present on hosts today, it is almost inevitable that some users will experience trouble installing a required patch. Of course, all due diligence should be taken to thoroughly test each required patch before enforcing it using NAC Appliance.

NAC Appliance includes built-in rules for Microsoft hotfixes and several antivirus and antispyware software vendors. If you choose to use these built-in rules, you give up some flexibility of having new patches from these vendors optional before making them required. In effect, all requirements put together using the built-in rules will automatically start enforcing any new updates released by the supported vendors. This is because NAC Appliance checks with Cisco every hour to see whether the supported vendors have released any new patches. If NAC Appliance finds new updates, it automatically adds them to the existing security checks for that vendor. In some environments, this works well; in others, it can be a help desk nightmare. It is important to note that for antivirus vendor built-in rules, you can set your policy to allow the antivirus data file to be x days out of date before marking it out of compliance. Use the proof of concept phase and even the pilot phase to determine what works best for your environment.

Summary

A solid, phased deployment plan agreed to by all relevant stakeholders is crucial to the success of a NAC Appliance deployment. The main phases are pre-deployment, proof of concept, pilot, and production. The production phase is divided into three subphases. This phased approach should ensure that your NAC Appliance deployment goes well. The sample deployment plan outlines given in this chapter are geared toward larger NAC Appliance environments but can be easily tailored to meet the needs of smaller organizations. It is also important to note that NAC Appliance deployment plans can vary greatly in scope, complexity, and content, and the ones presented to you in this chapter may or may not be appropriate for your environment. It is hoped that the deployment plans presented in this chapter have given you the information, best practice methods, and ideas necessary for you to develop your own customized plan. Overall, Cisco NAC Appliance is a relatively straightforward solution to deploy, but like most things worth doing well, it requires some forethought and planning. Always keep in mind that planning is vital but should not be so daunting in scope that it prevents actually doing something.

PART VI

Cisco NAC Appliance Monitoring and Troubleshooting

This chapter covers the following topics:

- Understanding the Various Monitoring Pages and Event Logs
- Understanding Monitoring of Web Login and Clean Access Agents
- Monitoring the Status of NAC Appliance Manager and NAC Appliance Servers

CHAPTER 14

Understanding Cisco NAC Appliance Monitoring

This chapter covers the most common monitoring techniques and tools available for NAC Appliance. This chapter is written with both the administrator and help desk support tech in mind. It also contains useful information for those who need to test a new installation of NAC Appliance. The pages, logs, and tools discussed here will help the support tech to locate, monitor, maintain, and troubleshoot the various components of the NAC Appliance solution. This includes the client, the web login and agent, the server, and the manager.

Understanding the Various Monitoring Pages and Event Logs

The NAC Appliance solution has several monitoring pages and support logs available. Most of these pages are accessed using the web GUI for NAC Appliance Manager. Many of them are found under the Monitoring section shown in Figure 14-1.

Figure 14-1 *Monitoring Section*

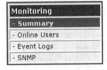

Other pages and logs require the use of the command-line interface (CLI) or the server's direct access web console. The purpose of these pages and log files is to provide administrators with operational information regarding their NAC Appliance environment. This includes clients, servers, system events, and others.

Summary Page

The Summary page is a good place to go to find out, at a high level, how many users, hosts, and NAC Appliance Servers are online. It is also a good place to go to see what Clean Access Agent version is installed. But the primary purpose of the Summary page is to display the online users who are both in-band (IB) and out-of-band (OOB). The Summary page shown in Figure 14-2 gives an example of this. It shows that one user is currently online out-of-band in the Employee user role. The number **1** is a hyperlink that, if clicked, takes you to the out-of-band online users list for the user role Employee. This allows you to quickly obtain additional detail for each user online in a particular role.

Figure 14-2 *Summary Page*

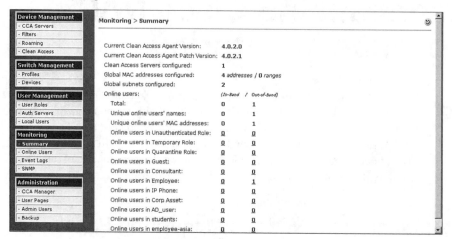

The Summary page shown in Figure 14-2 has several fields, described in Table 14-1.

Table 14-1 *Summary Page Fields*

Field	Description
Current Clean Access Agent Version	The latest version of the Clean Access Agent installed.
Current Clean Access Agent Patch Version	The latest patch version installed and available to clients via auto-upgrade.
Clean Access Servers Configured	The number of Clean Access Servers successfully configured to communicate with the manager. This does not represent how many are online or operational.
Global MAC Addresses Configured	Displays the number of MAC addresses and ranges configured under **Device Management > Filters > Devices**. These devices are set up with alternate access types and do not require authentication.
Global Subnets Configured	Displays the number of subnets configured under **Device Management > Filters > Subnets**. These subnets are set up with alternate access types and do not require authentication.
Online Users (In-Band/Out-of-Band)	Displays the total number of users online and the number of users online in each configured user role. Also provides the number of unique usernames and MAC addresses online.

Discovered Clients and Online Users Pages

The View Online Users page is actually broken down into two separate pages: an In-Band page and an Out-of-Band page. Each page shows the users who are online and using the respective mode of operation. When trying to track down an online user in an out-of-band environment, it is important to understand where a client can be monitored at each stage of its certification. For monitoring OOB clients, you need to be aware of three stages. Each stage requires you to view a different monitoring page to obtain client information at that stage. Table 14-2 shows each stage and its corresponding monitoring page.

Table 14-2   *OOB Monitoring Stages and Pages*

Stage	Certification Stage Description	Monitoring Page
1	Pre-Authentication. Host is moved to the authentication VLAN.	**Switch Management > Devices > Discovered Clients**
2	Post-Authentication. Host posture assessment is performed. Client is in the Temporary or Quarantine role.	**Monitoring > Online Users > View Online Users > In-Band**
3	Client is certified and on its Access VLAN.	**Monitoring > Online Users > View Online Users > Out-of-Band**

The following is an example of how you follow the monitoring of an OOB client as it progresses through the authentication and certification stages of NAC Appliance. Understanding this flow is essential for efficiently troubleshooting clients.

Stage 1   The client plugs into the network; the switch tells NAC Appliance Manager it has a new user on a particular port. The Manager then learns the MAC address of the host. The Manager instructs the switch to move the client's switch port into the authentication VLAN. At this point, the client is not online and therefore will not show up on any of the online user pages.

To monitor a client at stage 1, it is necessary to view the OOB Discovered Clients page. This page shows all the clients discovered from Simple Network Management Protocol (SNMP) MAC-notification or linkup and linkdown traps sent from controlled switch ports.

Stage 2   Relevant only for hosts that fail requirements or are presented with a User Agreement Page (UAP). If the host passes all requirements and no UAP is configured, it moves directly to stage 3. The user successfully authenticates to NAC Appliance. The access method used by the client, web login, or Clean Access Agent makes no difference to the monitoring pages flow. The client then moves to either the Temporary role (Clean Access Agents) or the Quarantine role (web login with network scanner clients). The client is now in-band with its respective NAC Appliance Server. While in quarantine, all traffic travels through NAC Appliance Server.

To monitor a client at stage 2, it is necessary to view the **View Online Users > In-Band** page. This page shows all clients that are actively in-band with NAC Appliance, such as clients in the Temporary and Quarantine user roles.

Stage 3 The client passes the posture assessment and remediation. The Manager instructs the switch to move the client's switch port into the proper access VLAN. At this stage, no client traffic flows through NAC Appliance; therefore, the client is said to be out-of-band.

Clients in stage 3 can be monitored using the Out-of-Band Online Users pages. This page displays all clients that are actively out-of-band with NAC Appliance.

A solid understanding of each of the monitoring pages just discussed is necessary. To that end, each page will be discussed in detail starting with the Discovered Clients page.

Discovered Clients Page

The Discovered Clients page displays all the clients discovered from SNMP MAC-notification or linkup and linkdown traps sent from controlled switch ports. It serves as a location database, letting NAC Appliance Manager know which switch port a particular client (MAC address) is plugged into. The Manager uses this list when it needs to set a VLAN (authentication or access VLAN) for an out-of-band client. When a client first connects to a switch port, the switch sends an SNMP MAC-notification or linkup trap to NAC Appliance Manager. The Manager then adds the client's MAC address, switch IP, port number, and Auth VLAN to the Discovered Clients page. The other fields on the page update as the information becomes available to the Manager. The Manager then sends an SNMP Set request to the switch, instructing it to change the port's VLAN to the proper authentication VLAN. Figure 14-3 shows a sample Discovered Clients page.

Figure 14-3 *Discovered Clients Page*

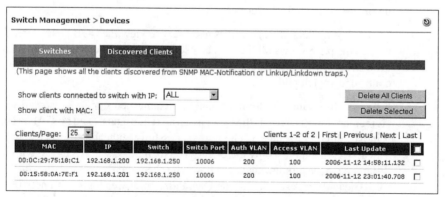

It is possible to delete an entry in the Discovered Clients page. However, this should rarely have to be done and should be used with care. Deleting an entry does not log out the client; it only removes the MAC address-to-switch port pairing. It will not affect a currently logged-in user. However, NAC Appliance Manager cannot set or change a client's VLAN if the client is not listed in the Discovered Clients list. An entry must exist in the Discovered Clients list for the Manager to determine which switch port a client resides on.

Online Users Page

When you are troubleshooting a client issue, the first place you usually start is the Online Users page. This page provides many of the details you will need to start to troubleshoot the issue. It is also the page you would use to log out or kick off a particular client. If a particular client is not found on one of the Online User pages, check the Discovered Clients page.

The Online Users page is broken up into two sections: one for in-band users and one for out-of-band users. The In-Band page shows all users currently authenticated and in-band. The Out-of-Band page shows only OOB users who are on their access VLAN (trusted side). This means that only users who have successfully authenticated and been certified will be shown here. Users in any other OOB state will be shown in the In-Band user pages. The pages of each are very similar. In fact, the only difference between them is that the OOB page has the switch and switch port information added. Figure 14-4 shows an example of an Online Users page for out-of-band clients.

Figure 14-4 *Online Users Page for Out-of-Band Clients*

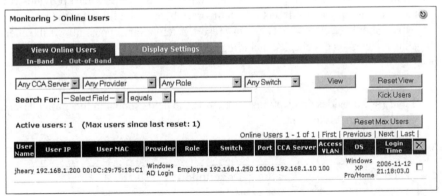

The Online Users page in Figure 14-4 shows that one user is currently online in Out-of-Band mode. This page is helpful for tracking users by IP, MAC, or username. If a network security device, such as an intrusion prevention system (IPS), alerts on a certain IP address, you can use this page to determine whether the address represents a NAC Appliance user. If it does, you can use the **Kick Users** button to remove it from the network.

Figure 14-5 shows an example of an Online Users page for in-band clients. This shows the client in the Temporary role. All users in a Temporary or Quarantine user role display with a green background.

Figure 14-5 *Online Users Page for In-Band Clients*

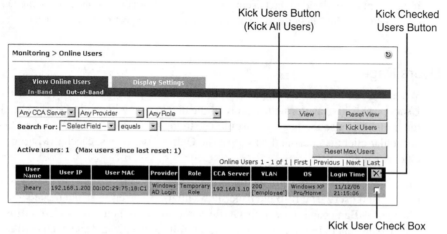

NOTE   Even if you deploy your NAC Appliance solution in Out-of-Band mode, be sure to check the In-Band page because any users stuck in the certification process will be shown there. From a troubleshooting standpoint, the information given there for each user is very valuable. It usually helps you to isolate the issue or at the very least provides you with all the information you need to build a temporary bypass condition for the user. A temporary bypass should be created only as a last resort. A temporary bypass allows the client to avoid all the Clean Access checks, including authentication.

Table 14-3 provides descriptions for each of the fields shown in the Online Users page, IB or OOB, from left to right.

Table 14-3   *Online Users Page Fields*

Field	Description
User Name	Name of the authenticated user. All users who logged in using the **Guest Access** web login button will show up with Guest as their username.
User IP	IP address of the client.
User MAC	MAC address of the client if applicable.
Provider	Authentication provider used.

Table 14-3 *Online Users Page Fields (Continued)*

Field	Description
Role	User role of the client.
Switch	LAN switch that the client is plugged into.
Port	Port on the LAN switch that the client is plugged into. Note: This port number is given in index format. To get the normal format, such as "fastEthernet 0/1/1", go to **Switch Management > Devices > Switch > Ports**.
CCA Server	The NAC Appliance Server that the user is behind.
Access VLAN/VLAN	Gives the VLAN that the client is currently a member of.
OS	Operating system of the client.
Login Time	Time that the user successfully passed authentication.
Kick User check box	When the Delete Checked Entries ![X button] button is clicked, all clients with checks in the Kick User check boxes are logged out (see Figure 14-5).

Both the IB and OOB pages have the capability to filter the page view and search for online users based on criteria you select. The filter options are indicated in Figure 14-6.

Figure 14-6 *Online User Page Filter and Search Criteria*

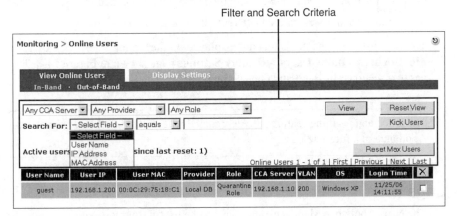

To change your Online Users page view, you can filter on NAC Appliance Server, authentication provider, and user role. To search the online user database, you first choose a search type: client IP address, MAC address, or username. Then you pick an operator, such as equals, starts with, ends with, or contains. Finally, you enter the text or string to search for. For example, Figure 14-7 shows the OOB Online Users view restricted using both view and search criteria. The view shown is filtered using the following criteria:

- NAC Appliance Server = 192.168.1.10
- Provider = Windows AD Login
- User role = Employee
- Switch = 192.168.1.250
- Only IP addresses starting with 192.168.1

Figure 14-7 *Online Users Page Filter and Search Example*

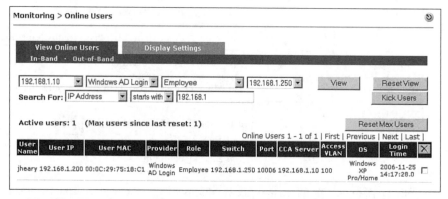

The **Kick Users** button will log out only users displayed on the screen. This means that you can use the search and view filters to narrow down the users who you want to log out. Unlike the ![X] button, which removes only those users with checked boxes, the **Kick Users** button removes all users on the page regardless of their check box status.

You can customize the fields that are displayed on the Online Users page by going to the **Monitoring > Online Users > Display Settings** page shown in Figure 14-8. This page has two sections: In-Band and Out-of-Band.

NOTE   The IPsec and roaming features are deprecated features and will be removed from NAC Appliance in a future release.

Event Logs

The NAC Appliance Manager event logs can be useful troubleshooting and auditing tools. The Manager's event logs can be found under **Monitoring > Event Logs**. There are three tabs here: View Logs, Logs Setting, and Syslog Settings.

The View Logs page presents all the events generated by the Manager, with the most recent events at the top. You can customize the view by changing the search criteria as shown in Figure 14-9.

Figure 14-8 *Display Settings Page*

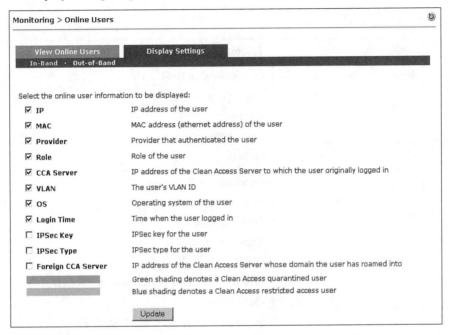

Figure 14-9 *View Logs Page*

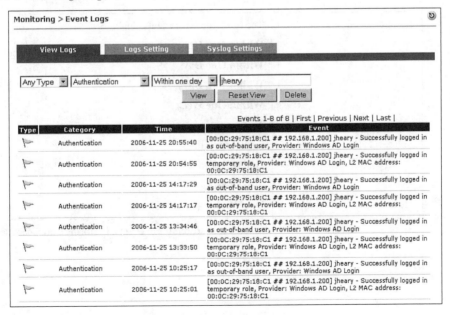

The search criteria available are described in Table 14-4.

Table 14-4   *Event Logs Search Criteria*

Field	Values
Type	Events can be of type **Any type** (all types) **Failure** **Information** **Success**
Category	Events can be of category **Any Category** **Authentication** **Administration** **Client** **CleanAccessServer** (NAC Appliance Server) **CleanAccess** **SW_Management** (Switch Management) **Miscellaneous** **DHCP**
Timeframe	The time frame for events can be **Within One Hour** **Within One Day** **Within Two Days** **Within One Week** **Anytime** **One Hour Ago** **One Day Ago** **Two Days Ago** **One Week Ago**
Event Search string	Enter text to search for in events. Performs a non–case sensitive fuzzy search.

Deleting an event from this page permanently deletes the event from NAC Appliance Manager.

The events are shown below the search criteria and are separated into four columns: Type, Category, Time, and Event. The values for the Type column are represented by the following different colored flags :

- **Red flag** Failure event. Indicates an error or failed operation, such as an authentication failure.
- **Green flag** Success event. Indicates a normal condition or successful operation, such as a successful authentication.
- **Yellow flag** Informational event. Indicates system performance and load information, including those reported by NAC Appliance Servers.

The Logs Setting page under **Monitoring > Event Logs > Logs Setting** has only one setting. The only setting is Maximum Event Logs. This setting specifies how many events should be kept in the Manager's event database. When full, the database will start to overwrite the oldest events first. The value defaults to a value of 30,000 and has a maximum value of 200,000 events.

To have your event messages forwarded to a syslog server, you must configure the parameters under **Monitoring > Event Logs > Syslog Settings**. The following three fields must be configured:

- **Syslog Server Address** This is the IP address of a syslog server.
- **Syslog Server Port** This is the User Datagram Protocol (UDP) port that the syslog server is listening on. The default is 514.
- **System Health Log Interval** This is the interval, in minutes, between system status events. This setting determines how frequently system status messages from NAC Appliance Manager and the NAC Appliance Servers are generated.

The event logs are stored in NAC Appliance Manager's database with the table name of log_info. The locations of other useful logs are shown in Table 14-5. These logs can be accessed via the Linux CLI or via the web GUI. On the Manager, navigate to **Administration > Clean Access Manager > Support Logs** and click the **Download Technical Support Logs** button. On the Server, open the direct access web GUI (https://<Server eth0 IP>/admin), navigate to **Monitoring > Support Logs**, and click the **Download** button. To change the logging level for these files, see the "Understanding and Changing Logging Levels of NAC Appliance" section that follows. The most important files for troubleshooting purposes are the files found in the /perfigo/logs directory on both NAC Appliance Manager and NAC Appliance Servers.

Table 14-5 *NAC Appliance Manager and Server Log Locations*

Log File	Description	File Located On
/var/log/messages	Startup and operating system messages.	Manager and Server
/var/log/dhcplog	DHCP relay, DHCP logs.	Server
/perfigo/logs/perfigo-log0-.log.0	General services logs file. Excellent for troubleshooting. Used for troubleshooting CAM/CAS communication problems, certificate errors, and troubleshooting OOB and database issues. Contains switch management events if logging level is set to Info or finer in the **Administration > Clean Access Manager > Support Logs** page.	Manager
/perfigo/logs/perfigo-redirect-log0.log.0	These are the general Server log files. Excellent for troubleshooting. Used for troubleshooting CAM/CAS communication problems, Active Directory[1], and certificate-related connection errors.	Server
/var/nessus/logs/nessusd.messages	Nessus plug-in test logs.	Manager and Server
/perfigo/control/apache/logs/*	Manager SSL (certificate), Apache error log.	Manager
/perfigo/access/apache/logs/*	Server SSL (certificate), Appache error log.	Server
/perfigo/control/tomcat/logs/localhost*	Manager Tomcat, redirect, and JSP logs.	Manager
/perfigo/access/tomcat/logs/*	Server Tomcat, redirect, and JSP logs.	Server
/var/log/ha-log	High-availability logs.	Manager and Server

1.   AD = Active Directory

Understanding and Changing Logging Levels of NAC Appliance

NAC Appliance Manager and Server have three logging levels available for support logs. They are Severe (the default), Info, and All. These levels can be changed on the Manager using the **Administration > Clean Access Manager > Support Logs** page. They are changed on NAC Appliance Server by using the **Monitoring > Support Logs** page. This page can be accessed only by using the Server's direct access web console found at https://<server IP>/admin. Altering these settings changes the level of detail recorded in the support files found in the /perfigo/logs directory of both the Manager and Servers.

NOTE   Changing the logging level on the Support Log page does *not* affect the events shown in **Monitoring > Event Logs**.

In most cases, if you are troubleshooting a problem, it is recommended that you change the logging level to All. The All logging level should be used with care because it causes the log file to grow very quickly. In addition, the All logging level can use significant system resources. The logging level should be reset to Severe, the default, after troubleshooting has been completed. Logging settings will be reset to default values after a NAC Appliance reboot/restart.

To access the generated log events, you have two options:

- Open an SSH (Secure Shell) connection to NAC Appliance and use the Linux CLI. The files are stored in the /perfigo/logs directory.

- Download the support logs to your PC from the Manager by clicking the **Download** button shown in Figure 14-10, and from the Server by clicking the **Download** button shown in Figure 14-11.

Figure 14-10 shows the Support Logs configuration page for NAC Appliance Manager.

Figure 14-10 *Support Logs Configuration Page for NAC Appliance Manager*

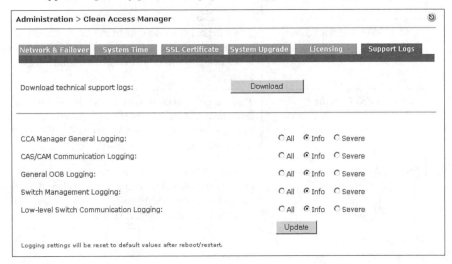

Figure 14-11 *Support Logs Configuration Page for NAC Appliance Server*

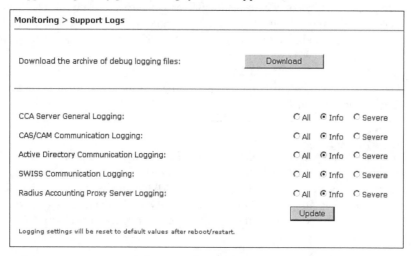

Table 14-6 provides a description of the different log categories found on the Manager.

Table 14-6 *Log Categories for NAC Appliance Manager*

Log Category	Description
CCA Manager General Logging	This category contains the majority of logging events for the system. Any log event not contained in the other four categories listed in this table will be found under CCA Manager General Logging (for example, authentication failures).
CAS/CAM Communication Logging	This category contains CAM/CAS configuration or communication errors. For example, if the CAM's attempt to publish information to the CAS fails, the event will be logged.
General OOB Logging	This category contains generic SNMP errors that can arise from the CAM directly communicating with the switch, such as if the CAM receives an SNMP trap for which the community string does not match.
Switch Management Logging	This category contains general OOB errors that may arise from incorrect settings on the CAM, such as if the system cannot process an SNMP linkup trap from a switch because it is not configured on the CAM or is overloaded.
Low-Level Switch Communication Logging	This category contains OOB errors for specific switch models.

Figure 14-11 shows the Support Logs configuration page for NAC Appliance Server. You will notice that the logging categories on NAC Appliance Server differ from those found on NAC Appliance Manager. Understanding what is logged where will help you during troubleshooting.

Table 14-7 provides a description of the different log categories found on NAC Appliance Server.

Table 14-7   *Log Categories for NAC Appliance Server*

Log Category	Description
CCA Server General Logging	This category contains general logging events for this CAS not contained in the other three categories listed in the rest of this table. For example, a user who logs in (needs to post a request to the CAM) will be logged here.
CAS/CAM Communication Logging	This category contains the majority of relevant logs: CAM/CAS configuration or communication errors specific to this CAS. For example, if the CAM's attempt to publish information to this CAS fails, the event will be logged here.
Active Directory Communication Logging	This category contains log events related to AD communication. For example, if the AD Single Sign-on fails to start, the event will be logged here.
SWISS Communication Logging	This category contains log events related to SWISS (a proprietary communication protocol) packets sent between this CAS and the Clean Access Agent.
Radius Accounting Proxy Server Logging	This category contains RADIUS accounting log events related to Single Sign-On (SSO) for this CAS when integrated with a Cisco VPN Server.

SNMP

Most environments have an SNMP-monitoring tool, such as HP OpenView or SolarWinds, monitoring their network devices. This is done using a combination of SNMP polling and SNMP trap receiving. It is recommended to have your SNMP-monitoring tool poll and receive SNMP traps from NAC Appliance. This is done by configuring SNMP on NAC Appliance Manager under **Monitoring > SNMP**. Note that NAC Appliance supports only SNMP version 1 and SNMP is disabled by default. Clicking the **Enable** button next to SNMP Traps, shown at the top of Figure 14-12, enables both SNMP polling and traps on NAC Appliance Manager. Figure 14-12 shows an example of the SNMP configuration page.

Figure 14-12 *SNMP Configuration Page*

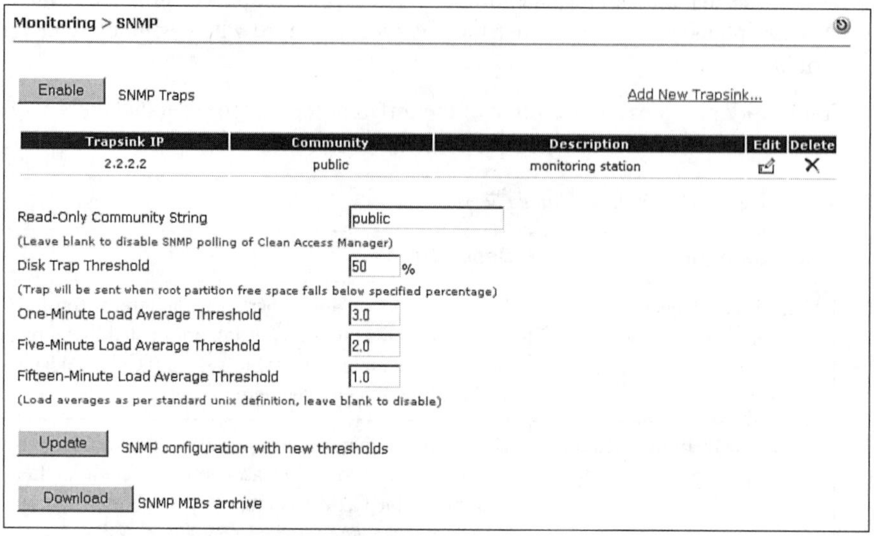

To configure SNMP polling, perform the following:

Step 1 Go to the **Monitoring > SNMP** configuration page.

Step 2 Enter a string value in the **Read-Only Community String** field. NAC Appliance Manager will respond to snmpget and snmpwalk requests sent with the correct community string. Leave the field blank to disable SNMP polling.

To configure SNMP traps, perform the following:

Step 1 Go to the **Monitoring > SNMP** configuration page.

Step 2 Click the **Add New Trapsink** link. A new configuration page opens. You can add multiple trap destination servers in this way.

Step 3 Enter the IP address of the receiving trapsink server.

Step 4 Enter the SNMP community string that all traps should be sent with.

Step 5 Enter an optional description of the trapsink server.

Step 6 Click the **Update SNMP Trapsink Table** button.

Step 7   Specify values for the following fields:

> — **Disk Trap Threshold (%)**   The default is 50%. An SNMP trap will be sent when the root partition's free disk space falls below the specified percentage.

> — **One-Minute Load Average Threshold**   The default is 3.0. An SNMP trap will be sent when the One-Minute Load Average exceeds the threshold specified. This is the same load value that you would find if you issued the **uptime** command from the Linux console of the Manager. For example, a value of 2.0 means that over a one-minute period, two processes were stuck waiting for system resources (CPU, disk, or network) to free up. If the value specified is exceeded, a trap is generated. Leave blank to disable.

> — **Five-Minute Load Average Threshold**   The default is 2.0. This setting is the same as One-Minute Load Average Threshold except that it monitors a five-minute period.

> — **Fifteen-Minute Load Average Threshold**   The default is 1.0. This setting is the same as One-Minute Load Average Threshold except that it monitors a 15-minute period.

Step 8   Click the **Update** button next to the SNMP Configuration with New Thresholds text.

When enabled, the SNMP module monitors the following processes:

- SSH daemon
- Postgres database
- Clean Access Manager
- Apache Web Server

An SNMP trap will also be sent when the following events occur:

- NAC Appliance Manager comes online.
- NAC Appliance Manager shuts down.
- NAC Appliance Manager becomes connected or disconnected to any NAC Appliance Server it manages.
- The SNMP service starts.

Understanding Monitoring of Web Login and Clean Access Agents

Several new monitoring pages become available to you when clients use the host posture assessment features, found under **Device Management > Clean Access**. These features provide insight into the certification process performed for each client. There are also reports that can be generated for auditing purposes. Given that the use of the posture assessment features is highly recommended for most deployments, you should familiarize yourself with their corresponding agent-monitoring pages. There are two main monitoring pages: the Certified list and the Reports page. This section will go into detail surrounding the best pages to use for troubleshooting, help desk support, and general auditing of clients using the posture assessment features through either the Clean Access Agent or web login.

Clean Access Agent Reports

The Clean Access Agent Reports page is an indispensable resource for troubleshooting why clients who use the Clean Access Agent are failing certification. These reports are not available to web login clients. It also serves as a nice auditing and reporting tool. The Reports page shown in Figure 14-13 lists the agent reports. The report list includes the following information: username, user key, user IP, user MAC, user operating system, login time, and Report View icon. Reports from clients that have failed one or more required checks are highlighted with an orange background.

Figure 14-13 *Clean Access Agent Reports Page*

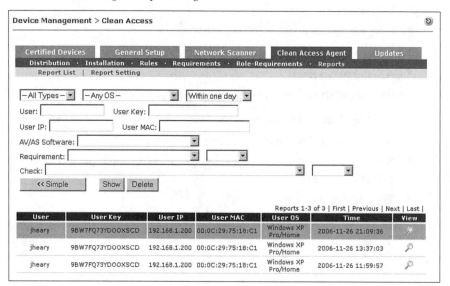

The search criteria shown allows you to customize the view to your needs. For example, a user calls the help desk reporting that he is failing some of the posture assessment checks and wants to know why. To speed things up, you perform a custom search like the one shown in Figure 14-14.

Figure 14-14 *Customized Clean Access Agent Reports View*

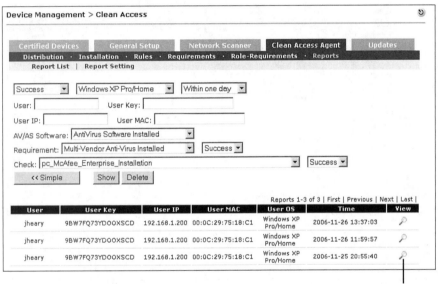

Report View Icon

To find reports efficiently in environments with many clients, using custom views becomes a mandatory practice. You can also use the report search for auditing purposes. For example, you could run a search to find all users who failed the up-to-date antivirus (AV) software requirement. Or you could run a search to find all the users who have the corporate antivirus software installed but not active. Another common use is to search to find the number of users still failing an optional requirement. This will help you gauge what the potential impact might be if you were to start making the requirement mandatory. Ideally, you would like to have the majority of your users passing the requirement before you make it mandatory. This will help minimize the disruption to your user community and your help desk staff.

After you have found the report you would like to examine, click the Report View icon; it looks like the magnifying glass indicated in Figure 14-14. This opens the report, like the one in Figure 14-15, in a separate window.

Figure 14-15 *Clean Access Agent Report View*

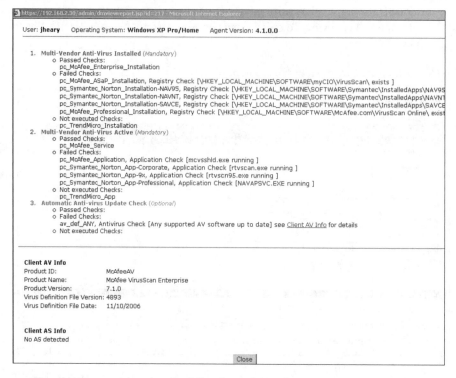

The Agent report contains the following information:

- At the top of the page:
  - Username
  - Operating system type
  - Agent version

- In the middle of the page:
  - Each requirement checked is listed in order. Green is used if the requirement passed, red if the requirement failed. The keyword Optional or Mandatory at the end of the requirement name indicates the enforcement level of the requirement.
  - Under each requirement, the Passed, Failed, and Not Executed Checks that make up the requirement are listed. Failed Checks may be the result of an "or" operation. Checks found under Not Executed are typically there because they do not apply to the client operating system type.

- At the bottom of the page:
  - Client AV Info: This information can be very valuable when troubleshooting failed antivirus requirements and checks.

— Client AS Info: This information can be very valuable when troubleshooting failed antispyware requirements and checks.

The report shown in Figure 14-15 shows the failed optional requirement called Automatic Anti-virus Update Check. This shows up in red on the interface. This is a requirement that checks to make sure the client has up-to-date AV software. As shown, the check looks for any supported AV software that is up to date.

If you look into this further to find out why the check failed, you see that the client AV info indicates that the client is running McAfee VirusScan Enterprise 7.1.0. The virus definition file version is 4893 with a date of 11/10/2006. Next compare this information against what NAC Appliance thinks the latest virus definition file should be to be up to date. To do this, go to the **Device Management > Clean Access > Rules > AV/AS Support** info page shown in Figure 14-16. This page allows you to search the NAC Appliance database to find the latest AV/AS product information. NAC Appliance frequently checks back with Cisco.com to make sure that this database is kept current.

Figure 14-16 *AV/AS Support Info Page*

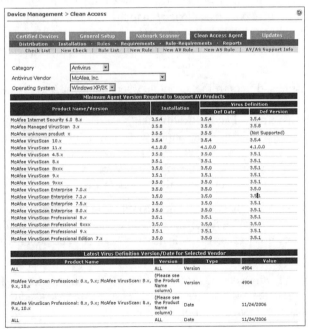

At the bottom of the AV/AS support page, the latest virus definition version and date information are shown for the vendor selected. As you can see, the up-to-date version for All McAfee products is 4904 with a date of 11/24/2006. Because this version is newer than the one found on the client, 4893 with a date of 11/10/2006, the check failed.

Certified List

The Certified list found at **Device Management > Clean Access > Certified Devices > Certified List** shows all the clients that have successfully passed authentication, scanning, and agent certification (posture assessment). This list shows both Clean Access Agent and web login clients. To be in the Certified list, you must have passed user authentication, passed network scanning (if configured), and passed agent certification checks (if using a Clean Access Agent).

When a host reconnects to the network or logs in to NAC Appliance, NAC Appliance Manager checks to see if the host is already listed in the Certified list. If the host is on the list, network scanning (if configured for the user's role) is not repeated until the client leaves the list. However, Clean Access Agents still go through requirement checks regardless of whether they are on the certified list. The only process bypassed by devices on the certified list is network scanning. All other authentication and posture assessment processes happen normally.

If a certified client roams to another NAC Appliance Server and logs in, it will be forced to go through the certification process again. The Certified list is specific to individual servers. A device is certified only when logged in to the server it originally certified on. Given that scanning requirements can be configured to vary from server to server in a NAC Appliance deployment, forcing recertification ensures that the client is rescanned using the local server's policy.

The Certified list differs from the Online Users list in the way clients are added and removed. All clients that have passed authentication are added to the Online Users list. Only clients that have passed authentication and posture assessment are added to the Certified list. For example, a client in quarantine will show up in the Online Users list but not the Certified list. Clients manually removed from the Online Users list are not removed from the Certified list. Conversely, clients manually removed from the Certified list are also automatically removed from the Online Users list.

Another difference is that the Certified list relies on the client's MAC address, whereas the Online Users list relies on the client's IP address and login credentials. If the client's MAC address is not known to NAC Appliance, it cannot be added to the Certified list. This can be the case in some Layer 3 adjacency deployments of NAC Appliance.

The Certified List is a device list based on the host's MAC address. Because the list is not based on username, it is possible to have a host (unique MAC address) remain on the Certified list even though the user on the host changes.

For example, a shared PC using web login has several different users throughout the day logging in to the network and, therefore, logging in to NAC Appliance. If you want to perform a network scan of each PC only once a day, set the certified devices timer recurrence to 1 day. This will clear the Certified list once every 24 hours. The first person of the day to use the shared PC will be scanned, adding the device to the Certified list. Subsequent users will still have to be authenticated but will not be scanned because the host's MAC address is already registered in the Certified list. When the day ends, NAC Appliance Manager clears the list. On the next day, the process repeats itself. Remember that being on the Certified list affects only network scanner execution, not authentication or agent requirement checks; these are always performed.

Figure 14-17 displays the Certified list and the pop-up for device location. The device location pop-up is available only for OOB clients and is accessed by clicking the icon in the Switch column.

Figure 14-17 *Certified List and the Pop-Up for Device Location*

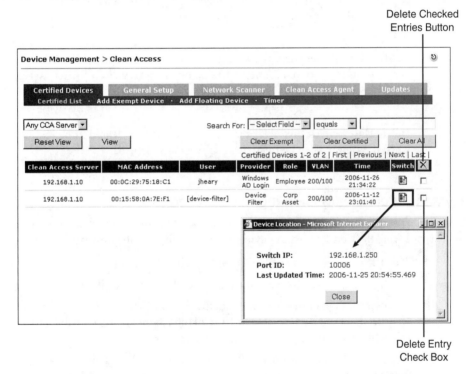

The Certified List page has the following components:

- **Clean Access Server**   Shows the NAC Appliance Server that the client is behind.
- **MAC Address**   The client's MAC address. If not known, 00:00:00:00:00:00 will be displayed.
- **User**   For clients using Clean Access Agent, this column will always show the currently logged-in user. For web login, the username of the first user to log in with this device is shown. If **Certify at Every Login** is enabled for web login, this field will show the current user.
- **Provider**   Authentication source or server used.

- **Role**   The user's role.

- **VLAN**   Relevant only for OOB clients. The format is authentication VLAN/access VLAN; for example, 200/100. For web login clients, only the access VLAN is shown; for example, /100.

- **Time**   This field shows the time at which the original certification of the device took place. It does not show the time the last user logged in. For that information, you would use the Online Users page.

- **Switch**   Relevant only for OOB clients. When the icon in this column is clicked, it pops up a dialog box showing the device's location. The switch IP, port ID (in index format), and last updated time are also shown.

Note   To match the index style port ID (10006) to its port name (FastEthernet 1/1, for example), go to the **Switch Management > Devices > Switches** page and click **Ports** next to the relevant switch.

- **Delete Entry check box**   All checked devices will be cleared from the Certified list when the **Delete Checked Entries** [X] icon is clicked.

Manually and Automatically Clearing the Certified List

If you want to ensure that users are periodically network scanned, you must remove the device from the Certified list. A device remains on the Certified list until

- The list or device is manually cleared by an administrator.

- The list is automatically cleared using the certified devices timer.

- The user logs out or disconnects from the network. The device is cleared only if the **Require Users to Be Certified at Every Web Login** feature is enabled for the user's role. Otherwise, the device remains on the certified list.

You can clear the Certified list manually or automatically. To manually clear the list, you have four options:

- Check the **Delete Entry** check box next to the devices you want to remove and click the **Delete Checked Entries** [X] button.

- Clear all certified devices by clicking the **Clear Certified** button shown in Figure 14-17.

- The **Clear All** button clears both exempt devices and certified devices from the list. This will require you to re-enter any previously exempt MAC addresses using the Add Exempt Device page.

- Clear all exempt devices by clicking the **Clear Exempt** button shown in Figure 14-17. Exempt devices are manually added or added via the API interface of an external program. Devices on the Exempt list are not checked for Clean Access requirements.

CAUTION   If you manually or automatically remove a device that is connected using Out-of-Band mode, NAC Appliance will immediately change the device's switch port back to the authentication VLAN. As a result, if port bouncing is not enabled, the client will be left with a DHCP-obtained IP address relevant only for the access VLAN. It is then necessary to manually issue a DHCP release/renew on the client or wait for the DHCP lease to time out before the client can communicate and log in again. Therefore, a best practice is to clear the certified list only during nonpeak times, such as 1 a.m., weekends, or in emergency cases. This will be fixed in a future release of NAC Appliance. In-band clients do not have this issue, nor do clients in OOB when port bouncing is enabled.

To clear the Certified list automatically, you must create a certified devices timer as shown in Figure 14-18.

Figure 14-18 *Creating a New Certified Devices Timer*

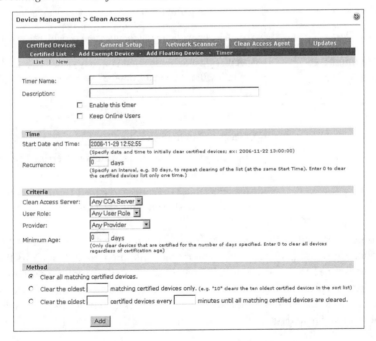

The list will be initially cleared at the start date entered. It will be subsequently cleared according to the recurrence interval you configure. Table 14-8 describes the options found on the Timer configuration page (see Figure 14-18).

Table 14-8 *Certified Device Timer Options*

Option	Description
Timer Name	Arbitrary name.
Enable This Timer check box	If enabled, the timer is active.
Keep Online Users check box	If checked, users who are online will not be removed from the Certified list until they log out or a linkdown trap is received (OOB).
Start Date and Time	Specifies the date and time to initially clear the list.
Recurrence (days)	Specifies how often to repeat clearing the list at the same initial start time. Enter **0** to disable recurrence.
Clean Access Server	Specifies the particular NAC Appliance Server that devices will be cleared from.
User Role	Specifies the particular user role that you want cleared.
Provider	Specifies the particular authentication provider that you want cleared.
Minimum Age (days)	Specifies the minimum number of days a device must be certified before it will be cleared from the list. Enter **0** to clear all devices regardless of their age.
Method	Has three options: **Clear All Matching Certified Devices.** **Clear the Oldest** <number> **Matching Certified Devices Only.** Example: clear the 50 oldest devices. **Clear the Oldest** <number> **Certified Devices Every** <number> **Minutes Until All Matching Certified Devices Are Cleared.**

It is possible, and likely, that you will configure multiple device timers in your NAC Appliance solution. For example, you might configure a timer that clears the list once a month for the Employee user role and have a separate timer for the Guest user role that clears the list once a day. It is also very common to create a timer on a per Cisco NAC Appliance Server basis. Each timer is then set to clear on different days. This lessens the impact on the database and help desk, scales better, and creates a kind of rolling refresh effect.

Requiring Certification for Every Login

If you have a shared PC or a multiuser device, such as a VPN concentrator or wireless controller, and you want each user to be network scanned regardless of the device's presence on the Certified list, you have two options:

- Configure the device as a floating device.

- Check **Require Users to Be Certified at Every Web Login** on the **Device Management > Clean Access > General Setup > Web Login** page for the user role or roles considered necessary. This works only for web login clients.

For shared PCs using either the web login or agent method, it is recommended to enable the **Require Users to Be Certified at Every Web Login** feature.

TIP   Even though the feature reads and configures as if it works for only web login, it also works for Clean Access Agents configured to use network scanning. When configured, this forces every agent user to be recertified and network scanned at every login.

For non-PC devices, it is recommended that you use the floating device method. To configure a floating device, follow these steps:

Step 1   Navigate to **Device Management > Clean Access > Certified Devices > Add Floating Device**.

Step 2   Enter the MAC address, type, and description of the floating device. There are two types available: 0 and 1. Their descriptions are as follows:

— Enter a device with type set to 0 to allow it to be certified for only the duration of a single user session. After user logout, the device must be certified again by the next user.

— Set type to 1 to never exempt the device from certification. This is useful for nonuser devices that channel traffic from multiple users to the network, such as dial-up routers and VPN concentrators.

See Figure 14-19 for a sample configuration of the floating device page.

Figure 14-19 *Sample Configuration of the Floating Device Page*

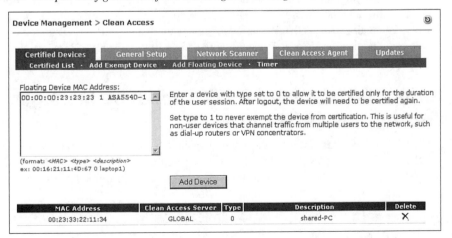

Summary of the Behavior of the Certified List

Here is a summary of the characteristics of the Certified list. This summary includes details for its operation using both the Clean Access Agent and the web login.

- Clean Access Agents always perform posture assessment in the form of checks and requirements at every login.

- For network scanning, a device does not perform network scanning if already on the Certified list. However, if **Require Users to Be Certified at Every Web Login** is enabled, network scanning is always performed.

- For web login, if a device is already on the Certified list, subsequent users of the same host are not forced to recertify the device. This per-user role default behavior can be changed by enabling the **Require Users to Be Certified at Every Web Login** feature. Remember that every user is still required to pass a unique user authentication process. The preceding applies only to network scanning of the device the user is using.

- It only records the username of the client that originally performed the certification. It does not necessarily display the currently logged-in user. To find the currently logged-in user, go to the Online Users list.

- Clean Access Agent always sends the client MAC address to NAC Appliance. This ensures that a client using the agent will always show up in the Certified list regardless of whether it is Layer 2 or 3 adjacent to NAC Appliance Server.

- By default, web login does not send the client's MAC address to NAC Appliance. However, you can enable the optional web client to detect the client's MAC address and operating system. The web client is an ActiveX or Java applet that loads with the Web Login page.

- Manually removing a device from the Certified list also removes it from the Online Users list. However, removing a user from the Online Users list does not remove that user from the Certified list.

- When you remove an OOB client, the client's switch port is immediately moved back to the authentication VLAN. However, if port bouncing is not enabled, the client must manually issue a DHCP release and renew to obtain an IP address in the authentication VLAN. This will be fixed in a future release of NAC Appliance.

Monitoring the Status of NAC Appliance Manager and NAC Appliance Servers

NAC Appliance has several pages where you can obtain the status of the Manager and the Servers. This section will explore the most useful monitoring pages available to you. These pages can come in handy when troubleshooting issues or just monitoring performance.

Manager and Server Monitoring Using the Linux CLI

Both the Manager and Server run Linux operating systems. Specifically, they run Fedora Core 4 with a proprietary kernel. As a result, most of the built-in Linux monitoring commands are available to you via the CLI. If you want more information about the usage of a command, the manual pages are available to you, such as **man netstat**. You can access the CLI via an SSHv2 session to either the Manager or Server. Be sure to log in as root. The most useful CLI monitoring commands are as follows:

- **ifconfig**   Displays the status and configuration information for all Ethernet ports. The interface is connected properly if it displays *UP* and *RUNNING* in the output and shows no packet errors; see Example 14-1 for an example. Note: A small number of packet errors is no cause for alarm.

Example 14-1 ifconfig *Output Example*

```
[root@NAC-Manager perfigo]# ifconfig

eth0    Link encap:Ethernet  HWaddr 00:0C:29:92:C6:05
        inet addr:192.168.3.10  Bcast:192.168.3.255  Mask:255.255.255.0
        UP BROADCAST RUNNING MULTICAST  MTU:1500  Metric:1
        RX packets:180388 errors:0 dropped:0 overruns:0 frame:0
        TX packets:321123 errors:0 dropped:0 overruns:0 carrier:0
        collisions:0 txqueuelen:1000
        RX bytes:18154301 (17.3 MiB)  TX bytes:78289696 (74.6 MiB)
Interrupt:10 Base address:0x1080
```

- **top**   Displays the CPU and memory utilization. It also displays the average load on the device. This command updates/runs continuously; to stop it, press **Ctrl-c**. If your users are complaining of slow NAC Appliance performance, this is an excellent command to run. It will show you the total system utilization as well as the processes using the most CPU and memory.

- **netstat**   If used with the **–rn** arguments, it shows the routing table of the device, such as **netstat –rn**. If run with no arguments, it shows you all the TCP and UDP connections that are active. Under normal conditions, you should see at least two connections between the Manager and Server, similar to the ones shown in Example 14-2.

Example 14-2 netstat *Output Example*

```
[root@NAC-Manager perfigo]# netstat
Active Internet connections (w/o servers)
Proto Recv-Q Send-Q Local Address        Foreign Address           State
tcp        0      0 NAC-Manager:https    nac-server.jheary.com:10285 ESTABLISHED
tcp        0      0 NAC-Manager:32861    nac-server.jheary.com:8995  ESTABLISHED
```

- **cat /perfigo/build**   This command displays the current version of NAC Appliance.

Several other Linux monitoring commands are available, but these are typically the most used.

Manager and Server Monitoring Using the Web GUI

There are almost no pages devoted to monitoring NAC Appliance Manager itself in the web GUI. In fact, there are only two pages of note. The first one allows you view the active administrator sessions on the Manager, and the other allows you to obtain the Manager's version information. The Active Administrator Sessions page is located at **Administration > Admin Users > Active Sessions**. You can also set the auto-logout interval for inactive administrator sessions on this page.

To view the Manager's software version information, head to **Administration > Clean Access Manager > System Upgrade**. Along with the current version information is the list of upgrade logs and details.

NAC Appliance Server has a few more pages devoted to monitoring. These pages are found using the NAC Appliance Manager Web GUI. They are as follows:

- **Status page**   This page, shown in Figure 14-20, lists all NAC Appliance Servers configured to communicate to the Manager. Their current connection status is also shown. Under normal conditions, the page should display a status of Connected. If there is a problem, it will display Disconnected.

Figure 14-20 *List of Servers Status Page*

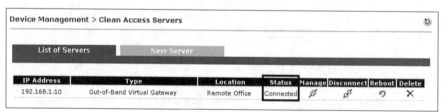

- **Server Process Status page**   This page, shown in Figure 14-21, displays the status of several services. Of particular note is the Active Directory SSO service. If its status displays as Started, you have properly configured AD SSO and it is successfully communicating with its AD domain controller. If AD SSO is not working, this service shows a status of Stopped.

Figure 14-21 *Server Process Status Page*

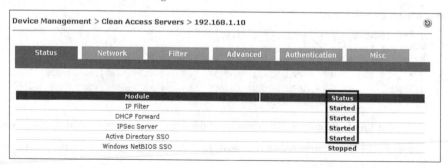

- **Server Version Info page**   To find the current version and the upgrade logs and details, go to **Device Management > Clean Access Servers > Manage > Misc > Update**.
- **Server Failover Status page**   This page, shown in Figure 14-22, shows the current failover state of the server, the status of its connection to the Manager, and its peer server's IP address. This page can only be accessed using the server's direct web access console (https://<server's IP>/admin).

Figure 14-22 *Server Failover Status Page*

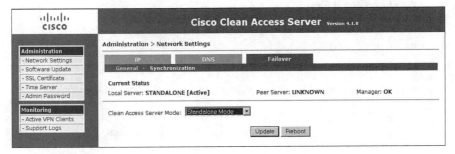

Summary

This chapter covered three main topics: understanding the various monitoring pages and event logs, understanding monitoring of Clean Access Agents, and monitoring the status of NAC Appliance Manager and Servers. The material covered in each topic will assist you in the efficient monitoring and troubleshooting of your NAC Appliance deployment.

This chapter covers the following topics:

- Licensing Issues
- Adding NAS to NAM
- Policy Issues
- Agent Issues
- Out-of-Band Issues
- Single Sign-On Issues
- High Availability Issues
- Useful Logs
- Common Issues Encountered by the Help Desk in the First 30 Days

CHAPTER 15

Troubleshooting Cisco NAC Appliance

This chapter goes through some common troubleshooting scenarios when deploying and working with NAC Appliance. You will learn general troubleshooting techniques and questions to ask when you see a problem with the operation of NAC Appliance.

Licensing Issues

License issues with the NAC Appliance are some of the most common reasons Technical Assistance Center (TAC) cases are opened. Most of the TAC cases are due to customer confusion on what is required to generate a valid license. Licensing with NAC Appliance has changed a few times over the past 2–3 years, and this has added to the confusion.

Prior to acquisition by Cisco, licenses were in the form of license keys, which were strings of letters and numbers. One key covered the license for NAC Appliance Manager (NAM) and NAC Appliance Servers (NAS). Failover capability, if required, was included in the same key.

After the acquisition by Cisco, licenses were put in the form of FlexLM license files. There are separate licenses for NAC Appliance Manager, NAC Appliance Server, and failover capability.

Also, for a short time, Cisco had separate licenses for in-band and out-of-band. Starting from release 3.6(1) (December 2005) onward, there is just one license for both in-band and out-of-band.

Customers receive a product authorization key when they receive the appliances. When requesting license files, the customers have to give the MAC addresses, and this is usually a large source of confusion.

The NAC Appliance Manager license is generated using the MAC address of the eth0 interface of NAC Appliance Manager. If a failover NAM license is required, the MAC addresses of the eth0 interfaces of both the primary and secondary NAMs are required.

The NAC Appliance Server license is generated using the MAC address of the eth0 interface of the NAM. Generating a failover license for NAS still requires the MAC address of the eth0 interface of NAM. This is the most common mistake people make when requesting licenses. *They usually request NAS licenses using the eth0 MAC address from NAS itself.* Also, with the FlexLM licenses, separate license files are required for each NAS. Therefore, if you have 40 NAS instances, you require 40 NAS license files.

If you have the older license keys and are adding more NASs, you will have to convert the license keys to the new FlexLM license files. Open a TAC case with the Cisco licensing team, and its members will convert the licenses for you.

The license page on NAC Appliance Manager has a **Remove All Licenses** button, as shown in Figure 15-1. In case you install an incorrect license file, you can remove all licenses and reinstall from scratch.

Figure 15-1 *NAC Appliance License Page*

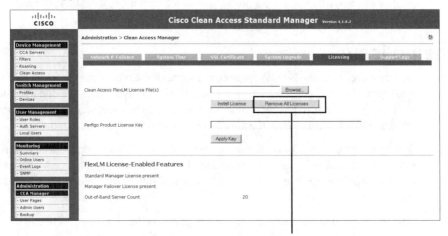

Remove All Licenses Button

Adding NAS to NAM

One of the initial steps in setting up NAC Appliance is adding NAS to NAM. The following are a few things to check if you are not successful in doing so:

Step 1   Make sure that NAM and NAS can reach each other. Go to the command-line interface (CLI) of NAM and see whether you can ping the eth0 IP address of NAS. Similarly, go to the CLI of NAS and see whether you can ping NAM. If this step fails, check the IP address, the subnet mask, the default gateway of the NAM and NAS, and other switch configuration to make sure that routing and switching are configured correctly.

Step 2   From the CLI of NAM, use Secure Shell (SSH) to log in to NAS and see whether any error messages come up. Similarly, from the CLI of NAS, use SSH to log in to the NAM and see whether you are successful.

Step 3   Make sure that the shared secret key on NAM and NAS are the same. You can check this on the NAM and NAS by looking at the .secret file in the root directory, such as cat /root/.secret.

The shared secret key will be a hashed value. However, if this hashed value matches on NAM and NAS, you can assume that the shared secret key has been correctly configured.

Step 4   Check the Secure Sockets Layer (SSL) certificate. For a temporary certificate, make sure that you use the eth0 IP address of NAM when generating the certificate for the NAM, and use the eth0 IP address of NAS when generating the certificate for NAS.

If using certificates based on the DNS name, make sure that NAM and NAS can resolve the Domain Name System (DNS) name to an IP. If NAM and NAS are unable to resolve the IP, you will not be able to add NAS to NAM.

Step 5   Check the licenses on NAM. Make sure that you have the NAS licenses installed for the number of NAS instances that you want to support using NAM.

Step 6   Check the date on both NAM and NAS. The date and time difference should not be more than 5 minutes.

To check the date and time on the NAM and NAS, the command is **date**.

To change the time on the NAM and NAS, the command is **service perfigo time**.

Step 7   If you're adding NAS in Virtual Gateway mode and NAS is connected in Central Deployment, make sure that you disable the eth1 interface before adding NAS to NAM. This is because when you add NAS to NAM, VLAN mapping is not configured yet and can cause a Layer 2 loop to occur in the network. Disable the eth1 interface, add NAS to NAM, configure VLAN mapping, and then you can enable the eth1 interface back up.

Step 8   If you're adding NAS in Virtual Gateway mode, NAM and NAS have to be on different subnets; otherwise, you will not be able to add NAS to NAM.

Step 9 If there is a firewall between NAS and NAM, you have to open up the following ports to allow communication between NAM and NAS:

For 3.6(x), 4.x: TCP 80, 443, 1099, 8995-8996

For 3.5(x) and earlier: TCP 80, 443, 1099, 32768-61000

Step 10 Check the event log on the NAM. This might give the reason NAS is not added to NAM.

Policy Issues

Everything on NAC Appliance is based on user roles. Each user role has a set of access control lists (ACLs) configured. These ACLs are called *policies* in NAC terminology. These policies define what privileges the user has on the network; for example, whether the user has restricted access, Internet access only, or full access. These policies are fully configurable by the network administrator.

When troubleshooting multiple different issues with NAC Appliance, many times you might suspect that NAS might be incorrectly dropping the packet. To quickly isolate the issue in these circumstances, you can configure the policies to allow all traffic to go through for all the user roles, as shown in Figure 15-2.

Figure 15-2 *Traffic Policies Page*

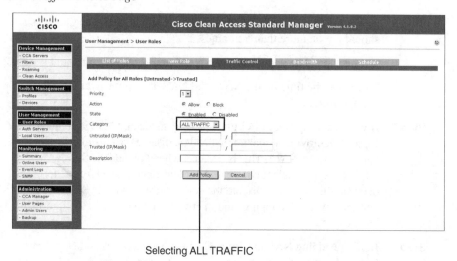

Selecting ALL TRAFFIC

If this is done, NAS will act as a bypass and will not drop traffic.

In the Unauthenticated role, many times you might have to poke holes and allow some traffic type to go through. Some examples are Windows Single Sign-On (SSO) and traffic for patch management applications. Many times you open up the ports for the correct protocols, but still the application doesn't work and you suspect that the NAS might be dropping packets incorrectly. To isolate the issue, you can open up the Unauthenticated role and allow all traffic to go through. If doing this fixes the issue, you know that you have to open up additional ports to make the application work correctly. At this point, you can capture a sniffer trace from the host and see what additional protocol traffic is being sent and open up additional ports on the NAS accordingly.

The NAS, by default, drops all IP fragmented traffic. In an Active Directory environment, some user profiles have additional attributes; therefore, when the Windows host is sending traffic out for authentication, it fragments the packets before sending it to the Active Directory (AD) server. By default, these packets are dropped by the NAS. Therefore, if this occurs, you need to configure a traffic policy to allow IP fragments to go through, as shown in Figure 15-3.

Figure 15-3 *Allowing IP Fragmented Traffic in the Unauthenticated Role*

Allowing IP Fragments

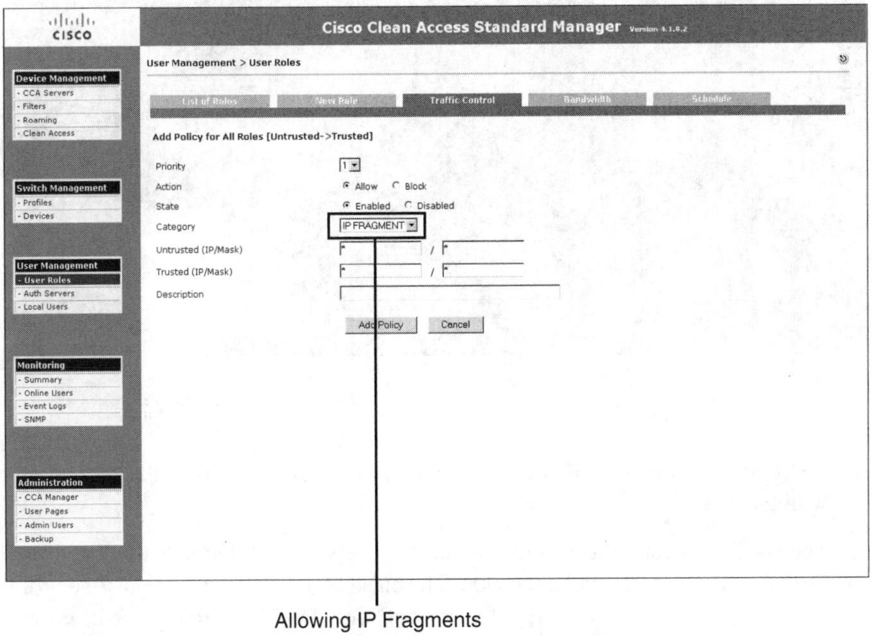

Agent Issues

One of the most common issues customers hit when deploying NAC Appliance is that NAC Appliance Agent does not pop up. On right-clicking the Agent icon on the taskbar, the **Login** button is grayed out, as shown in Figure 15-4.

Figure 15-4 *Login Prompt Grayed Out*

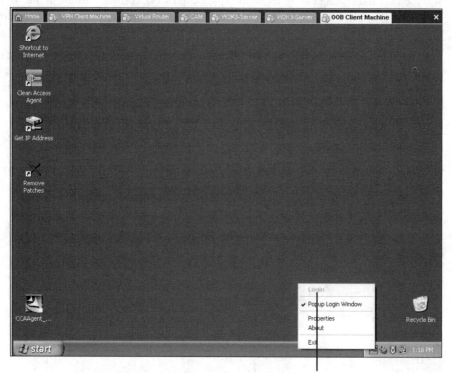

Login Button Grayed Out

To troubleshoot this issue, it is important to first understand how the agent communicates with the NAS.

The NAC Appliance Agent sends unicast packets every 5 seconds on User Datagram Protocol (UDP) ports 8905 and 8906. The packets on UDP 8905 are destined for the default gateway of the end-user device. The packets on UDP 8906 are destined for the IP address configured in the **Discovery Host** field. The discovery host configuration can be found at **Device Management > Clean Access > Clean Access Agent > Distribution**. By default, you populate the Discovery Host configuration with the IP address of NAM.

The agent discovery process takes place as follows:

1   The end user connects to the network and gets an IP address. The agent starts sending UDP packets on ports 8905 and 8906.

2   If the end user is L2 adjacent to NAS, the UDP 8905 packets sent to the default gateway IP will hit NAS before it is able to reach the default gateway. NAS uses these packets to discover the NAC Appliance Agent and instructs the NAC Appliance Agent to pop up on the end-user device. NAS doesn't forward these packets to the default gateway.

3   If the end user is one or multiple hops away (L3), and if NAC Appliance and networking has been configured correctly, for the UDP 8906 packets (from the untrusted side) to reach the NAM (which is on the trusted side), the packets will have to hit the NAS first and the NAS will discover the NAC Appliance Agent.

The discovery host can be configured to be any IP that exists on the trusted side of the network and is reachable and routable. By default, you prepopulate this with the NAM IP because you know that NAM exists on the trusted side of the network, and it has to exist for NAC Appliance to work.

This is also the reason that NAC Appliance Agent has to be downloaded from NAS and cannot be downloaded from Cisco.com to use for end users if the end users are L3 hops away. The NAC Appliance Agent file from Cisco.com will not have the discovery host configuration; therefore, NAC Appliance Agent will not know which destination IP to use for the UDP 8906 packets. You can view the discovery host IP by right-clicking the **NAC Appliance Agent** icon on the client taskbar and selecting **Properties**.

The key points to be noted here are that for NAC Appliance Agent to pop up, the NAC Appliance Agent discovery packets have to reach the NAS, and the NAS should be able to send packets back to the end-user device. The following are a few things to check if NAC Appliance Agent is not popping up:

Step 1   Check whether the user device is sending packets on UDP ports 8905 and 8906. You can take a quick sniffer trace using Ethereal or any other packet capture utility.

Step 2   Check whether there is a personal firewall on the user's device that might be blocking the NAC Appliance Agent discovery packets on UDP ports 8905 and 8906.

Step 3   Check whether the NAC Appliance Agent discovery packets are hitting the untrusted port of NAS. You can capture a sniffer trace on the switch port connecting the untrusted port of the NAS. This will show you if the NAC Appliance Agent discovery packets are actually sent toward NAS. Another way of checking this is to use the tcpdump utility on the NAS untrusted port. The tcpdump utility on NAS does not display any traffic that is sent through NAS. The agent discovery packets sent on UDP 8905 can be seen using the tcpdump utility, as shown in Example 15-1; however, the discovery packets on UDP 8906 cannot be seen with the tcpdump utility. Therefore, if NAS is L2 adjacent to the user, you can also use the tcpdump utility on NAS to check whether NAS is receiving the NAC Appliance Agent discovery packets.

Example 15-1 *TCPDump Showing UDP 8905 Packets*

```
[root@CAS_OOB ~]# tcpdump -i eth1 -vv
tcpdump: listening on eth1, link-type EN10MB (Ethernet), capture size 96 bytes
03:09:53.445063 IP (tos 0x0, ttl 128, id 9459, offset 0, flags [none], proto 17,
length: 99)
 10.60.60.6.1990 > 10.60.60.2.8905: UDP, length 71
03:09:58.500124 IP (tos 0x0, ttl 128, id 9474, offset 0, flags [none], proto 17,
length: 103)
 10.60.60.6.1991 > 10.60.60.2.8905: UDP, length 75
```

Step 4　If you don't see NAC Appliance Agent discovery packets hitting the untrusted port of NAS, you need to track down the path of these packets from the user and find out whether there is any network misconfiguration.

Step 5　If the user is L2 adjacent to the NAS, check whether managed subnets have been configured for the users subnet. Make sure that the managed subnet section has an IP address configured and not a subnet address. This is so that NAS has a virtual IP in that subnet to facilitate NAS getting an Address Resolution Protocol (ARP) entry for the user device. If managed subnets are not configured, NAS will not be able to determine the IP address-to-MAC address mapping of the user and will not be able to send return traffic back to the user.

Step 6　If the user is multiple hops (L3) away from the NAS, make sure that the user's subnet is not configured in the managed subnet section. However, you should configure static routes for the user subnet.

Step 7　Get a sniffer trace on the user's switch port and check whether return traffic from the NAS is reaching the user.

Step 8　If all else fails, the last thing to check is the Clean Access Agent debug logs.

The Clean Access Agent debug logs can be enabled and captured using the following procedure:

Step 1　Exit Clean Access Agent on the client by right-clicking the taskbar icon and selecting **Exit**.

Step 2   Edit the registry of the client by going to **Start > Run** and typing **regedit** in the **Open:** field of the Run dialog. The Registry Editor opens.

Step 3   Navigate to HKEY_CURRENT_USER\Software\Cisco\Clean Access Agent\ in the Registry Editor.

Note that for 3.6.0.0/3.6.0.1, and 3.5.10 and earlier, HKEY_LOCAL_MACHINE\Software\Cisco\Clean Access Agent\ is the correct location.

Step 4   If LogLevel is not already present in the directory, go to **Edit > New > String Value** and add a string to the Clean Access Agent key called **LogLevel**.

Step 5   Right-click **LogLevel** and select **Modify**. The Edit String dialog appears.

Step 6   Type **debug** in the Value data field and click **OK**. (This sets the value of the LogLevel string to "debug.")

Step 7   Restart Clean Access Agent by double-clicking the desktop shortcut.

Step 8   Re-log in to the Clean Access Agent.

Step 9   When a requirement fails, click the **Cancel** button in Clean Access Agent.

Step 10 Take the resulting event.log file from the home directory of the current user (for example, C:\Documents and Settings\<username>\Application Data\CiscoCAA\event.log) and send it to TAC customer support.

NOTE   For 3.6.0.0/3.6.0.1 and 3.5.10 and earlier, the event.log file is located in the Agent installation directory (for example, C:\Program Files\Cisco Systems\Clean Access Agent\).

For 3.5.0 and earlier, the Agent installation directory is C:\Program Files\Cisco\Clean Access\.

The debug file is not in readable format and can be decoded only by Cisco TAC.

For any other issues involving Windows Single Sign-On, posture assessment, or remediation carried out by the agent, TAC will always request that you enable agent debug logs and send them. Therefore, knowing the procedure to enable the debug logs is important.

Out-of-Band Issues

When troubleshooting out-of-band issues, looking at the out-of-band (OOB) process and finding out what process or phase of OOB is failing is recommended. Doing so will help you isolate the issue quickly and attack the problem.

Step 1   Check whether the user's switch port is moved to the authentication VLAN when the user first connected to the switch port. If the user is not being moved to the authentication VLAN, do the following:

(a) Check whether the switch is generating a Simple Network Management Protocol (SNMP) linkup or MAC-notification trap. This can be done by running SNMP debugs on the switch:

debug snmp header
debug snmp packet

— Check whether the trap is being received by NAM. This can be done by capturing a sniffer trace or by using tcpdump on NAM. If NAM correctly receives the SNMP trap from the switch, the device immediately shows up in the discovered clients list, as shown in Figure 15-5, which is located at **Switch Management > Devices > Discovered Clients**.

Figure 15-5 *Discovered Clients List Page*

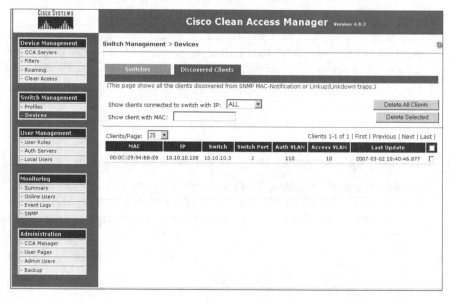

— Look at the support logs on NAM. For OOB, the main log file to look at is located at /perfigo/logs/perfigo-log0.log.0. This log file will give information on what happens if the SNMP trap is received by NAM.

— Check whether the user device already exists in the online user list. If the user already exists in the online user list, as shown in Figure 15-6, NAM will not instruct the switch port to be moved to the authentication VLAN.

Figure 15-6 *Online User List*

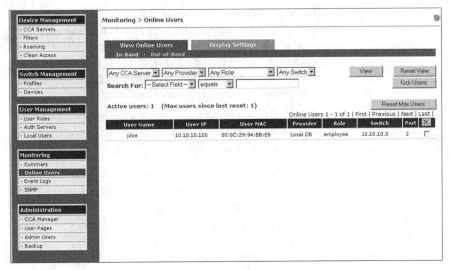

— Next, check whether NAM sends SNMP set messages to the switch to move the user to the authentication VLAN. Again, run SNMP debugs on the switch to see whether the switch is receiving these SNMP sets from NAM and if the switch processes these packets.

If the switch port VLAN is being changed to the authentication VLAN, go to the next step.

Step 2 Check whether the traffic from the user in the authentication VLAN is reaching the untrusted port of NAS.

The simplest way to check this is to get a sniffer trace on the switch port connecting the untrusted port of the NAS. To troubleshoot any networking misconfigurations, determine the IP and MAC of the end user device and then check the ARP and MAC address tables on the L2 and L3 switches to make sure that the entries look correct.

If you determine that traffic from the user in the authentication VLAN is hitting the untrusted port of the NAS, go to the next step.

Step 3   Ensure that managed subnet is configured for user subnets that are Layer 2 adjacent to NAS and static routes are configured for user subnets that are multiple hops away from the NAS. Check whether you can ping from the NAS to the host in the authentication VLAN.

Step 4   On the user device, open a browser and check whether you are redirected to a web login page. If HTTP or HTTPS packets from the user device reach NAS, it will be automatically redirected to the web login page. If NAS does not redirect you, check for the following:

> (a)   Check whether you have the right DNS server settings. Check whether the user device is able to resolve the URL to which it is trying to go. If the user device is unable to resolve the URL, it will not send HTTP/HTTPS packets out and will display a Page Not Found page, giving the impression that page redirect has failed.
>
> — Also check the log file located at /perfig/access/ apache/logs/error_log. If the certificate on the NAS is not valid, you will see an error message in the logs.
>
> — Check whether the httpd service has been started on the NAS. You can check this by the command **netstat –al | grep http** on NAS.
>
> ```
> netstat -al | grep http
> tcp        0        0 *:http          *:*          LISTEN
> tcp        0        0 *:https         *:*          LISTEN
> ```
>
> — Check whether a user page has been configured on the NAM.
>
> — Connect a test PC directly into the untrusted port of the NAS and check whether redirect to the web login page occurs. This will bypass any network issues and immediately prove whether it is a networking issue or an issue with NAS.
>
> — Check whether the user device has multiple network interface cards (NICs) enabled. At the time of writing this chapter, NAC Appliance did not have support for enabling multiple NICs on the user device.

Step 5   If the Agent does pop up or you are redirected to a web login page, the next step is to check whether the user is able to authenticate.

Step 6   The next step is to check whether the user shows up in the online user list and if the user shows up in the correct user role.

Step 7   Check the reports to get information regarding the posture of the end-user device, as shown in Figure 15-7.

Figure 15-7   *User Reports Page*

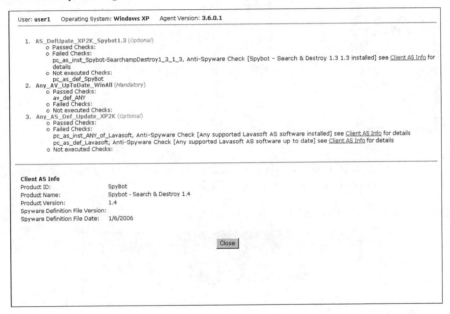

Step 8   Check whether the user has been moved to the correct access VLAN based on either port-based VLAN or user role–based VLAN mapping.

If you follow these troubleshooting steps, you will be able to isolate the issue in a logical manner and focus your attention on that particular phase of the out-of-band process. Later you will cover certain error conditions that occur with out-of-band.

The error message in Figure 15-8 shows up if the community string on the NAM configuration does not match the configuration on the switch.

Figure 15-8 *Error Message If Unable to Add Switch to NAC Appliance Manager*

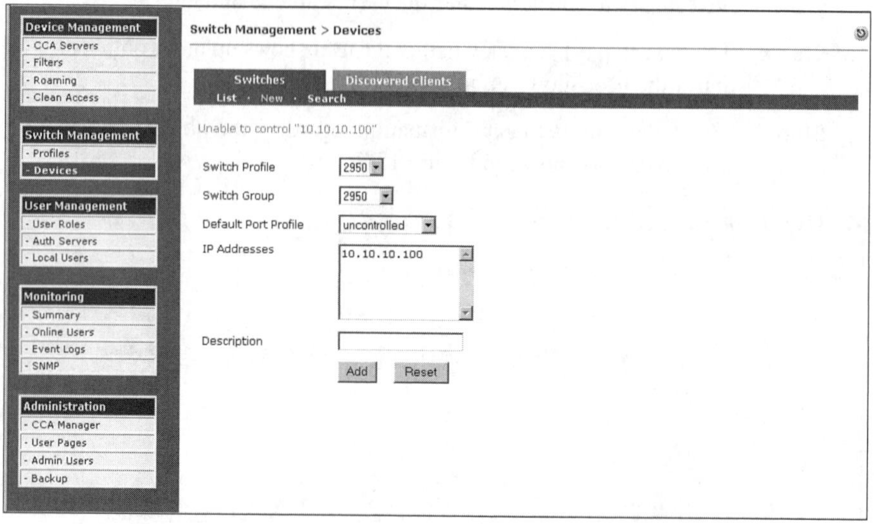

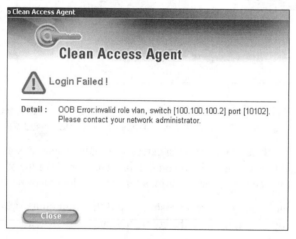

Another error that shows up is displayed in Figure 15-9. This occurs if user role–based VLAN assignment is being used with OOB.

Figure 15-9 *Error Message If OOB VLAN in the User Role Is Not Configured*

This message shows up if there is no OOB VLAN configured under the user role as shown in Figure 15-10.

Figure 15-10 *OOB VLAN Configuration on the User Role Page*

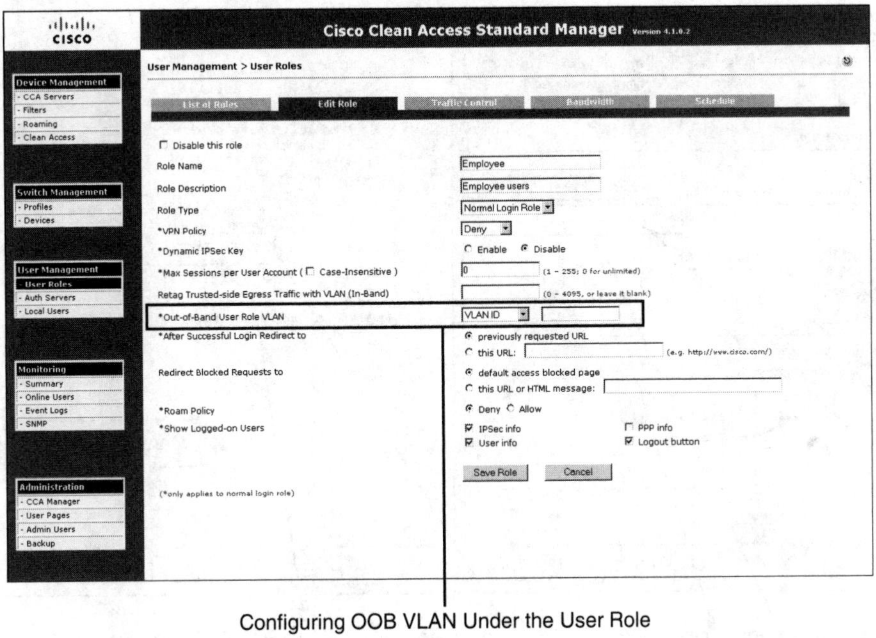

Configuring OOB VLAN Under the User Role

Single Sign-On Issues

This section covers single sign-on issues when configuring Windows Single Sign-On and virtual private networking (VPN) or Wireless Single Sign-On.

AD SSO

When configuring AD SSO, the most common mistake is not having the correct **ktpass** command.

Figure 15-11 shows a sample **ktpass** command. It shows you where the relevant information should be taken from. The computer name that is between the / and the @ should match case-by-case with the full computer name, as shown in Figure 15-11. The Realm Name, which is after the @ sign, should always be in capital letters.

Figure 15-11 *Sample* **ktpass** *Command*

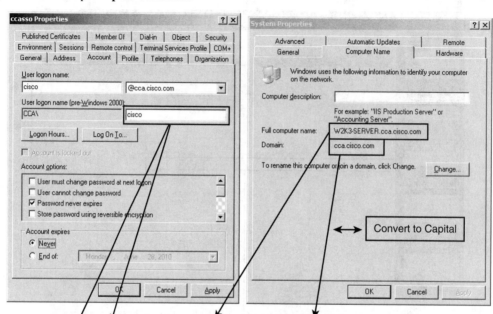

ktpass -princ cisco/W2K3-SERVER.cca.cisco.com@CCA.CISCO.COM -mapuser
cisco --pass Cisco123 - out c:\cca.keytab -ptype KRB5_NT_PRINCIPAL +DesOnly

In case any mistake is made in the **ktpass** command, the generated keytab file (cca.keytab, in this case) should be deleted before running the command again.

When configuring NAS for AD SSO, you might find that the AD service does not start. The error message in Figure 15-12 can show up due to several reasons.

The following are a few of the things that you will check if you see the error message in Figure 15-12:

- If the **ktpass** command was not run correctly on the domain controller, or the configuration parameters on NAS have been entered incorrectly, it will prevent the AD SSO service from starting on the NAS.

- The Active Directory has to be in capital letters.

- The Active Directory Server (fully qualified domain name [FQDN]) should match case-by-case as it appears on the Active Directory server.

- The FQDN cannot be an IP address. It has to be a DNS host name and should be resolvable by the NAS. Ping the DNS host name from the NAS and ensure that the NAS is able to resolve it and reach the AD server.

Figure 15-12 *SSO Service Unable to Start on NAC Appliance Server*

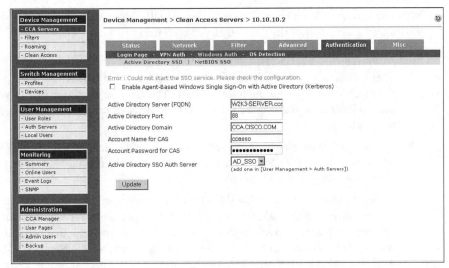

- Make sure that the time between NAS and the AD server is synchronized within 5 minutes.
- On the NAS support log page, increase the logging level for AD communication logging to the info level. Then re-create the issue and check the log file located at /perfigo/logs/perfigo-redirect-log0.log.0. This log file should give useful information regarding why the SSO service is not starting on the NAS.

Another issue that you might run into is on the user side. Assume that everything is configured correctly. However, on the agent PC, NAC Appliance Agent still asks for a manual login instead of using Single Sign-On. The following are some things to check if this happens:

- If there is some communication problem between the user's PC and the AD server, or between the NAS and the AD server, this issue can occur. Check whether there is connectivity between these devices.
- Confirm if you are logged in to the domain and the user has the correct Kerberos keys.
- On the NAC Appliance Unauthenticated user role, make sure that the correct ports are open to the AD server. Most AD servers use the standard ports; however, in some installations, custom ports might be used. Therefore, you might have to open ports in addition to the standard ports that Cisco recommends. The ports to be opened can be determined by taking a sniffer trace on the user's PC and checking what ports are being used for the authentication purposes.
- Capture the Agent debug logs.
- On NAS, check whether it is listening on port 8910.
- Check the TCP and UDP ports necessary for SSO to work in the Unauthenticated user role.

VPN and Wireless SSO

VPN and wireless SSO rely on NAS receiving RADIUS accounting packets. If SSO fails, the following are a few of the things that you can check:

- Check whether there is connectivity between the VPN or wireless device and NAS.

- Check whether the RADIUS accounting packet is reaching the NAS trusted port. This can be checked by capturing a sniffer trace. You can also check the /perfigo/logs/perfigo-redirect-log0.log.0 log file to see whether NAS received the RADIUS accounting packet.

- Check whether the shared secret settings match between the NAS and the VPN or wireless device. If they don't match, you will see an error message in the /perfigo/logs/perfigo-redirect-log0.log.0 log file.

- If NAS has successfully received RADIUS accounting information from the VPN or wireless device, it will add the user's information in a temporary table that it uses to determine whether it should do SSO for a subsequent user with that particular IP address. This table can be viewed at **Device Management > CCA Servers > Manage > Authentication > VPN Auth > Active Clients > Show All**, as shown in Figure 15-13.

Figure 15-13 *Active Clients Table*

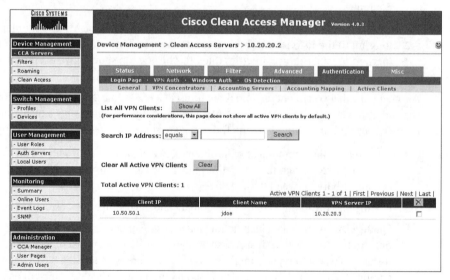

High Availability Issues

NAM and NAS rely on heartbeat packets for the high availability solution. Most issues occur due to heartbeat packets not reliably reaching the peers.

NAM GUIs on both the primary and the secondary NAM don't directly tell you whether they have the correct status of each other from an active/standby point of view. The GUI on the standby NAM does not show all the tabs on the left side of the page; therefore, you can deduce that it is the standby NAM.

You can look up the high availability configuration on the NAM by looking at the following files:

- /etc/ha.d/perfigo/conf
- /etc/ha.d/ha.cf

You can look up the HA status of a NAM from the CLI as follows:

Step 1   Go to the /store directory.

Step 2   Check whether there is an upgrade folder present, such as cca_upgrade-4.1.0.2.

Step 3   Inside the upgrade folder, you will find a script called fostate.sh. Run that script.

The active NAM will show the following output:

```
[root@cam1 cca_upgrade-4.1.0.2]# ./fostate.sh
My node is active, peer node is standby
```

The standby NAM will show the following output:

```
[root@cam2 cca_upgrade-4.1.0.2]# ./fostate.sh
My node is standby, peer node is active
```

If you have installed NAM using an ISO image and have not done any upgrades, you will not find an upgrade folder in the /store folder. In that case, you can find the HA status of the NAM as follows:

Step 1   Find the host names of the NAMs (nodes) from the /etc/ha.d/ha.cf file:

```
[root@cam1 ha.d]# more ha.cf
#Generated by make-hacf.pl
udpport          694
bcast            eth1
auto_failback    off
apiauth          default uid=root
log_badpack      false
debug            0
```

```
debugfile        /var/log/ha-debug
logfile          /var/log/ha-log
#logfacility     local0
watchdog         /dev/watchdog
keepalive        2
warntime         10
deadtime         15
node             cam1
node             cam2
```

Step 2   Run the command **/perfigo/control/bin/check-ha** *node* and see whether
the output shows up as "active":

```
[root@cam1 ~]# /perfigo/control/bin/check-ha cam1
active

[root@cam1 ~]# /perfigo/control/bin/check-ha cam2
active
```

Step 3   Go to /perfigo/contro/tomcat and type **ls -la**.

Step 4   If "webapps" is pointing to "normal-webapps," it is the primary NAM:

```
[root@cam1 tomcat]# ls -la
total 216
drwxr-xr-x  12 root root  4096 Sep 14 23:28 .
drwxr-xr-x   8 root root  4096 Aug 28 22:12 ..
drwxr-xr-x   4 root root  4096 Aug 28 22:12 admin-webapps
<output cut.....>
drwxr-xr-x   2 root root  4096 Aug 28 22:12 temp
lrwxrwxrwx   1 root root    38 Sep 14 23:28 webapps -> /perfigo/control/
tomcat/normal-webapps
drwxr-xr-x   3 root root  4096 Aug 28 15:15 work
```

Step 5   If "webapps" is pointing to "admin-webapps," it is the secondary NAM:

```
[root@cam2 tomcat]# ls -la
total 216
drwxr-xr-x  12 root root  4096 Sep 14 23:33 .
drwxr-xr-x   8 root root  4096 Sep 15  2006 ..
drwxr-xr-x   4 root root  4096 Sep 15  2006 admin-webapps
<output cut …>
drwxr-xr-x   2 root root  4096 Sep 15  2006 temp
lrwxrwxrwx   1 root root    37 Sep 14 23:33 webapps -> /perfigo/control/
tomcat/admin-webapps
drwxr-xr-x   3 root root  4096 Sep 14 23:25 work
```

If you determine that NAMs are not detecting each other in correct status, the following logs files will help you isolate the issue further:

- /var/log/ha-log
- /var/log/ha-debug

For NAC Appliance Server, the GUI shows the HA status on the NASs themselves. You can look up the HA config on the NAS CLI using the /etc/ha.d/perfigo.conf and /etc/ha.dha.cf files, as shown in Example 15-2.

Example 15-2   *HA Configuration as Seen via CLI*

```
 [root@cas1 ha.d]# more perfigo.conf
#linux-ha
#Mon Jan 16 18:50:15 PDT 2007
WIRELESS_SERVICEIP=10.10.20.4
PING_DEAD=25
HOSTNAME=cas1
HA_DEAD=15
PEERGUSSK=
PEERMAC=00\:16\:35\:BF\:FE\:67
PEERHOSTNAME=cas2
TRUSTED_PINGNODE=10.10.40.100
UNTRUSTED_PINGNODE=10.10.20.100
HAMODE=PRIMARY
PEERMAC0=00\:16\:35\:BF\:FE\:66
PEERHOSTIP=10.10.50.2
HA_FAILBACK=off
HA_UDP=eth2
WIRED_SERVICEIP=10.10.20.4
HA_SERIAL=ttyS0

[root@cas1 ha.d]# more ha.cf
# Generated by make-hacf-ss.pl
udpport         694
ucast           eth2 10.10.50.2
baud            19200
serial          /dev/ttyS0
keepalive       2
deadtime        15
deadping        25
auto_failback   off
apiauth         default uid=root
respawn         hacluster /usr/lib64/heartbeat/ipfail
ping            10.10.20.100
ping            10.10.40.100
log_badpack     false
warntime        10
debug           0
debugfile       /var/log/ha-debug
logfile         /var/log/ha-log
watchdog        /dev/watchdog
node            cas1
node            cas2
```

The HA status on the NAS CLI can be viewed similar to the way it is for NAM:

```
[root@cas1 cca_upgrade-4.1.0.2]# ./fostate.sh
My node is active, peer node is standby

[root@cas2 cca_upgrade-4.1.0.2]# ./fostate.sh
My node is standby, peer node is active
```

For further troubleshooting purposes, the following two files give important information:

* /var/log/ha-log
* /var/log/ha-debug

Useful Logs

This section lists some of the log on NAM and NAS that are useful for troubleshooting purposes.

NAM Logs

The following two logs files can be seen on NAM:

* **/var/log/messages**   This is a general log file and has information regarding driver- and system-level errors, messages seen during reboots, and kernel panic messages.

* **/perfigo/logs/perfigo-log0.log.0**   This is an important log file and shows whether there are any errors in NAM and NAS communication, all errors related to OOB, switch communication, and authentication.

NAS Logs

The following log files can be seen on NAS:

* **/var/log/messages**   This log file consists of the same information as the NAM log file.

* **/perfigo/logs/perfigo-redirect-log0.log.0**   This log file shows information regarding errors in NAM and NAS communication, errors related to single sign-on using RADIUS and for Windows Single Sign-On, user authentication errors, and certificate errors.

* **/perfigo/access/apache/logs/access_log**   This log file shows users accessing the web login page on NAS. If an end user is not getting redirected to a web login page, you can view this log to see whether NAS is receiving the user's HTTP or HTTPS traffic.

- **/var/log/dhcplog**   This log file shows all the DHCP events when NAS is configured in Real-IP Gateway mode and is configured to be the DHCP server. This log is good to see whether you're troubleshooting why a user is not getting an IP address.

- **/etc/sysconfig/network-scripts/ifcfg-eth0 or eth1**   This log file shows the configuration for the eth0 and the eth1 interfaces.

- **/proc/click/intern_arpq/table**   This log has the ARP entries for devices on the untrusted network, which are Layer 2 adjacent to NAS.

- **/proc/click/extern_arpq/table**   This log has the ARP entries for devices on the trusted network.

- **/proc/click/real_routing_table/table**   This log shows the routing table on NAS.

Additional Logs

The following are some additional logs that can be viewed on NAM and NAS for troubleshooting purposes:

- **netstat -an**   This command shows all active services running on NAM or NAS.

- **ifconfig**   This command shows information regarding the interfaces.

- **mii-tool**   This command gives the status of the interfaces.

- **top**   This command gives information regarding memory and CPU usage.

- **/var/log/ha-log and /var/log/ha-debug**   This log gives information regarding high availability.

Common Issues Encountered by the Help Desk in the First 30 Days

After NAC Appliance has been installed, configured, and deployed across your user base, the most common issues that come to your help desk will be related to the following:

- Users not being able to get a web login page or the NAC Appliance Agent not popping up

- Users not being able to authenticate

- Users getting stuck in the Quarantine or Temporary role

- Users not being put in the correct VLAN or not getting access to certain resources

The following sections discuss each of these common issues.

Users Not Being Able to Get a Web Login Page, or the NAC Appliance Agent Not Popping

When a user connects to the network and opens the browser, it should be redirected to a web login page hosted by the NAS. If a user calls in saying that he is not being redirected, the following are a few things to check:

- Check whether the user has the correct IP address and default gateway information.

- Check the switch port the user is connected to and see whether the user is in the correct VLAN.

- Ask the user to browse to an IP address that exists on the trusted network and see whether the user gets redirected to a web login page. Most times, users have a DNS name as the default home page when they open a browser. If the user has incorrect DNS server settings or is unable to resolve the DNS name for any reason, the user's device will not send out any HTTP or HTTPS packets; therefore, the NAS is unable to redirect the user to the web login page. Browsing to an IP instead of a DNS name forces the user's device to send out HTTP or HTTPS packets. If this fixes the issue, you know that the user has some DNS issues.

- Check the perfigo/access/apache/logs/access_log log file on NAS to see whether NAS is seeing HTTP or HTTPS packets from the user.

- Check whether user pages have been configured on the NAM GUI at **Administration > User Pages**.

- If no HTTP or HTTPS packets are reaching NAS, you must further troubleshoot the network to see the path of the packet from the user to the network and the NAS, and see whether the user's packets might be getting forwarded through some other route.

For a scenario in which users have NAC Appliance Agent and it is not popping up, follow the troubleshooting steps listed in the "Agent Issues" section of this chapter.

Users Not Being Able to Authenticate

If a user is successful in getting a web login page or the NAC Appliance Agent does pop up but is unable to authenticate, you can check the following:

- Check whether the user is choosing the correct provider from the drop-down menu. Sometimes you might have multiple authentication providers and users might have to choose an authentication provider specific for themselves.

- On the NAM GUI, you can go to **User Management > Auth Servers > Auth Test** and do an authentication test for the user's username and password, as shown in Figure 15-14.

Figure 15-14 *Authentication Test Page*

- Check the /perfigo/logs/perfigo-redirect-log-.log.0 log file on NAS and the /perfigo/logs/perfigo-logs0.log.0 file on NAM for any error messages.

Users Getting Stuck in the Quarantine or Temporary Role

If a user is stuck in the Quarantine or Temporary role, it's most likely because that user does not meet a requirement and is unable to remediate. The following is what the help desk professional should do:

- Ask the user to exit out of the agent. As long as the user has the agent up, no report will be generated on the NAM GUI.

- Go to **Device Management > Clean Access > Clean Access Agent > Reports**. Find the report for the particular user and see what checks the user is failing.

- Find out exactly what that particular check is checking for, whether it is registry key, file, application, or service. Accordingly, you can ask the user to check for the missing piece and troubleshoot why the user is not able to remediate.

- Check the policies in the quarantine or temporary role to ensure that you are allowing access to the remediation resources.

- If the user is stuck due to issues with an antivirus or antispyware application, ask the user to right-click the **Agent** icon on the taskbar and then click **Properties**. The agent window will show what antivirus and antispyware application it detects, as shown in Figure 15-15.

Figure 15-15 *Agent Properties Page*

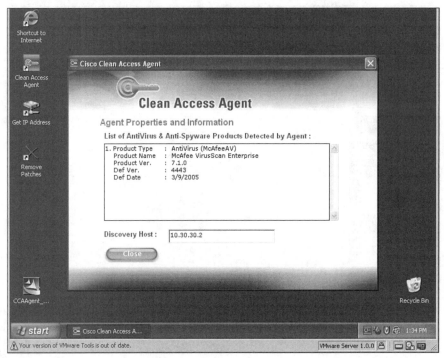

- If you're getting some other error messages on the agent window, capture agent debug logs and open a TAC case so that TAC can decode the log file and isolate the issue.

Users Not Being Put in the Correct VLAN or Not Getting Access to Certain Resources

If a user is able to authenticate, is compliant, and is still not able to get access to resources on the trusted network, you can check for the following:

- Check the online user list and make sure that the user shows up there and has the correct user role.

- Check the VLAN on the switch port and see whether the user is moved to the correct VLAN (if this is OOB mode).

- Check the policies on the user's user role and make sure that the correct ACLs have been configured.

- Check the user device's IP address and make sure that the user has the correct IP address in the access VLAN.

- If everything looks correct, further troubleshooting on the network will be needed to track the path of the packet and to see where the packet might be getting dropped.

Summary

Always follow a logical troubleshooting path when troubleshooting any NAC Appliance issues. Many times the symptoms may point to the NAC Appliance being the issue; however, it is important to always follow the process that NAC Appliance takes after a user has connected to the network. Follow the process the user has to go through during authentication, posture assessment, remediation, and when NAC Appliance puts the user into the correct user role VLAN. Step-by-step troubleshooting at each stage of the process is critical. This will help you isolate the issue faster and focusing on the problem at hand. The content in this chapter gave you some idea of what questions to ask, what steps to take, and some logs to investigate when troubleshooting the different scenarios with NAC Appliance.

This appendix covers the following topics:

- Sample NAC Appliance Requirement Change Notification E-mail
- Sample NAC Appliance Notice for Bulletin Board or Poster
- Sample NAC Appliance Letter to Students

Sample User Community Deployment Messaging Material

This appendix provides sample messaging that you can use to get the word out to your user population on what NAC Appliance is, how to use it, and where to get help. This messaging is tailored for the education environment, but it can be easily tailored for use in other environments.

Sample NAC Appliance Requirement Change Notification E-Mail

This e-mail sample is meant to be sent out to the user community prior to the enforcement of a new requirement or check in NAC Appliance. This e-mail assumes that the Cisco NAC Appliance solution and agents have already been rolled out to and are in use by the user community. It is recommended that all new requirements be first rolled out as optional. After a set amount of time, the requirements should be made mandatory. Sending this e-mail should coincide with the implementation of the optional requirement. You should send a reminder prior to the requirements being made mandatory.

To:	All Students and Faculty
From:	ITD
Subject:	New PC security updates required

Faculty and Students,

Starting today, September 20th, there will be two new security requirements for all Windows PCs connected to the residential network. Upon connection to the network, you might see Clean Access prompt you to install these new security updates on your PC. Please follow the instructions given to install these updates. You have a two-week discretionary period within which to install the new updates before enforcement begins, at which time compliance will be required for network access.

In order to ensure uninterrupted network access, it is strongly recommended that you install the new updates during the discretionary period. Please keep in mind that these updates can take from 5 to 30 minutes to install, depending on the performance of your PC. Starting October 6th, the Clean Access system will initiate the enforcement of the new security updates. Once enforcement begins, any PC not running the required security updates will be forced to install them before being allowed full network access.

If you have any questions or need technical assistance, please go to the ITD Clean Access support page at www.univ.com/nac/support or call the helpdesk at x4000.

Thank you,
IT Management

Sample NAC Appliance Notice for Bulletin Board or Poster

This announcement can be posted on internal websites, posted on bulletin boards, or handed out as flyers. Your implementation may differ, so please use this only as a guideline. The objectives of this announcement are as follows:

- Inform the user community that the NAC Appliance solution is in place and why.
- Inform users how to use the system.
- Set expectations for its use.
- Give references for obtaining more information.

Sample NAC Appliance Notice

Connecting to the Campus Network

In an effort to reduce the threats posed by viruses and worms to the campus network, the university has implemented the Cisco Clean Access network admission control solution.

Here's What Students Need to Know:

- All PCs of students living in the residence halls will be required to go through the Clean Access process to gain access to the campus network.

- Students with Windows and Mac PCs are required to install the Clean Access Agent security software.

- Students are required to authenticate to the network using their campus username and password.

- The PC being used will be checked by Clean Access to make sure that it has the necessary security software and system patches installed before being allowed on the network.

- Any PC that does not meet the security requirements will dynamically be placed into network quarantine and provided the necessary instructions and security software. After the PC is certified, full network access will be restored.

- The Cisco Clean Access solution does *not* access your personal files, block any applications, or monitor your network traffic.

Why Is Cisco Clean Access Necessary?

Nearly all network outages or brownouts experienced on the campus network are the result of virus-infected or severely compromised student PCs accessing the network. As a result, it has become necessary for the university to implement a network security system to minimize the risk posed by students who connect infected PCs to the campus network. This security solution will keep your computers much more secure, empowering them to resist the infection of viruses that could destroy your documents or render your PC unusable.

How to Obtain the Clean Access Agent:

1 Plug in to the campus network.

2 Open your web browser. You will be redirected to the university login page.

3 Log in using your campus username and password.

    4 You will be directed to install the Clean Access Agent.

    5 Click the **Download Clean Access Agent** button and follow the installation wizard's instructions to install the software. Installation does not require a reboot.

How to Log In to the Network:

    1 Login is done using the Clean Access Agent.

    2 After Clean Access Agent is installed, the agent login window will appear automatically whenever your computer attempts to access the campus network.

    3 Enter your username and password and click **login**.

    4 Follow the instructions given to remediate any failed checks found on your PC.

    5 After your PC is certified, you will gain full network access.

Who to Contact for Help:

Help Desk at x4000

http://www.university.com/nac/support

Email: Support@university.com

Additional information can be found at http://www.university.com/nac/support.

Sample NAC Appliance Letter to Students

This sample letter is intended to be added to a university's student handbook that is typically sent to students before the beginning of the new school year. The letter serves two purposes: to inform students about the NAC Appliance solution and to instruct students how to obtain the Clean Access Agent prior to arriving on campus.

Dear Student,

This letter is to inform you that the university's campus network is protected using a system called Cisco NAC Appliance, Clean Access. This security solution was put into place in an effort to decrease the threat posed by viruses and worms on the university's network. The vast majority of previous network outages or slowness can be attributed directly to the outbreak of a computer virus or worm. These outbreaks also resulted in the widespread damage or loss of data on student PCs. An effective method of combating these outbreaks is to ensure that every PC connecting to the network is running an up-to-date antivirus software package and has all the latest Windows security patches installed. The Cisco NAC Appliance security solution provides this capability to the university.

To be ready for the school year, you will need to download and install the Clean Access Agent on your Windows- or Mac-based computer. Please make every effort to install the agent prior to arriving on campus. This will help make your arrival go that much smoother. The agent is available for download at http://www.university.com/agent. Just follow the instructions provided to complete the simple installation. Should you have any questions or need technical assistance, please call the university help desk at 800-333-3333.

Thank you,

The ITD Staff

INDEX

Symbols

/var/log/ha-debug log, 517
/var/log/ha-log log, 517

Numerics

3500XL Edge Layer 2 switch, configuring AD
SSO, 354–355

A

access to resources, troubleshooting issues, 520
access VLANs, 54
ACLs. *See also* policies
   Layer 3 OOB traffic control, 59–60
Active Administrator Sessions page, 492
Active Directory SSO, 93
   operation, 94–95
   prerequisites, 94
AD server, configuring for AD SSO, 360–363
AD SSO (Active Directory Single Sign-On), 345
   3500XL Edge Layer 2 switch, configuring,
      354–355
   AD SSO authentication server, adding, 357
   Agent-based Windows SSO, enabling, 364
   configuring, 347
   DHCP, enabling in NAS, 379–381
   domain structure, 346
   GPO updates, enabling, 364
   Layer 3 3550 core switch, configuring, 352–354
   mapping users to multiple roles, 366–368
      user attributes, 370–371, 374, 378–379
   NAC Agent, downloading, 382, 384
   NAM, configuring, 348–349
   NAS
      configuring, 349–351
      user account, creating, 361
   ports, configuring, 358
   supported devices, 345
   traffic policies, configuring, 358
   troubleshooting, 509–511
   Windows 2003 support tools, installing, 362

Add Exempt Device page (Certified Devices tab),
   configuring, 246
Add Floating Device page (Certified Devices tab),
   configuring, 246
adding
   CA-signed certificate to NAM, 413–414
   checks, rules, and requirements to HSP,
      150–151
   external authentication servers
      LDAP/AD, 224–225
      RADIUS, 223
   NAS appliances
      to network, 201
      to NAM, 496–498
      to NAM in L3OOB deployment, 322
      to NAM in OOB deployment, 289
   switch to NAM in L3OOB mode, 328
adjacency mode, effect on OOB operation, 56–58
admin group, creating, 220
admin user account, creating, 222
agent distribution, configuring, 255–257
agent issues, troubleshooting, 500–503
Agent Login page (General Setup tab),
   configuring, 243–245
agent policy enforcement, configuring, 239–241
   agent login, configuring, 243–245
   certified devices, configuring, 245–246, 249
   web login, configuring, 242–243
Agent-based Windows SSO, enabling for AD SSO
   configuration, 364
agentless authentication, 14
antivirus update requirements, configuring, 259
API for guest access, 236
applying
   NAS logs to troubleshooting process, 516–517
   requirements to HSP user roles, 153
assigning roles to local users, 207–208
   by external authentication source attribute, 219
   by MAC/IP address, 213, 217
   by subnet, 217–218
   by VLAN ID, 209–211
attributes, mapping users to user roles, 90–91
AUPs (acceptable use policies), 138
   components of, 139
   enforcing, 139, 142
   samples, 139

M

S

T

U

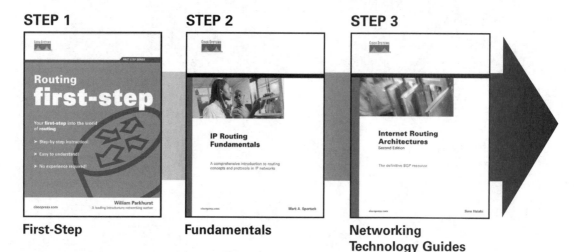

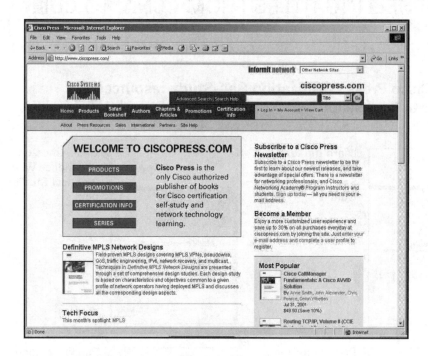
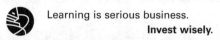

SEARCH THOUSANDS OF BOOKS FROM LEADING PUBLISHERS

Safari® Bookshelf is a searchable electronic reference library for IT professionals that features more than 2,000 titles from technical publishers, including Cisco Press.

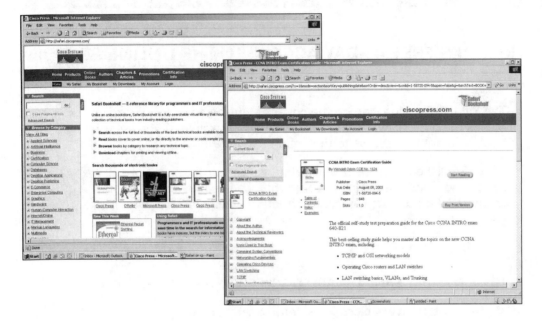

With Safari Bookshelf you can

- **Search** the full text of thousands of technical books, including more than 70 Cisco Press titles from authors such as Wendell Odom, Jeff Doyle, Bill Parkhurst, Sam Halabi, and Karl Solie.

- **Read** the books on My Bookshelf from cover to cover, or just flip to the information you need.

- **Browse** books by category to research any technical topic.

- **Download** chapters for printing and viewing offline.

With a customized library, you'll have access to your books when and where you need them—and all you need is a user name and password.

TRY SAFARI BOOKSHELF FREE FOR 14 DAYS!

You can sign up to get a 10-slot Bookshelf free for the first 14 days. Visit **http://safari.ciscopress.com** to register.